KNOWLEDGE-BASED INFORMATION SYSTEMS

D. Partridge
University of Exeter
UK

K. M. Hussain
Professor Emeritus
New Mexico State University
USA

McGRAW-HILL BOOK COMPANY

London · New York · St Louis · San Francisco · Auckland
Bogotá · Caracas · Lisbon · Madrid · Mexico
Milan · Montreal · New Delhi · Panama · Paris · San Juan
São Paulo · Singapore · Sydney · Tokyo · Toronto

Published by
McGRAW-HILL Book Company Europe
Shoppenhangers Road, Maidenhead, Berkshire, SL6 2QL, England
Telephone 01628 23432
Fax 01628 770224

British Library Cataloguing in Publication Data

Partridge, D.
  Knowledge-based Information Systems
  I. Title   II. Hussain, K. M.
  006.33
  ISBN 0-07-707624-9

Library of Congress Cataloging-in-Publication Data

Partridge, D. (Derek),
  Knowledge-based information systems/D. Partridge, K.M. Hussain.
    p.   cm.
  Includes bibliographical references and index.
  ISBN 0-07-707624-9
    1. Expert systems (Computer science)   I. Hussain, K. M. (Khateeb M.)   II. Title.
QA76.76.E95P273 1994   94-20437
006.3′3–dc20   CIP

1234   BL   9765

Typeset by Computape (Pickering) Ltd, North Yorkshire
and printed and bound in Great Britain by Biddles Ltd, Guildford

CONTENTS

LIST OF CASES

PREFACE

The results of a questionnaire and personalized letter sent to the chief executive officers of the 1657 largest US and Canadian corporations elicited 382 responses; 94 per cent of the CEOs either had never heard of artificial intelligence or did not think it feasible, and only 6 per cent were already using it at one or more levels in their companies. This was the situation in North America in 1988. Given the typical lag time in take-up of innovative uses of information technology between Europe and the United States, it could well be a fairly accurate picture of the current situation in Europe.

The responses to this survey remind us of a story of three shoe salesmen who were sent to a remote tropical island to sell shoes to the indigenous population. The Italian salesman faxed back to Milan that the people did not wear shoes, and so he was returning home. The British salesman similarly contacted his home base, reporting that the people did not need shoes, and seeking permission to return home. The American faxed back that the people did not wear shoes and did not think they needed any. He saw a tremendous potential market and demanded that 10 000 sample shoes were rushed to him.

We react to the survey outcome in a manner that might be described as half-British and half-American (which just happens to be the national composition of this book's authorship). We feel that CEOs do not (and cannot be expected to) know what they need with regard to the details of the latest technological developments, and we try, in this book, to tell them how and why they need knowledge-based systems technology.

Chief executive officers are not stupid, nor are they unaware (in a general sense) of technological innovations that can be taken on board to swell the corporate profits. So why do we seem to see so little uptake of artificial intelligence and knowledge-based systems technology?

Much is probably hidden beneath the bare facts of the questionnaire and of the two results presented. Artificial intelligence is a diverse, multifaceted topic, and so it can be both true that artificial intelligence is not feasible, and that artificial intelligence is a practical and potentially valuable technology—it all depends upon what is really being referred to by use of the blanket term 'artificial intelligence'. A general-purpose office-cleaning robot should not enter into any planning exercise that does not go way beyond the end of the current century. But an intelligent file-management system could be available tomorow, and a listening typewriter in the not-too-distant future.

Artificial intelligence technology, particularly knowledge-based systems technology, is here now, and can be used to great advantage throughout the commercial world. It is just a matter of knowing what is currently feasible, and of circumscribing closely the scope and limitations of its use within the company.

Within this book we survey the scope of knowledge-based information systems—repositories of information (e.g. personnel files, sales records, product designs, company plans, financial projections, or analyses) that are managed in some way by means of this innovative technology. We cover the complete spectrum from the currently available (and therefore demonstrably feasible) to the more speculative forays into what the future promise may be, but always stressing the current status of what is being presented.

In a fast-moving field like information technology wise decisions can only be made with a well-grounded appreciation of the currently feasible together with some clear indications of what is soon to be feasible. Thus we integrate all aspects of the technology surrounding knowledge-based information systems—basic artificial intelligence, necessary support systems (hardware, software, and personnel), development strategies—and present it as a coherent whole. Such a broad sweep through some seemingly disparate topics is the only way to gain a proper appreciation of what is a complex, detailed, ever-changing, but potentially very rewarding application of artificial intelligence technology.

Study of the many facets of this technology is facilitated by supplementing the textual material with both case studies on selected subtopics and sets of review and discussion questions concluding each chapter. The discussion questions do not always have clear-cut right and wrong answers, but they can be answered after proper study of the chapter and associated support material.

ACKNOWLEDGEMENTS

A number of chapters are based on, and contain excerpts from, *A New Guide to AI*, by D. Partridge. These excerpts are reprinted with permission from Ablex Publishing Corporation. Parts of Chapters 6 and 12, as well as Figs 3.4, 6.3, 15.3, and 15.4 are from D. Partridge, *Engineering AI Software*, Intellect Books, Oxford (1992).

ACKNOWLEDGMENTS

1

INTRODUCTION TO KNOWLEDGE-BASED SYSTEMS

At the end of the century, the use of words and general educated opinion will have changed so much that one is able to speak of 'machines thinking' without expecting to be contradicted.

A. Turing, 1950

FROM FILE-SERVER TO KNOWLEDGE-SERVER

Knowledge is more than data. Knowledge is data plus information necessary to make inferences and reach conclusions necessary for decision making and problem solving. Once knowledge is organized and represented in a structure that can be recognized by a programming language (and often a specialized one), it can be used to yield opinions often as good or better than a human expert. This relationship constitutes the bare bones of a *knowledge-based information system* (also referred to as *knowledge-based system* and the acronyms of *KBIS* or *KBS*) as shown in Fig. 1.1.

A KBIS could be a stand-alone system generating all its needed information as input. Alternatively, a KBIS could use information generated by a data-processing system as shown before the mark X in Fig. 1.1.

The hierarchy of data, information, and knowledge can be seen in Fig. 1.2. Here we have data being transformed by processing (data processing) into information which when combined with the necessary heuristics and rules will yield knowledge. This knowledge when tempered by judgement and a value system (of the problem-solver and decision-maker) and supplemented by experience and learning will yield wisdom. We do not

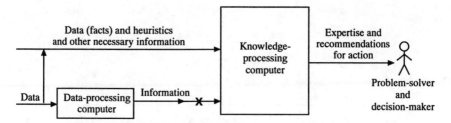

Figure 1.1 Data processing and knowledge processing.

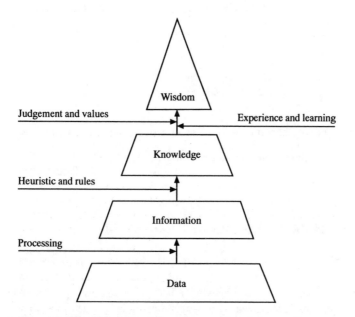

Figure 1.2 Hierarchy of data, information, and knowledge structure.

achieve this high level of wisdom in most cases, but it could well be an objective of a KBIS.

Another view of knowledge and wisdom can be seen in Fig. 1.3 where we compare knowledge and wisdom with intuition and instincts in a matrix with cognitive complexity and domain generality. Intuition (as well as data and information processing) has low cognitive complexity and low domain generality (i.e. high domain specificity), while instincts have low cognitive complexity but high generality. In contrast, knowledge has higher cognitive complexity and low generality (i.e. high domain specificity), and wisdom has both higher cognitive complexity and higher generality. In terms of structure (and definition), knowledge and wisdom have low structure (i.e.

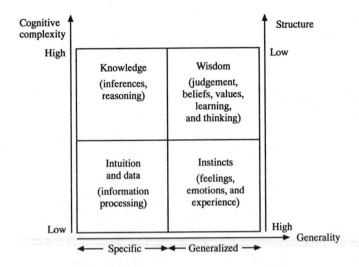

Figure 1.3 Matrix of intuition, instincts, knowledge, and judgement.

ill-structured, semi-structured, and unstructured), while intuition (and data and information processing) as well as instincts have high structure (i.e. can be highly structured and well defined).

The topic area of this book is knowledge and knowledge-based systems, which in terms of Fig. 1.3 is concerned with problem areas of medium to high cognitive complexity, domain specific, and medium to low structure, i.e. semi-structured, ill-structured, and perhaps even unstructured problem environments. For a KBIS, this is the primary area of jurisdiction, but it does not necessarily exclude areas of some overlap such as areas of low cognitive complexity where intuition and data and information processing are typically used.

We will define knowledge and a KBIS more formally in a later chapter (Chapter 5). In Chapter 3 we will consider the basic components and functions of a KBIS. We will also compare a KBIS with data transactional systems and with a decision support system (DSS).

A KBIS is largely the product of the discipline of artificial intelligence (AI), especially through its most successful commercial product, the expert system (ES). Expert systems are discussed in great detail in Chapter 3, after a discussion of AI in Chapter 2. Although the expert system is sometimes equated with AI, there is much in AI other than an expert system. Techniques of search, reasoning, and learning have important applications in other techniques of problem solving and are used in many disciplines, especially in business and engineering. These problem-solving techniques are discussed in Chapter 4. It is here that we define many of the concepts and terminology that will be invoked repeatedly in chapters to follow when we discuss the development of a KBIS. It also provides us with the vocabulary to describe and define a KBIS (after examining the nature and scope of 'knowledge') which is the subject of Chapter 5.

OUTLINE OF BOOK

The main thrust of this book is the development of a KBIS which starts in Part II. Part I is an introduction of basic concepts and terminology which a reader versed in problem-solving technology like operations research (OR) may wish to skip. Part II starts with the development process. The methodology and much of the process is conceptually no different from that of any other system, whether it be a transactional system or a DSS. In all cases we start with a feasibility study, user specification, overall design, and we end up with an acceptance test of the system. What happens in between is of course unique to each system. In this book we emphasize the in-between, which is the detailed design and implementation, for each subsystem. We start with knowledge acquisition in Chapter 7 after an overview of the development of a KBIS in Chapter 6.

All systems have the problem of knowledge acquisition, so is it different for a KBIS? It is not different when it comes to the concept of GIGO: garbage in–garbage out. Input is crucial in a KBIS too. What is different is that in a KBIS the main source of information is not a scanner as in a retail store or a sensor in a process control system. In a KBIS the main source is a domain expert. The expert, being human, has all the frailties of a human and may even have additional characteristics of reticence, shyness, and a hesitation to part with and share information. Eliciting and extracting information from a human expert is not a technical computer science problem but more one of psychology and group dynamics. And yet the information must be extracted by a computer scientist trained in the technology of a KBIS and called a *knowledge engineer*. This is because it is the knowledge engineer who must represent all this information in a machine-usable form to be operated on by a computer program that then makes the necessary inferences and recommends actions.

Knowledge acquisition (discussed in Chapter 7) is difficult and may even be slow. But once achieved, the data must be represented in a knowledge-base. Unfortunately, the traditional data-representation models for a transactional system are not always appropriate for a knowledge-base and so special models of data representation have to be used. These are discussed in Chapter 8.

Once knowledge has been represented and stored in a knowledge-base, it is then possible to write programs to draw inferences from the knowledge-base. Again unfortunately, traditional technology is not adequate for a KBIS. Despite the hundreds (yes hundreds!) of programming languages, special ones often have to be used for a KBIS. These languages or alternatives such as software packages or toolkits or programming environments, which may be object-oriented systems, are all discussed in detail in Part III. Part II of this book is on development, and we discuss the technology of making inferences and reaching conclusions. This is done in Chapter 9. If there is an environment with uncertainty and the information is incomplete or unknown, then we may use fuzzy sets to manage the uncertainty. This is the subject of Chapter 10. Fuzzy sets may sound vague but are based on a formal approach to quantifying the fuzziness and vagueness in values of variables such as high, low, long, short, very short, very long, etc. This enables us to handle problems involving uncertainty.

Once the output is theoretically available, there is the problem of accessing the output. This is certainly not a new problem for it is faced in both transactional systems and in a DSS—and for all levels of end-users. But the user interface for a KBIS, as discussed in Chapter 11, is different in two important ways. Firstly, great emphasis is placed on end-user friendliness. The end-user is assumed to be possibly naïve about computers and often a casual user with no time for training as a transactional clerk would have. The end-user of a KBIS may have a high level of computer anxiety and may even be hostile to computers. The end-user is assumed to be always right and the KBIS goes out of its way to help and even humour the end-user. All useful techniques from *ergonomics* (considering the physiological factors) and from *human factors* (considering primarily the psychological factors) are employed. The presentation module is often interactive and would typically possess many features to help the end-user.

The other unique feature of the *presentation module* and *end-user interface* for a KBIS is that it has the capability of justifying everything it does. It will explain all knowledge and heuristics that it used, and explain why they are used. The logic is automatically traced. The end-user is taken into full confidence by the system. Again, all this is often done interactively and very politely. The attitude is that the end-user is always correct and has the right to question and even challenge the system. This is a far cry from traditional systems, even from the DSSs designed for managers, who were never allowed to question the system. They often would not dare. They were intimidated. They were awed. But with a KBIS the end-user is encouraged to question without any limitations and conditions. This is a change in aproach that could well be adopted by other system designers, and indeed that may well happen for we have here what economists call the 'demonstration effect': 'If the neighbour has it, why not me?' 'If they can do it, why can we not do it?' If this happens, KBIS technology will have made an important contribution to problem solving making a computer system more acceptable and accessible to the casual and non-technical end-user.

The presentation module and knowledge-delivery systems are to be end-user centred. They are configured with interactive software mixing menus and commands, supported by a readily available 'help' routine and helpful error messages. The hardware should have graphic capabilities including attributes (lines, areas, and colour), primitives (polygon and area fills) and transformations (scale and rotate).

Once the presentation module is ready and tested satisfactorily (individually and with other subsystems), then the development of the KBIS is complete. What remains to be discussed are matters of development that were skipped over, including the need for special computer equipment. It is often the case that the available central processing unit (CPU) is inadequate for the type of inference processing that is needed. Special computers such as LISP machines and even parallel processors are required. These are discussed in Part III, starting with Chapter 13.

There is currently quite a debate raging between the supporters of the programming language LISP and its competitor PROLOG. This debate will be joined and both sides of the argument are presented in Chapter 14, in which examples of coding for both LISP and PROLOG are offered. But this is not a traditional chapter on programming languages. Instead, Chapter 14 matches the nature and structure of input available, the nature of the output desired, and then matches them with a coding structure that can perform the necessary non-procedural, symbolic manipulation.

Sometimes a programming language is too costly (in development time if not money) and a packaged program called a *shell* is quite adequate. Sometimes a *programming language environment* with supporting software appropriate for a KBIS is better than either a programming language or a shell. Sometimes a *toolkit* is appropriate. These alternatives are discussed in Chapter 15.

More recently a whole new approach to a KBIS has emerged. This approach is not just for programming but also for data structuring, systems design, and development. This is based on an 'object' as a unit of data and code the development methodology is referred to as 'object-oriented'. This is the subject of Chapter 16.

The last but not least important resource of a KBIS is the human resource. We have mentioned the domain expert and the knowledge engineer. The knowledge engineer is an emerging new profession and has its own educational and training requirements. The knowledge engineer as well as other AI personnel do raise the organizational question as to where they should reside in the corporate structure. Should they be with other computer personnel, with OR and problem-solving personnel, or should they be separate? Are they different from the computer personnel? How does one select a potentially promising knowledge engineer? How is the knowledge engineer to be trained? How can a knowledge engineer be retained? These and other related issues are the topics of Chapter 17.

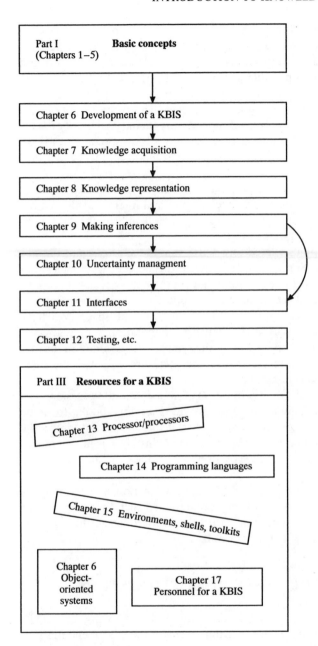

Figure 1.4 Sequence of chapters.

A possible sequence for the reading of selected chapters is offered in Fig. 1.4. All the chapters in Part II should be read in order except perhaps Chapter 10, 'Uncertainty Management', which could be skipped in a first reading of the book. This possible 'jump ahead' is indicated by the arrow in Fig. 1.4. The chapter on uncertainty management is not crucial to the basic understanding of a KBIS but is important when there is uncertainty in the problem environment. The topic of uncertainty management does have many applications in environments other than a KBIS especially in a DSS environment and hence may be a topic that should not be skipped altogether.

The chapters in Part III are modular and can be read in any sequence or not read at all depending on the background and interest of the reader. This possible randomness in the reading sequence is indicated by the non-sequential order of the chapters in Fig. 1.4.

There are many topics related to a KBIS that are very relevant but not discussed in this book. Some are listed later in this chapter. The topics that are discussed are not always covered at the depth that we would like. This lack of depth and the deletion of certain topics is not because they are unimportant but because we are restricted in terms of space. We have traded some of these topics and depth for annotations to a selected bibliography for each chapter (after this one). These annotations are designed to guide the serious reader to the literature and in some cases substantial information is presented.

Each chapter that follows has questions for review and discussion. The answers to all the questions are not provided in this book; to some questions, there are perhaps no answers yet. But this should not inhibit the reader from thinking about them. The purpose of this book is not merely to provide some answers but to make you think about the contemporary issues relating to a KBIS.

Each of the following chapters has an introduction and a summary section. There is some overlap but they are designed such that when all the introductions and all the summaries are read in a sequence, they provide two separate summaries of the entire book.

APPLICATIONS OF KNOWLEDGE-BASED SYSTEMS

Listing the applications of a KBIS is like trying to hit a moving target. The range of applications is increasing continuously and there is no end in sight. The applications of a KBIS (and currently it is mostly applications of expert systems) are almost paralleling early applications of computers: it is across the board for all functional departments and across the spectrum of commerce and industry. There are, of course, environments where a KBIS is suitable and environments when it is not desirable or appropriate. The necessary conditions for the feasibility of a KBIS are discussed in great detail as part of Chapter 6, 'Development of a KBIS'.

A KBIS is not designed to replace the structured processing of a transactional system like a payroll, financial transactional reporting, etc. Nor will it replace all the modelling systems and query processing of the type done in a typical DSS using OR models. But it may replace some of the information processing and analytical reporting done in a DSS and add intelligence to others, especially those that are concerned with ill-structured environments and with uncertainty. This relationship and coexistence of systems (including different hardware and programming language configurations) other than a KBIS is shown in Fig. 1.5. Such coexistence raises serious problems of integration, issues that are still unresolved with the emergence of a KBIS unless specific action has been taken to properly integrate the KBIS.

Whether as an integrated system or a stand-alone system, the KBIS may encounter many obstacles before it can be used effectively. One obstacle is that KBISs are closely associated with AI—and the image of AI is one of abstract quality and mysticism. This image will change with greater applications of KBISs but there may be fewer applications to start with because of the bad image. Working through this circular relationship may take time.

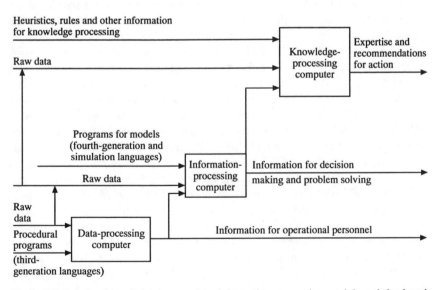

Figure 1.5 Relationship of data processing, information processing, and knowledge-based processing.

Another obstacle to the greater use of KBISs is that they have often been greatly oversold, with the result that user expectations are unrealistically high. There is too much hype and often many charlatans. Failure to achieve unrealistically high expectations results in disappointment, disenchantment, and a bad image.

Another obstacle to a greater use of KBISs is the deficiency of the scientific methodology of making inferences. In addition, there are pragmatic difficulties in implementing a KBIS that are largely the result of a lack of personnel trained and experienced in a KBIS as well as a lack of support from top management. But despite these difficulties, applications will soon be daily performing cognitive tasks, aiding human memory, scanning and searching knowledge libraries, and even communicating with other KBISs. A KBIS will help us to make intelligent use of a mass of data and knowledge, and relieve us from being inundated with voluminous newspapers, advertisements, and magazines as well relieve us from loud radios and televisions. Access to knowledge and the flow of knowledge to all those in need of the knowledge could be far simpler than it currently is, and certainly quieter. The KBIS will not only perform the secretarial tasks and the necessary number crunching but also perform some intellectual tasks in many value-laden problem domains.

A comparison of a KBIS to a transactional system has been implied above. A more formal comparison is shown in Table 1.1 and offers a good base for comparing the transactional system, the earliest of all information systems, with the KBIS, the most recent of all information systems.

The application of a KBIS plays an important role in its own lifecycle by continuously improving and enhancing its performance and usability. Applications are an important part of the feedback loop as shown in Fig. 1.6. We see that one loop contributes to a better understanding of cognitive sciences, which in turn (through advances in the research in cognitive sciences) contribute to a better development of a KBIS. Another loop creates new demands for a KBIS which feeds into KBIS technology. Other inputs to KBIS technology are advances in distributed processing (including networking) and KBIS management which would include better interface management. There are also inputs from advances in specialized processors (parallel and neural processors) and software for a KBIS as well as from research in the human factors affecting a KBIS. Human considerations are yet another input to the development process, making it more human-centred. Advances in the implementing and processing of richer knowledge-bases, which includes knowledge acquisition and knowledge representation, also provide input.

Table 1.1 Comparison of a KBIS with a transactional system

	Transactional system	KBIS
Objective	To facilitate operations	To replicate human decision making and to transfer expertise
Type of task	Clerical Number-crunching	Intellectual
Unit of processing	Data	Knowledge
Scope	Across the board	Narrow domain
Nature of task	Well-defined Well-structured	Ill-defined Ill- or semi-structured
When invoked	Regularly Repetitive	*Ad hoc* Repetitive
Levels of management served primarily	Operational management Operational personnel	Middle management Professional personnel
Mother discipline	Data processing	Artificial intelligence
Personnel involved	Systems analyst Programmer	Domain expert Knowledge engineer
Computer	PC to mainframe	PC to mainframe and LISP computer
Programming	3GL procedural	3GL and AI languages

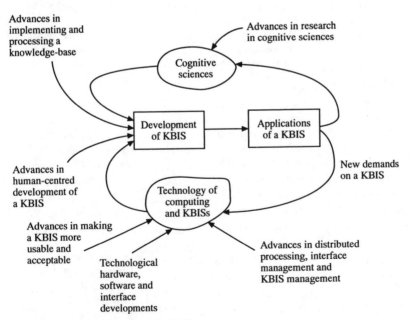

Figure 1.6 Role of applications of a KBIS.

CURRENT LIMITATIONS OF KNOWLEDGE-BASED SYSTEMS

What we now see in the early 1990s are the first generations of KBISs. There are many limitations of the current KBISs that are already the subject of intense research and study. One is the problem of integration, which must occur at all levels of operations and management. There must be integration between the knowledge-base and the most efficient and effective algorithms of problem solving. There must also be integration between the KBIS and other information systems not just in the organization but between selected systems in the industry, regionally and nationally. The integration must allow the flow of truly relevant knowledge both backwards and forwards as the needs arise.

In tracing the limitations of KBISs, one should look at the source of their strength. This strength lies in the knowledge elicited by the knowledge

Table 1.2 Comparison of a neural net with a KBIS

	Neural Net	KBIS
Objective	To be trained to exhibit the desired behaviour	To be built to replicate human decision making and to transform expertise
Type of task	Analyse data after previous training or learning sets	Analysis with conventional and KBIS approaches
Driver	Numeric data	Knowledge and symbols
Scope	Self-organizing (largely unknown)	Narrow domain and closed
Nature of task	Well-defined Well-structured (in order to provide learning sets)	Semi-, ill- and well-defined and structured
When invoked	For massive parallel processing and pattern recognition	Sequential, logic-based repetitive symbolic manipulation
Interface	Not so friendly	Very friendly
Reasoning	Associative	Logical
Testing	Fast and easy	Slow and difficult
Mother discipline	Biological science Neuroscience	Artificial intelligence
Personnel involved	Neurocomputing engineer	Domain expert Knowledge engineer
Computer	Parallel processors (ideally)	PC to mainframe and LISP computer
Programming	C	3GL and AI languages

engineer from the domain expert. There exists a serious gap in our technology for knowledge acquisition and elicitation. Much more research needs to be done in understanding the importance and role of the human expert and the process of knowledge acquisition.

We also have problems relating to cognition. We need to understand better the cognitive processes of our problem-solvers. We need to understand better the principles and laws that govern the mind, especially those that make decisions and solve problems in business and industry. We need to comprehend better how and why domain experts form their expert opinions and gain their expertise in successfully performing the tasks in their domains. We need to understand human behaviour and intelligent behaviour better, especially as they pertain to decision making and problem solving, and how such behaviour could be influenced. We need a better conceptualization of knowledge systems and how people think and learn when they make decisions and solve problems in varying degrees of complexity of problem environments.

The KBIS has done a great deal in making systems more end-user friendly. But more needs to be done. Our problem-solving algorithms need to be re-examined from the point of view of effective human-oriented presentation. A system must create no (or little) computer anxiety amongst its users; instead it must anticipate the users' needs and reactions to a computer system, especially a KBIS. A system must recognize the problem-solving characteristics of its users and communicate with them at their level of comprehension and understanding.

The communication between a user and a KBIS must be truly interactive, with the system doing all the search and number crunching while maintaining the necessary security and privacy. It must also warn the user of findings that may be unethical or even illegal. The system must not replace human judgement but must instead help the user to make the necessary judgements. The system must help the user to use the domain knowledge available and the ever-changing knowledge-base without inhibiting the user from discovering unexpected and unanticipated solutions to more and more complex problems. Such complexity will arise in problems such as those in computer-aided design/computer-integrated manufacturing (CAD/CIM), natural-language textual processing, and in the handling of multimedia knowledge-bases.

TOPICS NOT COVERED

The thrust of this book is on the development (design and implementation) of KBISs. A KBIS is developed to be used. Unfortunately, we do not get to discuss the applications of a KBIS or its many implications for the organization, the workplace, the workforce, and for the problem-solvers and decision-makers. Nor do we discuss the many implications of a KBIS for society, such as the impact on employment and displacement, for leisure, and for the lifestyle of society. We have also omitted many topics relating to the management of a KBIS, such as the operations of KBISs, the role of a KBIS in the corporate culture; the success and failure factors of a KBIS; and the management of change resulting from a KBIS. The omission of topics from this book is no reflection of their importance: coverage is strictly dictated by the constraints of space.

FUTURE OF KNOWLEDGE-BASED SYSTEMS

Before making any predictions one should remember the caution of Niels Bohr, the eminent Danish physicist: 'It is hard to predict—especially the future.' But there are some things that one can predict with great confidence, and one such prediction is that there will continue to be a growth of data and knowledge. In 1990 there were over three million databases around the world, though admittedly most of these were small PC databases. The size, number, and complexity of these databases will certainly increase, and the rates of increase will also increase. It is estimated that information in the world doubles every 20 months. In some countries, databases are increasing—in terms of quantity, size, complexity, and number of end-users—by 40 per cent a year. The problem is not only one of efficiently organizing and managing the growth, but also one of extracting knowledge from this vast reserve of data and information, knowledge that is useful and meaningful to decision-makers and problem-solvers in problem environments of varying degrees of complexity.

We can safely expect that future KBISs will contain not just hundreds and thousands but millions of facts, heuristics, hypothesis, and relationships. We must improve our ability to access them, to use them with the relevant decision-making algorithms, and to enhance their utility. The access should be partly automatic; it should simply happen when needed, as one aspect of the growing automation of our capability just as access to and use of computerized knowledge has become commonplace.

We need to be able to access truly relevant knowledge quickly and easily, and for this we need to be able to classify knowledge of all types, not just domain knowledge but also functional knowledge, empirical knowledge, experimental knowledge, casual knowledge, pragmatic knowledge, teleological knowledge, etc. What we would also like to do is to use efficiently and effectively the knowledge-base that we have to create new knowledge, formulate new rules and heuristics, state new hypotheses, and discover new concepts that would enhance our problem-solving abilities.

SUMMARY AND CONCLUSIONS

It can be said that a KBIS is a logical evolution from an information system, and that an information system is a logical evolution from a functionally oriented transactional system. Each of these systems can be associated with an 'age' and 'revolution'. Thus looking forward, one can say that the early computer revolution with the transactional system evolved into an information revolution, which in turn evolved into a knowledge revolution. This relationship is shown in Fig. 1.7. One cannot predict with any certainty what the knowledge system will evolve into and when that will happen. There are, however, good reasons to expect and hope that the knowledge revolution and KBISs will become truly intelligent not only in their problem-solving abilities but also in their interfaces, especially with the end-user. It is these possibilities and the development of KBISs that we will explore in this book.

A view of the growth of problem-solving techniques is shown in Fig. 1.8. Also shown is the growth and popularity of end-user friendliness, which has shown a steeper rate of growth in the 1980s and will continue in the 1990s. Historically, end-user computing was non-existent and even had a negative value in the 1950s and 1960s (i.e. systems were distinctly end-user unfriendly). End-user friendliness started to be recognized as important

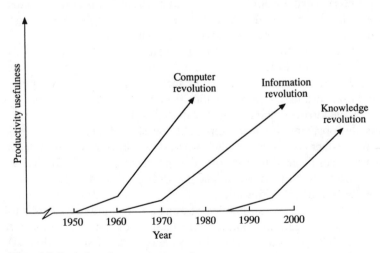

Figure 1.7 Evolution of computer processing.

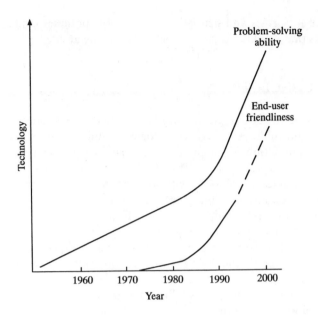

Figure 1.8 Problem-solving ability and end-user friendliness over time.

only in the 1970s. The growth curve took a sharp turn upwards in the 1980s partly because of the emergence of expert systems and its innovation of justification and explanation interfaces. This capability should continue to increase with the use of KBISs and increase further as ergonomics and human factors are applied to KBISs.

Our problem-solving abilities and the number of computing systems have increased over the decades. The history of computing reveals a high rate of innovation and a higher rate of obsolescence. These innovations and advances in computing are shown in Fig. 1.9 as they relate to a KBIS. This trend will continue with KBISs that enable us to solve more complex problems and to apply the problem-solving techniques developed ever more widely, to business and industry. Artificial intelligence and disciplines in engineering have also brought an understanding of fuzzy sets for example, to address the problems of uncertainty. At the same time, we have had advances in the technology of parallel processing, object-oriented systems (OOSs), and neural nets to support the processing in KBISs. These advances in the context of the development of KBISs are some of the topics to be discussed in Part III of this book.

Another view of the evolution of computing and computer systems is to view it in relation to data/information and its control. This perspective is shown in Fig. 1.10. We start with data systems in the SW (south-west) corner of the diagram. These are systems that process data under the

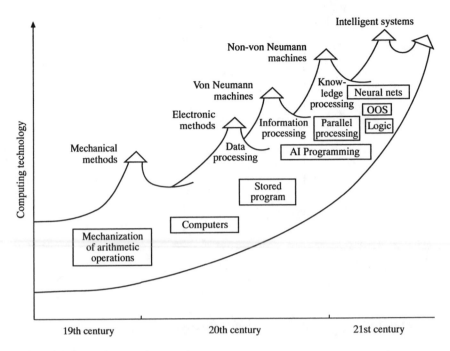

Figure 1.9 Computing over the centuries.

exclusive control of the technical personnel in the electronic data processing (EDP) department. These were transactional functional systems processed in batch mode, i.e. once started the system ran to completion with no opportunity for significant user interaction. These systems were superseded by information-processing systems (NW quadrant of Fig. 1.10). These systems were often on-line and sometimes on-line, real-time (OLRT). They were still under the control of technical computer personnel. The processing was more extended and included word processing and graphic processing and reached from the plant floor into the office. And now information processing is being replaced by knowledge processing (NE quadrant) where knowledge is processed and inferences are made. But there is another important shift in the processing paradigm: the shift of control from the technical personnel to the end-user. This shift was not sudden as none of the quadrants in Fig. 1.10 have strict boundaries. The shift came even with the dominance of the transactional systems. This shift was a result partly of the change in the end-user who became more computer literate—not just able but also willing to take responsibility for the control of processing. Part of the shift was a response to the long backlogs in jobs to be processed because of the dependence on technical personnel who were the liaison between the computing power and the end-user. Much of the shift was a result of

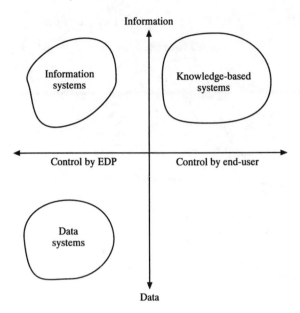

Figure 1.10 Evolution of computer systems with changing control.

technology: computers became smaller, more powerful, and cheap enough to be affordable for every desk-top; computers were interconnected through telecommunications and networks; processing became distributed and the end-user was liberated. The end-user became more demanding and was no longer willing to look at the computer system as a black box. Instead, the end-user began to demand explanations of the processing that was done, the assumptions that were made in the processing, and the rules that were used in the processing. This is why an explanation and justification module is now an essential part of a KBIS, and why the end-user is no longer taken for granted. The physical and psychological aspects of processing are now important. The end-user no longer must do what the system demands; instead the system must do what the end-user wants.

Another view of this evolution of transactional systems to knowledge-based systems is to view these systems as part of the growth curves of computing. These are shown in Fig. 1.11. The first two lower curves are for data and information systems. These were first suggested by Nolan and are sometimes known as the Nolan growth curves. Actually they are S-shaped curves of learning, first suggested by the educationist Skinner. The S-curve represented learning in a human, which is very slow to start with, increases rapidly in the teen years, before flattening out or even drooping in old age. Such a growth is observed for computing systems with some overlap between each curve. The two Nolan curves are now overtaken by the curve

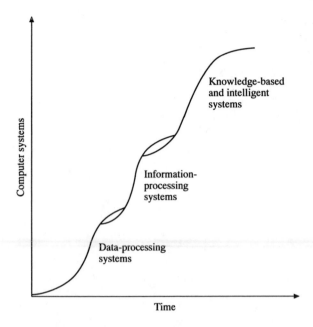

Figure 1.11 Growth curves for computing.

representing the knowledge-based system. In the 1990s, we are at the lower end of this curve. As we apply AI not just in making inferences and in expert systems, but also in all other aspects of computing including hardware and interfaces, we will approach an intelligent system. But this will require a better appreciation and application of AI, the subject of our next chapter where we will examine the nature, scope and promise of AI. However, our perspective will be somewhat limited: we are concerned with what is most relevant to a KBIS.

BIBLIOGRAPHY

Caudill, M. (1990) 'Using neural nets: making an expert network', *AI Expert*, **5** (6), 41–45.

Hillman, D. V. (1990) 'Integrating neural nets and expert systems', *AI Expert*, **5** (6), 54–59.

Rowe, A. J. and P. R. Watkins (1992) 'Beyond expert systems—reasoning, judgement, and wisdom', *Expert Systems with Applications*, **4** (1), 1–10.

Tafti, M. H. A. (1992) 'Neural networks: a new dimension in expert systems applications'. *Database*, **23** (1), 51–54.

Wang, L., A. L. Porter and S. Cunningham (1991) 'Expert systems: present and future', *Expert Systems with Applications*, **3** (4), 383–396.

Weizel, R. (ed.) (1990) *The Age of Intelligent Machines*, MIT Press, Cambridge MA.

Part I

Basic Concepts

In this first part of the book, we review the fundamental ideas underlying the notion of a KBIS. This will provide a proper basis for the details to be found in Parts II and III.

2

ARTIFICIAL INTELLIGENCE

Machines can and do transcend some of the limitations of their designers, and . . . in doing so they can be both effective and dangerous.

Norbert Weiner

People in every field will start asking themselves AI type questions about how they . . . model the knowledge in their field in the form of an understanding system . . . AI will change the questions people ask and the methods they use.

Roger Schank, *The Cognitive Computer*

INTRODUCTION

Let us consider a robot. Early robots were electro-mechanical devices, each designed to do a very specific and limited task. Later, robots used computers, but they were essentially '*dumb*'—that is to say, they operated in a limited domain and could only perform carefully prespecified tasks.

Nevertheless, early robots had many applications. They were, for example, used in factories to pick up objects and put them on a machine or on an assembly line. Robots belonging to this class, called *pick-and-put* robots, were particularly useful in situations where working conditions were poor (e.g. where fumes might threaten the health of human workers), or where tasks were dangerous (such as the handling of hot steel or nuclear waste). Robots worked tirelessly without demands to management for a rise in wages or fringe benefits. They had perfect memory as well as accuracy and speed in computations—characteristics for which computers are well known. However, they lacked the adaptability of a human worker—a crucial capability when the job environment changes. For example, suppose that the object to be lifted by the robot was in an unexpected position or location. In such cases, the robot might miss the object altogether or grasp parts that could be damaged or broken under pressure. Whereas a human worker would have the vision to see a change in position, the ability to analyse the 'scene', and the intelligence to modify grasping position, or lifting technique, pick-and-put robots would continue to lift and put as programmed even though those actions were no longer appropriate.

What factory managers wanted was robots that combined the memory, accuracy, and speed of computers with the intelligence and flexibility of humans. They wanted robots to adapt to changed conditions without having to be reprogrammed, a time-consuming and costly process. In effect, they wanted *machine intelligence*. To many people such intelligence is unnatural, artificial, which explains why the term *artificial intelligence (AI)* was coined. An AI application might give the robot the intelligence and ability to adapt to changed conditions, to understand voice commands, or to follow natural-language instructions. Other applications might give the robot image-processing and *scene analysis* capabilities.

The field of *expert systems* represents the first large commercial AI application that enables a computer to deliver advice in limited-domain problems like a human expert might do. Most of the rest of this book is spent discussing the extension of an expert system into a knowledge-based information system (KBIS). But first, we must introduce you to the fundamentals of AI.

We shall begin by tracing the evolution of AI, then examine the ability of computers to exhibit intelligent activity such as learning. We next identify the characteristics and limitations of AI and compare the capabilities of a human with that of a computer. Having established a basic AI vocabulary, we then examine some definitions of AI. We close the chapter by looking at issues that remain controversial among AI personnel, computer science practitioners, and end-users of computer systems.

THE EVOLUTION OF ARTIFICIAL INTELLIGENCE

In 1956 a summer institute was organized at Dartmouth College in the United States to exchange ideas about ways of making computers behave intelligently. All of the scientists attending the conference believed that thinking could indeed take place outside the human brain. All agreed that the digital computer would be the best non-human instrument for that purpose. Many of the conference participants were already engaged in projects to enhance the problem-solving capabilities of computers. Some were programming computers to play games and prove theorems, activities that require reasoning. Others were interested in *pattern recognition* (recognition of forms, shapes, or configurations by automatic means) as well as *language processing* (translation and understanding of human language by computer). At Dartmouth, participants reported on the progress of their work and discussed directions for future research.

Today in the 1990s, one finds AI still evolving, somewhat in the spirit of the Dartmouth conference. Many disciplines in the hard and soft sciences are contributors, including cognitive psychology, formal logic, symbolic programming, propositional calculus, learning and heuristics. Their products constitute subdisciplines of AI including expert systems, natural-language processing (NLP), machine translation (MT), intelligence robots, as well as voice, vision, and image processing. Each of these subdisciplines can be viewed as branches of the tree of AI, whilst the disciplines contributing to AI can be viewed as the roots of AI. This view is illustrated in Fig. 2.1.

Some of the disciplines can be viewed as subdividing into subdisciplines, such as NLP branching into NLP analysers and NLP synthesizers. These are shown in Fig. 2.1, which also identifies inputs to AI applications (analogous to the fertilizer for a tree), and include parallel processors as well as AI programming languages and software. These resources along with the personnel resources needed are the subject of Part III of this book.

The disciplines and techniques that provided the theoretical foundations for AI, analogous to the roots of the AI tree, are many. They include cognitive science, symbolic programming (LISP, PROLOG, and Smalltalk), formal logic, heuristics as well as search, reasoning and learning techniques.

Many expressions were used at the Dartmouth conference to describe complex information processing and machine learning, including the term 'artificial intelligence'. This term has gained widespread popularity in spite of the fact that there is nothing artificial about artificial intelligence. In fact, AI is a terrible name for any subject to have to live with. The word 'artificial' almost ensures that the success of AI will be viewed as the production of some inferior substitute for the real thing. John McCarthy, a professor of computer science at Stanford University, is generally credited with devising the term for the Dartmouth meeting, and this name has resisted all attempts to displace it, despite widespread agreement that it is a poor one. Machine intelligence and computational intelligence are just two labels that various pressure groups have championed to replace AI, but all such attempts have failed miserably.

Quite apart from what to call this discipline, there is the question of what it covers. No definition of AI has been universally accepted. We shall introduce a few definitions later in this chapter, but first we need to discuss basic terms like 'thinking', 'learning', and of course, 'intelligence'.

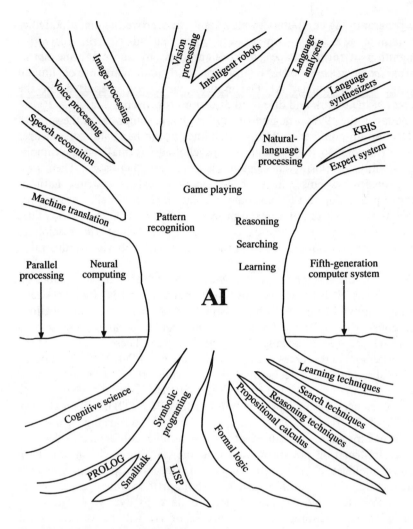

Figure 2.1 A tree representation of AI.

One problem with existing definitions is that they are stated in terms of other undefined and often controversial terms. Thus, for example, *Webster's Dictionary* defines intelligence as the ability to learn or understand from experience. The faculty of reasoning, the ability to perceive relationships, and the power of thought are also given as attributes. Other lexicographers add creativity and originality as essential components of intelligence

Most definitions only add to the problem of defining intelligence since they only lengthen the list of terms that need to be defined, leaving questions like: What constitutes 'learning'? What is meant by 'thinking'? What is creativity? How can learning, thinking, and creativity be measured?

It is argued that computers have demonstrated intelligence by proving theorems in geometry (including Pythagoras' theorem) and finding solutions to problems in logic and integral calculus. Computers have been programmed to rediscover laws such as Archimedes' law of displacement and Ohm's law for electric circuits. As early as the 1960s, computers have also composed music, produced graphic art, and even designed an electric motor. Certainly we would attribute intelligence to humans performing the same activities. But can computers think and learn and be creative, or must all the credit be given to their programmers?

CAN COMPUTERS THINK?

Can machines (computers) think? This is the type of question that philosophers like to debate. A practical approach may be to argue that since humans think, one way of deciding whether a machine can think is to see whether a machine can be mistaken for a human. Alan Turing, a British mathematician challenged by the problems of developing a criterion of thinking, suggested such a test. He proposed a 'conversation' over a teleprinter circuit between a human and an unseen respondent. Turing argued that if the average human could not correctly decide whether the respondent was a person or machine, it would have to be admitted that the respondent was 'thinking' (see Fig. 2.2).

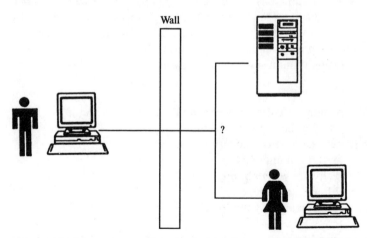

Figure 2.2 The Turing test. In the Turing test a human communicates with an unseen respondent through a terminal, not knowing if the respondent is a person or a machine. If the tester mistakes computer answers for human answers, the computer successfully passes the Turing test.

If one accepts the validity of this test, better known as the *Turing test*, a chess match in 1978 might be used to support the thesis that machines can think. In this match a computer program, Chess 4.7, was challenged by David Levy, a chess champion of some repute. Levy commented after the game that the defeated computer responded as a human would have done.

The responses of a computer in a Turing test depend on the programming used and the database stored in the computer's memory. Unless programmed to calculate, say, an average of numbers, a computer cannot figure the average of 2 and 6 although this is a very simple problem. Unless updated with the stock market quotations, a computer cannot give the current price of, say, an IBM stock. Of course, a computer can be programmed to give evasive answers, such as 'I'm not interested in the stock market' or 'The price of the stock is too volatile to quote.' And it might fool an interrogator when asked such questions such as 'What is the colour of your hair?' by bragging about its charms. The nature of the test prevents the interrogator from demanding a demonstration that such charms exist. Conversely, if it is to appear human, it will have to pretend that its simple mathematical skills are not as good as they really are.

Many anecdotes can be cited of computers fooling people for short periods of time into believing they are human respondents, not machines. But no computer has yet been built and programmed that can imitate humans indefinitely. However, inability to pass the Turing test does not mean that computers do not think, nor does it mean that passing the Turing test proves that computers do think. It could also be argued that the test in itself is not a valid test of thinking and that the nature of the questions may be biased.

Joseph Weizenbaum has produced a family of programs called DOCTOR that make it possible for patients to converse quite naturally with a computer through a computer terminal. For example, his program ELIZA provides responses similar to those given by some psychotherapists simply by rephrasing human statements in giving standard replies, as in this exchange:

ELIZA's opening statement (appears on the terminal screen):
Do you have any problems
Human (types response on the terminal screen):
Yes, I am unhappy.
ELIZA: Why are you unhappy?
Human: My friend is mean to me.
ELIZA: Tell me about your friend.

ELIZA's capability of rephrasing (and its stock of stored sentences) has fooled many people into believing that they were conversing with a doctor, not a computer. But Weizenbaum cautions against relying on the simple and superficial language understanding of his DOCTOR programs and denounces the use of such programs in clinical situations.

In order for a computer truly to understand a natural language, the computer must know the meaning of words in context. It must understand

---

SUPPLEMENT 2.1   ELIZA PUT TO THE TEST

Upon arrival at work early one Saturday morning, a vice-president of Bolt, Beranek and Newman, Inc. found the following message attached to a PDP-1 computer teletype terminal: 'Type all messages into this teletype and end them with a period.'

Assuming that the teletype was linked to the home of a colleague, Dr Daniel Bobrow, the vice-president initiated the following conversation.

VP:	Do you think I can use the computer this morning?
Response:	Why do you ask?
VP:	I might be able to make some additional sales.
Response:	Why aren't you sure?
VP:	My prospective customers have never seen a demonstration of the system.
Response:	Does this mean very much to you?
VP:	Of course it does.
Response:	You seem very positive about that.
VP:	This is ridiculous.
Response:	What do you mean by ridiculous?
VP:	Is there any reason why I can't use the computer now?
Response:	Tell me about your prospective customers
VP:	Please dial me up on 491–1850

When the vice-president got no response or phone call (note the missing period), he was decidedly irritated. Thinking someone (human operator) was playing games with him, the vice-president phoned Dr Bobrow for an explanation, waking him from a sound sleep. Dr Bobrow burst into laughter when the vice-president related the teletype conversation. The teletype, Bobrow explained, was linked to a computer. The vice-president had been communicating with ELIZA.

Source: 'Newsletter of the Special Interest Group on Artificial Intelligence of the Association of Computing Machinery', December 1969, in Z. W. Pylyshyn, *Perspectives on the Computer Revolution*, Prentice Hall, Englewood Cliffs, NJ (1970) pp. 347–348.

metaphors, appreciate the unstated goals and beliefs of the speaker, be able to perceive inferences, and recognize the underlying motivations of the speaker in a given context. In addition, the computer must be able to handle inconsistent information, and judge the plausibility of sentences. For example, understanding the sentence 'John ate up the compliments' depends on the recognition that the object of John is, strictly speaking, inappropriate for its action and that the statement constitutes a kind of metaphor. Understanding the sentence 'Mary jumped ten feet high when she heard the news' requires the ability to recognize the nature of exaggeration. These problems are culture dependent and vary not only between countries but within a country. They constitute an important problem in natural-language understanding that has been of great theoretical interest to AI and has great import to the end-user, especially the casual and non-technical user who would love to communicate with a computer in their natural language.

CAN COMPUTERS LEARN?

If learning is an attribute of intelligence, perhaps machine intelligence can be demonstrated by showing that a computer can learn. With this partially in mind, in the 1950s Arthur Samuel programmed a computer to play draughts (checkers). His draughts program identified and stored winning game strategies (along with losing strategies) and revised such stored winning moves in subsequent plays (while avoiding losing moves). As a result, the program Samuel wrote soon played better than Samuel himself. In time, the computer program even beat regional draughts champions. The *Samuel draughts program* demonstrated that self-improvement could be programmed, that computers can learn from experience. It was a major contribution in early research, not only in machine learning but also in search and reasoning techniques.

When Samuel first began writing his program, he considered programming a decision tree. All possible paths from the starting point in the game would be delineated. The computer would be given the task of searching the various paths leading to the end of the game, and then selecting a path that would win. This technique is illustrated in Fig. 2.3 for noughts and crosses (tic-tac-toe), a simpler game than draughts. The paths possible are akin to the paths taken by branches of an inverted tree and hence this schema is referred to as a *tree* structure, in this case, a game tree. Only a partial tree is illustrated in Fig. 2.3 showing some of the possible path options that follow a single initial move. A more complex tree could be prepared showing all the game moves. If such a complex tree were input to a computer, the computer could be programmed to search all paths in the tree in order to identify a winning strategy after each move by the opponent.

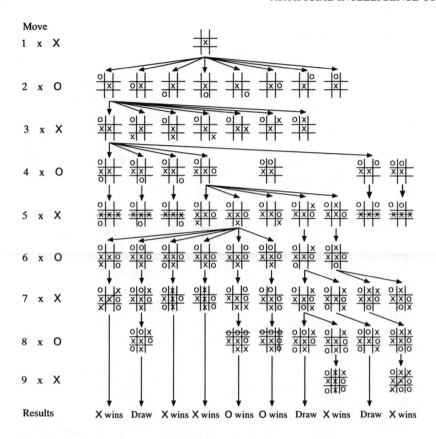

Figure 2.3 Partial decision tree for noughts and crosses. This diagram is a partial decision tree tracing one branch of the tree leading to a win for X, should the first move of X be the centre square. Row 1 shows the initial move of X. Row 2 shows the possible responses of 0. To simplify the diagram, row 3 takes one of these responses and lists all possible counter moves for X, while row 4 pursues options for 0 for some of the possible X choices in row 3. Rows 5, 6, 7, and 8 show possible winning game strategies for X after the move in row 4.

Given the speed of a computer, a noughts and crosses decision tree search does not take long. (This strategy is used in searching data tree structures for many simple business problems and we shall revisit this problem in Chapter 4.) However, a decision tree for a more demanding game is much more complex. Samuel calculated the need to search 10^{21} moves for a game of draughts. In chess, an exhaustive search of only three moves for each player from a given decision point involves a search of 1.8 billion possibilities. A computer could make such a search but it would be time consuming and costly, and certainly very inefficient.

Samuel decided that a more promising approach for programming the game of checkers would be to employ '*heuristics*' or rules of thumb to identify winning strategies. In *heuristic problem solving*, solutions are discovered by evaluating progress made towards the end result, a guided and controlled trial-and-error approach. Samuel argued that heuristic principles in the draughts program would shorten the decision tree search by pruning the tree. For example, by using heuristics, a computer might be programmed to take the centre square in noughts and crosses as soon as possible because it is crucial to many wins. Samuel's problem was to devise a set of rules for choosing promising paths of search, rules that would lead to a win and eliminate dead-end searches. (Rules-of-thumb heuristics can contribute to a game loss if they are ill conceived.)

SUPPLEMENT 2.2 FACTS VERSUS HEURISTICS

Fact: Plants need water.

Heuristic: Water houseplants when the soil feels dry to the finger.

Fact: Zinfandel is a full-bodied, dry, red wine.

Heuristic: Red wines are usually best with beef.

Fact: Rice increases in bulk when cooked in water.

Heuristic: Allow one cup of uncooked rice for four servings.

Fact: The height of a person depends on bone growth.

Heuristic: Double the height of a child at age $2\frac{1}{2}$ to determine the child's adult height.

One-way to eliminate unpromising alternatives is to formulate a strategy and investigate only those paths consistent with that strategy. For example, a fire chief who analyses past fires by type, time and place, and then trains fire-fighters to recognize and meet similar emergencies, has a strategy for training that eliminates preparation for unlikely situations. In the event of the unexpected, however, the plan for training may prove incomplete and inadequate. Samuel realized in writing his draughts program that both heuristics and a planned game strategy were possibly inadequate.

A third element was, therefore, added to his program, that of *pattern recognition*. Successful game players often make standard moves to common board positions or develop their own responses to familiar game patterns. Samuel programmed the computer to identify and store winning game patterns, including winning patterns used by opponents. These patterns were then used in game playing by the computer.

Samuel's programming of decision trees, searching of tree data structures, heuristics, learning capabilities, and pattern recognition resulted in a draughts program that could modify itself as a result of experience. The program improved its performance with each game by learning. Although never a world-class draughts master, a significant achievement was that the Samuel program consistently beat its designer and creator. Samuel had no pretensions to expertise in draughts, but he nevertheless did write a program that soon consistently trounced him. The program raised doubts about the significance of the adage that computers can only do what you tell them to do. Samuel did not instruct the program to beat him, but he did program the computer to play legal draughts and to improve its performance as a result of experience.

Samuel's work also demonstrated that in writing a complex program, especially a program with learning mechanisms, the full range of possible program behaviour cannot be predicted. This phenomenon, known as the *Samuel phenomenon*, plagues modern programmers. Because of the complexity of software today, many programmers lose track of instructions that they have written during program development, and often fail to foresee the consequences of their program once they put it into use. When you hear statements like 'Computers are literal-minded brutes and do exactly as they are told; no more and no less', treat such statements with caution: remember Samuel's learning program.

Since Samuel's pioneering work in AI, many other people have contributed to the store of knowledge about machine learning and to its many applications in business and industry. Researchers have approached the problem from two different angles. On the other hand, studies of the physiology of the human mind have resulted in attempts to construct computers that match the manner in which the brain appears to process information, a branch of computing referred to as *neural computing*. This explains the interest of researchers in *parallel processing*, i.e. processing with many processors all working at the same time. Others are searching for electronic solutions to problem solving that do not bear any obvious correspondence with the methods used by the brain. The emphasis is rather on designing hardware and software that will match the results of human thought.

One goal is to move beyond the traditional computer transactional applications that operate only on two levels—data and programs—to a *knowledge-based system*. Such a system will combine the following aspects:

1. The problem-solving ability of computers.
2. The algorithmic power of decision models.
3. The know-how of human experts in their domains of specialization.
4 A self-modification capability

For a KBIS to be feasible, computer systems must apply machine learning as well as searching and reasoning techniques to knowledge-bases.

Unlike present databases, knowledge-bases will consist of facts and data stored in computer memory plus heuristics and rules such as the IF–THEN rule that allows knowledge to be created from these facts and data. You will read about the development of such systems in the next part of this book. First, however, we need to examine a few more basic concepts, some in this chapter. Subsequently, the concepts of expert systems, problem solving, and the definition of knowledge and of a KBIS will be given in the following chapters.

THE NATURE OF ARTIFICIAL INTELLIGENCE PROBLEMS

AI problems are intractable problems. An *intractable problem* is one that cannot be correctly solved within the bounds of finite time and computational resources. 'If AI problems are insoluble', you might ask, 'then why are we bothered?' The reason is that they are insoluble only if we want to insist on a correct or optimum solution. If we are content with an adequate, satisfactory, or 'good enough' solution, then the story is very different. And that is what we are aiming for in AI problem solving.

Let us take an example from the business world. A sample problem is to construct a financial plan for a company. Is management hoping to develop 'the correct plan'? Before deciding whether AI is appropriate for solving this problem, one must question whether the notion of a correct plan makes any sense. There are clearly good plans and bad plans, but deciding between alternative quite good plans can be an impossible task without the introduction of human hunches and personal biases for which no solid rationalization can be given.

Continuing this example: how do we know that we have a good plan? Evaluation of the quality of an AI solution can be difficult. Often the only real course is to try out the proposed solution and then attempt to evaluate it after some experience has been gained in using it.

Now suppose that the use of the chosen financial plan ends with the company going bankrupt. Was it a bad financial plan? Not necessarily. There are many features that can lead to bankruptcy: an adverse change in tax laws, or in customer habits, or in world markets, or in employee productivity, etc. The financial plan might be still defendable as a good plan; the bankruptcy may be attributed to the 'world' behaving badly, as it sometimes does.

This example illustrates some important characteristics of AI problem solving: no 'correct' solutions, difficulty in choosing between alternative possible solutions, difficulty in evaluating the quality of a chosen solution because of a complex network of similarly intractable problems that will affect the solution. A summary of problems that computers are convention-

Table 2.1 Conventional Problems Versus AI Problems

Conventional problems	AI problems
1. Can be solved correctly → potential solutions can be tested for correctness → not much difficulty in choosing between alternative correct solutions	Cannot be solved correctly → potential solutions cannot be tested for correctness → difficult to choose between alternative, adequate solutions
2. A complete, abstract specification of the problem is feasible → can agree on a specification first, and then design a system to meet it → the correctness of the system with respect to the abstract specification will not change	Only a partial, behavioural specification is feasible in practice → must explore the behaviour of partial specifications in the search for an adequate approximation → must expect that the adequacy of a chosen approximation will degrade over time

The points of difference are numbered and followed by implications of these differences; each implication is introduced by an arrow '→'.

ally used to solve and types of problems that AI can address appears in Table 2.1.

TYPES OF PROBLEM SOLVING

Given that there are these two broad classes of problem, it should come as no surprise that there are two classes of problem solving, commonly called *algorithmic* and *heuristic*. Both of these types of problem solving are based on the notion of a search space. A *search space* is a structured representation of alternative partial solutions (or more precisely, partial potential solutions) to the problem under consideration.

Let us be more specific and consider some examples. A search space is typically characterized by a set of states—'initial states', 'goal states' and 'intermediate states'—and a set of 'operators' that can transform one state into another. Thus problem solving is represented as finding and applying a sequence of operators that will transform an 'initial state', through a sequence of 'intermediate states' (the partial solutions) into a 'goal state', a solution. And, of course, the starting point is one of the initial states which is a representation of the given problem.

So problem solving within a search space involves finding a path from the given state, through a sequence of intermediate states, to a goal state. Now if the task of problem solving is to find such a path in a search space, then clearly we could try all the possible paths until we find one that leads to the goal state. This is called an *exhaustive search*, and it is the simplest form of algorithmic problem solving. The algorithm that controls the search just has to ensure that all paths can be explored while looking for a goal state. Now given this view of problem solving, AI problems can be characterized by very large search spaces. In fact, they are so large that exhaustive search of the space is an intractable problem. So, in order to have some chance of solving AI problems, we must avoid exhaustive searches of the search space. Two common methods of pruning the search are as follows:

1. Ordering the operators such that the 'best' applicable operator is always tried first.
2. Devising a state-evaluation function that can be used to rank intermediate states with respect to their 'closeness' to a goal state; thus, one can always choose to move to the next intermediate state which is closest to the desired goal state.

The above two words in quotes are where most of the AI must be concentrated. Finding a 'best' ordering of the operators (static or dynamic), and finding a useful 'closeness' function are both difficult problems that are typically solved by the use of *heuristics*—rules of thumb—that are used for no other reason than they seem to work most of the time. If we can find a guaranteed decision procedure, one that does not make mistakes, then we have an algorithmic search strategy, and we probably do not have an AI problem.

Thus, *algorithmic problem solving* means that the selection of a solution path is guided by a guaranteed decision procedure. By way of contrast, *heuristic problem* solving means that the selection of a possible solution path is controlled by a heuristic (and therefore unguaranteed) decision procedure. A heuristic problem solver may fail to find goal nodes in a search space. In fact the measure of the quality of the heuristics used is derived directly from the number of times that it fails to find solutions as compared with the number of times that it succeeds.

Plausibly useful heuristics are many, ways to implement them, are legion, and analytical evaluations are scarce (although quite possible in a trivial, well-defined game like noughts and crosses). In general, the worth of such heuristics is an empirical question: try it and see, is the evaluation procedure.

Moving on to a more realistic domain, a useful heuristic in a business management application might be: go for growth when the economy is strong.

To incorporate a heuristic within a program, we generate an algorithm to approximate it—a heuristic algorithm. So an implementation of the above heuristic must include explicit code to perform the following tasks:

1. Decide if the economy is 'strong' or not; this will involve prerequisite decisions as to what economic indicators to feed into the decision procedure, and the detailed decision procedure itself.

2. Specify the kind and extent of the growth to go for; there are clearly many ways for a business to grow, and an infinite number of combinations of these different types of growth.

So not only do we have to come up with good heuristics, we have to make a further series of awkward, explicit decisions in order to render our heuristic machine executable. Having thought long and hard about the original heuristic, we come up with a more precise statement of the managerial behaviour required, say:

If inflation and interest rates are both low, then we should promote our product in new areas and take on extra staff to satisfy the expected increases in both production and distribution.

This appears to be a reasonable rule that could be appropriate. But although this statement of the heuristic would probably be sufficient if you were discussing managerial strategy with a colleague, it cannot be used within a computer system until it has been transformed into a precise algorithmic rule.

Let us try for a more precise statement:

If inflation is less than 2 per cent and interest rates are less than 10 per cent, then invest a sensible amount of capital in increased advertisement and expansion of staff numbers.

This reformulation is certainly more precise, especially with respect to what we mean by a strong economy. But has it moved us much closer to a computable decision procedure? Let us list some questions that would have to be answered before this heuristic attains the algorithmic specificity necessary in AI systems.

*   How is inflation to be measured?
*   What interest rate must be lower than 10 per cent?
*   What sort of guarantees do we require on the interest rate remaining low?
*   How do we compute 'a sensible amount of capital'?
*   How do we decide what staff to increase, and by how many?

As we said earlier, the questions are many, reasonable answers are legion, and correct answers are exceptional. But the questions must be paired with precise answers before we can obtain a machine-executable version of the original heuristic. The selection of a particular set of necessary, somewhat arbitrary answers will result in a particular algorithmic approximation of our original heuristic. There are very many such approximations, and a very few ways to choose between them.

So a heuristic implemented in an AI program is more accurately viewed as one of many possible algorithmic approximations to the heuristic—but this is an exceedingly clumsy and pedantic phrase, so we shall use instead the terms 'heuristic' and 'heuristic problem solving' as opposed to 'algorithmic problem solving', which is reserved for non-heuristic procedures.

The guarantees, or lack of them, are one thing, but where does the heuristic come from in the first place? The sources are varied and ill understood. Unfortunately, experts are no more expert at introspection than you or I. All indications are that they are full of expertise, replete with high-quality heuristics, but how to pour them out of the expert and into a program is a problem that is receiving a lot of attention. In a later chapter we shall describe several approaches to this transfer of expertise problem, known as the *knowledge acquisition problem*.

Provided that the first guess for a heuristic strategy focuses upon the significant dimensions of the problem domain, then there is every chance that the heuristic can be tuned to adequacy by means of an iterative process. This tuning process may be totally automatic, in which case it is described as *machine learning*, like the early, classic example of Samuel's draughts playing program described earlier in this chapter, or it may be man–machine symbiosis, and as such it is considered in a later chapter.

HUMANS VERSUS COMPUTERS

The previous section provided you with examples of differences between humans and computers—e.g. a human can devise new strategies of game playing; the computer is restricted to the improvement of a fixed strategy. We also discussed the ability of humans to improvise, while computers follow programmed instructions. In this section we will delve further into the comparison between humans and computers.

Humans have some capabilities that machines may never be able to duplicate. As Lewis Garrett (1977) put it:

> Man is inventive and flexible. He perceives, abstracts, and associates quite well, drawing on broad experience to make decisions and check reasonableness. However, he is forgetful of detail, inaccurate, and subject to boredom and fatigue.

The organic components of the human brain appear to function quite slowly and the brain is configured for general reliability at the cost of detailed precision. In contrast, electronic components of computers process

Table 2.2 Comparison between human brain and computers

Area of comparison	Computer			Human
	1960	1980	2000	
Memory density (bits/cm^3)	10^3	10^5	10^9	10^{16}
Computing power (switches/second)	10^{12}	10^{13}	10^{15}	10^{12}
Speed (cycles/second)	10^6	10^8	10^{10}	10^2
Total density (circuits/cm^2)	10	10^2	10^5	10^7
Accuracy	Superior, especially in numeric computation			
Visual domain				Superior
Auditory domain				Superior
Fatigue	No loss of efficiency and effectiveness because of fatigue			Tires easily
Breakdown	Breaks down completely if few connectors are destroyed			Has some of the same capabilities
Problem-solving strengths	Defined and well-structured problems			Ill-defined, ill-structured problems as well as well-structured problems
Ability to adapt to changed conditions	Limited			High
Life	5–30 years			75 years
Ability to correlate and analyse masses of data	Good			Poor

information at high speed with detailed precision. Other differences between humans and computers are listed in Table 2.2. The following maxim sums up these differences:

Humans: slow, sloppy, limited memory, but brilliant
Computers: fast, accurate, vast memory, but stupid

A major goal of workers in AI is to change the latter attribute stupid to smart, if not brilliant. Whether this can be done without degrading speed and accuracy is in question. Clearly, most workers in AI believe this is possible.

Given the strengths and weaknesses of humans and computers in information processing, most AI systems today are designed to complement workers on the job, not replace them. As will be pointed out repeatedly in this text, AI systems for business and industrial management allow tasks to be performed that could not be done in the past by either humans alone or

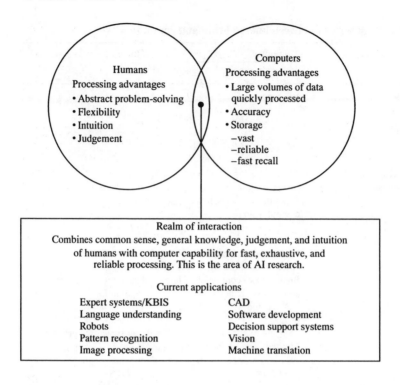

Figure 2.4 Areas of comparative advantage.

computers alone. Some of these applications that combine the comparative advantages of humans and computers are listed in Fig. 2.4.

Most often, AI systems augment human performance in pursuance of corporate goals. However, we still need the aesthetic and emotional sensitivity of people to temper machine rationality. In any case, as Lord Bowden, a distinguished British scientist, argued: it would be futile to try to duplicate humans with computers in a world already overpopulated by intelligent beings that are produced quite easily, relatively cheaply, and in an enjoyable way.

Some people prophesy a future in which the capacity of computers to learn will be used to design improvements in computer hardware and software—improvements that add to the capabilities of the machines. These new capabilities combined with learning may, in turn, trigger new design improvements, a cycle that may be repeated until 'ultra-intelligence machines (UIMs) have been developed.

Marvin Minsky, an MIT scientist, cautions that machine intelligence may cause problems as well as solve them:

It is unreasonable to think that machines will become 'nearly' as intelligent as we are and then stop, or to suppose that we will always be able to compete with them in wit or wisdom. Whether or not we could retain some sort of control of the machines, assuming that we would want to, the nature of our activities and aspirations would be changed utterly by the presence on earth of intellectually superior beings.   (quoted in Dorf, 1977: 405)

Although the number of commercial AI applications is currently limited, AI and KBIS offer great promise for information systems of the future. Research in the representation of knowledge and machine learning is progressing steadily. With progress in language and speech understanding—an area of research where researchers have made advances—natural language communication with computers may soon replace programming languages such as FORTRAN, COBOL, Pascal, and BASIC. As a result, computers will become more accessible to users, and the anxiety, technostress, and worker resistance commonly associated with computer use in the workplace will be reduced.

This should come as good news to business managers and *end-users* (ultimate uses of the system, as opposed to *users* who may be intermediate users such as the technical developers of systems). Analysts and programmers of information systems will benefit as well because they will be able to develop information systems that are more versatile and flexible. For example, they will be able to customize systems to the backgrounds, preferences, and even idiosyncrasies of individual workers. Computer systems will also become more tolerant of common human errors and allow user choice in the way the systems operate. Input will not have to be keyed in; voice commands in English, French and other natural languages, blueprints, pictures, printed matter, and handwriting will be accepted as well.

The jobs of computer analysts, designers, and programmers will change in the future. No longer will these workers be needed as technical intermediaries between computer users and computer systems. End-users will even be able to develop new systems on their own using new AI tools. Relieved of development duties, computer technicians, will spend more time on computer system infrastructure, such as integrated databases and applications for interconnected networks. The goal is higher levels of systems performance and increased end-user satisfaction.

IS THERE A DEFINITION OF ARTIFICIAL INTELLIGENCE?

The short answer to this question is 'no'. And, although accurate and concise, this answer has little else to recommend it. If we wish to develop an appreciation for the theories and programs that are typically labelled with

AI, then we need to explore a few of the proposed definitions and see why and where they fail.

The anonymous, but widely used, definition is: AI is the study of computers doing tasks that would be considered to require intelligence if a human did them. So AI tasks are playing chess, proving theorems, diagnosing diseases, and so on. But what about conversing in English, cleaning a house, and going shopping? These appear to be much harder computational problems, but they are not ones that we typically associate with human intelligence. And what about vast mental calculations? Complex mental arithmetic is certainly a scarce skill and one that is likely to be associated with human intelligence. Yet nothing could be easier computationally. Clearly some of this mess can be tidied up by separating out the various meanings of that slippery word *intelligence*. But having done that, we still would not expect this definition to come out sharp and shiny.

A somewhat anti-intellectualist definition is given by Minsky: intelligence is a collection of kludges (i.e. tricks that are used simply because they work, and different tricks are needed for different occasions). The most recent exposition of this line of argument is in his book *The Society of Mind* (Minsky, 1986). So AI becomes the process of identifying these tricks and how they fit together. A similar view offered by Chandrasekaran (1990) has had a considerable airing: intelligence is not one thing, it is really a collection of strategies—generic functional strategies to be more precise (see below for an explication of these ponderous objects). 'The task of AI as the science of intelligence is to identify these strategies concretely, and understand how they integrate into coherent wholes.'

One popular AI text (Rich, 1983) offers the following definition: 'AI is the study of how to make computers do things at which, at the moment, people are better.' This is another moving definition, and also one that exhibits the customary nebulousness, both of which points Rich draws to our attention. She admits that it is ephemeral because of reference to the current state of the art in computer science, but in actuality, she claims, it is surprisingly stable and avoids the philosophical issues that plague attempts to define the meaning of either *artificial* or *intelligence*. And she has a point there. But, of course, it also has its weaknesses. Thus, there are many things that humans do much better than computers, such as walking and swimming, but attempts to build machines with similar capabilities would only be peripheral AI work. For example, a swimming and walking robot would be a major breakthrough, but the central problems of swimming and walking are not similarly central AI problems. They are problems of balance, motor coordination, and timing; these are primarily engineering problems, although a satisfactory level of solution *may* draw heavily on AI.

At this point we hope that it is clear that AI is the name of a body of work that is not at all easy to define in any simple and clear-cut way.

DIRECTIONS OF ARTIFICIAL INTELLIGENCE

Clearly, most of the problems associated with constructing intelligent systems remain to be solved. There are fairly clear-cut technical problems of, for example, representation of information (or even knowledge!) to support intelligent decision making, and there is the generating of inferences from such information when it is both incomplete and probabalistic in nature. We humans do these things all the time, even fairly mundane-seeming tasks do, in fact, demand this sophistication of problem-solving behaviour. But what about the less-easy-to-specify facets of intelligence: the expert who does 'what feels right', the machine operator who just 'knows that a weld is weak', etc.? Are these aspects of human intelligence important? Are they mechaniz-able? Can we ignore them and still have useful and effective applications of AI in the business world? These are all open questions, but they have generated much speculation over the years with a variety of outcomes. In this chapter we shall conclude with a brief review of just a few of the more influential arguments about these sorts of questions.

The first major compendium of dissension was the book *What Computers Can't Do* by Hubert Dreyfus, published in 1972, but many of the technical arguments in this early critique are quite weak and have now been either discarded or superseded in his later contributions to these issues.

Joseph Weizenbaum's famous critique, *Computer Power and Human Reason*, published in 1976, was motivated, in part at least, by the desire to 'get it right'—although it did not, in fact, turn out that way. The other, and perhaps the major, impetus behind the production of Weizenbaum's landmark critique of AI was the persistent misconceptions of a crude demonstration program that Weizenbaum had written—the ELIZA program that we mentioned earlier.

In sum, Weizenbaum did not argue (like Dreyfus's original book) that certain things cannot be done by computers, but that certain things *should not* be done, either because we have not yet understood the phenomenon and solved the problems sufficiently well, or because it is just something that we should never pursue—it is 'obscene' (e.g. wiring electronic circuits to animal brains).

In his more recent book with his brother, Stuart, *Mind over Machine* (1986), Hubert Dreyfus has considerably narrowed his attack on AI and the specific target selected is expert systems technology (EST). In broad outline, the Dreyfus brothers maintain that EST has failed to deliver expert systems (and the few that have progressed beyond the prototype stage display a level of behaviour that might be called competent rather than expert). The reason for this signal failure is, they claim, that the underlying theory is wrong: human expertise is not based upon an inferencing mechanism operating with a set of independent rules.

The novice uses simple rules. The move to expertise requires abandonment of such rule-based behaviour and the development of sophisticated 'situational' knowledge—an automatic 'knowing' what to do from an appreciation of the totality of each individual situation. This rather difficult argument can be readily appreciated, we think, from consideration of a familiar class of expertise, car driving. When you first learn to drive a car you do operate according to rules such as 'change from first gear to second gear at 20 m.p.h.' Such rules enable you to begin driving, but they must be abandoned in order to become an expert driver. Practice in driving, which is necessary in order to become expert, enables you to replace such simplistic rules by a subtly context-sensitive and largely unconscious skill, such that you just know when it is right to change gear.

Now, none of this proves that the basis for EST is wrong, but it is all very suggestive of its erroneous nature, and in the hands of the Dreyfus brothers the arguments have much more force than is apparent in the short synopsis we have been able to present.

One last contribution to this final, grand-scale critique of AI and all that it has attempted to achieve over the last few decades can be found in the book by Winograd and Flores first published in 1986 and entitled *Understanding Computers and Cognition*. They write that 'current thinking about computers and their impact on society has been shaped by a rationalistic tradition that needs to be re-examined and challenged as a source of understanding'. Quite rightly, they reject the common belief that computer decision-making systems may be preferable to human ones because the computer system will be free of prejudice and bias. All in all, they are highly critical of the current and past approaches to the building of computer systems for use in business as well as elsewhere. They charge that the pure rationalist approach to the design of such systems has led us to view, say, decision making in business as a situation within which we continually try to select the best option from a predefined set of alternative choices. Much real-world decision making, they claim, is not like this; there is no predefined set of alternatives at each choice point. The construction of any set of alternative choices only comes from a prior application of bias and prejudices concerning the situation at hand. By preselecting and building in our systems all these sets of alternatives, we build in (in a non-explicit way) our biases about the problem. This generates systems with a 'blindness' (their word) to a larger realm of concern for human behaviour—and fails to produce systems that do a good job.

And, although Winograd and Flores are highly critical of current technology, they are not pessimistic about the future applications of computer technology. They propose a new approach to the design of computer systems. System flexibility is of prime importance, they claim, as there will always be unanticipated 'breakdowns' in the matching of the computer system to the real-world situation that it was designed to cope with. They see computer technology being used to help us explore the adequacy and the breakdowns of preselected sets of alternative possibilities in, say, a decision-support system. They freely admit that there are appropriate domains for useful application of the current, inflexible technology, but, they caution us, there is also a danger of seeing them as capable of doing too much.

And this is the message that we would like to leave you with at the end of this book. Computer technology, employing AI techniques, holds much promise for the production of radically new types of computer systems in all spheres of the business world. But, given the known limitations of the current technology, appropriate problems must be selected with care and the technology applied in a well-thought-out way. All manner of dangers lurk in an ill-conceived usage of computer technology and of AI technology. There are out-and-out technical problems that we do not yet know how to solve; there are societal problems that a radical change in technology always engenders; and there are even ethical problems, once we introduce a new species of intelligence into our midst. Luckily, at our current crude level of AI technology, the problems are mostly technical with some social aspects.

So, with much promise, but many problems, the introduction of AI technology to support new, and more advanced, KBISs will be an exciting area to work in.

SUMMARY AND CONCLUSIONS

In this chapter we have presented a number of ideas about what AI really is. As you have seen, there are a wide variety of interpretations of AI, and there is no simple and accurate definition. As a result, there is no simple test or decision procedure for determining whether a computer system embodies AI or not. One side-effect from reading the rest of the book should be that you will begin to appreciate the tools and techniques that are typically associated with knowledge-based systems and AI systems. What we hope you will gain from reading this book is a sound realization of what the scope and limitations of AI really are, as well as a feeling for what might be possible in the near future. The lack of a neat definition, and all the nice things that it entails, is unfortunate but clearly of lesser importance. The most important consideration is the 'bottom line' of AI and all the research and development in AI.

The results and fruits of AI research and development can be viewed by returning to the analogy of the tree presented earlier in the discussion of the evolution of AI. Each fruit or product of AI is in a different state of maturity, as depicted in Fig. 2.5. The fruit of expert systems, already a

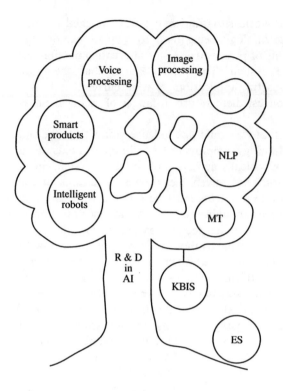

Figure 2.5 The tree of AI research and development.

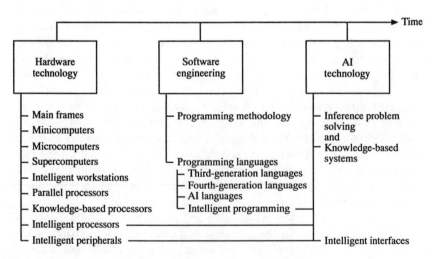

Figure 2.6 Resources of computer technology that support a KBIS.

commercial success, has been plucked. A KBIS, an extension of an expert system and the subject of this book, is near ripe for public harvesting and commercial use. Some AI fruits and products will become embedded in other products, for use in the home, office, and the factory. Some AI fruits have not yet got their names. To paraphrase the late Rear-Admiral Grace Hopper, a computer scientist of some note, you haven't seen anything yet. There is much more to come.

There are many resources needed for a KBIS, most important being those of hardware and software technology, and these are shown in Fig. 2.6. Most of these resources are discussed in Part III of this book. Before discussing them we need to discuss the development of a KBIS which is done in Part II. But first, we need to discuss a few more basic concepts which are the subject of the remaining part of this part of the book. We start with the expert system, the basic foundation for a KBIS.

CASE 2.1 ARTIFICIAL INTELLIGENCE IN THE UNITED KINGDOM

In 1973, the Lighthill Report on Artificial Intelligence argued that AI was a theoreticians' toy and had little potential for the business world. In 1981, the SGCS system in Japan highlighted the potential applications of AI. A 10-year programme under John Alvey was funded by the British Government for £200 million for the first five years. Alvey recommended a major investment in an intelligent knowledge-based system (IKBS), which had as its central plank close collaboration between industry and academia. Awareness Clubs were created and some were specialized for functional fields such as the 'Alvey Financial Expert Systems Club'. Through such clubs and by funding projects directly, the Alvey programme contributed greatly to the establishment in the United Kingdom of a community of firms and academia interested in applying AI to business and industry.

The Alvey Programme was conceived, planned, and initiated by a Conservative government under the assumption that world market forces left to themselves would not necessarily work to the United Kingdom's advantage in relation to information technology.

Sources: N. Ostler (1990) 'The Alvey Programme: Footnotes', *Knowledge Engineering Review*, **5** (4), 295–301; B. Oakley and K. Owen, *Britain's Strategic Computing Initiative* (1990).

QUESTIONS

1. Is the damage to the cause of a KBIS of the type caused by the

Lighthill Report too difficult to overcome? What steps would you propose?

2 Is government intervention such as the Alvey Programme essential for the development of AI and KBISs in a country? If so, why? If not, what are the alternatives that you suggest? What are the variables involved?

3. When is close collaboration between academia and industry essential for the encouragement of AI technology in a country? When is independence between academia and industry desirable?

4. When would you recommend the formation of 'Awareness Clubs'? Why? What are the limitations? Should they be organized along functional lines? Explain your position.

5. Under what conditions would market forces be relied upon for the development of AI technology as was the case in the United States?

CASE 2.2 ESKORT IN DENMARK

ESKORT is an expert system for auditing implemented for the Danish Customs Service in 1988. ESKORT audits value-added tax (VAT) and has produced time savings of about 20 per cent, besides improving the quality of the audits, which are both better and more uniform. These benefits must be considered against the cost of 18 million kroner that the system cost over five years.

ESKORT also saved the customs authorities 'about 500 new officers that would have been needed . . . and that training alone would occupy 60% of the existing officers' time for a long period'.

Besides savings in training and an increase in efficiency of the auditing activities, the evaluation report mentioned the advantage of 'improving the appearance of the Danish Customs Authorities as a modern and efficient organization'.

Source: E. Hollnagel (1991) 'The pragmatic and academic view on expert systems', *Expert Systems with Applications,* **3** (2), 179–186.

QUESTIONS

1. How does one evaluate the monetary benefits of an improvement in quality of audits?

2. If the system were not justified on economic grounds, how would one monetarize the benefits of the improved 'appearance' and 'image'.

3. Were the non-monetary benefits of savings in training and in

improved image a surprise? What other political advantages could emerge from an expert system?

4. How does one determine when the system is no longer relevant? For example, could changes in the VAT process or rate make the system irrelevant? How does one monitor the existence of relevancy?

REVIEW AND DISCUSSION QUESTIONS

2.1 Which of the 'definitions' of AI do you prefer? Explain why it is preferred, and also indicate what its weaknesses are.

2.2 Why is machine learning 'the quintessential AI issue' for Schank? Do you agree? Explain your reasons.

2.3 Consider the rock game as a possible alternative to the Turing test. When people put their toes through a hole in a screen either someone stamps on them (the toes that is) or else they drop a rock on them (still the toes). Now if these brutalized people cannot generally distinguish between the impact of a rock and that of a person on their pedal appendages, then are we going to have to admit that the rock embodies intelligence? If your answer is 'yes', then discuss the implications for the Turing test as a decision procedure for machine intelligence; if the answer is 'no', then explain why the imitation game is a valid test and the rock game is not.

2.4 Describe briefly a job that you are familiar with, and then try to imagine how it would change if sophisticated AI systems were available within this work environment.

2.5 Why might computers and AI be considered dehumanizing? What is your view on this question? Explain and justify it.

2.6 Whose view of the dangers of computerization (i.e. Weizenbaum, the Dreyfus brothers, or Winograd and Flores) do you see as most important and accurate? Why? Also explain why you view it as superior to the other two viewpoints presented.

2.7 What does it mean to say that AI systems can function as intelligence amplifiers?

2.8 The AI revolution and a knowledge-based system in the business world will clearly cause great changes. List and describe six important changes in a business area of your choice, three changes for the better and three changes for the worst.

2.9 Applications of AI technology must be introduced with care. In what ways can the computer technologist and the business manager guard against some of the potentially bad effects of this new technology in the business world?

BIBLIOGRAPHY AND REFERENCES

'Artificial intelligence: a debate' (1990) *Scientific American*, **262** (1), 26–31 and 32–37.
    A contribution to the continuing debate on 'can machines think?' composed of two contrary views from philosophers of AI.
Bobrow, D. G. and P. J. Hayes (1985) 'Artificial intelligence—where are we?', *Artificial Intelligence*, **25** (3), 374–417.
    A special edition of this journal to mark its 25th volume. A variety of leading figures in AI were invited to answer a number of leading questions about the nature of AI. It makes very interesting reading.

Bundy, A. (1990) 'What kind of field is AI?', in D. Partridge and Y. Wilks (eds), *The Foundation of AI: A Source Book*, Cambridge University Press, Cambridge, pp. 215–22.

Bundy explains three types of AI: pure AI, cognitive science and applied AI. The sourcebook itself is a collection of fundamental papers on AI—formal, methodological, and philosophical.

Chandrasekaran, B. (1990) 'What kind of information processing is intelligence?' in D. Partridge and Y. Wilks (eds), *The Foundations of AI: A Sourcebook*, Cambridge University Press, Cambridge, pp. 14–46.

This paper lays out in historical perspective the different methodological frameworks within which AI projects have, at different times and in different places, been pursued.

Coleman, K. (1993) 'The AI market in the year 2000', *AI Expert*, **8** (1), 35–47.

A survey analyses questions like: What do people think about AI? Where is the market going?

de Garis, H. (1989) 'What if AI succeeds? The rise of the 21st century artilect', *AI Magazine*, **10** (2), 16–26.

A discussion of rival political and technological scenarios about the rise of the 'artilect' (artificial intellect), and its impact on society.

Dorf, R. (1977) *Computers and Man*, Boyd & Fraser, San Francisco.

Dreyfus, H. L. (1979) *What Computers Can't Do*, 2nd edn., Harper & Row, New York.

A landmark in AI despite the community's attempt to ignore it.

Dreyfus, H. L. and S. E. Dreyfus (1986) *Mind Over Machine*, Macmillan Free Press, New York.

A powerful indictment of current expert systems technology and the hype that surrounds it.

Epstein, R. (1992) 'Can machines think?', *AI Magazine*, **13** (2), 80–91.

Dr Epstein, Director Emeritus of the Cambridge Center for Behavioral Studies, collects presentations at the first round of the Turing test of machine intelligence held in 1991.

Garrett, L. E. (1977) 'Primer on artificial intelligence', in *The Best of Creative Computing*, vol. 2, Creative Computing Press, Morristown, NJ.

Germain, E. (1992) 'Introducing natural language processing', *AI Expert*, **7** (8), 30–35.

'It would be a lot easier if we could talk to computers. Sooner or later we'll be able to— and it could be sooner.'

Hall, R. P. and Kibler, D. F. (1985) 'Differing methodological perspectives in AI research', *AI Magazine*, **6** (3), 166–178.

An attempt to lay out a taxonomy for the different sorts of AI work. The *AI Magazine* is a quarterly publication of the American Association for AI and is a glossy magazine containing up-to-date technical articles as well as notices of new products from AI software vendors.

Halpern, M. (1987) 'Turing's test and the ideology of artificial intelligence', *AI Review*, **1** (2), 79–93.

A hard look at the nature of Turing's famous test for AI. Halpern examines the outcomes when the test is not passed by a machine and finds the whole framework sadly lacking in terms of what this test can really tell the scientist.

The Handbook of Artificial Intelligence (1981–1982) Ed. A. Barr and E. A. Feigenbaum (vols 1 and 2) and P. R. Cohen and E. A. Feigenbaum (vol. 3), William Kaufmann, Los Altos, CA.

Hofstadter, D. R. (1979) *Godel, Escher, Bach: An Eternal Golden Braid*, Basic Books, New York.

A classic read, it does not cover all of AI but it blends the treatment in with many other concerns (e.g. music and art). Very easy to read at one level, and very difficult to fully grasp at another.

McCorduck, P. (1979) *Machines Who Think*, Freeman, San Francisco.
Solely a casual reading book, devoid of technical content but full of fascinating anecdotes about the founders of AI and the history of AI in general.

McRobbie, M. A. and J. H. Siekmann (1991) 'Artificial intelligence: perspectives and predictions', *Applied Artificial Intelligence*, **5** (2), 187–207.
After a brief introduction to AI, the author makes predictions over a timespan of around 'two years about future developments in each of what are arguably the major subfields of AI'.

Michie, D. (1982) 'The state of the art in machine learning', In D. Michie (ed.), *Introductory Readings in Expert Systems*, Gordon & Breach, London, pp. 208–229.
In this chapter Michie introduces his own, somewhat novel, solution to the 'knowledge acquisition' problem—i.e. the problem of extracting from human experts the information upon which their expertise is based. This general problem and the proposals for dealing with it are addressed later in this book (Chapter 9).

Michie, D. (1991) 'Machine intelligence and the human window', *Applied Artificial Intelligence*, **5** (1) 1–10.
The well-known British author starts with the theme of the computer as a learner and among other things discusses inductive learning as found in fifth-generation computer systems.

Minsky, M. (1986) *The Society of Mind*, Simon & Schuster, New York.
In this book Minsky presents a non-technical treatment of his quite unique view of the nature of human intelligence. He views human intelligence as the outcome of the somewhat anarchic interaction of a society of competing and conflicting agents. The book makes interesting reading, but it is difficult to begin to see how his ideas could be explored through computer programs.

Partridge, D. (1991) *A New Guide to Artificial Intelligence*, Ablex, Norwood, NJ.
An introduction to AI including a comprehensive review of the connectionist approach.

Partridge, D. and Y. Wilks (eds) (1990) *The Foundations of Artificial Intelligence: A Sourcebook*, Cambridge University Press, Cambridge.
The subtitle is very appropriate. This is a source book and a good one. It is a collection of papers and their follow-up discussions at a conference held in 1986 on 'Foundations of AI'. The selection of papers covers a wide range of important topics in AI including correctness, connectionism, role of representations, rational reconstructions, as well as the role and limitations of AI. It also has a 48-page annotated bibliography on the foundations of AI.

Rich, E. (1983) *Artificial Intelligence*, McGraw-Hill, New York.
One of the popular textbooks. A measured and fairly restrained introduction to the field.

Schank, R. C. (1990) 'What is AI anyway?', in D. Partridge and Y. Wilks (eds), *The Foundations of AI: A Sourcebook*, Cambridge University Press, Cambridge, pp. 3–13.
Schank discusses the nature of AI and presents it, not as a single coherent subject, but more as a way of approaching the computerization of other subjects—e.g. business and management problems.

Schank, R. C. (1991) 'Where's the AI?', *AI Expert*, **12** (4), 38–49.
The move from toy domains into concrete ones has three big consequences for the development of AI. First, it will force software designers to face the idiosyncrasies of its users. Second, it will act as an important reality check between the language of the machine, the software, and the user. Third, the scaled-up programs will become templates of the future.'

Simon, H. A. (1991) 'Artificial intelligence: where has it been, and where is it going?', *Transactions on Knowledge and Data Engineering*, **3** (1), 128–136.
An excellent overview by a Nobel Laureate and practitioner of AI.

Weizenbaum, J. (1976) *Computer Power and Human Reason*, San Francisco.

This book was begun as an attempt to repeat Dreyfus's argument, 'but do it right'; it turned out to be something rather different. Rather than argue about the technological limitations of AI, Weizenbaum argues that certain types of AI research should not be pursued because they are immoral or 'obscene'—a difficult argument to make, but one that is well worth attempting.

Winograd, T. and F. Flores (1986) *Understanding Computers and Cognition*, Ablex, Norwood, NJ.

The very different backgrounds of the two authors is explained in the preface: 'The philosophical ideas of thinkers such as Heidegger, Gadamer, Maturana, and Austin provided a framework to integrate what we had previously learnt through our practical experience'.

3

EXPERT SYSTEMS

Knowledge is power and permits the wise to conquer without bloodshed and to accomplish deeds surpassing all others.

Sun Tzu, *Art of War*, ca 4th century BC

'No, no! The adventures first', said the Gryphon in an impatient tone: 'explanations take such a dreadful time!'

Lewis Carroll, *Alice's Adventures in Wonderland*

INTRODUCTION

An *expert system* (ES) is a computer program that draws upon the knowledge of human experts captured in a knowledge-base to solve problems that normally require human expertise. Unlike conventional programming, an ES does not follow an algorithm that details a precise series of steps to yield a precise result. Instead, processing is based on rules called *heuristics*, often called rules of thumb, that state relationships that are likely, but not guaranteed, to yield an outcome in an environment where information is uncertain or incomplete. Consider the thought process of a banker in deciding whether a loan applicant is a good credit risk. After examining hard data, the banker will intuitively evaluate the likelihood of repayment. This is the type of problem that ESs are designed to address— problems that cannot be reduced to mathematical formulas. Well-designed expert systems imitate the reasoning process of human experts in solving specific problems within specific domains of knowledge.

In this chapter we first introduce the reasons why ESs are developed,

, then look at the components of such systems. We also describe the benefits, limitations, and use of ESs. The chapter concludes with a comparison of ESs with decision support systems and presents ways to combine the two to enhance management decision-making.

WHY DEVELOP AN EXPERT SYSTEM?

Every organization has valued employees who are more proficient in their jobs than others—people who have acquired knowledge and experience that makes them experts in their fields. A decision to implement an ES is often triggered by the pending retirement of such an expert and the need to preserve that person's expertise.

The idea is to 'clone' the individual's skill in a computer program so that even after retirement, his or her expertise is available to the organization on a continuing basis. For example, the person who replaces the retiree on the job might use the ES in problem solving. The system might help train junior staff to think the way experienced professionals do. Perhaps the system can automate decision-making in certain domains, freeing staff for assignment to other activities. An ES ensures that work quality is consistent since the program is not subject to human failings like fatigue. Above all, scarce, expensive expertise for performing a task is stored in an active form, a knowledge-base, not lost to the organization or stored in a passive form, like a manual or textbook.

COMPONENTS OF EXPERT SYSTEMS

Expert systems have three basic parts: a knowledge-base, an inference engine, and a set of interfaces (for knowledge acquisition and a consultative interface for the end-user). Each component will be discussed in later chapters. Here, we will introduce these components, which are shown in Fig. 3.1.

The *knowledge-base* contains facts, theories, relationships, attributes, observations, definitions, and other types of information about the problem area gleaned from one or more experts in a given field and supporting textbooks and manuals. (Figure 3.2 illustrates different kinds of knowledge stored in a knowledge-base. The collection of this knowledge is called knowledge acquisition.) Usually a specially trained professional known as a *knowledge engineer* interviews an expert (or experts) in the problem area for which the system is being designed to learn what is known about the problem—knowledge that is then organized for representation in a computer and transferred to the knowledge-base. The building of a

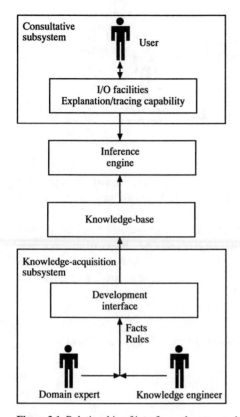

Figure 3.1 Relationship of interface subsystem to inference engine and knowledge-base.

Figure 3.2 Kinds of knowledge in a knowledge-base.

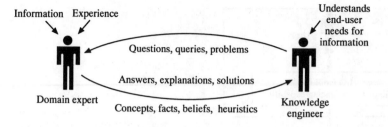

Information Experience

Questions, queries, problems

Answers, explanations, solutions

Domain expert

Concepts, facts, beliefs, heuristics

Understands
end-user
needs for
information

Knowledge
engineer

Figure 3.3 Building a knowledge-base.

knowledge-base is a result of interactions between the knowledge engineer and the domain expert as shown in Fig. 3.3. We will say more on the knowledge-base in a series of chapters later.

The knowledge engineer also ascertains subconscious rules of thumb and acquired instincts that are applied to the facts or observations to reach a solution. These rules, usually stated in an IF–THEN format, are also included in the knowledge-base. For example, a rule in an ES to diagnose engine failures might look like this:

IF   the engine is idle, and the fuel pressure is less than 38 p.s.i., and
        the gauge is accurate
THEN   there is a fuel system fault.

An ES for a simple task may have one or two dozen such rules; an ES for a complicated task, hundreds or thousands of rules. The complexity of the activity determines the number of rules and the amount of data to be stored in the knowledge-base. Memory capacity is one constraint in choosing ES hardware; CPU speed is another: a large rule-based ES can take a lot of CPU time.

The component of the ES that searches, reasons, and makes inferences from the facts and rules in the knowledge database is called the *inference engine*. The inference engine consists of a computer program that provides the methodology for reasoning about information in the knowledge-base and instructions that control processing. In other words, the inference engine selects what rules to use (in a rule-based system), accesses and executes those rules, and determines when an acceptable solution has been found. No wonder the inference engine is sometimes called the 'control structure' or 'rule interpreter'. Inference approaches used in ESs include logical deduction, reasoning by analogy, and procedural reasoning (use of mathematical models or simulation). We will have more to say about the inference engine in two later chapters.

MODES AND APPLICATIONS OF EXPERT SYSTEMS

Initial problems for a potential user of ES technology are to determine the type of problem, and the style of ES to be employed. Answers will provide information that can help in making the right decision about which shell to purchase for your particular ES problem. Two initial questions need to be answered: what sort of application is it (e.g. diagnostic or predictive); and in what way are you going to apply ES technology to the problem (e.g. will it be highly interactive, or stand-alone once the input data has been supplied?).

First, let us look at the range of types of generic problem solving to which ES technology might be applied.

Harmon and King (1985: 94) list the following types of application:

1. *Interpretation*—inferring situation descriptions from sensor data.
2. *Prediction*—inferring likely consequences of given situations.
3. *Diagnosis*—inferring system malfunctions from observables.
4. *Design*—configuring objects under constraints.
5. *Planning*—designing actions.
6. *Monitoring*—comparing observations to plan vulnerabilities.
7. *Debugging*—prescribing remedies for malfunctions.
8. *Repair*—executing a plan to administer a prescribed remedy.
9. *Instruction*—diagnosing, debugging, and repairing system behaviour.
10. *Control*—interpreting, predicting, repairing, and monitoring system behaviour.

So, if you are planning to purchase a shell or tool to facilitate the construction of an ES, one of the important clues to finding an appropriate one is to determine the mode and type of application of your proposed ES. The next move is to locate shells and tools that have been used successfully to construct the sort of ES that you are contemplating, or that have been derived from an ES of the type you are considering.

Thus the EMYCIN shell was derived from the medical diagnostic ES MYCIN. So, if it is a medical diagnosis problem that you want to tackle, EMYCIN is a shell to examine in detail. Several words of warning should be issued at this point.

Firstly, if your proposed ES is a diagnosis problem, but not medical diagnosis (which seems quite likely in the average business context), a shell such as EMYCIN may not be appropriate at all. It depends on your particular diagnosis problem and the way you propose to address it. Is diagnosing faults in complex machinery just like diagnosing diseases in the human body? The answer is 'no', but they do have a number of similarities. It is your task to evaluate the extent and the importance of the similarities.

Do not be blindly led to purchase the wrong tool just because a generic term like *diagnosis* is used for a number of rather different phenomena.

Secondly, do not commit yourself to a particular tool just because the mode and type of application seem to match perfectly. This just provides a preliminary selection procedure; you must still look at the desired and available detailed features and assure yourself that there is a substantial overlap.

And lastly, there is no well-defined way to select the 'right' shell or tool for the job. A thorough investigation both of your proposed application and of the available shells and tools can add considerably to the probability that you will make a good choice, but there are no guarantees. Decision procedures are improving, but currently they are rather loose and *ad hoc*. This is one of the costs of using technology at the cutting edge.

APPROPRIATE PROBLEM ENVIRONMENTS

An ES is appropriate when the task to be performed requires expertise, logic rather than computations alone for solution, and heuristic techniques in the decision process. And when the task is either so complex or so variable that traditional information systems fail to help the decision-maker. The problem domain should be well defined and stable so that the knowledge-base does not need frequent maintenance or restructuring. In addition, the task should be performed often enough to warrant an ES.

The general areas where expert systems are of value are as follows:

1. *Diagnosis*. To identify a problem given a set of symptoms or malfunctions. For example, an ES to diagnose reasons for engine failure.
2. *Interpretation*. To infer a situation from sensory data. For example, an ES to estimate molecular structure of unknown compounds by analysing mass spectrographic and other data.
3. *Prediction*. To predict a future state from a set of data or observations. For example, an ES to evaluate the likelihood of oil or mineral deposits given soil samples.
4. *Design*. To develop configurations that satisfy constraints of a design problem. For example, an ES to configure minicomputers.
5. *Planning*, both long and short term in areas such as project management, product development, or financial planning. For example, an ES to plan tax shelters.
6. *Monitoring*. To check performance and flag exceptions. For example, an ES to determine whether a bank is complying with regulations on overdrafting and cash transaction reporting.
7. *Control*. To collect and evaluate evidence and form opinions on that

evidence. For example, an ES to judge the adequacy of a loan loss reserve for a bank.

8. *Instruction.* To train students and correct their performance. For example, an ES to give medical students experience diagnosing illness.

9. *Debugging.* To identify and prescribe remedies for malfunctions. For example, an ES to identify errors in an automated teller machine network and ways to correct the errors.

Table 3.1 lists sample ESs currently in use or under development.

Table 3.1 Examples of expert systems currently in use or under development

System	Knowledge domain	Function performed
AQ11	Medicine	Diagnosis of plant diseases
CAD/CAE/CAM	Engineering	Automated engineering design
Capital Investment	Management	Capital investment
CASNET	Medicine	Medical consulting, infectious diseases
Concept	Management	Marketing simulation, consumer behaviour, integration DSS/ES
CONGEN	Chemistry	Determining chemical structure of an unknown compound
Counsellor	Agriculture	Agricultural advice, diagnosis, economic analysis for farmers
DENDRAL	Chemistry	Hypothesizing molecular structure from mass spectrograms
Dipmeter Adviser	Oil industry	Oil exploration
EL	Electrical industry	Analysing electrical circuits
Financial Adviser	Management	Capital budgeting
FX	Management	Foreign exchange trading
Guidon	Medicine	Computer-aided instruction (CAI)
HASP (SU/X)	Machine acoustics	Problem solving
HASP/SIAP	Defence	Passive sonar surveillance system
Hiring Edge	Management	Personnel management
Internist/Cadeceus	Medicine	Consultant in internal medicine
Leading Effectively	Management	Effectiveness, productivity
Logician	Computer industry	Electronic design
Macsyma	Mathematics	Mathematical formula manipulation
Management Edge	Management	Management sales and training
Mecho	Machine industry	Problem solving and planning
MLES	Manufacturing	Manufacturing and logistics
MOLGEN	Biology	Planning DNA elements and genetic engineering
MORE	Management	Selecting potential customers from large lists
MYCIN	Medicine	Infectious disease treatment
Negotiation Edge	Management	Personnel, labour, labour relations
PECOS	Programming	Problem solving
PowerPlan	Management	Financial planning
Production	Manufacturing	Integrated factory management
Project Management	Management	Software project management

Table 3.1 (*continued*)

System	Knowledge domain	Function performed
Prospector	Mining industry	Mineral exploration
Puff	Medicine	Diagnosis of lung diseases
Questware	Management	Selecting PC hardware and software
R1	Computer industry	Computer configurations (VAX 11/780 systems)
Resource 1	Management	Productivity, time management
SACON	Engineering	Diagnosis
Sales Edge	Management	Advertising
SECS	Chemistry	Complex organic molecule synthesis
SMP	Mathematics	Mathematical problem solving
Sophie	Electronics	CAI
Synchem	Chemistry	Complex organic molecule synthesis
VM	Medicine	Measurement and interpretation

SUPPLEMENT 3.1 EXPERT SYSTEM FOR CREDIT APPROVAL

Unlike other credit card companies, American Express does not assign credit limitations to its card-holders. Each credit card transaction must receive approval. Several years ago, a mainframe credit authorization system was implemented to approve simple transactions, leaving complex transactions to the more than 300 human authorizers in the company's employ.

As the number of American Express card-holders has grown in recent years, credit losses have multiplied, in part because of faulty authorization decisions traced to inexperienced human authorizers. An expert system called Authorizer's Assistant was initiated in late 1985 to remedy this situation. The original knowledge-base codified the expertise of a group of expert authorizers in approximately 500 rules. The rules were subsequently fine tuned and expanded during a test period during which the authorization decisions of the ES were compared with decisions of human experts using actual case data. The system was put into service after demonstrating that it was accurate 96.5 per cent of the time compared with 85 per cent of the average human authorizer.

The role of Authorizer's Assistant is to approve unusual credit requests. For example, the computer might approve the purchase of a £3000 oriental rug for a card-holder with a prudent spending record, but refuse the same purchase to a cardholder on a spending spree. In a recent review of 2500 cases, 50 per cent fewer approvals judged questionable were made by Authorizer's Assistant than by human authorizers. In addition, the ES was rated 20 per cent more efficient than its human counterparts and realized an average 20 per cent improvement in service time to cardholders and merchants.

Source: P. Hessinger (1987) 'Giving credit to an expert system', *Computerworld,* **21** (47), S7.

Table 3.2   A representative list of commercial applications of expert systems

Financial services
Claim estimation
Credit analysis
Tax advisor
Financial statement analysis
Financial planning advisor
Retail bank services advisor

Data processing and MIS
Front-end to statistical analysis package
Front-end to a large software package
(several applications)
Database management system selection
Software services consultant

Finance and administration
Legal analysis of contract claims
Loan application assistant for school
administrators
Performance evaluation of dealerships
Conflict-of-interest consultant
Inventory management advisor

Manufacturing
Maintenance advisor for multimillion-
pound hydraulic system
Continuous-process manufacturing advisor
Tooling selection for machining (several
applications)
Drilling advisor for machining
Material selection (chemical)
Procedure advisor for oil well drilling
operations (several applications)
Electrical system fault diagnosis
Gas turbine engine fault diagnosis
Electronic equipment fault diagnosis
(several applications)
Power supply fault diagnosis
Mechanical equipment fault diagnosis
(several applications)
Refinery process control
Sensor verification for power generation
equipment

Field service
Software system troubleshooter
Fault diagnosis of electronic systems from
event traces (several applications)
Fault diagnosis of automotive subsystems
(several applications)
Computer network fault diagnosis

Education
Problem diagnosis training aid
Speech pathology advisor
Test result interpreter
Worksheet generation based on students'
prior performance
Student behaviour consultant
Learning disability classification advisor
Textbook selection advisor

Sales and marketing
Selection of components from an
engineering catalogue
Qualification of sales leads

Engineering
Design of motor components (output
engineering drawings)
Fastener selection (several applications)
Material selection for manufacturing
process (several applications)
Front-end for complex computer
simulation program
Front-end for engineering design package
Engineering change order manager
Weight estimator for evolving designs
Statistical analysis tool selector
Front-end to structural analysis software
system
Construction project planning and
evaluation
Structural analysis of buildings
Sensor interpretation for drilling
Robot sensor interpretation

Source: TRANSFER, IJCAI, show edition, Teknowledge, Inc. (August 1985)

Successful ESs are usually implemented in response to an immediate need. The task to be automated should be important enough to make a difference in the effectiveness of corporate operations. Before development is initiated, management should ask what the organizational payoff is likely to be. Of course, management must ensure the availability of knowledge engineers and knowledge-based systems designers, a prerequisite to a custom-developed ES. Shortage of these professionals is a major bottleneck to growth of commercial applications of ES technology.

Some applications of an ES are shown in Table 3.2. All these applications, many enhanced, are available in a KBIS, a knowledge-based information system.

ADVANTAGES AND LIMITATIONS OF EXPERT SYSTEMS

The characteristics of ESs, which we have already presented, do imply their advantages and limitations. Nevertheless, we feel that it is useful to state them explicitly.

Advantages

1. The ES is a repository of valuable information that might otherwise be lost and inaccessible to the firm creating the system and even a loss to society as a whole.
2. The ES can be indispensable when human expertise is not accessible. This could be critical in disciplines such as medicine and in remote areas.
3. Expert systems could be more efficient and cost effective than human systems, and will become increasingly so as wages of human professionals rise.
4. The ES could be better than local and even national human experts if the expertise of world-renowned experts is captured within the knowledge-base of the system.
5. An ES that is predictive can be particularly valuable when the predictions are generated fast and tirelessly.
6. A flexible, adaptable ES can grow modularly and be constantly kept up to date. Human expertise often lags way behind the state of the art when the human lacks both time and inclination to assimilate new knowledge.
7. An ES can be used for training future human experts. One such system can be duplicated, at very little cost, to yield as many copies as are required.
8. An ES will always be able to (and be prepared to) explain its premises and lines of reasoning if so requested. It will readily explain the why and

how of its conclusions and predictions. This adds to system credibility and user friendliness.

9. An ES deals with uncertainty and fuzzy data in an explicit manner. Its methods in such ill-understood areas are open to inspection; a human expert's are not.

10. An ES can be particularly useful in an organization with high employee turnover, low human performance, and a rapidly changing product mix.

11. Expert systems may be in high demand in developing countries where human expertise (such as agricultural or medical experts) is rare and expensive, where education levels are low, and where professional expertise is limited or substandard when available.

12. Advice from ESs in an organization will be consistent; it could even be faster and more efficient.

Limitations

1. An ES cannot reason on the basis of a human 'gut feeling', of intuition, or even of common sense, because these modes of reasoning are not easily representable as a knowledge-base of rules and facts.

2. An ES is confined to a restricted domain of expertise; it cannot easily integrate expertise from other domains, nor can it generalize reliably.

3. Many of the conceptually complex and tough problems in business, industry, and society (e.g. high-level planning decision making) do not appear to be applicable to current ES technology.

4. There are whole classes of problems in our society, especially procedural and behavioural problems (e.g. evaluating people for their future performance and behaviour, especially at hiring time), for which we have few (or no?) human experts, and hence, little or no chance to acquire a knowledge-base for an ES.

5. Expert systems do not learn as humans do, at least not yet. The benefit of human learning can be used to update a knowledge database, but the process is not automatic.

6. Current ESs cannot reason reliably from theories or from analysis.

7. The knowledge in an ES is highly dependent upon the human expert expressing and articulating knowledge in the form that can be used in a knowledge-base.

EXPERT SYSTEMS VERSUS TRADITIONAL SYSTEMS

In examining the advantages and limitations of ESs, it is clear that they are different from traditional systems for data processing, and from conventional approaches to computer programming. We conclude this introduction to ESs by examining some of these differences.

1. What most differentiates an ES from traditional and conventional systems is the basis of symbolic processing as opposed to numeric processing that dominates most traditional systems.
2. Expert systems are driven by heuristics rather than guaranteed algorithms (i.e. they use strategies, or rules of thumb, just because they 'work', rather than algorithms that are in some sense 'correct').
3. Expert systems are interactive; explanations, in particular, are usually obtainable at any point in a run of the system. This can be contrasted with many batch-processing, transactional systems where mid-run feedback is unobtainable.
4. Expert systems must be created and maintained by relatively scarce knowledge engineers while traditional computer systems analysts and programmers perform this role with conventional data-processing systems.
5. The knowledge-base of an ES is often more flexible and easier to modify than many a conventional database.
6. Processing within an ES is an open inferential process when compared with the fixed-operation, repetitive nature of data processing systems.
7. An ES must operate under uncertainty and with incomplete information.
8. As for data, ESs have to deal with 'fuzzy' data—i.e. data that are qualitative and derived from a consensus of expert opinion.

THE LESSONS OF EXPERT SYSTEMS

An important cache of examples of practical ES software is to be found at the Digital Equipment Corporation (DEC). For well over ten years, DEC has been collaborating with researchers at Carnegie Mellon University with the express aim of developing ESs to tackle various problems associated with the selling of sophisticated computer systems. The fruits of this collaborative effort have the somewhat cryptic names of R1, XSEL, XCON, etc. The R1 system, for example, checks customer orders of computer systems. It is designed to minimize the shipping out of wrong or incompatible components. This example is of particular interest for a number of reasons: firstly, ES technology was explicitly employed to address an outstanding problem that a conventional software engineering approach failed to solve; secondly, the benefits of the R1 system were easily quantifiable (at least in terms of money saved as a result of fewer incorrect orders being shipped out); and thirdly, the system has now been successfully used for many years and a lot of empirical data has been collected and published (e.g. frequency of occurrence of errors, ease of maintainability).

This last point is particularly important because so very few ESs have been subjected to close study during prolonged usage, and we know that maintenance (i.e. post-delivery activities) is an extremely important element of practical software technology. It is one thing to build a piece of software that passes all acceptance tests for immediate use; it is quite another for that software to be amenable to subsequent modification (either to remove the residual errors as and when they surface, or to enhance its functionality in response to changing needs). DEC's ESs seem to satisfy both sorts of requirement. Figure 3.4 gives us some data from the R1 ES collected over a period of three years. It illustrates the contention that basic software problems (such as the number of different kinds of situations that R1 did not deal effectively with—graphed as 'total distinct problems') are no worse

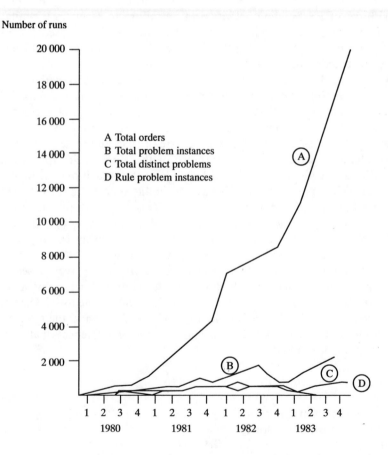

Figure 3.4 Sketch of R1's performance. *(From McDermott and Bachant, 1984: 31.)*

for ESs than they are for conventional software. This discovery is not one that is greeted with great jubilation but it is, nevertheless, quite a comfort within a technology as new and untried, and potentially unstable, as that of ESs.

A general introduction to this family of expert systems and the full results of empirical study of the R1 system can be found in McDermott (1981) and in McDermott and Bachant (1984). And a long-term study of XSEL is provided by Mumford and MacDonald (1989).

A second lesson, with more immediate impact but still quite general, is that the development of ES software cannot be squeezed into the conventional mould. We must come to grips with the notions of partial specifications whose adequacy is explored by means of working prototype systems. And we must similarly learn to do without the comfort of thinking that system behaviour is provably correct even in principle. The relatively recent flurry of ES building activity and its failure to result in a similar flurry of practical ESs should teach us that the problems posed by ES software are not to be taken lightly. They are deep and difficult problems, and we must recognize this fact.

A further twist to the conventional wisdom that experience with expert systems has exemplified is the importance of the HOW in building ES software. It is important that the system's reasoning is (or can be presented as if it is) analogous to human reasoning in similar situations. Expert system technology, based as it is on a knowledge-base of rules and a mechanism of logical inference, shows us the importance of this point. Self-explanation capabilities are made much of in ES technology (too much of, but that is beside the current point). Many ESs have the ability to 'explain' their line of reasoning that led to a particular outcome. This 'explanation' of how a specific conclusion was generated, which is a simple chaining of IF–THEN–IF–THEN . . . from the rules that the inference mechanism employed, is designed to be easy for the human expert to understand.

As an example, a car engine diagnosis system when given a set of symptoms (such as 'engine won't start' and 'turns over slowly') might, *en route* to a diagnosis, ask the question 'are the lights dim?' The user is then at liberty to ask the ES 'why are you asking this question?', and the system's explanation will come from the particular chain of inferences that it is building. It might respond:

It has been established that

1. the car won't start, and
2. the engine turns over slowly
Therefore, if
2. the engine turns over slowly, and

3. the lights are dim
then
there is evidence that the problem is
4. the battery is flat [Rule 123].

Of course, the reasoning is likely to be much more complex than this, but the point is that a fairly good explanation can be automatically generated from a rule-based and logical-inference-driven system. In the above example, the clauses numbered 2, 3, and 4 constitute one of the car-engine diagnostic rules in the rule-base. If we can suspend disbelief for one moment and assume that the explanation is not transparently obvious, the user might want to clarify further this explanation. Further probing can typically be done using HOW queries. For example, 'how did you know that the engine turns over slowly?' In this case the system should respond that 'the engine turns over slowly was a given fact', but it might have been an inference from another rule in which case the system would have retrieved and displayed the relevant rule. This could in turn suggest more HOW queries and so the system–user explanatory dialogue can continue.

The importance of this HOW constraint on AI software function stems from the nature of the basic problems. Iterative system development requires that someone can understand the specific system behaviour in terms of general system structure—the closer the human developer can relate to the way the computer system is operating, the easier it is to achieve the necessary understanding. So the HOW constraint is necessary for system development. It is also necessary for both validation and use of an adequate system. Validation of ES software is problematic. A long-term process of building confidence in the behaviour of the system seems to be an essential component of ES software validation, and a major feature of this confidence-building process is for the human experts to 'see' how the behaviour is generated. In addition, an ES is expected to produce surprising results, but this class of results is composed of two different categories which must be clearly separated: there are surprising results because of intelligent reasoning that the human overlooked, and there are surprising results from problems within the system—not just outright errors but possibly a generally good heuristic having a bad moment (as they necessarily will from time to time). Again an understanding of the system's reasoning behind the surprising result will provide the basis for the necessary discrimination.

A third lesson from experience with ESs is that part (perhaps a large part) of the secret of success is choosing the right sort of problem, and the fact that most ES projects do not get beyond the prototype stage, tells us that it is all too easy to make the wrong choice. So, do we know what the characteristics of an appropriate problem are? We know that configuration of complex computer systems was an appropriate choice, and we know that medical diagnosis was not. But do we know why, in general, this is so? A number of people have tried to provide the general characterization that we now seek. Luger and Stubblefield (1989) present the following criteria for selecting a problem for ES development:

1. The need for the solution justifies the cost and effort of building an ES.
2. Human expertise is not available in all situations where it is needed.
3. The problem does not require either perceptual or motor skills—i.e. it is a purely cognitive problem.
4. The problem is relatively self-contained—in particular, high-quality solutions do not require common-sense reasoning.
5. The problem cannot be solved as a conventional software engineering problem.
6. Cooperative and articulate experts exist in the problem domain.
7. The problem can be limited in scope and still be usefully solvable—it can be fitted within the current scope of the technology, say, a few hundred rules per module (knowledge-base partition).

SUPPLEMENT 3.2 SAMPLE EXPERT SYSTEM SUCCESS AND FAILURE

With transaction volume in the foreign exchange trading department of Chemical Bank on the increase, management supported the development of an expert system to monitor trade. The ES, called Auditing Assistant, flags irregular trading patterns that could indicate improprieties like embezzlement or kickbacks. The system, which cost £105 000 to develop and install, originally checked New York-based trades in dollars and pounds. However, recently deutschmark and yen trades have been added. Soon London-based traders will also be checked by the system.

Auditing Assistant, developed from an expert system shell, runs on a LISP processor. To avoid having to solve problems of connectivity, the system is independent. Someone must physically carry information stored on tape to the LISP processor for loading in order to transfer data from desktop terminals to the ES. Because the system is user-friendly, eases workloads, and does not threaten the jobs of auditors, there has been no resistance to this ES in the workplace.

Contrast this successful ES with K:Base, a system for Shearson American Express to match major borrowers who might be interested in interest-rate swapping. In order to save development costs, a K:Base prototype was first built on a personal computer, but its slow speed made the system useless on Wall Street. Although a LISP version was planned, support for the system soon vanished. One reason was trader resistance. (The K:Base system required traders to share their leads with others in the company.) A merger with Lehman Brothers was an additional reason to discontinue development: Lehman had a different swapping strategy that made the ES unnecessary. Besides, corporate managers were overburdened by problems associated with the merger and were unwilling to invest in expensive new technology. Another factor leading to the demise of the system was the resignation of the original mentor of K:Base who departed to another job. According to one Shearson Lehman executive: 'The system was like an orphan; when the parent left, no one adopted it.'

Source: A. Kozlov (1988) 'Rethinking artificial intelligence', *High Technology*, **8** (5), 24–25.

SUPPLEMENT 3.3 MICROCOMPUTER-BASED EXPERT SYSTEMS

No longer is a mainframe, minicomputer, or a special LISP machine required for an ES. Today, ES shells that typically support from 200 to 2000 rules are available for microcomputers. One rule of thumb to identify tasks appropriate for such systems is the following: a micro-based ES is appropriate if the problem to be solved can be done by a novice after a half-hour give-and-take conversation with a human expert.

Another way of evaluating potential ES applications for a microcomputer is to consider the training time and cost of developing an in-house expert to perform the task at hand. 'Micro-based ESs best solve routine judgement problems, problems for which you might ordinarily train someone for one to two months to do a job and where you have a high turnover', says one software developer.

A sample micro-based ES is used at the help desk of Travelers Corp., an insurance and financial firm, to diagnose failures in the company's 560 IBM 8100 controllers. Almost every day a malfunction occurs in one of these machines, resulting in a call to the data-processing help desk for advice on ways to return the controller to service. Unable to justify the permanent assignment of a maintenance expert to the help desk, the company created a 70-rule program called DIAG8100 to help regular staff members respond to requests for help. The result? Downtime of the company's 8100s has decreased. Instead of being out of commission from 30 minutes to 2 hours, machines today are typically down only 5–10 minutes.

Many micro-based ESs evolve to meet a specific need like this. Many such systems evolve haphazardly, not included in long-range plans of the information services department.

Source: B. Cronin (1986) 'Micro-based systems pave low-cost route to commercial AI', *Computerworld*, **20** (2), 55–56.

A fourth lesson to be learnt is that the so-called knowledge acquisition problem is far from solved. The codification of the information upon which human expertise is widely believed to be founded—i.e. the knowledge acquisition problem—has proved to be surprisingly resistant to the straightforward strategy of inducing the expert to simply articulate his or her rules and heuristics. As a consequence, we might observe that within the ES community there are substantial breakaway groups who are employing alternative tactics to solve this problem. Automatically inducing a general decision tree from a set of tutorial examples is one such alternative approach that we shall see in a subsequent chapter. Another group of alternatives is based upon traditional psychological techniques of collecting large amounts of relatively simple data from the experts (e.g. judgements from the experts of relatedness of pairs of specific concepts), and applying statistics to yield an appropriate representation of the knowledge (see Cooke, 1990, for a representative example). There are also radically different approaches which deny the existence of rule-based knowledge (e.g. Dreyfus and Dreyfus, 1986) and thus champion fundamentally different solution strategies (e.g. PDP implementations, such as the 'harmony theory' model of electronic circuit expertise constructed by Smolensky, 1986).

In sum, the very existence of practical ESs should boost our confidence that the many (very many) problems to be faced by the developer of practical ES software are not insurmountable. But at the same time, the ratio of ESs started to systems as delivered products is sufficiently large (perhaps 100:1) to warn us against overconfidence. The few successes do not, we believe, encapsulate the silver bullet that AI software developers might hope to discover. Success with ES technology must be predicated upon the right choice of problem, a supportive exploratory programming environment (i.e. the right basic tools and continual behavioural feedback from the experts), and, we suspect, no small measure of sheer good fortune. And what we can gain from experience with this technology (both successes and failures) is not a neat new methodology for ES software development, but only a knowledge of where much of the conventional wisdom on software development is deficient and where future emphasis needs to be placed—e.g. in evolutionary prototyping, in in-use validation.

A last, but very important point, which is further explored in Chapter 15, is that the leap in software development complexity that the move from conventional to ES development entails has given considerable impetus to efforts to produce software development tools. We now see a plethora of ES building tools and shells on the market. One of the most important decisions for the novice ES builder is which, if any, tool or shells to purchase. Having the right tool (or shell) for the job can make the difference between having a working prototype to explore at an early stage, and becoming bogged down in knowledge-base and inference-engine implementation details so that time, patience and money run out before any working system is forthcoming.

SUMMARY AND CONCLUSIONS

The basic components of an ES are the knowledge database, consisting of facts and rules, and the inference engine, which generates inferences and conclusions after symbolic processing of the knowledge database.

There are two interfaces to the basic components of the ES. One is the development interface, used by the domain expert and the knowledge engineer during the development of the knowledge database. The other interface is for the user; it controls the dialogue with the user by asking questions and providing expert answers, as well as explanations where required. This is discussed in Chapter 11.

The main characteristic of an ES is its ability to manipulate information at a high level of skill but within only a very narrow domain. It can also respond to questions about how it arrived at its opinions, its intermediate conclusions, and its lines of reasoning in general.

Expert systems are very valuable when human experts in the domain are not easily accessible or are not cost effective, where there is higher demand than supply, or where the supply is substandard—e.g. in remote areas or in developing countries.

The limitations of ESs are that they cannot respond to complex, generalized, real-world problems, nor can they easily incorporate subjective and qualitative values, including intuition and common sense, into their reasoning strategies. In addition, they cannot form nor reason from theories, axioms, and analogies, but are dependent upon human experts to provide the necessary knowledge in a form that can be inferred from by the inference engine.

An ES varies greatly from conventional data-processing systems, and these differences are summarized in Table 3.3.

Table 3.3 The differences between traditional information systems and expert systems

Characteristics	Differences	
	Traditional transactional data processing	Expert systems
Nature of processing	Numeric algorithms	Symbolic
	Sequential and repetitive	Heuristic
Mode of processing	Usually batch	Always interactive
Nature of data	Quantitative true/false	Qualitative fuzzy
	Complete certainty	Incomplete
	or probabilistic	Uncertainty
Personnel required	Systems analyst	Knowledge engineer
	and programmers	and expert
Driven by Data	External	Internal 'knowledge'
Database	Structured	Amorphous
Inference capacity	None or little	Considerable
Needs of users	Diverse	Specific

Other processing systems and problem-solving approaches are the subject of our next chapter.

CASE STUDY 3.1 EXPERT SYSTEM FOR UK CEREAL GRAIN FARMERS

Imperial Chemical Industries (ICI) sells a variety of fertilizers and pesticides to cereal grain farmers throughout the British Isles. Choice of chemical, the amount, and time of the application depend on factors such as previous cropping, soil conditions, pH, and weather. In the past, farmers often called company headquarters for expert advice, knowing that the financial return from their fields depended on astute application of the chemicals. The lengthy phone conversations were costly to the company and took ICI personnel away from their assigned duties. In addition, the advice given was not uniform for the same conditions since a number of different employees answered the phones. The result was loss of confidence in ICI advice.

To remedy this situation, ICI developed a rule-based ES, called Crop Adviser, which farmers can access by modem from their own desktop computers. After farmers enter pertinent crop, weather, and field data, the system provides varying financial return projections for different application rates for a choice of chemicals. The advice of the system is statistically based. If the problem is beyond the system's expertise, the farmer is referred to a human expert.

Source: L. F. Whitney (1989) 'What expert systems can do for the food industry', *Food Technology*, **43** (5), 135–136.

Questions

1. How can Crop Adviser help farmers? How does the system benefit ICI?
2. How can ICI ensure that the system gives accurate advice? Should the company be responsible if the advice is in error? Explain your position.
3. Suppose a farmer loses money following the system's advice. Who should be liable?
4. What responsibility does ICI have to update its knowledge-base and rules as new products are introduced or new information comes to light?
5. Can a system similar to Crop Adviser be used in developing countries? What hardware and software problems might arise?
6. How might Crop Adviser be used as an educational tool?

REVIEW AND DISCUSSION QUESTIONS

3.1 What is an expert system? What advantages does an ES have over a human expert and vice versa?

3.2 What is the meaning of the term 'heuristic'? What is the relationship of heuristics to ESs?

3.3 What are the reasons an organization may choose to develop an ES?

3.4 What clues or indicators suggest that an ES is appropriate for a given task? What criteria should be used in deciding whether to initiate development of an ES? What factors determine whether an ES is economically feasible?

3.5 What are the major components of ESs?

3.6 Is the process used to create a database for a transactional information system the same as that for building a knowledge-base for an ES? Explain. Who is responsible for database creation for these two systems?

3.7 What is the role of an inference engine in an ES?

3.8 How do users interface with ESs?

3.9 What is the difference between a rule-based knowledge-base and the storage of knowledge in frames?

3.10 What is the purpose of the explanation facility of an ES? How does this facility serve the users?

3.11 Give examples of ESs for functional applications (finance, production, marketing, and so on). For what type of business problems are ESs appropriate?

3.12 What is an ES shell? Why might a company choose to purchase an ES shell instead of developing a custom ES?

3.13 Compare an ES shell with an ES application package. Describe their similarities and differences.

3.14 What are the benefits of an ES? What are the limitations?

3.15 What factors may hamper or prevent the development of a successful ES?

3.16 Describe how ESs and decision support systems contribute to management. What are the differences between the two systems?

3.17 What is the advantage of ES and DSS integration? How can ES subsystems in a DSS contribute to system intelligence?

3.18 Discuss problems of integrating ES with:
  (*a*) transactional systems; and
  (*b*) DSSs.

3.19 Would you expect to find resistance to ES? If so, why? How can it be managed?

EXERCISES

3.1 Select a task where an ES would be appropriate but none exists. Conduct a feasibility study for this ES. Indicate what resources would be necessary and discuss their availability. What would be the costs and benefits of the ES? (Conduct the study even if financial data are not available basing your study on economic, technological, and organizational considerations.)

3.2 Interview a person using an ES. Determine what were the original expectations for the system and whether these expectations have been met. Describe unexpected benefits, limitations and problems encountered by end-users.

3.3 Consider a task in a firm, office, shop, or restaurant done by an expert. Now consider yourself a knowledge engineer. Prepare questions to ask the expert and draw a decision table showing at least three rules that could be automated for an ES.

3.4 Search the literature of the last two years to find an example of an ES used in business. Describe the system briefly and critique it.

3.5 From a literature search, identify an unsuccessful ES. Describe the system briefly and analyse the reasons for its failure.

BIBLIOGRAPHY AND REFERENCES

Beckman, T. J. (1991) 'Selecting expert-systems applications', *AI Expert*, **6** (2), 42–48.
  The author gives a checklist that 'addresses both the technical and practical aspects of application evaluation'.
Bench-Capron, T. and R. Rada (1991) 'Expert systems in the UK: from AI to KBS', *Expert Systems with Applications*, **1**, 397–402.
  ' . . . substantial practical contributions in the development of expert systems' are discussed.
Brown, C. E. (ed.) (1991) *Expert Systems with Applications*, **3** (1).
  This special issue is on applications in business including the use of artificial neural networks and semantic knowledge-bases.
Cooke, N. J. (1990) 'Using Pathfinder as a knowledge elicitation tool: link interpretation', in

R. W. Schvaneveldt (ed.), *Pathfinder Associative Networks*, Ablex, Norwood, NJ, pp. 227–239.

Craig, K. T. and J. F. George (1993) 'The implementation of expert systems: a survey of successful systems', *Database*, **24** (1), 5–10.
This article presents survey results of 45 ES projects. Practices associated with success were: 'commitment to the ES project, user participation, and management support'.

Dreyfus, H. L. and S. E. Dreyfus (1986) *Mind Over Machine*, Free Press, New York.

Dubas, M. (1990) 'Expert systems in industrial practice: advantages and drawbacks', *Expert Systems*, **7** (3), 150–156.
Factors that influence the choice of software and hardware are presented. Knowledge elicitation and implementation topics are also discussed.

Davis, R. (1989) 'Expert systems: how far can they go?', *AI Magazine*, **10** (3), 65–76.
This is the second of a series of reports on a panel discussion. A good range of opinions of learned and experienced panelists.

Harmon, P. and D. King (1985) *Expert Systems: Artificial Intelligence in Business*, Wiley, New York.

Liebowitz, J. (1989) 'How much "artificial stupidity" do expert systems possess?' *Information Age*, **11** (6), 225-228.
The author answers the question: how smart are AI systems? It offers a general discussion of how expert systems could be improved.

Luger, G. F. and W. A. Stubblefeld (1989) *Artificial Intelligence and the Design of Expert Systems*, Benjamin/Cummings, Redwood City, CA.

McDermott, J. (1981) 'R1, the formative years', *AI Magazine*, **2** (2), 21–29.

McDermott, J. and J. Bachant (1984) 'R1 revisited: four years in the trenches', *AI Magazine*, **5** (3), 21–32.

Mumford, E. and W. R. MacDonald (1989) *XSEL's Progress: The Continuing Journey of an Expert System*, Wiley, Chichester.

Phillips, G. C. and H. K. Schultz (1990) 'What's happening with expert systems?', *AI Expert*, **5** (11), 57–59.
'A survey of expert-system users reveals a range of outlooks and concerns.' Has nine informative tables.

Rada, R. (1990) 'Expert systems in the UK', *IEEE Expert*, **5** (4), 12–17.
Instead of migrating to the US, experts on expert systems are now focusing on European connections because of 'new economic movements in Europe, which are now becoming political movements as well'.

Smolensky, P. (1986) 'Formal modelling of subsymbolic processes: an introduction to harmony theory', in N. E. Sharkely (ed.), *Advances in Cognitive Science 1*. Ellis Horwood, Chichester, pp. 204–235.

van Weelderen, J. A. (1993) 'Medess: a methodology for designing expert support systems', *Interfaces*, **23** (3), 51–61.
Two Dutch professors used MEDESS to ask the why, what, how, and with what questions as they relate to design.

4

PROBLEM SOLVING

One of the main reasons why so many problems are intractable, is that they are formulated in such a way as to defeat any solution.

Stafford Beer

INTRODUCTION

From its very inception, artificial intelligence (AI) has had a great commitment to and interest in problem solving. It has increased our understanding of many of the issues involved, and developed techniques that are not only applicable to AI problems but have considerable portability to problems in managerial decision making. Take, for instance, the problem of search. Techniques of search are not only important to AI problems in say image and voice processing but have great relevance to searching for an optimum and feasible solution in a large solution space for problems in business and industry. Similarly, techniques of reasoning and inferring are important not only to, say, expert systems in AI but also to problems in operations research/management science (OR/MS). A similar expansion can be seen in the notion of learning, which started with interest in machine learning in AI but has developed great potential for learning by managers in their decision-making process.

There are situations where all three techniques—reasoning, search, and learning—are needed for the same problem. This happened with the AI researcher Arthur Samuel who developed the first learning program and had to develop approaches to search as well as techniques of reasoning and learning. But his motivation was not pure or applied research, but rather the desire to impress the top administrators at the University of Illinois so that they would fund his work in constructing a computer. He did not achieve his goal before he moved to IBM. One might imagine that 'Big Blue' would have helped him but those were the days when AI was shunned by even the brave: it was considered unnatural (and even sacrilegious) because it was seen as threatening to replace natural and god-given intelligence. Samuel had to work on his learning program on the sly, and test it on computers early in the morning before the machines were shipped to customers. But whatever the motivation, we have made great strides in machine learning. Would this please all business managers? No: some are petrified that intelligent computers that can learn to play championship draughts (and chess) may some day learn to make business decisions and replace the manager. This, of course, is an unfounded fear: the word-processor, for example, has not replaced the secretary. Instead, the learning computer and other techniques of problem solving developed in AI could aid the business manager in making more and better decisions and in solving more complex problems—problems that have hitherto been unsolvable. It is these potentials and fears that we will explore in this chapter. We will start, however, with a taxonomy of problem solving and discuss briefly some of the approaches and techniques of problem solving. This chapter is an introduction to terms and concepts that will be used extensively in the chapters that follow.

TAXONOMIES OF PROBLEM SOLVING

Algorithms, Heuristics, or Simulation

Algorithmic problem solving is perhaps the oldest and still most common form of problem solving. This method involves the use of algorithms, where an *algorithm* is a step-by-step iterative procedure that solves a problem in a finite number of steps. Improvements are made towards an objective in each step until typically an *optimal* or best solution is reached. When an algorithm is not available, then *heuristic problem solving* is used (as in many problems of AI). A *heuristic* is a rule-of-thumb procedure that determines a good but not necessarily an optimal solution to the problem. In the case of the transportation problem in (OR/MS), we have the *greedy algorithm* which is a heuristic implemented as an algorithm that yields a fast and often good solution but not necessarily an optimal solution. Not finding an optimal solution, however, may not be serious. Herbert Simon argued in his book *Administrative Behavior* that most managers do not optimize any way, they *satisfice* because of bounded rationality. And so, heuristic problem solving is useful in applying customized logic to problems where the objective is to obtain only satisficing, but computationally efficient, solutions. Sometimes, however, neither algorithmic nor heuristic problem solving is possible; *simulation* is then used. This is where the problem is solved for a given set of parameters and the results are analysed. If the solution is satisfactory, it is used; if not, another solution is simulated. Again note that the solution may or may not be optimal. But this approach allows the problem-solver and perhaps the manager to experiment with different parameters and values of variables in order to find a satisfactory solution. The manager can then ask 'What if?' questions, like: 'What would happen if I changed the values of these variables?' The consequences are computed and if not satisfactory then other values can be changed until a satisfactory solution is reached.

Let us examine this problem a little more closely. Consider finding the minimum value of a total cost curve such as the one shown in Fig. 4.1. This shows the shape of a total cost curve that we will encounter in inventory control or queuing problems. In many cases, the total cost function would be differentiated and the equation set to zero, yielding the minimum total cost point. But then this is not possible if the function has probability variables as we shall assume in the case of Fig. 4.1. In this case we must simulate for different values of, say, X. Suppose that we are start at point A and increase the variable X move to point B. This change is in the desired direction (of reducing the cost) and so we make another increase in X and arrive at point C. Now the direction of the cost value has increased

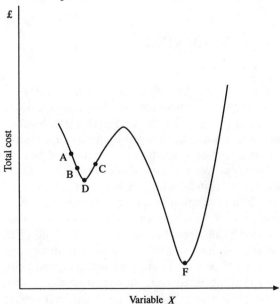

Variable X

Figure 4.1 Simulating a total cost function.

instead of decreasing, and so we go back to point B and repeat the process but with smaller increases in X so long as the cost value decreases until we reach the point D. This is the minimum point around D and so we are perhaps satisfied. But this is not the best or optimal solution; it is a *local optimum* but not the *global optimum* (point F). Thus if we want the global optimum or something near it, then we must search further. One possibility is to look at all the possible solutions and find the best or most satisfactory solution. This process of *total enumeration* is the *brute-force approach*, which even in these days of fast and low computing unit costs may be time consuming and cost ineffective. What we need is a clever way of searching the most profitable area of solutions. Such searching is not only important in operations research/management science (OR/MS) problems but also in many problems in AI, like pattern recognition and knowledge-based and expert systems. Hence we will discuss searching techniques later in this chapter; they were introduced in the chapter on expert systems. Meanwhile, we must return to the taxonomies of problem solving.

Weakly or Strongly Formulated Problems

Weakly formulated problems are the opposite of *strongly formulated problems*, which have a complete and well-formulated problem specification. The importance of strong problem formulation, i.e. complete and well defined, is not only important to AI as well as OR/MS but also to information systems. Many studies have shown that an important weak spot in all information systems is not the lack of good hardware or software or even techniques of design, but the lack of good user specifications. The reason for the importance is, of course, the fact that design and implementation start with the user specification and problem formulation. If this is incomplete or incorrect then the system that follows cannot be satisfactory and effective, let alone efficient. And the reasons for the incomplete and incorrect problem formulation is partly the 'noise' and lack of communication between the problem owner and the analyst solving the problem; partly the ambiguity and 'fuzziness' in the manager-user's articulation; partly the changing of the problem during implementation and the inability of the system to accommodate and adapt to the changes; and partly the lack of good techniques for specifying a complete and accurate problem formulation of the user's needs. Some of these problems are being resolved with techniques of prototyping which involve the user in a process of problem reformulation. In addition, changes in the attitudes of problem-owners, who are becoming increasingly more knowledgeable and sophisticated about problem-solving techniques, will lead to better-formulated problems.

One approach to the difficulties of the formulation of large and complex problems is *decomposition*, or *problem reduction*, i.e. breaking down the problem into subproblems and the goals into subgoals. The solving of a small number of subproblems for their corresponding subgoals may be easier to achieve than solving the original large problem—divide and conquer is the general idea. The difficulty with such an approach is that there is no guarantee that by solving the subproblems one has satisfactorily solved the larger problem. Optimizing subproblems need not lead to an optimization of the original organizational problem. Coordination between solving the various subproblems may be required and the approach necessary will vary with the model of OR/MS that is used.

Soft or Strong Methodologies

A *soft methodology* is concerned with the solving of problems that are ill-structured and messy with a vague problem situation where the 'various stakeholders may hold different subjective perceptions of "the problem" and its context, and where they may be no agreement on objectives' (Dallenbach, 1992). This is in contrast to the *hard methodologies* such as *operations research, management science,* or *systems engineering.* Here the problem is well-structured or at least better structured, with definable objectives and constraints. The solution is found by *modelling* the problem and using mathematical and statistical techniques to find a solution. In operations research (OR) the solution one seeks is preferably an optimal one, but if that is not possible, then simulation is used for a near-optimal or satisfactory solution.

While hard systems methodologies attempt to answer the question of how to achieve these objectives, soft systems methodologies also address the question of what the needs or objectives ought to be (Dallenbach, 1992).

General Problem Solving and Means–Ends Analysis

General problem solving (GPS) is one of the earliest research areas in AI, and was originally concerned with the psychology of thinking and human cognition. The research done by Newell, Shaw and Simon was related to the field of information processing and the construction of intelligent automata.

GPS relies on a strategy of selecting operators, where an *operator* performs the action of transforming one *state* (data structure of a problem at one stage of a solution) description to another. These operators are selected to reduce the difference between the current state and the goal state. The concept thus goes under the alias *means–ends analysis,* and involves determining the 'difference' between the initial and goal states, and selecting that instance of a particular operator that would reduce the difference. The path from the initial state to the goal then defines a *plan.* The idea is to apply a sequence of operators (means) until the goal (end) is reached.

Means–ends analysis is often preferred by decision-makers in business but the GPS concept of having a generalized approach to all problem solving has not been very successful. One reason is that many problems cannot be solved by successfully reducing differences, e.g. the 'best' route from the office to the bank may involve first increasing your distance from the bank. However, research in human cognition and the unique cognition styles of business decision-makers is still on-going and active.

Transactional to Strategic

Problem solving can also be classified by the levels of personnel in the organization that uses the solutions of problem solving. This is shown in Fig. 4.2 where the lowest level is that of the clerks and workers. Here problem solving is done on daily transactions referred to as *transactional processing* and constitutes the largest volume of processing in most business organizations. Such processing—also referred to as *business computing*—has the characteristic of repetitive processing of high volumes of input and output and very simple calculations. For example, the processing in most payrolls primarily requires simple additions and multiplications, a lot of file handling, and formatting of results. In contrast, as one moves up the hierarchy of the organization, which for simplicity is represented in Fig. 4.2 by a triangle, the nature of problem solving changes and involves very sophisticated models such as those found in OR/MS. This problem solving

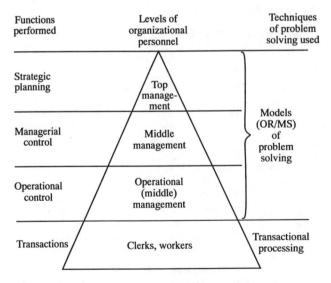

Figure 4.2 Types of problem solving at different levels of organization and different functions performed.

is much like *scientific computing* where the input, output, and file handling is small and not too repetitive, but the computations are many and very mathematical as in the case of linear programming which requires a lot of matrix algebra manipulations.

The applications of problem solving by management varies with the level of management, such as operational control, management control, or strategic planning. The problem solving and decisions can also be classified in terms of the nature of the problem such as *structured*, where the variables involved and their relationships are well known; *unstructured* or *non-structured* at the top management and strategic level, where the variables and their relationships are unknown or/and not easily quantified; or *semi-structured* or *ill-structured*, which is something in between. Ill-structured problems are also referred to as ill-defined or ill-formed, while unstructured problems are referred to as 'wicked'—perhaps to reflect their difficulty and the possibility that some 'tricks' will be involved in solving such problems effectively.

Some of the applications at these three levels of management have been classified by the degree of structure by Keene and Morton (1978) and are shown in Table 4.1. These applications are mostly data driven and do not include applications now possible because of AI and knowledge-based systems. As stated by Keene and Morton (1978: 86), such problem solving involves

> decisions where managerial judgment will not be adequate, perhaps because of the size of the problem or the computational complexity and precision needed to solve it. On the other hand, the models of data alone are also inadequate because the solution involves judgment and subjective analysis. Under these conditions the manager plus the system can provide a more effective solution than either alone.

Table 4.1 Sample decisions classified by level of decision making

Type of decision	Operational control	Management control	Strategic planning
Structured	Inventory control Accounts payable Accounts receivable Queuing Sequencing Plant scheduling Transportation models Assignment models	PERT/GERT for project control Linear and mathematical programming for resource allocation Prediction models Inventory control Break-even, marginal, or instrumental analyses	Resource allocation using mathematical programming
Semistructured	Cash management Bond trading	Short-term forecasting Budgeting Marketing models Long-term forecasting	Capital acquisition Portfolio analyses New product planning Mergers and acquisitions
Unstructured	Designing products	Hiring and firing Predicting consumer preference	R&D planning

Keene and Morton point out that there are no rigid divisions between the cells of their tabular classification. Factors such as time and effort available for problem solving and techniques of OR/MS could continually blur the arbitrary divisions: yesterday's ill-structured problem may be solvable tomorrow.

Programmed and Non-programmed

Another classification of decisions made by management is offered by Herbert Simon. He identified decisions as being *programmed decisions* in the sense that computer programs can be used to solve the problem as in the case of structured problems. In contrast, non-programmed decisions are required for non-structured problems and some ill-structured problems. An example would be the hiring, layoff, and assignment of personnel; these are non-programmed management control decisions for which, at the present time, no decision theory or problem-solving technique exists that would make such decisions programmable. However, this may change. In 1945, Simon predicted that in 1985 'we shall have acquired an extensive and empirically tested theory of human cognition processes and their interaction with human emotions, attitudes and values'. Norbert Wiener (1948) predicted that whatever humans can do, computers of the future will also do, though Wiener does not specify a point in time when this would occur.

Simon's framework for programmed and non-programmed decisions is shown in Fig. 4.3. The shaded area is what is currently programmed and will vary with industries and also over time. There is a large area of decision making that is theoretically non-programmable and also an area that is theoretically programmable but is, in practice, not programmable. But as foreseen by Keene and Morton, this is expected to change with technological progress. And indeed we are seeing this happen. The use of AI in knowledge-based systems and expert systems will increase the shaded area

Function Type of decision	Operational control	Management control	Strategic planning
Programmed	1	3	5
Nonprogrammed	2	4	6

Note Though all problems in cells 1, 3 and 5 are theoretically programmable, the shaded area approximates the current computerized problem-solving effort.

Figure 4.3 Classification of decisions.

in Fig. 4.3 as hitherto data-driven systems progress towards becoming knowledge-driven systems. How this may be done is, of course, the subject of much of the rest of this book.

Simple versus Complex Problem Solving

Our final taxonomy is that between a simple and complex problem. When is a problem complex enough to make problem solving impossible, or if possible, not worth the time and effort required to solve the problem?

There are many factors that could contribute to making a problem complex. Some of these are as follows:

- Objectives undefined or nebulous.
- Numerous and non-homogeneous end-users and developers.
- Search space is large or/and unknown.
- Problem is very unstructured or/and is not well known and understood.
- Unreliable data or knowledge (facts + beliefs + heuristics) because they are:
  —varying with time;
  —very fuzzy;
  —from too many multiple unreliable sources;
  —not subject to any one clear line of reasoning.
- Relationships between variables are too many and are mostly unknown.
- Guessing is required for a solution.
- All single models are too weak for problem.
- Too many diverse specialists are required.
- Need for integration with other information systems.
- Boundaries of systems and subsystems are unspecified or unknown.

Some of the above factors did exist in some of the problems faced by researchers in AI such as image understanding, text comprehension, automatic programming, task planning and scheduling, and protein crystallography. Generally speaking, however, when many of the above factors exist in a problem simultaneously, then certainly the problem is a complex one and may be *intractable*. Such is the case in some problems in pattern recognition in AI and the 'travelling salesman problem' in OR/MS. (The latter problem is to determine how a salesperson, vehicle, or other entity can travel from point to point, visiting each one only once, so as to minimize the total distance covered.) However, when even one or two factors contributing to complexity exist, then the problem must be approached with caution. Examples of complex problems in the areas of both AI and OR/MS are listed in Table 4.2.

Problems that were once deemed intractable and unprogrammable are now becoming tractable and programmable. An example is the case of linear programming (LP). To make it tractable and solvable for a large

Table 4.2 Examples of complexity in problem solving

Artificial intelligence	Business/industry
Test comprehension	Travelling salesperson/s problem
Image comprehension	Crystallography of proteins
Language comprehension (NLP)	Medicine/healthcare
Automatic programming	Task planning
	Scheduling
	Computer-aided design
	Computer-integrated manufacturing
	Weather forecasting
	Macro-economic forecasting

number of products and constraints, it was necessary to make two assumptions: one, that the objective function and the constraints are all linear; and two, that the coefficients and resource constraints are known with certainty. Relaxing these assumptions typically leads to combinatorial explosion. But this is exactly the situation that corresponds to the real world of uncertainty. In one industrial case, the problem matrix had 1034 columns (products) and 1093 rows (constraints) with over a million values that were not known with certainty. This problem was solved by using decomposition and importance sampling. It took 687 minutes on a PC to yield a solution; given computing power and clever techniques, an otherwise intractable problem was made tractable.

We take a slight diversion to share part of the folklore in linear programming. The story as told by George Dantzig, the father of LP, is that the Pharaoh of Egypt had two dreams that he wanted interpreted. The first dream involved seven fat sheep; the other dream had seven lean sheep that quickly consumed the fat ones but stayed lean. The interpretation was that the fat sheep represented years of plenty and the lean sheep, years of drought and famine. The lean years consume the fat of the surplus years but survive and stay lean. Transformed to policy, the dream led to the building of warehouses to store grain from the surplus years. Thus when famine next struck the land there was enough in the warehouses to feed the citizens and they all survived. The Pharoah rewarded the dream interpreter and asked for his secret. 'Simple', was the answer, 'It was lean year programming for uncertainty.' (If you don't get it, try reading it fast and listen hard.)

P/NP A formal approach to complexity is the *P/NP* problem, where P is the class of binary, yes/no, problems where there exists a deterministic polynomial time solution. The NP (non-deterministic polynomial) is the class of yes/no problems where there exists a non-deterministic algorithm whose worst-case time complexity is bounded by a polynomial. Goldberg and Pohl (1984: 45) state further:

> In a certain sense, a problem which is NP-complete is among the hardest problems in NP. If an NP-complete problem is solvable in polynomial time, then all problems in NP are. Remarkably, this class contains hundreds of important combinatorial problems from logic, language theory, database, automata theory, graph theory, and optimization theory. The existence of a polynomial time algorithm for any one of them yields polynomial algorithms for each of them.

We conclude this discussion of taxonomies with a summary diagram in Fig. 4.4.

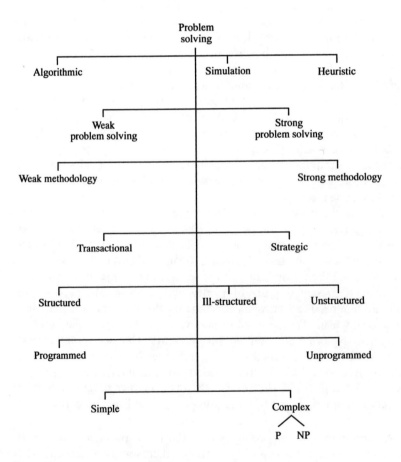

Figure 4.4 Taxonomies of problem-solving techniques.

PROCESS OF PROBLEM SOLVING

In cases of very simple problems all the problem solving can be compressed into a single choice for a solution. In more complex cases, however, a set of steps must be followed. We have already encountered some such steps like that of problem formulation in the discussion of strong or weak methods and the need to search as in the discussion of simulation. These and other steps in problem solving are shown in Fig. 4.5. There will be no attempt to discuss these steps in much detail. Our interest is only to introduce the

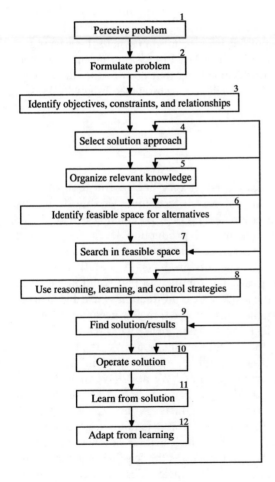

Figure 4.5 Activities in problem solving.

reader to the principles involved and their importance to problem solving and decision making.

In Fig. 4.5 we provide a schematic overview of a generic structure for problem solving. We start with the problem perception (box 1 in Fig. 4.5) and then proceed to the problem formulation (box 2) and the identification of objectives and constraints relevant to the problem domain (box 3). This is followed by the selection of a solution approach or model (box 4) and the collection of relevant data and knowledge relevant to the problem (box 5). The feasible space for alternatives is identified (box 6) and searched for a solution (box 7). In some models the search for a solution is part of the process of finding a solution and yielding a desired result as in the case of LP. In some models this is not possible and reasoning and learning is necessary (box 8) before a result is obtained (box 9). Once a result is found it is used in operations (box 10) and learning may occur (box 11). This learning is adapted (box 12) and fed back to a point where the learning is relevant (boxes 4–10). We note from the above discussion that there are two important phases or stages in problem solving that need further discussion, namely searching and learning. Each will now be discussed briefly.

SEARCHING

Search Space

We will discuss techniques of search, albeit very briefly. But first we must discuss the need and applicability of search techniques. To illustrate this need, we shall examine two situations from OR/MS. The first is that of LP. This involves finding the optimal mix of production levels for a linear objective function given a linear set of constraints. In our example we will consider a simple case of producing two products, A and B, and three resources, 1, 2, and 3. Before searching for the optimal solution we must define our *feasible space*, i.e. the space where production is feasible. This is shown in Fig. 4.6. We know that any production for negative values of products A and B are physically impossible and hence what remains feasible is the corner north-east of the origin in Fig. 4.6. We then draw the constraint lines for resources 1–3, and these lines show the infeasibility of production beyond those resource constraints. We now have the remaining area, OWXYZ, which is the *feasible region*. In this region lies the optimal solution. But what combination of products A and B is optimal? Fortunately our search for the optimal solution is facilitated greatly by the SIMPLEX method algorithm, which is, in fact, neither simple conceptually nor computationally. This algorithm recognizes the feasible region as being a convex body, and by exploiting the characteristics of a convex body knows that the optimal solution lies on the boundaries (including corners)

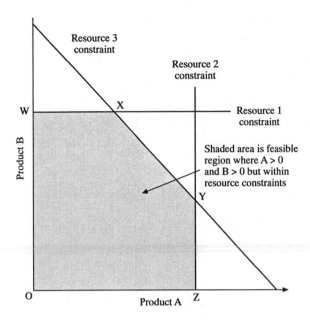

Figure 4.6 Feasible space for a linear programming problem.

of the feasible region. The algorithm goes from corner to corner, calculates the value of the objective function, and then identifies the optimal value.

Unfortunately, not many models, either in OR/MS or in AI, have algorithms that yield optimal values, and so the feasible region must be searched systematically and methodically. This is also true for the whole class of simulation models which, as we learned earlier, is necessary when algorithms are not applicable because of probabilistic variables. We shall look at one such example, that of inventory control. In this actual case study, we have probabilistic functions for demand, supply, and delays in delivery, and we have to determine the minimum total cost of inventory. The model shows that the total cost needs to be simulated for different combinations of order quantity (Q) and reorder point (ROP). It was determined (by the analyst and inventory control manager) that reasonable simulation values would be $Q = 10-80$ and $ROP = 5-20$. Assuming only integer values of Q and ROP, we still have a search space of over 1000 points. This is not a trivial amount of computation since each point computation is non-trivial in itself, given that probability distributions are involved. It was then decided to simulate for values of $Q = 10(10)80$, i.e. starting at 10 and ending at 80 with intervals of 10. Likewise, the simulated values for ROP were determined to be $ROP = 5(2)19$. This gave a set of 64 values to be simulated, which was quite reasonable. The calculation was

ROP → Q ↓	5	7	9	11	13	15	17	19
10	80.9	55.2	36.3	21.1	20.1	15.3	14.6	15.4
20	46.8	35.1	13.7	12.0	12.7	12.2	13	12.7
30	15.9	13.7	11.8	13.5	13.8	14	14.5	16.2
40	15.2	13.1	13.8	15.4	15.7	16	17.1	18.2
50	15.4	16.8	16.9	17	17.2	18.8	19.0	19.9
60	17.2	18.0	18.4	18.6	19.1	21.5	22.3	23.6
70	19.8	20.1	20.9	21.6	22.3	22.9	22.8	25.7
80	23.1	23.0	23	23.8	24.0	25.1	26.7	28.1

The circled value is the minimum value for this set of data. But further search should be pursued around this value as indicated by the tinted box.

Figure 4.7 Average total cost simulated for an inventory problem (in £10 000).

done, and the resulting average total costs/day are displayed in Fig. 4.7. Studying this matrix of values one can soon see that 11.8 (in 10 000 £) is the minimum value. But was this the optimum, the global optimum? Maybe! If we were lucky, we may at least have identified an area containing the global optimum. That assumption was made, thus identifying an area where a more detailed search should be made using smaller steps. Thus the next set of searches were for $R = 20(5)40$ and $ROP = 7(1)11$. These results were analysed and still further searches were made. This discussion is enough to illustrate the need for searching and the need for a search approach and technique. It does not necessarily yield the global optimum for there may well be a chasm or ridge (containing the actual global optimum) outside the area of detailed search which falls between our steps and so goes undetected. So there is a tradeoff: bigger step sizes minimize searching but increase the chances of missing the global optimum. In our example problem we were fortunate that the search space was only around 1000 points. In the case of searching for games of draughts and chess, the search space was estimated by Samuel (1963) to be 10^{40} and 10^{120}, respectively.

This was because of the phenomenon of *combinatorial explosion*, which results from a need to examine all sequences of n moves. If there are only two possible further moves after each move then a sequence n long involves a search space of 2^n. A brief tabulation of n and 2^n quickly shows how this leads to an explosion in the search space.

$$n = \quad 1 \quad 2 \quad 3 \quad 4 \quad \ldots$$
$$2^n = \quad 2 \quad 4 \quad 8 \quad 16 \quad \ldots$$

In this situation we say that the number of nodes in the game would *grow exponentially* with n. Studies based on games have demonstrated that exhaustive search of total enumeration by brute force is not feasible for non-trivial problems even when using mainframe computers. What we need are control strategies to help decide what to do next in searching. What we also need are efficient search techniques, suitable for each type of problem, that reduce the search and still yield satisfactory values. The efficiency of searching can be aided by the following approaches and strategies:

- Detecting profitable search areas and plausible paths of search.
- Avoiding 'blind alleys' and getting bogged down because one cannot see the 'trees from the forest'
- Eliminating redundant computations and reasoning at varying levels of abstraction.
- Pruning the search space early and effectively.

Not all search strategies satisfy all the desired criteria listed above but many are useful and will now be discussed briefly.

Search Strategies

Breadth-first search explores first the possibilities horizontally across each branch of a tree structure before moving to a different one. *Depth-first search* explores first the possibilities in depth, such as one branch in a tree structure through as many levels as possible. There is also a hybrid approach—some breadth first and then some depth repeatedly—which we encountered in the problem on inventory control. We will encounter similarities in forward and backward chaining in the chapter on the inference engine.

Another approach is *blind search* where one systematically searches all possibilities in the search space; this approach is, of course, exhaustive. Although blind search can always eventually find a solution, it may not be practical for large problems, and it is not practical when search space grows exponentially. In these cases we need domain-specific information that can guide the search process more efficiently, not just in terms of memory space but also in terms of the time required for a solution. Such information about the structure and nature of the problem domain could be heuristics that will not only help find a solution faster but know when to stop after a satisfactory solution is found rather than continue searching for an even better solution. One such *heuristic search* was performed by Samuel in his draughts program, which dealt with a binary tree structure. Samuel's heuristic was to select a branch and then immediately *prune* off the branch not used, thus cutting the search space by half. A heuristic in this context is essentially a rule of thumb or strategy that greatly reduces the search space. It offers 'solutions that are good enough most of the time'. A heuristic does not guarantee a solution, let alone an optimal solution, and should not be regarded as the opposite of foolproof. Heuristic search does, however, prevent combinatorial explosions of possible solutions as in the case of games of draughts and chess. It is just one example of an important contribution of AI to problem solving.

A comparison of heuristic search with blind search is well stated by Gardner (1988: 519):

> Blind search corresponds approximately to the systematic generation and testing of search-space elements, but it operates within a formalism that leaves room for additional information about the specific problem domain to be introduced, rather than excluding it by definition. If such information, going beyond that needed merely to formulate a class of problems, is in fact introduced, it may be possible to restrict search drastically. Whether or not the restriction is foolproof, the search is then called heuristic rather than blind.

Summary of Searching

We have examined a few strategies of reasoning and search. Such strategies are also used in the inference engine and so will be discussed later.

Whatever the strategy of search that is chosen and whatever the size or shape of the search space, there is a search process that should be implicitly or explicitly observed. This is shown in Fig. 4.8. All the terms and concepts used in this diagram have been defined earlier and hence the diagram is, hopefully, self-explanatory—except perhaps for the implicit topic of learning, which we now need to examine.

MACHINE LEARNING

Learning has long been of interest to the education profession. The AI community began to take an interest in 1963 when Arthur Samuel published his work on making a computer program learn to play better draughts. This first learning computer program was defeated in its early days by its author and programmer, but soon learned from and defeated many a draughts champion. What seemed a trivial pursuit turned out to

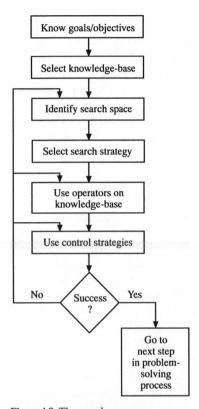

Figure 4.8 The search process.

incorporate many techniques of problem solving, including techniques of search, reasoning, and learning. Since then, machine learning has been applied to many subdisciplines of AI, including pattern recognition in speech, voice, vision and image processing, in natural language processing, and in expert systems. Machine learning has also been used in industry, especially in industrial process and production control, robotics, office automation, and in knowledge-based systems. It is of course of great interest to psychologists but also to the computer scientist and to the problem-solver. The greatest contribution of machine learning to problem solving is its development of mechanisms of automatic improvement that are applicable across many fields of study. We start with rote learning, the earliest technique and one that saw much experimentation and application in the learning of the game of draughts.

Rote Learning

Rote learning, also known as *caching*, is defined in *The Handbook of Artificial Intelligence* as 'memorization, it is saving new knowledge so that when it is needed again, the only problem will be retrieval, rather than a repeated computation, inference or query'. Learning is also an important part of intelligence and machine learning is essential to machine intelligence. Consequently, all learning and intelligent systems have a rote-learning process that stores, maintains, and retrieves information and knowledge from its knowledge-base. Conceptually, rote learning is simple but the mechanics of acquiring it can become cumbersome. One problem with rote learning is that too much memorization soon 'clogs up' the system, and a need for selective 'forgetting' is required.

Learning by Being Taught to Learning by Discovery

Closely related to rote learning is *learning by being taught*, where there is a teacher and a pupil. Of great interest to the AI researcher is the possibility of replacing the human teacher in the traditional scenario by a computer that would provide the same if not a better quality of teaching. This becomes complex because it involves knowing how people actually manage to learn. It is a subject that has engaged the educational community for many years without an answer that an AI practitioner can use. One possibility is that of *learning by analogy*; another is *learning by experience*, which is a 'completely unassisted method of knowledge acquisition. It is a continuous process in which existing knowledge is checked against reality for validity and efficiency' (Arnold and Bowie, 1986: 150). One of the problems with this and other methods is that of measurement. How does one measure successful learning? How does one measure efficient learning? How can one measure useful and successful feedback in learning?

Another approach is *learning by discovery*, which as stated by Arnold and Bowie (1986: 151) involves

> combining known facts together in previously untried ways to come up with new facts. Often the jump from the old facts to new conclusions required insight, which is not a well understood area of human cognition. . . . It has been successful in extremely regular and well defined domains. For example, one expert system successfully uses this method to discover mathematical concepts from a set of primitive axioms. It can do this because the domain of mathematics is extremely systematic.

Deductive and Inductive Learning

Knowledge from rote learning (and some other types of learning) can be used to compute *deductions*, and hence to proceed steps further than the basic information as with inferences from a knowledge-base. A deductive inference gives new specific information from general principles. One can also use algorithms or heuristics to make inductive inferences. *Inductive learning* involves the acquisition of general concepts from specific examples (positive or negative) and counter-examples of the concept being learned.

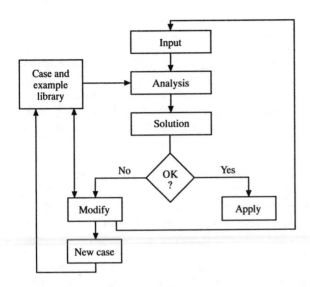

Figure 4.9 Learning by examples and cases.

Inductive techniques can give truly new information but the accuracy of this information can never be totally guaranteed. The use of examples, cases, or experience for learning may require some iteration of activities as displayed in Fig. 4.9.

Inductive learning is useful when acquiring new concepts is important. It is used extensively in pattern recognition and in expert systems. In contrast, deductive learning is best in environments that demand certainty and when new knowledge is not essential.

The Analytical Paradigm

Examples—the basis of inductive learning—are often unavailable or inadequate, and we then must supplement examples, or even one example, with a rich underlying domain theory. This is *analytical learning*; as stated by Carbonell (1983: 5), it is more deductive than inductive:

> utilizing past problem solving experience (the exemplars) to guide the deductive chains to perform when solving new problems, or to formulate search control rules that enable more efficient application of domain knowledge. Thus, analytical methods focus on improving the efficiency of a system without sacrificing accuracy or generality, rather than extending its library of concept descriptions.

Analytical learning is very appropriate in searching and in improving efficiency. It has applications in many areas of business and industry.

Neural Networks

Neural networks (or *NNets*) are a new approach but one with great prospects. These nets are constructed and process information in a way that is reminiscent of principles by which human brains organize and use knowledge. It is argued that if we want to make computers think and learn in order to help us in problem solving, then it may be wise to make machines think, learn, and act like human beings by copying the brain. In reality, however, current NNets are very crude approximations of the human brain.

Neural networks have lots of computing elements connected to lots of other elements arranged in a connection matrix. The detailed computations in NNets largely depend on the efficiency of these connections (hence NNets are also called *connectionist models*). As stated by Anderson and Rosenfeld (1988: xvii–xviii):

> In the learning phase, the connection strengths in the network are modified. Sometimes, if the constructor of the network is very clever or if the problem structure is so well defined that it allows it, it is possible to specify the connections strengths a priori. Otherwise, it is necessary to modify strengths using one of a number of useful algorithms.

It has been observed that it is not very difficult to train NNets to learn, even though we do not always know why the technology works the way it does. Neural networks have been used successfully in the training of speech recognition and pattern discrimination even though this training may be very time consuming.

Summary of Learning

A summary of the discussion on learning is displayed in Fig. 4.10. For an analytical comparison, see Table 4.3 and consider Carbonell (1983: 8):

> At the risk of oversimplification, one may make a general observation: Connectionist approaches are superior for single-step gestalt recognition in unstructured continuous domains, if very many training examples are present. At the opposite end of the spectrum, analytical models are best for well structured knowledge-rich domains that require deep reasoning and multi-step inference, even if few training examples are available. Inductive and genetic techniques are best in the center of the wide gulf between the two extremes.

SUMMARY AND CONCLUSIONS

There are summaries scattered throughout this chapter: Fig. 4.4 on taxonomies of problem solving; Fig. 4.8 on search processes; and Fig. 4.10

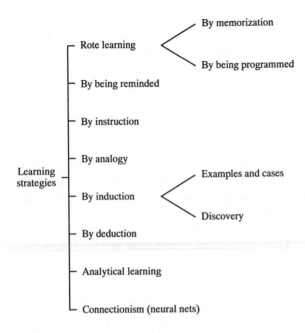

Figure 4.10 Approaches to machine learning.

and Table 4.3 on machine learning techniques. In discussing these techniques, we have advisedly selected examples of their use from areas in OR/MS and cited applications in AI. Our objective in the selection of examples is to emphasize that these techniques of problem solving are important, and are portable from AI to other fields of computing in commerce and industry. This chapter could well be in a book on OR/MS or in a book on AI.

Table 4.3 Comparison of selected approaches to learning

Learning approach	Comparative advantage	Appropriate application environment
Analytical	Searching Enhancing efficiency	Applications requiring —Search —Increased efficiency
Inductive	Acquiring new concepts	Discrete pattern recognition
Rote learning	Simple and straightforward	Can be cumbersome
Deductive	Certainty	No new knowledge acquired
Connection	Train to learn without understanding it	Need representative training sets

There is a fear on the part of managers that our techniques of problem solving, especially with the emergence of NNets and the maturing of machine learning, will replace management. This fear is unfounded. Our advances in the techniques of problem solving is greatly outpaced by the number and complexity of problems that need to be solved. Of those problems that can be solved given the state of the art of problem solving and computing power, we will be able to aid management in making decisions that are more rational leading to greater effectiveness and efficiency.

Learning, as once defined by Herbert Simon, is any process by which a system improves its performance. In this sense, we will certainly learn and improve not only our techniques of problem solving but also improve our overall performance in business and other computing activities.

Having discussed problem solving (as well as AI and expert systems) we are now ready to define a knowledge-based information system, the subject of our next chapter.

REVIEW AND DISCUSSION QUESTIONS

4.1 What is the difference between algorithmic and heuristic problem solving? How do they affect business decision making? In what business situations do each type have a comparative advantage? Explain your position.

4.2 Are algorithmic, simulation, and heuristic techniques mutually exclusive? Give examples from business and industry where they are not mutually exclusive.

4.3 Give examples of how means–ends analysis can be used in business decision making? What environmental conditions are necessary for it to be effective?

4.4 Give examples in business where problems are
   (a) structured;
   (b) ill-structured;
   (c) too complex to be intractable and 'wicked'.
   Explain the reasons for your choices.

4.5 Can managerial decisions be programmed? What decisions cannot be programmed? Why?

4.6 Give examples of programmed and non-programmed decisions in a business firm that is dependent on the business environment, such as where the primary activity is:
   (a) marketing;
   (b) production;
   (c) service;
   (d) financial;
   (e) personnel.

4.7 What is preventing unstructured problems becoming ill-structured and structured? How can these obstacles be removed?

4.8 Why is problem solving at the strategic level different from the control and transactional levels if all levels use much of the same data?

4.9 What are the constants in making problem solving more efficient and effective? Is it problem-solving techniques, computing power, educated personnel, or something else? Explain.

4.10 Why is it difficult for problem-solving techniques aided by computers to solve problems like humans do? What can we do about it?

4.11 What are the techniques of reasoning that are portable to business management? Give examples.

4.12 Give examples of situations in business where optimal decisions are possible and situations where satisfying decisions are possible and desirable?

4.13 'A problem well stated is a problem half solved.' Comment.

4.14 'The greater the power at our disposal, the greater the number of insoluble problems we can solve.' Comment.

4.15 Do learning computers threaten management? How and why? What can be done about it?

4.16 Can computers and problem-solving techniques make managerial decisions? How can unintentional decisions be avoided?

4.17 Is computing power a limit to our problem-solving ability? Or is it the lack of relevant and powerful techniques?

4.18 How has AI affected problem solving for business decision making?

4.19 'Computers and problem-solving techniques never have and never will solve the qualitative problems faced by business management.' Comment. Should we be concerned with the answer? Why?

4.20 'Rather than solve problems, it is clever to dissolve them.' Comment.

CASE 4.1 A KNOWLEDGE-BASED SYSTEM FOR FRENCH RAILWAYS

SNCF, the French railway company, had the problem in the late 1980s of distributing and reallocating railway carriages from regions with surpluses to regions that needed the carriages. The allocation was centred on an expert system that reproduces the distributors' reasoning. The distribution and rerouting involved 5280 variables for more than 100 types of carriage for a five-day plan, all with the objective of minimizing costs.

The allocation was done on the demand priority of the request and the supply priority (called usefulness) of the region, each being represented by a tree structure. Heuristics were used successfully without backtracking despite the highly combinatorial nature of the problem. The logic was represented by 800 rules in propositional logic and scanning the rules for a typical carriage allocation took 10 seconds of CPU time on an IBM AT computer.

The analysts overruled the integer programming model used by Swiss Railways because they felt that a 'rule-based approach is the only way we know to make multicriteria decisions with consideration for the context and for satisfaction levels.'

Source: P. Lévine and J.-C. Pomerol (1990) 'Railcar distribution at the French railways', *IEEE Expert*, **5** (5), 61–69.

Questions

1. Is this problem of allocation and routing not a standard OR problem rather than a problem for AI and KBIS?
2. What advantages does a KBIS solution have over the OR solution?
3. Is there a trend for OR problems to gravitate towards AI and the KBIS given the successful emergence of the expert systems?

Note: The above questions, especially (1), have been raised by the authors of the article cited above. You are invited to read the source article but only after attempting to answer the questions yourself.

EXERCISES

4.1 Calculate how a problem escalates to become complex because of combinatorial explosion. Take the example of a travelling vendor and show how the number of paths for the vendor increases as the number of nodes for travelling increases.

4.2 Suppose that you had to use the technique of 'examples for machine learning by example'. State your environment and then construct your example.

BIBLIOGRAPHY AND REFERENCES

Ackoff, R. L. (1978) *The Art of Problem Solving: Accompanied by Ackoff's Fables*, Wiley, New York.
  Let the subtitle not fool you into thinking that this is not a serious book. It is written by the co-author of the first book on operations research.
Andersen, J. A. and E. Rosenfeld (eds) (1988) *Neurocomputing*, MIT Press, Cambridge, MA.
Arnold, W. R. and J. S. Bowie (1986) *Artificial Intelligence: A Personal Commonsense Journey*, Prentice Hall, Englewood Cliffs, NJ.
  Chapter 7 is on 'Climbing the Learning Curve' and discusses the techniques of learning: learning by being programmed, by being taught, from experience and by discovery.
Bartree, T. C. (ed.) (1988) *Expert Systems and Artificial Intelligence: Applications and Management*. Howard W. Sams, Indianapolis.
  Chapter 4 is a tutorial on problem solving.
Carbonell, J. G. (1983) 'Introduction: paradigms for machine learning', in R. S. Michalski, J. G. Carbonell and T. M. Mitchell (eds), *Machine Learning: An Artificial Intelligence*

Approach, pp. 1–14, Tioga, Palo Alto, CA.

An excellent introduction to the subject.

Checkland, P. (1981) *Systems Thinking, Systems Practice*, Wiley, Chichester.

The author is the British guru on soft technology. He has expanded on what West Churchman, father of OR/MS, wrote in *The Systems Approach* in 1968. Checkland has co-authored, with J. Scholes, *Soft Systems Methodology in Action* (1990), in which the authors propose a general methodology of problem definition in addition to discussing soft-technology.

Cohen, P. R. and E. A. Feigenbaum (1982) *The Handbook of Artificial Intelligence*, Vol. 3, William Kaufmann, Los Altos, CA.

Chapter XIV is on 'Learning and Inductive Inference' and chapter XV is on 'Planning and Problem Solving'. You get what you should expect from such a scholarly handbook.

Dallenbach, H. G. (1992; in preparation) *Systems and Decision Making*, University of Canterbury, Christchurch, New Zealand.

Gardner, A. v. d. L. (1988) 'Search and overview', in R. Engelmore (ed.), *Readings from the AI Magazine, Volumes 1–5, 1980–1985*, pp. 515-519, American Association of Artificial Intelligence, Menlo Park, CA.

This volume also has other articles related to problem solving including 'Problem Solving Tactics' by Sacardoti (pp. 521–530) and 'Towards a Taxonomy of Problem Solving' by Chandrasekaran (pp. 521–529).

Goldberg, A. and I. Pohl (1984) 'Is complexity theory of use to AI?', in A. Elithorn and R. Banerjee (eds), *Artificial and Human Intelligence*, pp. 42–56, Elsevier, Amsterdam.

One of the few articles on the subject that is easily accessible.

Keene, P. G. W. and M. S. Scott Morton (1978) *Decision Support Systems: An Organizational Perspective*, Addison-Wesley, Reading, MA.

Outdated perhaps, but not on basic concepts of problem solving for business decision makers.

Kodratoff, Y. (1988) *Introduction to Machine Learning*, Morgan Kaufmann, London.

The author is the Research Director of the French National Scientific Research Council. He writes excellent English but this book uses many symbols and some mathematics. The author provides a thorough discussion of the subject interspersed with numerous thought-provoking exercises.

Palvia, S. C. and S. R. Gordon (1992) 'Tables, trees and formulas in decision analysis', *Communications of the ACM*, **35** (10), 104–113.

The authors demonstrate that the use of different techniques of problem solving result in varying degrees of difficulties in arriving at solutions, require different skills and provide different insights into input data, desired output/goals, and the solution.

Pearl, J. (1985) *Heuristics: Intelligent Search Strategies for Computer Problem Solving*, Addison-Wesley, Reading, MA.

Chapter 2 (pp. 33–42) is on 'Basic Heuristic-Search Procedures'. It is very formal and rather mathematical.

Polya, G. (1957) *How To Solve It*, Doubleday, New York.

A very popular book on problem solving addressed to the layman.

Rumelhart, D. E., B. Widrow and M. A. Lehr (1994) 'The basic ideas of neural networks', *Communications of the ACM*, **37** (3), 87–91.

A survey of the 'brain as a model of a parallel computational device very different from that of a traditional serial computer'.

Samuel, A. L. (1963) 'Some studies in machine learning using the game of checkers', in E. Feigenbaum and J. Feldman (eds), *Computers and Thought*, McGraw-Hill, New York, pp. 71–105.

Simon, H. A. (1945) *Administrative Behavior*, Free Press, New York.

Simon, A. H. (1991) *Models of My Life*, Basic Books, New York.

Yes, this is the same Simon that we encountered in the discussions of GPS and 'satisficing'. He is also partly responsible for the programming language IPL (Information Processing Language) and he is the winner of the Nobel Prize in 1978 for 'the dismal science' of economics. He brought behavioural science to problem solving and problem solving to the behavioural sciences. Simon also wrote 'Why Should Machines Learn?' in R. S. Michalski, J. G. Carbonell and T. M. Mitchell, *Machine Learning*, Vol. 1, Tioga, Los Altos, CA, pp. 25–37.

In *Models of My Life*, Simon discusses his academic and professional life and describes how his numerous professional interests became entangled and still remain entwined.

Wiener, N. (1948) *Cybernetics, or, Control and Communication in the Animal and the Machine*, Wiley, New York.

KNOWLEDGE-BASED INFORMATION SYSTEMS

> Knowledge, when wisdom is too weak to guide her,
> Is like a headstrong horse, that throws the rider.
> Francis Quarles

> In terms of government administration, KBS may be the single most significant development to emerge since the computer itself, for it offers a means of streamlining and improving decision-making to an unprecedented degree.
> Duffin

INTRODUCTION

In this chapter we will explore the question: what is a knowledge-based system? But first we need to consider knowledge—its types and manifestations, and its relevance to decision making and problem solving. We will leave the discussion of acquiring and representing knowledge to later chapters. It will be part of the development of a KBIS which is the subject of Part II. But first, let us examine the nature of knowledge.

KNOWLEDGE

What is knowledge? How is it used? These are deep philosophical questions that have been discussed for centuries. Our task is not so difficult. All we mean to do is to consider these questions with respect to modern computer systems. In this context, knowledge is used for problem solving and decision making. But so are data in many a transactional computer system. What is the difference? The difference is in the environment. In a transactional system the relevant data and the rules of manipulating the data are known with certainty. But in the real world, the relevant factual data and the rules of manipulation are not known with certainty. Also, in a transactional system manipulation may be required by known algorithms, while a knowledge-base is manipulated by inference mechanisms. Typically, there is often also the need for heuristics which are rules of thumb that enable reasonable inferences and hence conclusions, and subsequently actions to be made; actions that come close to what a human expert would have made.

A formal definition of *knowledge* is given by Frawley *et al.* (1992: 58):

> Given a set of facts (data) F, a language L, and some measure of certainty C, we define a *pattern* as a statement S in L that describes relationships among the subject F_S of F with a certainty C, such that S is simpler (in some sense) than the enumeration of all facts in F_S. A pattern that is interesting (according to a user-imposed interest measure) and certain enough (again according to certain user's criteria) is called *knowledge*.

The authors then define *discovered knowledge* as the 'output of a program that monitors the set of facts in a database and produces patterns'.

One related term that often appears in the literature is *knowledge engineering*. In many cases it is meant to include all the tools, techniques, and processes related to a KBIS. One author (Adeli, 1990) takes a broader view and includes applications of KBISs in AI as well as subdisciplines of AI such as machine learning, to be part of knowledge engineering.

Whatever definition you prefer, knowledge is a basic component of a KBIS. The important inputs to a KBIS are facts, heuristics, and rules that yield conclusions and recommendations for action. As an illustration, consider the heuristic that if it does not rain for three days and the maximum temperature is over 90°F, then one needs to water plants. Now consider the existence of a fact that it did not rain for three days and that the temperature was over 90°F. A KBIS will conclude that it is necessary to water the plants and such action is recommended. Whether this recommendation is acted upon or not is up to the end-user or decision-maker who must take other factors into consideration before deciding. But the KBIS can perform an important and useful function. This example may seem trivial but the principle and concept is important and has been used successfully in many problem environments in business and industry.

The 'bottom line' and the *raison d'être* of a KBIS is the expert opinion provided for the decision-maker and problem-solver. This is shown in Fig. 5.1. Much of the processing of number crunching, selection, sorting,

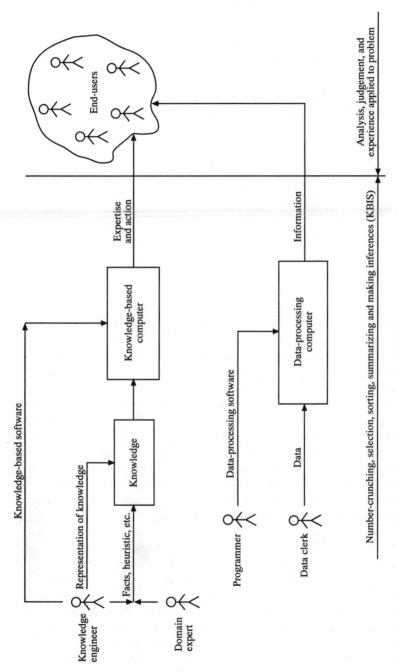

Figure 5.1 Inputs and outputs from a data-processing system and a KBIS.

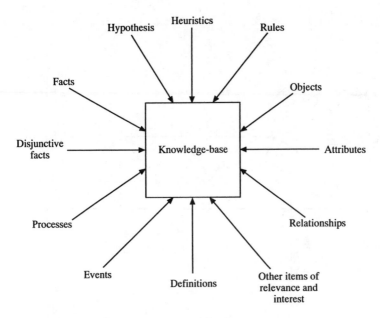

Figure 5.2 Kinds of knowledge in a knowledge-base.

summarizing, and the making of inferences are made by computer. This does not eliminate the analysis of inferences in light of organizational conditions (objectives, goals, and constraints) and external constraints that must still be done by humans, which in this case is the decision-maker and problem-solver.

We can see from Fig. 5.1 that the system is knowledge driven—hence the importance of knowledge. As stated earlier, knowledge is a collection of relevant information that may include facts, heuristics, rules, hypotheses, attributes, relationships, events, process information, and even definitions if not provided by a knowledge dictionary. This set of information is shown graphically in Fig. 5.2. Figure 5.2 shows the content of knowledge but in order to appreciate how it is processed, it is important to appreciate its many types and forms. This is our next topic.

Types of Knowledge

All information systems need knowledge, but expert systems need a special type of knowledge. These types of knowledge are discussed briefly below.

Domain dependent versus domain independent Knowledge that is *dependent* on a particular domain is largely derived from apprenticeship or experience. This knowledge could owe much to *domain-independent knowledge*, which is derived from first principles, theories, and axioms. It could also owe much to laws relating to the particular domain or to related domains or even unrelated domains.

Domain-independent knowledge is too broad for offering expert opinions. It would require a large knowledge-base to suggest an expert solution from domain-independent knowledge.

Facts and heuristics A *fact* is something real that is actual, objective, and demonstrable. A fact is knowledge that is widely available and universally agreed upon—it is documented in a book or can be substantiated in a library. In contrast, a *heuristic* is developed partly through the knowledge of the expert and partly through a study of the logic schema formed by rules.

Examples of heuristic rules about knowledge databases as given by Hayes-Roth *et al.* (1983) are:

1. A commercially practical system may require as few as 50 rules.
2. An expert in a narrow field requires about 500–1000 rules.
3. An expert in a profession requires about 10 000 rules.
4. The limit of human expertise is about 100 000 rules.

Heuristics are very important in solving ill-structured and ill-defined problems, or intractably large problems, for they rely on basic fundamentals and common sense. For example, every chess player knows that a knight on the base line (or any border line) has only half its potential movement. Thus a heuristic would be to move the knight from a border line where it has four potential moves to another position where it has eight potential moves. A combination of moves in a selected sequence could well result in achieving a goal, whether it be winning a game of chess or solving a problem in business.

Declarative versus procedural *Procedural knowledge* is a detailed set of instructions on how to carry out a procedure, whether it be fixing a car or performing brain surgery. Anyone doing computer programming in one of the higher-level languages like BASIC, COBOL, FORTRAN, or Pascal knows procedures. Every step in the procedure must be unambiguously stated in detail. Procedure states the 'how', while declarative knowledge states the 'what'. Procedure is the user's perspective. It encompasses everything that is dynamic about the world, e.g. actions, operations, inferences, applications, etc. It is *declarative knowledge* that is interpreted into a *procedure* by the interpreter of an expert system's inference engine.

Surface versus deep *Surface knowledge* is what is derived from experience and apprenticeship and consists of heuristics, all confined to a limited domain. In contrast, *deep knowledge* is derived from first principles, axioms,

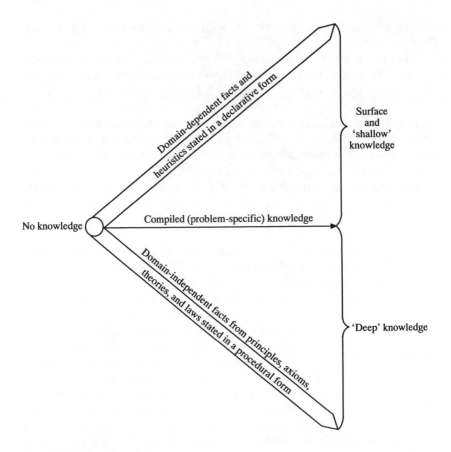

Figure 5.3 Types of knowledge.

and theories, and is possibly generalized over many domains. Surface knowledge, rather than deep knowledge is found in domain-specific databases of an expert system.

A mix of types There are other types of knowledge, but let us examine a mix of those already discussed, as displayed graphically in Fig. 5.2. The types of knowledge in expert systems are certainly domain dependent, heuristic, stated in the declarative form, and of a surface type. But this is one of the two extremes shown in Fig. 5.3. Some knowledge could well lie between the two extremes, like being procedural for example. The knowledge of expert systems may not always be well-structured or well-defined but may be ill-structured, ill-defined, and fuzzy. It may be between the extremes, but more on one side and of one type than the other. There are also other types of knowledge.

Prescriptive versus descriptive Descriptive and prescriptive notions are well known, especially to economists who have their own terminology: *descriptive* and *normative*. *Descriptive* is a description, such as 'a chair has four legs'; *normative* or *prescriptive* is not what you necessarily have or do not have but what you should have, e.g. 'your chair should have three legs', or 'the chair you need should have four casters'. Prescription is, of course, the role of an expert. One would not go to an expert for a description, although description may well be necessary for an expert knowledge database to make a prescription.

Specific versus general Expert systems are definitely specific; in fact, being specific is one of their characteristics. They are often criticized for being too specific to a domain, and so not general enough to be meaningful for some purposes. However, at a highly skilled, professional level, it is difficult to be a generalist, and being specific is necessary. One has to go no further than computer science or operations research to see a range of specialities within the field, like a specialist in integer programming, not just mathematical programming, or a specialist in COBOL, not just programming languages.

Uncertainty versus certainty The distinction between certainty and uncertainty can be traced to economists, who make a fine distinction between certainty, risk, and uncertainty. Complete *certainty* is where the probability of occurrence is known (i.e. a probability of 1). *Risk* is where the probability is known as a distribution. *Uncertainty* is where the probability is not known at all. Uncertainty often characterizes data and information in an expert system. Some data are known with certainty and risk, but uncertainty is also an important characteristic that cannot be ignored.

A difficulty with probability in situations of risk is that its values are difficult to determine. A well-known approach in statistics is Bayesian conditional probability estimates. Another approach, known after the statistician Schlaifer, is strictly subjective. In it, values are assigned based on the best information available. Another approach is to assign ordinal values for probabilities of certainty, $+1$ for complete certainty, -1 for complete uncertainty, and 0 for no opinion. Evidence with values in between for degrees of certainty are also referred to as *certainty factors*. One example of such a scale is shown in Fig. 5.4.

Another mix of types There are other mixes of types of knowledge, as shown in Fig. 5.5. Here, as in Fig. 5.3, and more so than in Fig. 5.4, the nature of the knowledge for an expert knowledge database would be in between the extreme of descriptive and prescriptive; general and specific; certainty and uncertainty.

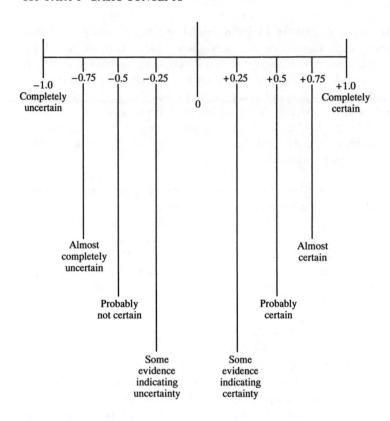

Figure 5.4 Degrees of certainty.

The expert may have factual knowledge that is necessary but not necessarily sufficient. This is supplemented by heuristics, which are represented symbolically in a declarative manner, but it is prescriptive, uncertain, and represents 'shallow' knowledge. In contrast, the generalist has a deep knowledge of facts that is domain independent, general, descriptively stated, and certain.

Chunks and Experts

Knowledge in large quantities must be organized to be efficiently and effectively accessible. One approach to the organization of knowledge is to arrange it in chunks, where *chunk* is a meaningful portion of knowledge that can be stored and retrieved as a functional unit.

A chunk has often been used as one measure of a domain expert, who would have 50 000–100 000 chunks of domain-specific knowledge organized and stored in long-term memory. The *long-term memory* is part of human memory that is 'permanent', and accessible when needed.

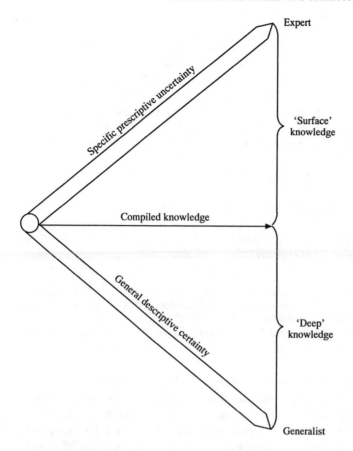

Figure 5.5 More types of knowledge.

DEFINITION OF A KNOWLEDGE-BASED SYSTEM

Having discussed and classified knowledge, we can now consider knowledge-based systems. There are many definitions of a knowledge-based system (KBS) or a knowledge-based information system (KBIS).

A number of authors imply that an ES and a KBS are equivalent: they claim that the notion behind KBSs is to capture the problem-solving expertise of a human being—an expert in a highly constrained problem area, called a problem domain—and represent this person's knowledge or expertise in a computer in such a way that the computer can approximate the expert's ability to solve a particular class of problems. This view is very close to the generally accepted definition of an ES. Similarly close is the definition by Mockler (1989a:2): A KBS is 'designed to replace the finctions performed by a human expert'.

Dym and Levitt (1991:11) explicitly make no distinction between a KBS and an ES. They define a knowledge-based (expert) system (KBES) as 'a computer program that performs a task normally done by an expert or consultant and which, in so doing, uses captured, heuristic knowledge'.

Szolovits (1986) also defines a KBS as many would define an ES. 'Knowledge-based systems are computer programs, usually based on technologies developed by AI research, which embody some aspects of human knowledge and expertise to perform tasks ordinarily done by human experts.' However, Szolovits has a somewhat open definition and his KBS could include systems other than an ES that would embody AI techniques other than ESs.

Of those that make an explicit distinction between a KBS and an ES, we start with Stratil and Hyball (1987: 138) who consider an ES as an application of a KBS concept. Howe (1991: 56) makes a sharper distinction between a KBS and other systems.

> 'Knowledge-based systems' (KBS) was coined for those systems in which the domain is explicit and separate from the program's other knowledge. It is a useful term to the layman since it tells him something specific about the kind of system, or subsystem, that is, enabling him to distinguish a KBS from conventional data processing or scientific computing systems.

But Howe does not explicitly differentiate between a KBS and an ES. He implies perhaps an equivalence but he could also imply that while a KBS is not conventional data processing or scientific computing, it includes other subsystems such as decision support systems (DSSs). Thus a KBS could well be more than an ES if the system were to use the domain knowledge and make inferences as do ESs. Such an open definition can be found with Hembry (1990: 274) 'Knowledge-based systems are tools for building applications that draw logical inferences from their stored knowledge of the problem domain.'

Davis (1986: 957) uses the terms knowledge-based systems or knowledge systems instead of expert systems in order to focus attention on the knowledge the systems carry, rather than the question of whether or not such knowledge constitutes expertise:

> ... the field came to be known as knowledge-based systems, in which work has come to focus on the accumulation, representation and use of knowledge specific to a particular task. The term knowledge-based is primarily a label for this focus and an indication of the source of the systems' power: task-specific knowledge, rather than the domain-independent methods used in early AI programs.

Botrow et al. (1986: 880) are more specific:

... the term knowledge-based is generally reserved for systems that have explicit knowledge bases and some flexibility in the uses of this knowledge. The problem with this definition is that there is no generally accepted definition of explicit versus implicit knowledge bases. But the definition does extend the boundaries of a KBS from an ES which uses explicit knowledge of a domain to other types of systems using implicit knowledge.

Thus far we have looked at the history of the definition of a KBS. How will this definition evolve? Evolve it will, since the use of ESs and knowledge-bases is increasing and they are expanding their boundaries. In an industrial environment, an engineer or an operations research/management science practitioner may well make inferences from a knowledge-base for an ES not for generating expertise information but for solving decision-making problems for management. Furthermore, techniques used by AI, such as the use of fuzzy sets in handling uncertainties, search, and learning techniques as those pioneered by AI practitioners like Arthur Samuel are all techniques that can be used for problem solving in a KBS environment. It is this broader definition of a KBS (that makes an ES a subset of a KBS) that will be used in this book.

SUPPLEMENT 5.1 MILESTONES RELATED DIRECTLY TO THE DEVELOPMENT OF A KBIS

1943   McCulloch and Pitts published the pioneering work that led to neural networks.

1950   Alan Turing's article that led to the Turing test.

1956   Newell, Simon, and Shaw developed the GPS (General Problem Solver) at Rand Corporation.

1958   McCarthy developed LISP at MIT.

1963   Samuel's article on the first learning computer program (Samuel's draughts program) and in the use of techniques of search and reasoning.

1970   Rousel and Colmerauer developed PROLOG.

1972   Newell and Simon's book *Human Problem Solving* introduced the general idea of production systems.

1973   Van Melle, Shortliffe, and Buchanan developed the EMYCIN shell from MYCIN.

1976   Minsky developed the concept of frames for knowledge representation.

1977   Forgy created OPS for programming expert systems.

1978 McDermott started developing R1 (later released as XCON, the first large commercial expert system) at Digital Corporation.

1980 Symbolics started the development of LISP machines.

The relationship of an ES with AI and with a KBS is illustrated in Fig. 5.6. In Fig. 5.6 we have a circle, sector A, representing an ES that is part of AI and also part of a KBS. Sector B represents all of AI that is not part of a KBS. Sectors C and D represent applications other than an ES that are part of a KBS and include speech, vision, image and natural-language processing. Then there is sector E which includes problem solving that makes inferences and uses a knowledge-base. Sector E also uses many of the AI techniques of problem solving such as techniques of search, reasoning, and learning. Such problem solving will be found in models of operations research (OR) such as inventory control, queuing, sequencing, etc.

There are also techniques used extensively in ESs that are also used in general problem solving that is not an ES. Examples include the techniques of handling uncertainty by fuzzy logic and the use of heuristics. The use of

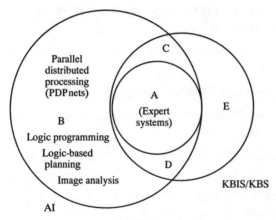

Note: not to scale

Key

A Expert system

B Non-KBIS applications of AI. e.g. image analysis, robotics, machine translation, PDP nets, logic programming

C, D Applications of AI and KBISs, e.g. speech, vision, image, and natural-language processing

E Applications of KBISs, not of AI, e.g. medical, engineering, business, and other

Figure 5.6 Relationship of AI to KBISs.

fuzzy logic was introduced and repeatedly articulated by Lofti Zadeh (1992) who is a computer scientist (also an electrical engineer and mathematician) with an expertise in ESs. Heuristics is a subject with many inputs, including some pioneering work by Herbert Simon who has also contributed to work on human cognitive processes, simulation of human thinking, heuristic programming, and the design of the programming language IPL. Simon is a social scientist who wrote the classic *Administrative Behavior* in 1945 and received the Nobel Prize for Economics in 1978. Simon and Zadeh are just two examples of how ideas, techniques, and research findings flow both ways across the boundary of AI and DSS.

Having suggested a boundary for a KBS, one should look at other views on the subject. One is by Harman and King (1986: 7):

> Today's knowledge systems are confined to well-circumscribed tasks. They are not able to reason broadly over a field of expertise. They cannot reason from axioms or general theories. They do not learn and, thus, they are limited to using the specific facts and heuristics that they were 'taught' by a human expert. They lack common sense, they cannot reason by analogy, and their performance deteriorates rapidly when problems extend beyond the narrow task that they were designed to perform.

The above quote was written in 1986. Perhaps the authors anticipated that 'today's' knowledge of 1986 will be extended by AI, for AI certainly has done much work and research in just these areas excluded from a KBS in 1986. Thus the work on learning programs, approaches to reasoning and problem solving, searching techniques, and the extensive use of heuristics are all relevant to a KBS and may well be applied to problem solving in a KBS context.

A further evolution of the term KBS (or KBIS) would be to integrate other AI applications such as natural language processing (NLP), voice processing and image processing into a KBS. These applications will give intelligent interfaces to the KBS and make it more end-user friendly. This would be very attractive to both end-users of an ES as well as problem-solvers because these end-users are often casual users with little or no computer background. With such an extension, a KBS may well embrace and apply most, if not all of AI that is relevant to a KBS. This relationship is shown in Fig. 5.6. KBS then includes many non-ES applications in AI such as processing of speech, vision, and natural language. In addition, a KBS will include many non-AI applications, such as those in medicine, engineering, and business.

Another view of a KBIS is to consider it just as another computerized information system. This classification is shown in Fig. 5.7. Here a KBS is distinct from a data-oriented system as found in most transactional systems. Data is also used in problem solving just as knowledge is used. Knowledge, of course, is used in many AI systems (discussed in Chapter 2) of which ESs are the best example of a commercial success (discussed in Chapter 3). We

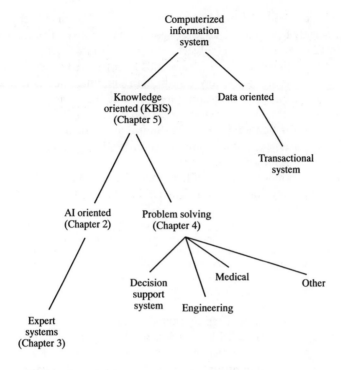

Figure 5.7   Classification of information systems.

did not discuss applications of ESs in any specificity since they are discussed in specialized books elsewhere such as Barr and Feigenbaum (1982) for the early medical applications; Dym and Levitt (1991) for engineering applications; Löf and Möller (1991) and Mockler (1989a,b) for business applications. A good discussion of KBIS in AI other than ESs is given in Howe (1991). We then discussed problem solving in Chapter 4. One type of problem solving used extensively in business and industry is the DSS. Since there could be an overlap in the problem jurisdiction of a KBIS and a DSS, we shall compare the two systems.

COMPARISON WITH A DECISION SUPPORT SYSTEM

We have already compared (albeit very briefly) a transactional data system with a KBIS. But how about a DSS? Both are concerned with ill-structured environments. So what are the differences? This short question has a long answer but we summarize the answer in Table 5.1. It is not crucial to the continuity of this book to follow all the nuances of Table 5.1 but it does

Table 5.1 Comparison of a KBIS with a DSS

	DSS	KBIS
Objective	Assist human decision making	Replicate and replace human decision making by a transference of expertise
Domain	General, broad, and complex	Narrow and limited (usually pre-suumes the closed-world assumption)
Nature of task	Ill-defined and unstructured *Ad hoc*	Ill-defined and very unstructured (fuzzy) Repetitive
Levels of management served	Middle and top	Middle, top, and operational
Function performed	Support decisions	Make decisions
'Mother' discipline	Operations research and management science	Artificial intelligence
Research emphasis	On decision-making activity and decision-makers	On cognitive processes, knowledge representation, inferential reasoning

provide points of reference which will become more meaningful as one reads through this book.

Table 5.1 shows the differences as they relate to decision making and problem solving. There are other differences as they relate to resources (hardware, software, and personnel), and these are discussed in Part III.

OVERVIEW OF A KNOWLEDGE-BASED SYSTEM

We conclude this section with a brief overview of a KBIS and identify the chapters where detailed discussions can be found. In this chapter, we have examined many definitions of knowledge and of a KBIS. Whatever definition you chose, the basic components of a KBIS as seen from the point of view of the end-user are shown in Fig. 5.8 (the interface from the point of view of the developer is discussed in the next chapter). The knowledge-base (box 1), consisting of facts, rules, heuristics, and other relevant information, is used by the inference mechanism (box 2) to provide expert opinion for the decision-maker and problem-solver through an interface (box 3). This interface must be end-user friendly to entice the end-user to use the systems. How this can be done is the subject of another chapter, as is the creation of the knowledge-base and the inference mechanism. These components have to be planned and designed before they are implemented. All this development is the subject of Part II.

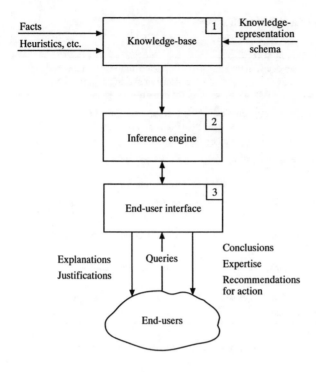

Figure 5.8 Basic components of a KBIS.

SUMMARY AND CONCLUSIONS

There are many kinds of knowledge partly because there are so many sources of knowledge. In a real-world KBIS, there is a mix of kinds and types of knowledge that make up the knowledge-base. The content of such knowledge is summarized in Fig. 5.9. The important types of knowledge are compared to Table 5.2. These different types of knowledge generate different knowledge-bases. We shall have much more to say about knowledge-bases (including how knowledge is acquired and represented) in later chapters.

Having discussed the structure of knowledge and the nature of a knowledge-based system, we are now ready to discuss its development, the subject of the next part of this book. We start in the next chapter with an overview of the development process. We emphasize the front-end (user-specifications and overall design) and identify the subsystems, which are then discussed in the following chapters.

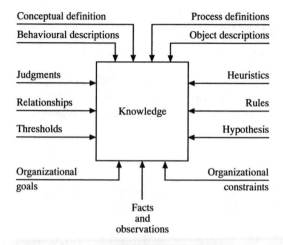

Figure 5.9 Content of knowledge.

Table 5.2 Comparison of selected kinds of knowledge

Kinds of knowledge	Characteristics	Output	Attributes	Relationship of knowledge to problem solving
Facts	Statement of existence	What is	Truth	Data
Heuristics	Rule of thumb	Why and why not	Discovery	Tactics
Rules	Relationship of factual conditions and conclusions	What should be	Conditions associated with actions and conclusions	Tactics
Procedure	How things work	How it is done	Algorithms	Procedure
Declarative (descriptive)	How things are	Why it is done	Association with truth	Strategies

CASE 5.1 THE RPFA IN THE UNITED KINGDOM

The RPFA stands for the Retirement Pension Forecast Advice Systems developed by Andersen Management Consultants for the UK Department of Social Security. The system used is a commercially available shell, ADS. The system was designed to support clerks advising people as to whether or not they could receive a retirement pension at an appropriate age and advising what payment to expect.

The case load was predicted at 300 000 cases per year with an expected savings estimated at over £1 million annually for an expert system which was expected to be developed quickly and be easy to maintain.

Source: S. Spirgel-Sinclair and G. Trevena (1988) 'The DHSS Retirement Pension Forecast and Advice System', in P. Duffin (ed.), *Knowledge-Based Systems: Applications in Administrative Government*, Ellis Horwood, Chichester, pp. 34–41.

Questions

1. Would you call this application a simple case of routine decisions that could be just another transactional information system? Explain.
2. Would you classify this system as a KBS or an intelligent knowledge-based system (IKBS), which is what it was originally expected to be; or would you call this a simple 'rule-based' system without any intelligence or knowledge-base?
3. This system has been referred to as the first major KBS to be 'used in anger by a government department'. Why the anger do you suppose?

CASE 5.2 KNOWLEDGE-BASED SYSTEMS IN DIFFERENT COUNTRIES

In the United Kingdom KBISs can be found mostly in banking, finance, and in engineering. In Germany, ESs are specialized in mechanical engineering and plant construction. In Japan, the emphasis is on heavy industries. In the United States, the early systems were medical but now they are across the board in all industries and businesses. In the EC, one project, AIM (Advanced Informatics in Medicine), has partners in the United Kingdom, Italy, Spain, France, Finland and Greece.

Source: T. Bench-Capon and R. Rada (1991) 'Expert systems in the UK: from AI to KBS', *Expert Systems with Applications*, **3**, 397–402.

Questions

1. Is specialization in one field a stepping stone for across-the-board applications in each country or region?
2. Why is the application such as the AIM a multinational effort? Why not a national effort?

3. Are applications of a KBS found mostly in developed countries; if so, why?
4. Is it a deliberate attempt for countries to specialize in specific application areas or is it inevitable because of world competition? Or are there other economic or technological reasons?
5. What seems to be constraining greater applications? Is it the lack of demand, or skilled personnel, of equipment and software; or is it the lack of adequate development technology?

REVIEW AND DISCUSSION QUESTIONS

5.1 What is a heuristic? Can heuristics for the same problem differ? If yes, then why?

5.2 Is there a best heuristic for a problem?

5.3 When should a heuristic be used and not be used in a KBIS?

5.4 Is surface knowledge or deep knowledge more relevant to a KBIS? Explain your reasoning.

5.5 What type of knowledge mix is most relevant to different KBIS environments? Is any mix harmful to a KBIS? Why?

5.6 What is the relevance of a hypothesis to a KBIS?

5.7 'Knowledge is a logical evolution from data, and knowledge systems an evolution of data systems.' Comment.

5.8 Can a knowledge-base be consistent with institutional databases? Explain.

5.9 Can a knowledge-base be integrated with an institutional transactional system? Explain some of the issues that may arise.

5.10 Who should be responsible for a knowledge-base? The end-user or the computer technician? Explain your choice.

5.11 What definition(s) of a KBIS do you like most? Explain why.

5.12 What definitions of a KBIS do you not agree with? Explain why.

5.13 Do you think that the definition of a KBIS has stabilized or is it still evolving? Explain your position.

5.14 Do you think the definition of 'knowledge' has stabilized or is that evolving too? Explain.

5.15 What is the most striking difference between a KBIS and (*a*) a transactional system; and (*b*) a decision support system?

5.16 In having a KBIS, who are the losers and who are the gainers (if any). Explain the losses or gains.

5.17 'Medical applications dominated the applications of KBISs in the early days. Now industrial and business applications will soon dominate.' Comment.

5.18 'Society is now ready for a KBIS because we have the technology and the proper attitudes.' Comment.

5.19 'We have not yet started even to consider the many social implications of a KBIS. We do so only at our grave peril.' Comment.

5.20 'A knowledge-base is an infrastructure for an entire organization to be used by all levels of management and end-users as well as all functional departments of a firm.' Comment.

Note: The answers to many of the questions listed above have not been discussed in this chapter. This should not, however, deter you from trying to answer them as best as you can. You may also wish to answer these questions after you have read this book. You may be pleasantly surprised.

BIBLIOGRAPHY AND REFERENCES

Adeli, H. (1990) *Knowledge Engineering*, vols 1 and 2, McGraw-Hill, New York.
This is a set of readings not only on fundamentals but also on applications of knowledge engineering.

Altenkrueger, D. E. (1990) 'KBMS: aspects, theory and implementation', *Information Systems*, **15** (1), 1–8.
An excellent overview and short tutorial. Also a good glossary.

Arnold, E. (1989) 'Artificial intelligence in the UK: the Alvey Intelligent Knowledge-based (IKBS) Programme', *AI Communications*, **2** (1), 18–19.
Needs updating but still good. Arnold identifies some of the lessons that he thinks should be exploited in future programs.

Barr, A. and E. A. Feigenbaum (1982) *The Handbook of Artificial Intelligence*, vols 1–4, William Kaufmann, Los Altos, CA.
Volume 2 has medical applications. All four volumes constitute a good reference set on AI.

Beach, S. S., S. Sickel and W. Gevarter (1991) 'Standards for evaluating expert systems tools', *Expert Systems with Applications*, **2** (4), 225–268.

Berry, D. and A. Hart (1991) 'User interface standards for expert systems: are they appropriate?', *Expert Systems with Applications*, **2** (4), 245–250.

Botrow, D. G., S. Mittal and M. J. Stefik (1986) 'Expert systems: perils and promise', *Communications of the ACM*, **29** (9), 880–894.

Copestake, A. and K. S. Jones (1990) 'Natural language interfaces to databases', *Knowledge Engineering Review*, **5** (4), 225–249.

Davis, R. (1986) 'Knowledge-based systems', *Science*, **231** (741), 957–963.

Dym, C. L. and R. E. Levitt (1991) *Knowledge-based Systems in Engineering*, McGraw-Hill, New York.
The theory and much of the implementation discussed is portable to systems other than engineering.

Frawley, W. J., G. Piatetsky-Shapiro and C. J. Matheus (1992) 'Knowledge discovery in databases: an overview', *AI Magazine*, **13** (3) 57–70.
Another good tutorial with a good section on future directions.

Gorney, D. J. and K. G. Coleman (1991) 'Expert systems development standards', *Expert Systems with Applications*, **2** (4), 239–244.

Harrison, P. R. and P. A. Ratcliffe (1991) 'Towards standards for validation of expert systems', *Expert Systems with Applications*, **2** (4), 251–258.

Harmon, P. and D. King (1985) *Expert Systems—Artificial Intelligence in Business*, Wiley-Interscience, New York.

Hayes-Roth, F. and N. Jacobstein (1994) 'The state of knowledge-based systems', *Communications of the ACM*, **37** (3), 27–39.
An excellent survey of the past and the current state of the art with a rosy picture of the future of KBIS.

Hayes-Roth, F., D. A. Waterman and D. B. Lenat (eds) (1983) *Building Expert Systems*, Addison-Wesley, Reading, MA.

Hembry, D. M. (1990) 'Knowledge-based systems in the AD/cycle environment', *IBM Systems Journal*, **29** (2), 274–286.

Discusses knowledge-based system from the point of view of improving productivity in the development of IBM's SAA (Systems Application Architecture).

Howe, J. (1991) 'Knowledge-based systems and artificial intelligence: emerging technology', *Future Generation Computer Systems*, **7**, 55–68.
Discusses the state of progress of applications of a KBIS in AI. Areas discussed are: vision, natural language processing and speech processing. The conclusion reached is that KBIS technology 'shows great promise for the future'.

Löf, S. and B. Möller (1991) 'Knowledge systems and management decision support', *Expert Systems with Applications*, **3**, 187–194.
Discusses how conventional tools combined with knowledge systems technology can create intelligent decision support systems.

Lowry, M. R. (1992) 'Software engineering in the twenty-first century', *AI Magazine*, **13** (9), 71–87.

Mockler, R. J. (1989a) *Knowledge-based systems for management decisions*, Prentice-Hall, Englewood Cliffs, NJ.
Mostly on 15 applications in business.

Mockler, R. J. (1989b) *Knowledge-based Systems for Strategic Planning*, Prentice Hall, Englewood Cliffs, NJ.
Mostly on implementation followed by seven cases.

Oakley, B. W. (1990) 'Intelligent knowledge-based systems: AI in the UK', in R. Kurzweil (ed.) *The Age of Intelligent Machines*, pp. 346–349, MIT Press, Cambridge, MA.
This article is a good excuse to read the many other articles that are worth reading especially those by Allen Newell, Marvin Minsky, Sherry Turkle, Seymour Papert, Margaret Boden, Roger Schank, and Edward Feigenbaum.

O'Docherty, M. H. and C. N. Daskalakis (1991) 'Multimedia information systems: the management and semantic retrieval of all electronic data types', *Computer Journal*, **34** (3), 225–238.

O'Leary, P. E. and P. K. Watkins (eds) (1992) *Expert Systems with Applications*, **4** (2), 175–227.
Special issue on 'Applied Artificial Intelligence/Expert Systems Program in Universities'.

Spectrum, **31**, no. 1 (1994). Special issue on technology.

Stratil, M. and C. Hyball (1987) 'Emerging methodology knowledge in engineering', paper presented at the KBS 87, Online, Pinner, UK.

Strok, D. (1992) 'Teaching artificial intelligence: an IEEE survey', *IEEE Expert*, **7** (2), 59–62.

Szolovits, P. (1986) 'Knowledge-based systems: a survey', in M. L. Brodie and J. Mylopoulos (eds), *On Knowledge-based Management Systems*, pp. 339–352, Springer Verlag, New York.
Starting with the roots of a KBIS, the author surveys the methodology through to an assessment of the current state of the art.

Turban, E. and R. Trippe (1990) 'Integrating expert systems with operations research: a conceptual framework', *Expert Systems with Applications*, **1** (4), 335–344.

Zadeh, L. A. (1992) *Fuzzy Logic for Management of Uncertainty*, Wiley, New York.

Part II

Development Cycle of a Knowledge-based Information System

This second part builds on the basic ideas presented in Part I. An overview of the chapters in Part II, and how they interrelate, is shown in Fig. II.1.

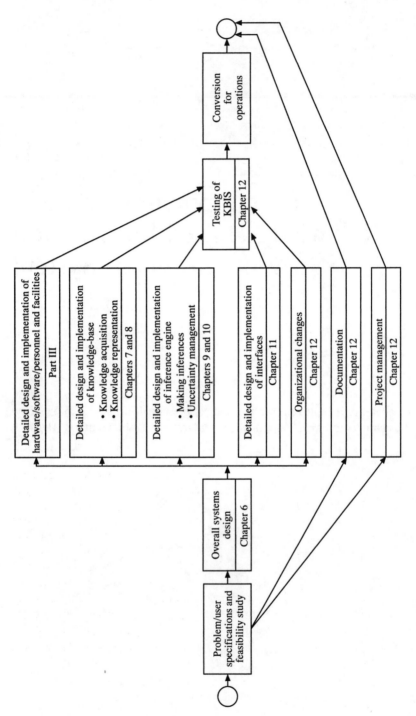

Figure II.1   An overview of Part II

6

DEVELOPMENT OF A KNOWLEDGE-BASED SYSTEM

The sooner you start programming, the longer it takes to finish.
H. F. Ledgard, *Programming proverbs*

INTRODUCTION

Development in the context of an information system is the process in which an information system is designed from a user's requirements, implemented, tested, and made ready for operation.

There are two main approaches to development: one is the *systems development lifecycle* (SDLC); and the other is through *prototyping*. The SDLC is appropriate for more comprehensive KBISs and is the focus of this chapter. It is a set of activities that must be followed in a prescribed sequence. In contrast to an SDLC—where the activities are distinct and formally separate—in prototyping many of the activities are intertwined. Thus in prototyping the design and implementation may be performed at one time or the design may evolve from a user specification that is also evolving in an interaction between the end-user and the knowledge engineer. Thus prototyping is particularly appropriate for certain subsystems and will be discussed later in the context of an appropriate application environment. In this chapter we will focus on the SDLC, which is often appropriate for larger KBISs and for some subsystems. For the SDLC, we shall identify and describe its many activities and discuss the nature and importance of sequencing between them. We shall, however, start our discussion by first considering briefly the nature of an SDLC as a development strategy.

DEVELOPMENT STRATEGIES

There are many development strategies. A stratified sample is compared in Table 6.1 with the traditional SDLC. First to be compared is the XCON system, the benchmark for all large commercial systems, which was used to configure computer systems' orders for Digital Equipment Corporation. The next comparison is with Waterman, a computer scientist and authority on expert systems, and finally, we have Turban, an author of books on ES and DSSs. Comparing these methodologies we find different terms used but the same basic stages of development as in a traditional SDLC. Therefore we will stay with the traditional SDLC while recognizing that this does not preclude the possibility that components of a KBIS can be developed using prototyping but all within the framework of an SDLC.

An overview of the development of a KBIS is shown in Fig. 6.1. It all looks very sequential but in reality there is much iteration and repetition among activities. Thus the design activity may be repeated many times before a design is agreed upon. In addition, repetition of an activity may cause reassessment of one or more previous activities. Thus one design may suggest a revised user specification or even a revised feasibility study. Such complex interaction is not shown in Fig. 6.1 in order to keep it simple.

It may also be necessary to repeat an entire SDLC for a KBIS by using one SDLC as a demonstration prototype for other progressively more complex and comprehensive ones, making the KBIS progressively more effective and useful. Or the repetition of an SDLC may result from redevelopment of a system after one has served its purpose and a new one is required. This spiralling of the SDLC is illustrated in Fig. 6.2. Whether spiralling or not, we have a set of main activities that will now be examined. The first important activity to be discussed is a feasibility study which follows the preparation of a systems plan.

The SDLC is particularly appropriate for large and complex systems. However, for small and simple systems it is often desirable to use prototyping or the run–understand–debug–edit (RUDE) cycle as an alternative development strategy. Also, prototyping could be used for a subsystem within an SDLC, and sometimes prototyping is used as part of the development of a subsystem such as the development of software. We will therefore take a small digression to discuss prototyping (Partridge, 1991: 51–53) and the RUDE cycle, and then return to the SDLC for a KBS.

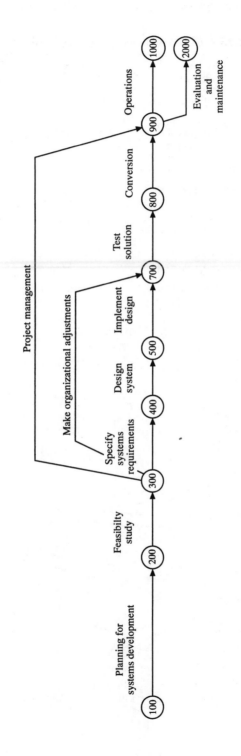

Figure 6.1 Development of a KBIS.

Table 6.1 Comparison of Development Strategies Used for a KBIS

SDLC	XCON (1980–1985)	Waterman (1986)	Turban (1990)
Feasibility	Initial program definition	Identification	Identification and justification
Systems Requirements specification	Build initial prototype	Conceptualization	Systems analysis and conceptualization
Design Conceptual Detailed	Design program plan Validate Education and user involvement Design documentation	Formalization	Hardware and software selection Systems design
Implementation Program Hardware	Implementation	Implementation	Systems construction Knowledge-base acquisition and representation
Testing and Conversion	Testing	Testing	Field testing Training Documentation Installation

Sources: Harman, P. and D. King (1985) *Expert Systems*, Wiley, New York, p. 156,
Waterman, D. (1986) *A Guide to Expert Systems*, Addison-Wesley, Reading, p. 137.
Turban, E. (1990) *Decision Support and Expert Systems*, Macmillan, New York. p. 446.

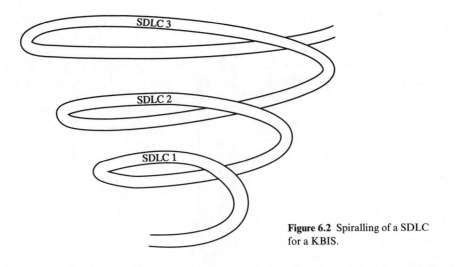

Figure 6.2 Spiralling of a SDLC for a KBIS.

Prototyping

A prototype is a small-scale version of the desired system, one that facilitates the exploration of a maximum of the implications of the specification with a minimum of resource commitment. As you will see, the name is something of a misnomer in the software context.

Floyd (1984) sees prototyping as consisting of four steps:

1. Functional selection
2. Construction
3. Evaluation
4. Further use

Step 1, functional selection, refers to the choice of functions (or range of features) that the prototype will exhibit—this will be some subset of the functionality of the final product. The difference in functional scope between the prototype and the final system can be delimited by two extremes (Floyd, 1984: 4):

- *Vertical prototyping*—'the system functions implemented are offered in their intended final form, but only selected functions are included'.
- *Horizontal prototyping*—'the functions are not implemented in detail as required in the final system; thus they can be used for demonstration, part of their effect being omitted or simulated'.

Thus a vertical prototype of the sorting problem (e.g. ordering a list of numbers) would be an implementation of the order-checking module without the permutation function preceding it. This prototype could be used to explore the accuracy and efficiency of say various order-checking strategies. Whereas if we implemented both modules such that they could deal with, say, lists of integers of length 10, then we would have a horizontal prototype. And, of course, all intermediate mixes are possible. The second step, construction, refers to the time and effort required to put the prototype together. Clearly, the amount of effort needed should be much less than for the final system, and this is achievable by judicious use of functional selection as well as use of prototyping tools. In prototyping, with respect to conventional software engineering, the emphasis is on the intended evaluation (what you are expecting to learn that will result in a better specification of the final system), not on long-term use—this may be obvious, but it is not true in KBIS development.

The evaluation step is the crucial one, for the whole point of the prototype is to gather information that will improve the development of the final system. What information is being sought from the prototype and how it will be gathered (e.g. by providing the necessary resources in terms of personnel and time) should all be clearly set out before the prototype is built. It should not be the case that we build a quick and dirty version of the proposed system and see what we can learn from it.

Further use of the prototype leads us into the domain of incremental system development methodologies. At one extreme, the prototype is a learning vehicle, and having learned all that we can from it, it is thrown away. There is not much choice about this in real engineering. The model building or model bridge can be broken up and discarded, or it can be put on display to gather dust, but what cannot be done with it is to use it as part of the actual building or bridge for which it was a prototype. But the software engineer has this option. A software prototype is exactly the same sort of thing as a software product: they are both software systems, programmed artefacts.

In fact, it can now take a considerable act of will-power for the software designer to throw away the prototype. However little time and effort was expended on the prototype. It was by no means negligible, so why waste it? The overriding temptation is to make maximal use of the prototype in the final system, and this is not necessarily a bad thing. It all depends on the sort of prototyping that you have embarked upon.

Three broad classes of prototyping are sometimes distinguished:

- *Prototyping for exploration*, where the emphasis is on clarifying requirements and desirable features of the target system and where alternative possibilities for solutions are discussed.
- *Prototyping for experimentation*, where the emphasis is on determining the adequacy of a proposed solution before investing in large-scale implementation of the target system.
- *Prototyping for evolution*, where the emphasis is on adapting the system gradually to changing requirements, which cannot reliably be determined in one early phase (Floyd, 1984: 6).

These three classes of prototyping are fuzzy—let us not try to hide that fact—but they are, nevertheless, a useful starting point. Exploratory prototyping is directed towards elucidating the system users' vision of the final product for the software engineer. It contributes primarily towards the construction of the specification. Experimental prototyping is the form that accords most closely with our introduction to the need for prototyping to uncover implicit features of a specification. It focuses on the behaviour of the specified system and allows a user to determine if the proposed system will in fact do what was envisaged and will not exhibit any undesired behaviour. The third class, evolutionary prototyping, is the one that will lead us onto the incremental development methodologies. It is not, in

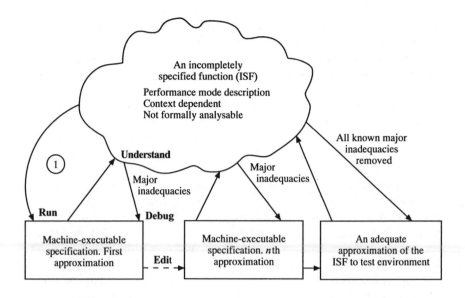

Figure 6.3 The RUDE cycle. (*From Partridge, 1991: 58.*)

fact, prototyping at all in a strict sense, and it is sometimes referred to as *versioning*. An evolutionary prototype is not built, evaluated, and discarded; it is built, evaluated, modified, and re-evaluated, which leads us to a RUDE cycle as a possible basis for system development. The RUDE cycle is shown in Fig. 6.3.

One can quite easily accept prototyping as a legitimate component of the software lifecycle, and yet utterly reject the incremental notion encapsulated in the RUDE cycle. Consider the case of the wax bell. If you want to make a bell, do you take a block of metal and carve away at it until it is a bell? No. You make a prototype out of wax. It is quick, cheap and easy to model with a wax prototype. But it also has some disadvantages: it will droop in hot weather. It goes 'phlub' instead of 'ding-dong', it is a fire hazard, bees will tend to nibble at it, etc. However, this is all beside the point, which is that when you are happy with your prototype you can take it to a foundry where they will make a metal bell out of it using various proven techniques. So, if you want a piece of complex software you do not want to hack it directly out of LISP (carving out a metal bell). It makes more sense to explore and model with a more humanly understandable, malleable, mathematical medium (the wax). Then conventional computer science can use established techniques to turn the mathematical description into a machine-executable form (the foundry). The RUDE approach, when exposed as the metal-carving exercise, looks to be clearly the wrong option to go for.

However, there is a response to this argument. Although it certainly appears to be eminently sensible to model with a wax bell rather than start carving away at a lump of metal from the outset, despite the disadvantages of wax as a medium for bells, certain disadvantages may be crucial. Take, for example, the tone disadvantage: a wax bell does not ring like a bell; in fact, it does not ring at all. Now the main reason for making a bell is usually to obtain an object that can produce a ringing sound. So exploration of potential bells using wax models may well allow us to find a pleasing-looking bell shape that is also within the technical and budgetary constraints. But the resultant metal bell may not ring with a pleasing sound. Indeed, it may not ring at all, in which case the project could hardly be counted as a success. The point here is that a prototype in a different (more convenient modelling) medium—i.e. a conventional engineering proto-type—may necessarily lack, by virtue of the prototyping medium used, one or more crucial features of the desired final product. This inadequacy of the modelling medium may be obvious, and therefore not a real problem, in the case of the wax bell, but will it always be so obvious when the goal is a large software system?

When we increase the complexity of what we are trying to build by several orders of magnitude over and above that exhibited by the bell problem, there may be aspects of the desired system that are not addressed by any conceivable prototype (partly because we cannot know all of the implications of a large and complex system before we have such a system). Thus prototyping in a more conventional engineering sense certainly has its advantages, but it also has its limitations. The ultimate prototype is some crude version of the final system that will itself become the final system as a result of evolutionary development.

One can argue about the virtues of various modelling mediums as vehicles to support a prototyping expedition (as we can similarly argue about so many of the claims in this field). There are, however, some empirical data available pertaining to the implications of prototyping as opposed to specifying as in an SDLC. The existence of real data is a rare occurrence in this area and thus we should not ignore it. Boehm *et al.* (1984) conducted an experiment to compare prototyping and specifying as techniques for software development. Seven teams each tackled the same project, consisting of 2000–4000 lines of source code. The specifying teams were constrained to produce a requirements specification and a design specification before any implementation. And the prototyping teams had to produce and exercise a prototype by week five (the midpoint of the overall project). The seven versions of the final system were compared both quantitatively (e.g. lines of code and pages of documentation) and qualitatively (e.g. maintainability and ease of use). Because of the small number of (small) teams involved and the use of limited subjective evaluation, the results should be thought of as no more than suggestive, certainly not definitive. But with this disclaimer in mind, it may be useful to see the major conclusions.

- Prototyping tended to produce a smaller product, with roughly equivalent performance, using less effort—almost half the size from almost half the effort. The specifiers often found themselves over-committed by their specifications. 'Words are cheap', they ruefully remarked.

- Prototyping did not tend to produce higher 'productivity' (measured as delivered source-code instructions per man-hour). However, when 'productivity' was measured in equivalent user satisfaction per man-hour, prototyping was superior.

- Prototyping did tend to provide expected benefits such as:
  —better human–machine interfaces;
  —always having something that works;
  —reduced deadline effect at the end of the project.

- Prototyping tended to create several negative effects such as:
  —less planning and designing, and more testing and fixing;
  —more difficult integration due to lack of interface specification;
  —a less coherent design.

The authors comment that these last negative effects from prototyping will become particularly critical on larger products. In summary, they say that both prototyping and the SDLC approach have valuable advantages that complement each other, and that for most large projects a mix of these two approaches is the best strategy.

FEASIBILITY STUDY FOR A KNOWLEDGE–BASED SYSTEM

Before any choice on a development strategy is contemplated, it is wise to invest resources in deciding whether development of a proposed KBIS promises to be a cost-effective exercise or not. This preliminary study explores the feasibility of the KBIS proposal.

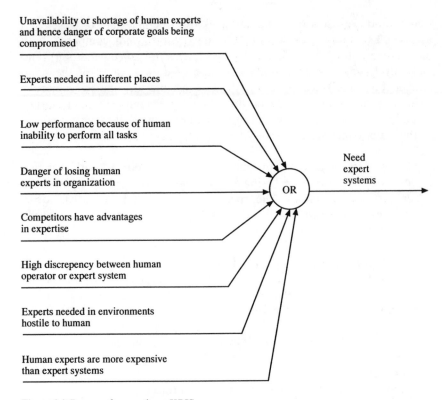

Unavailability or shortage of human experts
and hence danger of corporate goals being
compromised

Experts needed in different places

Low performance because of human
inability to perform all tasks

Danger of losing human
experts in organization

Competitors have advantages
in expertise

High discrepency between human
operator or expert system

Experts needed in environments
hostile to human

Human experts are more expensive
than expert systems

OR

Need
expert
systems

Figure 6.4 Reasons for wanting a KBIS.

A *feasibility study* is an analysis to determine whether or not desired objectives of a proposed project can be achieved within given constraints. The study could be part of the planning process and can be conducted by the planning department. Alternatively, a committee can be appointed for the task consisting of management that are interested in the proposed project's results. The project would be a response to the perception of a need for a KBIS which can result from one or more reasons as depicted in Fig. 6.4.

There are four main perspectives on feasibility: economic, financial, technological, and organizational. Each is the speciality of a different group of persons. Thus the economic feasibility is done by economists such as those in the planning department and accountants in the functional department for which the KBIS is being developed; the financial feasibility is done by financial experts and personnel from the comptroller's office; the technological feasibility is done by systems personnel with the help of AI personnel and perhaps consultants expert in the field; and the organizational feasibility is done by management, perhaps corporate management in consultation with managers of computing and of information systems. The general principles relating to feasibility of any information system do apply to a KBIS but there are some considerations that are specific to a KBIS. All these are summarized in Table 6.2.

And what if there were many KBIS projects that were all economically feasible and there was more than one KBIS project that could be

Table 6.2 Summary of Factors Affecting the Feasibility of a Knowledge-Based System

Nature of problem
Problem should
—be solvable by humans in 3–180 mins
—be primarily cognitive, requiring analysis and synthesis
—not involve a great deal of common-sense reasoning
—have well-known bounds and be well defined
—be confined to a narrow domain
—not be politically sensitive
—have a solution in real-time

Technological
Structure of problem appropriate to a KBIS
—involves heuristics and chains of reasoning
—requires symbolic manipulation
—domain well understood and constraints well defined

Economic
Benefits are greater or equal to costs and approaching 10:1
Improved quality
Increased competitiveness and market penetration
Increased expert productivity and expert capability
Expertise enhanced or at least preserved

Financial
Availability of funds for
—development of ESs
—maintenance of ESs

Organizational
Top and operational management support
Operational management understanding of AI
Organizational support
Willingness and availability of domain expert
Knowledge engineers with understanding of
—domain
—cognitive psychology
—group dynamics
Task knowledge and case studies that are reasonably stable and complete must be available
End-user involvement in development
Availability of project manager with
—technical appreciation
—top management support

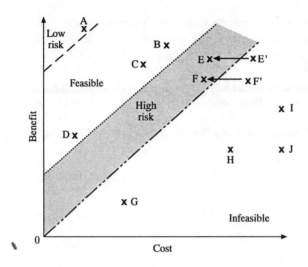

Figure 6.5 High-risk and low-risk zones.

implemented? Then one would select those that represented least risk. This can be illustrated in Fig. 6.5, where the diagonal through the origin O (dotted-dashed line) represents the break-even point where benefits equal costs. Points above the line were feasible. Point A has relatively high benefit compared to its costs and is the lowest risk project. B, C, and D are all economically feasible, with projects E and F also being feasible but in the high-risk area (shown shaded in Fig. 6.5). Projects G, H, I, and J are all infeasible. E′ and F′ are also infeasible and may represent projects using traditional software technology. However, using KBIS technology they are shifted to points E and F respectively but into the high-risk area. Of these two, F is closest to the break-even point and represents the highest risk and must only be implemented at the bottom of the economically feasible list. Thus within the area of feasible problems, both high-risk and low-risk applications occur. Clearly, when all else is equal, the low-risk applications are to be preferred.

The following are some potential problems with the feasibility of a KBIS:

- KBIS technology is still relatively new and unknown.
- Difficulty in identifying meaningful applications.
- Resistance to AI and KBISs is not uncommon.
- Unrealistic expectations of end-users.
- Difficulty in integrating a KBIS with existing information systems.
- Lack (relative) of skills required for a KBIS implementation.
- Gaining commitment of:
  —senior/top management;

—operational management and end-users;
—domain experts.

USER SPECIFICATION OF A KNOWLEDGE-BASED SYSTEM

Once it has been determined that a KBIS project is feasible (in relation to a set of constraints), then it is time to determine, as precisely as possible, what the proposed system should (and should not) do. This is the requirement and specification stage.

Problem specification, closely related to *user's requirements*, *user specification*, or *systems specifications*, can vary from a one-line statement on the cognitive tasks to be performed to a detailed manual that may even specify the domain expert or knowledge engineer that should be used in the project. In cases of doubt it is better to overstate than understate. To illustrate the problem, consider this case study: An application was delivered by a programmer to the supervisor who looked at the coding and asked why PL/1 was chosen when it was not the only language appropriate for the application, and besides was not a language maintained by the organization. The answer was: 'I know that PL/1 is not maintained here but I have never used the language and thought it would be fun to program an important application in it.' But the programmer soon left the company, as is to be expected in a profession with a high turnover and high mobility, with the result that the entire application had to be redeveloped. However, this time the problem specification was constructed to conform to company standards. A lesson was learned the hard way.

It is important not to overspecify in the specification stage because this reduces the flexibility open to the designer and developer. It is also important that the system not be underspecified. The specifications should be complete and well articulated with no ambiguities to be misinterpreted by the designer. And what should be articulated? The objectives and constraints for the system. Or else the system may well be delivered with unstated constraints being violated and objectives not being met because they were not specified.

Who makes the specifications? The ultimate source is the end-user of course, helped perhaps by the manager (if not the same person) and perhaps by the project sponsor, who may well be from another department and at a higher level of management. But the systems analyst and the knowledge engineer can also make significant contributions. They can ask questions about possible objectives and constraints based on their past experience with similar projects. They must persuade the end-users to make specifications that are complete and operational. It is not sufficient to say that one wants 'more' and 'better' information or an 'effective' and 'efficient' system unless these terms are defined operationally. This is difficult to do because end-users who are managers are people with many calls on their time. However, they must be convinced of the importance of the specification stage because it is crucial to a successful final system.

Another person who can help in the user and problem specification is the domain expert, either from within the organization or from outside. And the outside domain expert, as a consultant, could bring experience from other KBISs and, of course, can offer objectivity, especially to an organization that is inwardly oriented.

Part of user specifications may be left to the design stage but factors that may be specified in the user specifications stage may include those listed in Table 6.3.

Another approach to the content of a user's specifications is taken by Ince (1990: 261). Ince lists the properties that every software system specification should exhibit:

- It should be unambiguous.
- It should be free of design and implementation directives.
- It should enable the developer to reason about the properties of the system it describes.
- It should be free of extraneous detail.
- It should be partitioned.
- It should be understandable by the customer.

This is something of a wish list: it is a list of features that we would like our specifications to exhibit, and we should strive to construct them in accordance with this list. It is a list of tendencies whose presence within a specification we should attempt to maximize rather than a list of clear goals to be achieved. However, it is well-known that specifications and implementations tend to intertwine. So the second of the above-listed desiderata is not achievable in an absolute sense, but (all other things being equal) the fewer implementation directives that we have in a specification the better.

This section concentrates not on the technical issues of formal specification, but on issues that stem from the necessary interrelationships between a formal specification and the relevant humans—system designers and users.

A specification for a large software system is a large and complex document, and is, moreover, a document that contains many implicit consequences—i.e. a specification will specify many problem features implicitly. In a trivial sorting problem, the specification might imply that there is a well-defined order relation for list elements. This is nowhere explicitly said in the specification, but is implicitly specified in the

Table 6.3 Some Factors to Include in User Specifications

Output
Format
Content
Availability
Response time
Retention time

Processing
Inference mechanism
    Inference 'rules'
Approach to knowledge acquisition
Approach to knowledge representation
Uncertainty management approach
Programming language/shell/environment to be used

Input
Sources
Media
Procedures
Validity checks

Back-up
Items needing back-up
Procedures

Security
Define unauthorized access
What is to be controlled?
Control of access
    Procedures
Auditing
Internal or external or both?

Maintenance
When to maintain?
When to redevelop?
Mechanism to maintain

Personnel
Specification of domain experts
    Number
    Who?
Training
    Who?
    What?

Testing
Approaches to testing
Content of testing
Who performs the testing?

specification by the stipulation that the resultant list be an ordered permutation of the original list.

In a large and complex specification, such as for a KBIS, it is difficult enough to comprehend all that is specified explicitly, and it is, of course, much more difficult to gain full knowledge of all that is specified implicitly. So, there is a big difference between having a precise specification of a problem, and having a full grasp of all that is in fact specified.

Compounding the problem is the fact that a specification typically specifies only what is true—or, put another way, it specifies what the eventual system will do, and says nothing about what it will not do. So our specification for sorting does not specify that it will not sort tree structures, and that it will not sort lists of images, etc. There are clearly many more things that a given software system will not do than it will do. Hence, it would make little sense to attempt to specify explicitly what the system will not do, as well as what it will do. But, having said that, there are some aspects of what a specification excludes that may be worth explicitly stating, perhaps because they may be loosely implied by the specification, or perhaps because it would be particularly damaging to wrongly assume them, etc. A specification for a sorting problem, for example, is probably not expected to cover the possibility of infinite lists. It may not have explicitly excluded this possibility, but its exclusion is implicit in, for example, the exhaustive check for ordering. If exclusion of infinite lists is an intended constraint (and one suspects that it is) then maybe it should be explicitly excluded in the specification. On the other hand, if this exclusion is thought too obvious (in that it makes no sense to include infinite lists), then explicit inclusion of this list-length constraint within the specification might be viewed as unnecessary clutter. Unfortunately, one person's unnecessary clutter is another's essential detail—this is a rider on the fourth-listed desideratum given above.

The third of the desirable properties listed—i.e. the one concerning facilitation of reasoning about the properties of the specified system— addresses yet another point of communication between specification and the interested human parties. In this case we are concerned to provide the system developer with the facility to link by reasoned argument the specification (which is the developer's major interest and responsibility) with the behavioural properties of the desired system (the customer's major interest). This sort of linkage is necessary in order to check that the system specified is indeed the system that the customer ordered.

Now, we can extend our statement, about the difference between having a specification and having a full grasp of all that is specified, to encompass also full knowledge of what has been excluded from the desired system's behaviour. In sum, we have to avoid equating the possession of a specification (formal or not) with knowing what has, and what has not, been specified. This might sound like really bad news, and in truth, it is nothing to rejoice about. But is it a special problem for developers. The accurate answer is both 'no' and 'yes'.

No, it is a problem that occurs with the development of any complex computer system. The specification (if we can use that word in this context) of a building or a bridge will similarly embody unforeseen implications in the resultant artefact. What do they do about it? In part, the engineer tackles this problem by building models, prototypes, in order to explore the implicit features of the specification and this is possible, as we have seen earlier, even for a KBIS.

And now for the 'yes' answer. The problem of system features and limitations hidden within the folds of the specification is generally much worse for the knowledge engineer than the real engineer. And this aggravation of the problem is due to the tight constraints on acceptable functionality typically found in KBISs but not in, say, buildings or bridges. The upshot of this crucial difference is that the constructional engineer has considerable freedom to make adjustments while the structure is being built—i.e. as the implicit features of the specification are elaborated, by the construction, and thus become manifest as specific problems. In the world of tight and highly interrelated constraints to be found in KBIS systems, knowledge engineers dabble at their peril with individual, specific problems as they arise in their implementation. Such a procedure is a recipe for chaos.

So how is the knowledge engineer to explore the hidden feature of a specification? By building prototype systems, a subject discussed earlier.

The Myth of Complete Specification

The myth about complete specification of software problems has been discussed at length by Waters (1989), and we can do no better than quote from his argument. He begins by asserting that the purpose of a specification 'is to state the minimally acceptable behaviour of a program completely and exactly. The implementor is allowed to create any program that satisfies the specification.' It is often said that a specification functions like a contract between the two, but, as Waters points out, 'contracts only work well when both parties are making a good faith effort to work toward a common end. If good faith breaks down, it is always possible for one party to cheat the other without violating the contract.'

The problem with specifications (and contracts) is that it is not possible for them to be complete. This is true because no matter how trivial the program in question, there is essentially no limit to what you have to say. You do not just want some particular input/output relationship. You want a certain level of space and time efficiency. You want reasonable treatment of erroneous input. You want compatibility with other programs you have.

You want documentation and other collateral work products. You want modifiability of the program in the face of change. You want the implementation process to be completed at a reasonable cost. You want feedback from the implementor about the contradictions in what you want.

The only way to deal with the impossibility of consistently nailing down everything you want is to assign specifications a different role in the programming process. Instead of setting them up as a defensive measure between adversaries, use them as a tool for communication between colleagues. Under the assumption that the implementor will make a real effort to create a quality program, many of the points outlined above can go unsaid. In addition, things should be set up to encourage the implementor to help evolve the specification into a good one.

Requirements analysis can, and should, go a long way towards uncovering and resolving the hidden features of the proposed software systems, but it can never be exhaustive. In fact, Rich and Waters, (1988) argue at length for the 'Myth: requirements can be complete'. They choose the example of withdrawing money from a bank teller machine; the initial requirements might be:

> After the customer has inserted the bank card, entered the correct password, and specified how much is to be withdrawn, the correct account must be identified, debited by the specified amount and the cash dispensed to the customer, etc.

This is, of course, nowhere near complete, but could it ever be?

> To start with, a lot of details are missing regarding the user interface: What kinds of directions are displayed to the customer? How is the customer to select among various accounts? What kind of acknowledgement is produced? To be complete, these details must include the layout of every screen and printout, or at least a set of criteria for judging acceptability of these layouts. Even after the interface details are all specified, the requirement is still far from complete. For example, consider just the operation of checking the customer's password. What are passwords to be compared against? If this involves a central repository of password information, how is this to be protected against potential fraud within the bank? What kind of response time is required? Is anything to be done to prevent possible tampering with bank cards? Looking deeper, a truly complete requirement would have to list every possible error that could occur—in the customer's input, the teller machine, the central bank computer, the communication lines—and state exactly how each error should be handled.[*]

For Rich and Waters, 'At best, requirements are only approximations'. and the subsequent specifications cannot be expected to fill in the holes by

---

[*] C. Rich and R. Waters, 'Automatic programming', *IEEE Computer*, **21** (8), 42. © IEEE 1988.

merely a move to more formal precision. This viewpoint causes them to see software development as a process in which the developer must be oriented towards making reasonable assumptions about unspecified properties, rather than trying to minimally satisfy specified properties.

A closely related point is whether specification can be completed before implementation begins, for the model that requires complete specification prior to implementation clearly implies that complete specification is possible. 'This model', write Swartout and Balzer (1982).

> is overly naive, and does not match reality. Specification and implementation are, in fact, intimately intertwined because they are, respectively, the already-fixed and the yet-to-be-done portions of a multi-step system development. . . . It was then natural [i.e. when multi-step methodologies were accepted], though naive, to partition this multi-step development process into two disjoint partitions: specification and implementation. But this partitioning is entirely arbitrary. Every specification is an implementation at some other higher level specification.

Swartout and Balzer (1988: 27) emphasize that it is still of the utmost importance to keep unnecessary implementation decisions out of specifications and to perform maintenance by

> modifying the specification and reoptimizing the altered definition. These observations should indicate that the specification process is more complex and evolutionary than previously believed and they raise the question of the viability of the pervasive view of a specification as a fixed contract between a client and an implementer.

There are clearly some grounds for challenging the key notion of complete specification; it is thus all the more surprising that so little debate and discussion surrounds this central question. The question of the myth of complete specification merits more than expressions of belief or disbelief, and efforts to implement practical AI software will force the necessary further discussion upon the software community.

One often hears of the plea for more 'formal methods' in software design and development. The origin of this advocacy for a more formal approach was perhaps the general, and quite justified, dissatisfaction with software specifications couched in natural language. There are several good critiques that expose the weaknesses of specifications resting on the inherent informality of say, English, however assiduous the specifiers are in their vain attempts to chase away errors of omission, ambiguities, contradictions, etc. Meyer (1985) lists the following 'seven sins of the specifier' and uses them to highlight the weaknesses of natural-language specification and then the strengths of formal specification:

The seven sins of the specifier

- *Noise*—an element that does not carry information relevant to any feature of the problem; variants; redundancy, remorse.
- *Silence*—a feature of the problem that is not covered by any element of the text.
- *Overspecification*—an element that corresponds not to a feature of the problem but to a feature of a possible solution.
- *Contradiction*—two or more elements that define a feature of the system in an incomplete way.
- *Ambiguity*—an element that makes it possible to interpret a feature of the problem in at least two different ways.
- *Forward reference*—an element that uses features of the problem not defined until later in the text.
- *Wishful thinking*—an element that defines a feature of the problem in such a way that a candidate solution cannot realistically be validated with respect to this feature.

DESIGN AND USER SPECIFICATION

Design is the stage between the stages of problem specification and implementation. Much of what is done in the design stage depends on the completeness and detail of the user specification stage. Design, then, is in part the elaboration of the user specification stage, and in part the stating of the remaining necessary specification details. Design is the stage that precedes the implementation stage. This is reflected in Fig. 6.6(a) in which each activity or stage of development flows into another, which gives it the name of the 'waterfall' model. In Fig. 6.6(a) we show merely one part of the total waterfall of development. Here the design stage includes both the overall and the detailed design. As the system gets complex, the detailed design is separated from the overall design as shown in Fig. 6.6(b). Here the detailed design depends on the overall design specification document. This approach works well for relatively small systems but as the system gets more complex it becomes impractical (perhaps impossible) to do all the detailed design at one time. It then makes more sense to do the detailed design for each subsystem separately. This alternative is shown in Fig. 6.7. Here all the implementation is done at one time for the whole system. This may prove to be difficult for much the same reasons that all the detailed design is not done all at once but for each subsystem separately. Thus it also makes sense to do the implementation separately for each subsystem. In other words, one could do the detailed design and its implementation for each subsystem separately and in parallel. This is shown

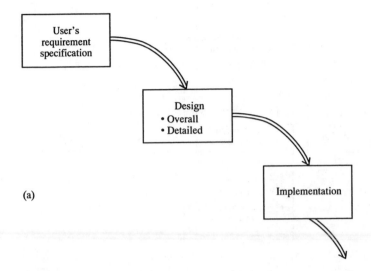

Figure 6.6(a) Overview of design showing the preceding and succeeding activities of a partial waterfall model of development.

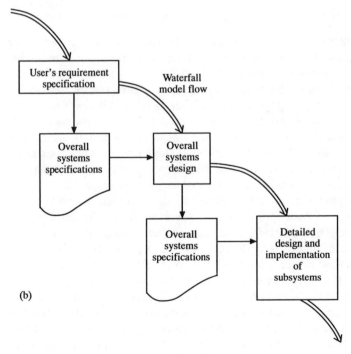

Figure 6.6(b) Detailed design and implementation.

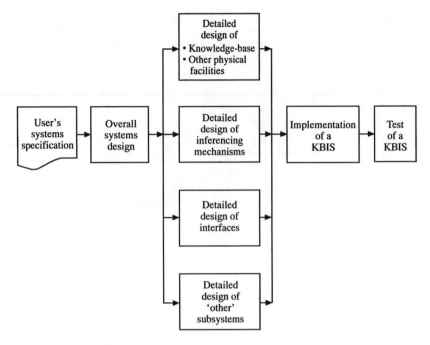

Figure 6.7 Detailed design and implementation of subsystems in a partial waterfall model.

in Fig. 6.8 for each of the subsystems of facilities (such as hardware and personnel), knowledge-base, inference engine, and interfaces. This makes sense since each subsystem requires a different set of personnel, tools, and techniques, and even programming languages. This subsystems approach is also appealing from pedagogical point of view because it is easier to discuss and explain. It is therefore the approach that we will follow in this text while recognizing that there are other approaches to combining design with implementation. In the concluding section of this chapter we will look at the overall design and implementation of the system, identifying other chapters in this book where the details for each subsystem will be discussed.

This subsystems approach requires close coordination, both in the design and the implementation stages. An example of the coordination needed is the selection of LISP as the language for making inferences, which must then be coordinated with the personnel responsible for hardware since the LISP language is much more efficient on specialized hardware; it will also require LISP programmers to develop and maintain the system. The necessary coordination can come from a coordinator or project manager or through knowledge engineers working on more than one team for a set of activities. This approach (cf. Fig. 6.8) allows for the division of labour necessary in large systems, but the coordination and integration of the subsystems then becomes critical.

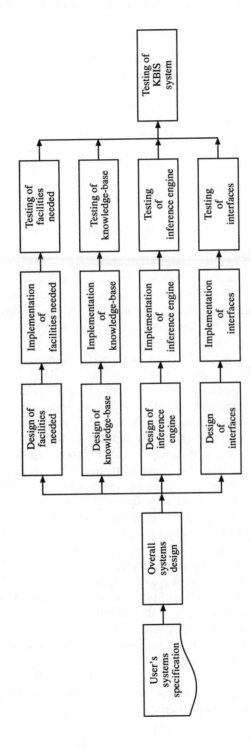

Figure 6.8 Detailed design and implementation of subsystems of a KBISl.

Integration of the subsystems of a KBIS is just one of the problems of integration. The other integration problem is that of integrating the KBIS with other information systems and subsystems in the organization—assuming such integration is desirable. Such systems or subsystems must be identified, and strategies for their integration must be part of the overall systems design, which becomes the basis for the detailed design of subsystems. Other topics for design decisions include the selection of the language, environment, shell or toolkit to be used. These will be discussed in some detail below.

ACTIVITIES OF DETAILED DESIGN

Physical Design

An approach that distinguishes between physical design and logical design is useful, for it separates activities that require different resources, both human and technological. Thus the *physical design* would include the design of hardware and data resources, while the *logical design* would include the design of software. In large and complex systems these sets of activities may require different types of personnel, and the resources needed are also different. Thus in the physical design, one may need to consider the requirements of a knowledge-based system as well as those of hardware for the end-user. In a KBIS, the needs of output forms and output printers are not so important as in a transactional system, but a KBIS needs a good capability for input and output involving soft data. Sometimes we need a specialized central processing unit (CPU) as, for example, in the case of the decision to use LISP, which might require a LISP machine. Technically speaking, the generation of soft input and soft output is not just a function of hardware but also of software support systems. For most practical purposes such supporting software often comes packaged with hardware, as is the case of a programming environment.

The activities for the development of the physical and logical systems are shown in Fig. 6.9, which is not inconsistent with Fig. 6.8 but there are differences of detail. The physical design is the design of not just the hardware resource needs but the design of the knowledge-base, which includes the knowledge-acquisition component as well as knowledge representation. Thereafter the implementation and testing of the hardware and knowledge-base subsystems are carried out (often by different sets of personnel). Only after the subsystems are tested satisfactorily are they ready to be tested with the outcome of the logical design. These subsystems will be discussed in detail in later chapters.

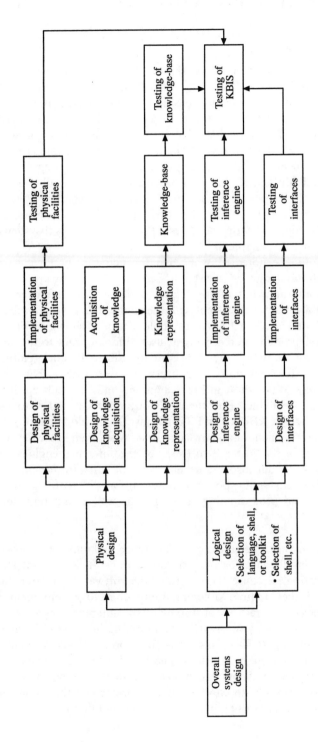

Note: Feedback loops (all interactions between activities) *not* shown

Figure 6.9 Development of a KBIS.

151

Logical Design

The logical design of a KBIS, shown in Fig. 6.9 parallels the design of the physical system. We start with the overall logical design, which includes decisions about the selection of a language as opposed to an environment, a shell, or a toolkit (these topics will be discussed later in this chapter). There are issues of integration as well as of security and control that must be resolved. There are also specifications of resources, operations, testing, and even output and input formatting that may need to be explicitly stated. In addition, there is the overall design of both the inference engine and the interfaces. This overall system design is followed by detail design, implementation, and testing of each sub-system. Again, as with the physical design, these subsystems will be discussed in later chapters.

It should be noted, though, that the activities of logical design and implementation can be viewed as activities of software development. Actually, the activities of the logical design of the inference engine are similar and certainly consistent with the common and popular diagrams for the development of an ES. An example of this is shown in Fig. 6.10. The logical design of an inference engine uses different terms to the design of an ES but the activities are conceptually alike. It does emphasize the possibilities for repetition of subactivities, a concept that we strongly embrace but do not show in Fig. 6.8 and 6.9 in order to keep the diagrams simple and readable. But there is an important point to make: the development of a KBIS or an ES is not just the development of software but also the development of a knowledge-base. Also, even in the development of software, it is not just the software of the inference engine that we are concerned with but also the development of software for interfaces, with each subsystem quite possibly requiring a different set of resources (hardware and programming languages) as well as different development techniques.

Inference making The software for inference making in a knowledge-based system is developed in parallel to that of the software for interfaces. Why the separation? Because the nature of the software is different in the two cases, and they require different approaches to development (interface development may require prototyping; the inference engine usually does not). These are likely to involve programming in different languages. Why different languages? This brings us to the problem of selecting languages, an environment, a shell, or a toolkit. The nature of these software alternatives is the subject of two later chapters. Here, however, we will discuss them in a comparative mode with enough detail to appreciate the importance of the selection process at this point in the development of a KBIS.

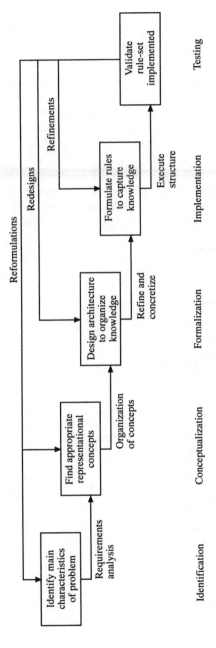

Figure 6.10 Stages and flow paths in the logical design and implementation of expert systems. (Based on Hayes-Roth *et al.* (1983), *Building Expert Systems*, Addison-Wesley, Reading, MA.)

Selection of language, shell, or toolkit It is excusable to think that the programming of an inference engine should be done in a language that facilitates inference making, such as LISP or PROLOG. But even in an inference engine, there is need for number crunching and computing that could well, and sometimes best, be done by a conventional procedural language, like the third-generation languages FORTRAN and Pascal. This situation arises in some engineering and business problems where ratios and formulas must be used to do basic computations followed by some necessary inferencing requiring more than one programming language. This would be especially true in a KBIS that is more than an ES and is integrated with a DSS. Also, programming is needed for the interfaces, and this could be done with prototyping in an interactive mode, which may require yet another type of programming language, perhaps even a fourth-generation language. Thus in a KBIS one may need a whole range of programming languages, and a designer must be prepared to consider different alternatives. The spectrum of programming languages currently available to the designer of a KBIS are summarized in Fig. 6.11.

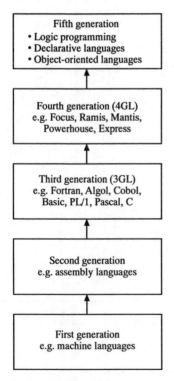

Figure 6.11 Generations of programming languages.

The selection of a programming language would depend on factors such as the following: internal storage required, time (compile and execution) required to run, ease of maintenance, ability to manipulate symbols, and built-in functions available. Consideration of these factors is desirable, but full consideration is somewhat idealistic. What happens in reality is that the ability to use the language without much resource outlay, and the personal preferences of the knowledge engineer will often supersede all other factors.

There are alternatives to selection of specific programming languages such as programming environments, shells, toolkits, and the object-oriented environment. These are the subjects of later chapters in the next part of this book.

Design of Interfaces

Interfaces are the last modules of a KBIS that need to be designed. Design specifications for each set of interfaces—for the developer and for the end-user—can be stated separately. Alternatively, the design can be left to the implementation phase to be developed in an interactive, prototyping mode. This delegation of responsibility may seem a very democratic way of doing things and it may result in a very responsive system, but there is the great danger that the resulting system may not be standard or portable. In a large organization, the system may have to be used at geographically separated sites and thus needs to be portable. The system also needs to be portable in a small organization since users will vary over time. It may therefore be deemed desirable, and even necessary, to specify certain minimum standards of performance and user-friendliness for the interfaces, rather than customize them to whoever happens to be user at the time of the initial system development.

Some of the factors that may have to be specified are as follows:

- Features of WIMP (*w*indows, *i*cons, *m*ouse, and *p*ointers).
- Menu or/and command interface.
- Types of menus to be offered (e.g. pop-up or pull-down).
- Screen design.
- Good screen-handling facilities.
- Nature of interaction and interactive dialogue.
- Nature and level of HELP facilities available.
- How the explanations for the 'what', 'why', and 'how' questions are provided.
- Nature and type of textual explanations.
- Importance of graphics and animation in making explanations.
- Profile of end-user to be expected (e.g. novice or experienced, or both).

- Editing facilities.
- Ability to make global changes.
- Debugging facilities.
- Security features.
- Tolerance levels of end-users for the phrasing of questions and answers.
- 'User-friendliness' of interface facilities.

SUMMARY AND CONCLUSIONS

This chapter concerns the development of a KBIS. The first activity considered is the feasibility study, in which one needs to spend a great deal of time thinking about the many unique factors relating to the feasibility of a KBIS. Why? Partly because KBISs is a new field and we have relatively little experience in the area of assessing the benefits and risks involved. And partly because a KBIS is a great consumer of resources—equipment, software, and time of specialized personnel.

Once the feasibility study is performed there may still be a problem if the feasible projects cannot all be implemented because there are not enough resources. All the feasible projects must then be evaluated, scored, and weighted (Laufmann *et al.* 1990). Some of the factors already considered, such as profitability, may be reconsidered along with factors such as opportunity, contribution to organizational goals, task appropriateness, risk inherent in the project, aversion to risk by decision-maker, time required for implementation and even political factors. The latter may involve the consideration of the project sponsors and end-users. Are they high in the hierarchy of the organization? Do they shout loud and long? Do they hold the purse-strings? Thus the choice of a project may start as being very rational, scientific, and even mathematical, but may end up being shaped by political and subjective decisions.

A major task in developing a KBIS is knowledge acquisition. The process requires technology transfer: to transfer relevant knowledge from a domain expert to a knowledge-base. One difficulty is that human experts may not have the time, ability, or will to articulate their expertise. Another difficulty concerns communicating the expertise to a knowledge engineer who may have a very different repertoire of concepts and definitions. These problems make it difficult for the experts to specify the rules specifically enough to be correct and meaningful. It is up to the knowledge engineer to extract the specifications of knowledge and represent it in a structure with a set of rules that generate useful advice.

The computational heart of the KBIS is the inference engine. This sounds like a piece of hardware, but it is not. It is software that enables us to make inferences from the knowledge-base. Depending on the knowledge

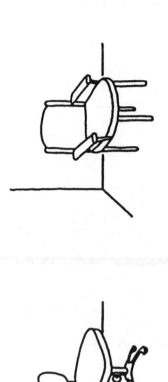

Product perceived in the
feasibility study

As specified in user
need specification

As viewed by the
knowledge engineer

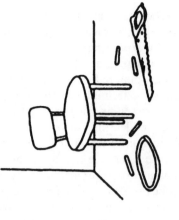

As envisioned by
the project manager

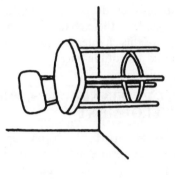

As interpreted by the
domain expert

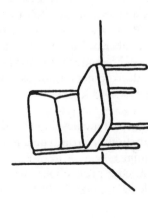

As delivered to the
end-user

Figure 6.12 Different perspectives of a project for development.

representation, we need a programming language if we do not use a shell. If the knowledge-base is rule based, then we can use algorithmic languages like the third-generation languages. If the knowledge is model-based, then we use a functional language and logic programming of which LISP and PROLOG are the most common. For these languages we need specialized hardware and large memories—technologies that we will discuss in later chapters. They are often not a constraining factor. What we need most is a better understanding of heuristics and learning theory—more specifically machine learning that is adaptable to human experience and new knowledge. That is perhaps the most important obstacle to a better and faster performance of a KBIS that exhibits human expertise close to the quality of a human expert.

Another problem arising in development is that of miscommunication. In a SDLC there are many stages and different people involved. Each person brings a different perspective to each stage of development and as a consequence there is often 'noise' and misinterpretation. This problem is reflected in a cartoon shown in Fig. 6.12.

In this chapter we have discussed the overview of development and have left details of design and implementation of subsystems to later chapters. A guide to these chapters is shown in the figure at the start of Part II. The spirit of this chapter is to offer an overview and review of what is yet to come in this part of the book.

CASE 6.1 A FINNISH BANKING EXPERT SYSTEM— 1: DEVELOPMENT

Matias is an expert system developed by the Okobank in Finland to provide 'fast service for farmers in need of long-term, low-interest loans'. The traditional wait of 2–3 weeks for processing a loan application was reduced to 15 minutes and the quality of decisions was also improved.

The Matias system consists of 350 rules divided into approximately 40 knowledge-bases and run on MS-DOS with 69 kbytes of memory. A shell, Xi Plus, was used but since this was 1987–8, the shell was new and a large number of bugs were discovered which were fixed quickly with the help of the vendor for the shell.

The development required 3 man-years of effort. The schedule for the project was as follows:

1. First prototype developing inference rules   4 months
2. Evaluation of prototype and detailed project
   planning   4 months
3. Knowledge acquisition, knowledge-base design and
   implementation   4 months

4. Interfaces design and implementation and systems and testing   6 months

Source: J. Konito (1991) Matias: development and maintenance of a large but well defined application, *Expert Systems with Applications*, **3** 241–248.

Questions

1. How is the development schedule of Matias different from a 'typical' development schedule for a KBIS?
2. How can the detailed planning after the prototyping be justified?
3. Is the design and implementation along with knowledge acquisition somewhat confusing? Should all these activities be done separately and in a prescribed sequence. If yes, what should the disaggregation of activities and the desired sequence. Explain your reasoning.
4. Is the design and implementation of the interfaces in parallel to the systems testing desirable? What are its advantages and limitations?

CASE 6.2 MANUFACTURING IN MEXICO— 1: PROJECT SELECTION

In 1987, CYDSA, a chemical and textile corporation with annual sales of $600 million, were persuaded by the CAI (Center for Artificial Intelligence) to develop KBISs for their manufacturing and repairing plants. Four problems were selected, all on diagnosis, and one for each plant. In making selection of the project to be implemented, the following 'questions' were answered:

1. Is the expertise being lost?
2. Is the problem domain narrow and well defined?
3. Is heuristic knowledge used in problem solution? Is it structured and well defined?
4. Are there experts? Can they explain their methods? What is their time availability? Do they agree on solution?
5. Are solutions based on common sense reasoning and knowledge? Are they based on symbolic reasoning? Is the reasoning non-monotonic?
6. Is the solution too complex? Too trivial?
7. Is the knowledge very dynamic? What is the return on investment? In what period is the return on investment expected?
8. Who are the users? What benefits will they have? Will they be aware of them?

Source: F. J. Cantu-Ortiz (1991) Expert systems in manufacturing: an experience in Mexico, *Expert Systems with Applications*, **3**, 45–55.

Questions

1. It is quite possible that some project candidates will score high on some criteria and low on some. How are they weighed?
2. Who does the weighting?
3. How do you measure a criterion that is very subjective. For example, take the benefit part of no. 8. How does one measure benefits of a KBIS?

CASE 6.3 R1/XCON—1: DEVELOPMENT

In 1980, XCON became the first large expert system to be used. It was developed by Digital Equipment Corporation (DEC), making VAX computers. XCON used a customer's purchase order to determine what, if any, substitutions had to be made to the 'typical' configuration of 50–100 components for the system to be complete and consistent with the needs of the customer.

The system was originally called R1 in its formative stages, started in 1978 by John McDermott and associates at the Carnegie Mellon University. Ever since, the system has been under continuous development. The group of professionals working on the system grew from five in 1980 to 77 in 1984, working on eight knowledge-based systems, one of them being R1. The system now has over 5500 component descriptions and the number of rules has grown from 750 in 1979 to 3250 in 1983.

> If R1's supporters had not emerged when they did, R1 could have easily sunk out of sight. But for R1 to survive, not having enemies was as important as having some strong supporters. R1's place in Digital was tenuous enough that if a few people had believed that exploring R1's potential was a serious mistake, the exploration would have stopped.

Several factors kept the all-pervasive caution from turning into hostility:

1. the degree of difficulty was just right for the VAX 11/780s, then the computer sold by Digital;
2. 'the number of people involved was quite small and grew very gradually'; and
3. 'the people who were the spokesmen for the project . . . worked hard to manage people's expectations to ensure that no one would count on more than it could deliver'.

Once developed, XCON soon became part of the manufacturing process at DEC. With XCON, DEC was able to configure equipment accurately 98 per cent of the time, compared to 65 per cent by the manual system. Manufacturing operations benefited from accurate systems configurations because of:

- Better use of materials in inventory.
- Increase throughput order rate.
- Fewer shipment delays because of fewer configuration errors.
- Faster response time to orders.
- Greater user satisfaction.
- Reduced cost of manufacturing and assembly.

In the 1980s, XCON expanded not just in depth but also in scope. Its current configuration of subsystems is shown in Fig. 6.13.

Source: J. Barchant and J. McDermott (1984) RI revisited: four years in the trenches, *AI Magazine*, **3**, 21–34; and J. McDermott (1981) R1: the formative years, *AI Magazine*, **2**, 21–29.

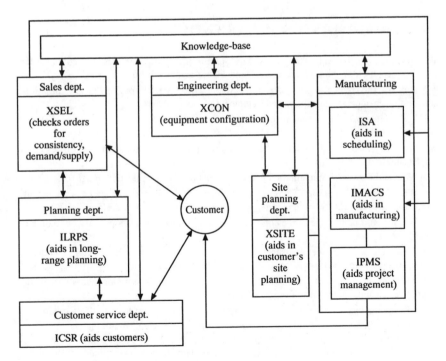

Figure 6.13 XCON

Questions

1. Is the XCON expertise typical for the 1990s? Why not?
2. What can one learn from the experiences in development and growth of the XCON system?
3. Is this transfer of technology from XCON only valid for large systems and only rule-based environments?
4. Should the close association of academia and industry be a model for future development of KBISs? Under what conditions is it desirable and not so desirable?
5. Is the tenuousness of successful projects such as XCON typical of a KBIS?
6. The size of the development team and its slow growth were important for XCON's survival during the development stage. Why was that?
7. The supporters of XCON kept the expectations lower than was justified. How can that be accomplished?

REVIEW AND DISCUSSION QUESTIONS

6.1 How are objectives important to the development of a KBIS? Are these objectives for the KBIS project itself or should there also be some higher organizational objectives?

6.2 How are the constraints related to the development of a KBIS project? Give examples of different types of constraints for each development phase involved?

6.3 Is the process of development of a KBIS different from any other information systems? Why and how?

6.4 To what extent is the user specification more or less important than that of design or implementation?

6.5 What is the role of documentation in the phases of (a) user specification and (b) design?

6.6 What should be the role (if any) of a consultant in the different stages of development? What are the disadvantages and limitations of having a consultant for a KBIS project?

6.7 What should be the role of the end-user in a KBIS project? Is this a primary or secondary role? Explain.

6.8 'Designing and implementing subsystems raises many problems of coordination.' Describe and give examples of the types of coordination problems that may arise.

6.9 'Detailed design follows an overall design.' How does one determine what is part of the overall design and what is part of the detailed design?

6.10 'Designing by committee is slow and dangerous.' Is this relevant for a KBIS? Explain.

6.11 Suppose that there were a large and complex KBIS to be designed and integrated with an existing DSS and transactional information systems. Further, it was decided that a team would do the designing and you are the leader of that team. How large a team would you have and what type of personnel would you want on your team?

6.12 Should maintainability be a consideration during the design stage? Or during the user-specification stage? Or both? If so why?

6.13 Give examples of necessary iteration and feedback loops. Explain why the repetition is necessary.

6.14 Should a domain expert be involved in the design stage? If so, why and should the person be internal to the organization or external to it? Explain your answer.

6.15 Should the end-user interface be specified in the design stage or left to prototyping by the user, the knowledge engineer, and the domain expert? Justify your answer.

6.16 Would you like to have a natural-language interface for your KBIS? Whatever your answer, please explain yourself.

6.17 Do you advocate standards for:

(*a*) Overall design?

(*b*) Detailed design?

(*c*) Development?

Would this help or hinder relatively new systems like the KBIS?

6.18 What is the role of planning and the corporate planning department in the development of a KBIS?

6.19 What is the difference (if any) in the perspectives of an end-user from that of the

(*a*) the knowledge engineer and

(*b*) the domain expert?

EXERCISES

6.1 Draw a diagram of the user specification and design process (assuming subsystems) for a KBIS showing (*a*) where and what documentation is created; and (*b*) different personnel participating (assume that consultants are used).

6.2 Draw a diagram for all the activities of overall design and user specification (assuming subsystems being designed) and show all the iterative repetition that may be necessary.

BIBLIOGRAPHY AND REFERENCES

Altenkrueger, D. E. (1990) 'KBMS: aspects, theory and implementation', *Information Systems*, **5**, 1–7.
  An excellent overview of a KBIS. It has a good section of types of programming languages for a KBIS and a good glossary.

Boehm, B. W. (1988) 'A spiral model of software development', *IEEE Computer*, **21**, 61–72.

Boehm, B. W., T. E. Gray and T. Seewaldt (1984) 'Prototyping versus Verifying: a multiproject experiment', *IEEE Transactions on Software Engineering*, **10**, 290–302.

Cupello, J. M. and D. J. Mishelevich (1988) 'Managing prototype knowledge/expert systems projects', *Communications of the ACM*, **31** 534–545.
  Fundamental issues of technology transfer, training, problem selection, staffing, corporate politics, and more, are explored.'

Edwards, J. S. (1991) *Building Knowledge-based Systems: Towards a Methodology*, Pitman, London.

Another excellent overview. This is by an academician writing from experiences in developing many expert systems and the KBIS project of Intellipse developed under the national Alvey Directorate in the UK. The author paints a 'rich picture' of a KBIS that is both a broad and detailed, and enhanced by his flair for good diagrams.

Floyd, C. (1984) 'A systematic look at prototyping', in R. Budde, K. Kuhlenkamp, L. Mathiassen and H. Züllighoven (eds) *Approaches to Prototyping*, Springer-Verlag, Berlin, pp. 1–18.

Both the article and the book in which it appears are good on prototyping.

Gorney, D. G. and K. G. Coleman (1991) 'Expert system standards', *Expert Systems with Applications*, **2**, 245–250.

An excellent survey of work being done in this important area for development and for KBISs.

Hardgrave, B. C., E. Reed Doke and N. E. Swanson (1993) 'Prototyping effects on systems development life cycle: an empirical study', *Journal of Computer Information Systems* **XXXIII**, 16–19.

This study examines managers in Fortune 1000 companies to investigate the importance, support, and replacement by prototyping of each phase of the SDLC.

Hilal, D. K. and H. Soltan (1993) 'Towards a comprehensive methodology for KBS development', *Expert Systems*, **10**, 75–89.

A critique of an 'articulation of the major schools of thought in developing KBS; their implicit assumptions and philosophies, especially the prototyping options'.

Huws, H., M. Wintrub and N. Martin (1992) 'Knowledge-based systems development', *Journal of Information Systems Management*, **9**, 51–56.

The authors describe 'One methodology that offers solutions to many of the management problems confronting those responsible for knowledge-based systems development and implementation efforts.

Iivari, J. (1990) 'Implementability of in-house developed vs. application package based information systems', *Database*, **2**, 1–9.

This article is not specifically for a KBIS but then are there any such articles? The principles discussed herein apply well to a shell or a toolkit.

Ince, D. (1990) 'Z and system specification', in D. Ince and D. Andrews (eds), *The Software Cycle*. Butterworths, London, pp. 260–277.

Z is a specification language developed at Oxford University. Ince offers an excellent short tutorial on Z.

Irgon, A., J. Zelnowski, K. J. Murray and M. G. Bellcore (1990) 'Expert system development: a retrospective view of five systems', *IEEE Expert*, **5**, 25–39.

This article discusses lessons learned from development especially those in training, development environment, knowledge acquisition, SDLC, integration with conventional software systems, ES acceptance, and ES project management.

Krcmar, H. (1988) 'Caution of criteria: on the context dependency of selection criteria for expert systems projects', *Database* **19**, 39–41.

A good discussion of the methodology for assessing the useability of expert systems.

Laufmann, S. C., D. Michael De Vaney and Mark Whiting (1991) 'A Methodology for evaluating potential KBS applications', *IEEE Expert*, **5**, 43–67.

An excellent article on project selection. The article includes the worksheet for evaluating some 120 questions relevant to scoring each project. There are three cases illustrating the scoring and weighting method for identifying the 'best', projects. The cases are too complex for inclusion as mini cases but are well worth looking at.

McTear, M. F. and T. J. Anderson (eds) (1990) *Understanding Knowledge Engineering*, Ellis Horwood, Chichester.

Eleven authors, many from the University of Ulster in Northern Ireland, give an excellent coverage of the development of a KBIS including its project management.

Moulin, B. (1990) 'Strategic planning for expert systems', *IEEE Expert*, **5**, 69–74.
Discusses project planning as part of strategic planning.
Meyer, B. (1985) 'On formalism in specifications', *IEEE Software*, **2**, 6–26.
O'Leary, T. J., M. Goul, K. E. Moffit and E. E. Radwan (1990) 'Validating expert systems', *IEEE Expert*, **5**, 51–67.
Defines and describes validation, verification, and evaluation of a KBIS.
O'Neill, M. and A. Morris (1989) 'Expert systems in the United Kingdom: an evaluation of development methodologies', *Expert Systems*, **6**, 74–89.
This article reports on a survey which focuses on the impact of human input, consultation procedures, the skills and attributes of a KE, and methodologies of an ES.
Partridge, D. (1992) *Engineering Artificial Intelligence Software*, Intellect, Oxford.
Price, C. J. (1990) *Knowledge Engineering Toolkits*, Ellis Horwood, New York.
Price poses a number of problems and answers them in the spirit of a dialogue à la Plato. Price also discusses four cases using toolkits. This book has a high substantive content-to-page ratio.
Rich, C. and R. C. Waters (1986) *Readings in Artificial Intelligence and Software Engineering*, Morgan Kaufmann, Los Altos, CA.
Salvendy, G. and M. J. Smith (eds) (1989) *Designing and Using Human–Computer Interfaces and Knowledge Based Systems*. Elsevier, Amsterdam.
These are proceedings of a conference held in 1989 represented by 26 countries. Papers range from the highly technical, directed to a fairly specialized audience, to the largely descriptive paper aimed at a much wider readership. It has good articles on the effect of VDUs on users of a KBIS.
Swartout, W. and R. Blazer (1988) On the inevitable intertwining of specification and implementation', *Communications of the ACM*, **25**, 438–40.
Stylianou, A., G. R. Madley and R. Smith (1992) 'Selection criteria for expert system shells: a socio-technical framework'. *Communications of the ACM*, **35**, 30–48.
Has numerous lists of selection criteria and a good explanation of them.
Tuthill, G. S. (1990) *Knowledge Engineering*, TAB Professional and Reference Books, Blue Ridge Summit, PA.
Chapter 9 is good on 'Preliminary Exploration and Requirements Analysis'.
Walters, J. and N. R. Nielsen (1988) *Crafting Knowledge-based Systems*, J. Wiley, New York,
Chapter 6 is on 'Crafting a Systems Design' and chapter 9 is on 'Crafting the Prototype Application'.
Waters, R. C. (1989) *Programming in the Year 2009*, University of Exeter, Exeter, pp. 1–5.
Weitzel, J. R. and L. K. Kertschberg (1989) 'Developing knowledge-based systems development life cycle', *Communications of the ACM*, **32**, 482–489.
The authors describe a methodology and claim 'processes replace phases and stages and during systems development, dynamic activation of processes allows the system to evolve'.
Yoon, Y. and T. Guimares (1993) 'Selecting expert system development techniques', *Information and Management*, **24**, 209–242.
The appropriateness of each development technique and its available supporting tools are discussed.

7

KNOWLEDGE ACQUISITION

He that increaseth knowledge increaseth sorrow.
Ecclesiastes, 1:18

Who shall decide when doctors disagree?
Alexander Pope

INTRODUCTION

Knowledge acquisition is the first step in creating a knowledge-base. It requires storage capacity and programming code to store the knowledge in machine-readable form ready for the making of inferences. But the problems of knowledge acquisition are not hardware or software problems but problems of human-ware. Knowledge acquisition is a very labour-intensive activity. It is almost an art-form with questions arising for which there are no algorithms or computer programs. For example, questions arise such as: how many domain experts are needed to provide the necessary knowledge and how should they be identified and selected? What sources of knowledge other than humans should be used? How should knowledge be organized? Should cases be used? How is knowledge to be elicited? What techniques and instruments of knowledge elicitation should be used? When should this elicitation start and end? What happens if there is more than one domain expert providing the knowledge and the experts differ? How should the knowledge elicited be verified and validated?

Fortunately, there is a *process* of knowledge acquisition that makes the acquisition orderly, effective, and perhaps even efficient. This process starts with *organizing* for the knowledge-base, followed by *knowledge elicitation* from the different relevant sources of knowledge. Different *instruments* of analysis and knowledge collections are used to facilitate the formulation of knowledge ready for knowledge representation and encoding into a knowledge-base. The knowledge-base is then *tested* for *validation* and *verification*; if it passes the test, it is ready for the testing of the knowledge-based information system with other subsystems like the inference engine and the presentation module. It is these stages of knowledge acquisition that are discussed in this chapter, very much in the order introduced above. The stages of knowledge representation and knowledge coding are discussed in Chapter 8.

We conclude this chapter with the identification of the many personnel involved in the knowledge acquisition process, and discuss the distribution of effort and responsibilities among these personnel.

OVERVIEW OF THE PROCESS

We start with an overview of the entire process of creating a knowledge-base which includes knowledge acquisition (KA). This overview is shown in Fig. 7.1. It starts with planning for the knowledge-base (box 1 in Fig. 7.1): it is here that the task for the knowledge base is defined if not already done in the previous stages of user specification and overall system design. Concepts, functions, relationships, interactions, dependencies, as well as the systems knowledge dictionary and vocabulary for planning of the knowledge-base are all specified. The content of the knowledge-base as well as its modules are identified along with all the relevant inputs and outputs to the knowledge-base. Also, standards and strategies for testing the knowledge-base must be specified. Finally, strategies for knowledge acquisition and representation need to be selected.

One important strategy in the organization for KA (box 2) are the decisions relating to the selection of the personnel required for the KA process, which includes one or more domain experts and a knowledge engineer responsible for the knowledge-base. Another important strategy in the organization of KA relates to the sources of knowledge and techniques of knowledge elicitation required to acquire the necessary knowledge (box 3). Once knowledge is elicited and expertise articulated, it then becomes the input for the formulation of knowledge and its representation necessary for inference making (box 4). Instruments for formulating the knowledge will be discussed in this chapter, while approaches to knowledge representation will be discussed in another chapter. The encoding of knowledge and the implementation of the knowledge-base (box 5) will also be discussed in a

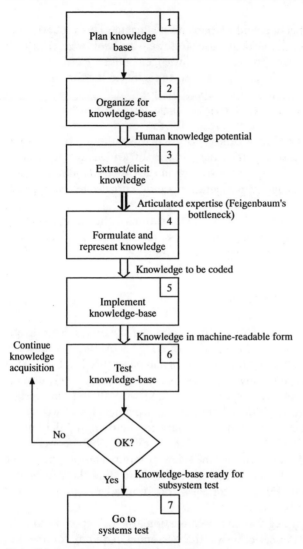

Figure 7.1 Overview of knowledge acquisition.

later chapter. Now the flow of knowledge increases as it does progressively after the knowledge elicitation stage (box 3). It is the knowledge elicitation stage that is often the biggest constraint in the process of creating the knowledge-base (as indicated by the narrow exit from box 3) and hence it is perhaps rightfully called the *Feigenbaum bottleneck*, named after Edward Feigenbaum who first identified the phenomenon.

Once the knowledge base is created, it must be tested (box 6). If the test is unsatisfactory, the process of knowledge acquisition may have to be repeated ('No' exit after box 6). If the testing is satisfactory ('Yes' exit after box 6), only then is the knowledge-base ready for systems testing along with the other subsystems.

ORGANIZING FOR KNOWLEDGE ACQUISITION (KA)

The first step in KA is to marshal all the potential sources of knowledge, which are summarized in Fig. 7.2. They include a lot of knowledge lying on the top of many a desk but buried in books, reference manuals, research papers, and case studies. Some attempts have been made with computer programs for text comprehension but much of the work of extraction requires sophisticated searching and is still very much an experimental process. There is also much knowledge, especially as to the local conditions, that can be derived from organizational personnel like the end-user, project sponsor, and the operations manager for the completed project. The consultant is an external source that can bring outside views not just of the industry but of the technology in general. The most important source of knowledge is, of course, the domain expert, or experts. In the case of a small and simple knowledge-based system, one domain expert may be all that is available or desirable. But as the systems get large and complex, multiple domain experts must be considered. They have the advantage of offering a greater distribution of labour and of varied counsel. A synergy through the

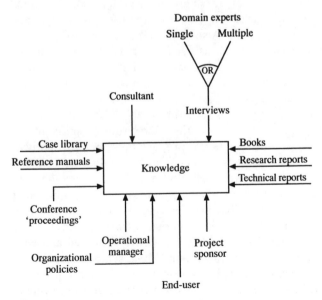

Figure 7.2 Sources of knowledge.

open and frank discussions and group interaction between domain experts can give a completeness to the knowledge-base that would otherwise not easily be achieved.

Multiple domain experts also help reduce individual bias and offer alternative lines of reasoning, which is important when the target system is contentious. The greater the variety of opinions and points of view the better, as this may produce greater sensitivity to the local and organizational problems. But the advantages are not without some accompanying problems and costs. One cost of multiple experts is that of committing more human resources to the project and the possible cost of disruption in the on-going functioning of the organization. Also, the more the sources of opinion, the greater the interpersonal interralationships and the greater the problems of group dynamics and logistics—and the more complicated becomes the process of KA, especially when many conflicting views have to be reconciled. Multiple domain experts do raise the need for special KA techniques as well as issues of group leadership and group problem solving. The group dynamics problem arises not only between the multiple domain experts but between the domain experts and the knowledge engineer. Hence, the problems of communication and understanding increase as well as the need for compatibility and motivation among the domain experts. The type and quality of the interrelationships will have an important influence on the success of the KA process, and on the creation of a relevant and useful knowledge-base.

Whether domain experts are used singly or in groups, some essential traits are important in their selection, namely expertise, knowledge, and experience in the target domain. Also important is the attitude and motivation to share expertise, as well as personal traits of being outgoing and relating well to others in a group situation. Thus the domain expert must not only have knowledge of the domain but must be willing to share it—and share it in an interactive mode with a knowledge engineer. This process can be time consuming and is sometimes very difficult to articulate even if you are willing to do so. But then the problem shifts to the knowledge engineer, who must create the proper atmosphere to motivate the domain expert to share knowledge. Sometimes a good listener is all that domain experts need for they are basically proud (and may be even flattered) to be the repository of the domain knowledge now being recognized and in great demand. The interviewing skills of the knowledge engineer are an important asset, aided perhaps by a background in cognitive psychology. Also, to know what knowledge is needed and what questions to ask requires a background in modelling, symbolic representation, the nature of knowledge, search and reasoning techniques, programming languages, and lots of basic computer science. An understanding of the process of knowing, learning, and thinking is also relevant. The knowledge engineer must also learn about the domain and the problem environment from the domain expert, and about the expected performance of the knowledge-based system from the end-users and project sponsors.

The availability of the domain expert is also important. Not having time for the knowledge engineer may not only delay the project but will not help the working atmosphere or relationship with the knowledge engineer. Domain engineers must be released from their on-going responsibilities for the project and must have the support of their immediate superiors. Both parties must be convinced or persuaded of the importance of the contribution of sharing knowledge for the overall benefit of the organization. A domain expert who is very protective and proprietary will not make the knowledge elicitation easy or pleasant.

Who selects the domain expert or experts? The project manager and the project sponsor will, of course, have an important role in this decision. The managers involved in releasing the domain experts will also have to agree. And finally there is the knowledge engineer. If one takes a participative view of management, one must involve the knowledge engineer in the selection of domain experts because it is the chemistry between the two groups that is crucial to any successful knowledge-base. The two groups must bring complementary qualities and characteristics to the KA process. And each can often help the other. For example, a domain expert can often make important contributions to the process of reasoning and search, the subjects of expertise of the knowledge engineer. Why and how? Because the domain expert knows the domain well and hence is in an excellent position to identify short-cuts and time-saving ways of reasoning and searching in the target domain.

The comparative advantages and the characteristics of the knowledge engineer and the domain expert for purposes of KA are summarized in Fig. 7.3.

The knowledge engineer will be discussed again in the chapter on the technical personnel needed for a KBIS because the knowledge engineer has responsibilities other than KA. But for the process of KA, the knowledge engineer has tasks that include getting acquainted with the domain, interviewing the domain expert, as well as analysing, evaluating, and documenting the knowledge acquired. To the task of KA, the knowledge engineer brings technological skills and an ability to learn quickly about a domain; the domain expert brings knowledge and experience of the target domain. Both must have strong interpersonal skills and a willingness to share their skills. The domain expert must have the ability to articulate, while the knowledge engineer must know how to listen and ask the relevant questions in a way that will not threaten the domain expert but instead tease and squeeze out of the domain expert all the knowledge necessary for constructing the knowledge-base. A lot depends on the skills and techniques of KA, which is our next topic.

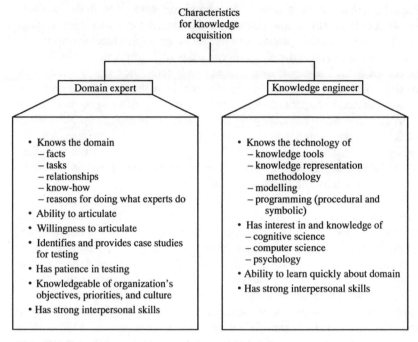

Figure 7.3 Characteristics of domain expert and knowledge engineer needed for knowledge acquisition.

But first, we shall raise and answer a commonly asked question: why could not a domain expert also be the knowledge engineer, much like a manager uses a spreadsheet and is also the programmer and analyst? Such a move would eliminate the in-between person and thereby reduce both the loss in communication and the time and cost for development of a KBS. The answer should lie partly in Fig. 7.3, which shows the many different qualifications and skills that are needed and are seldom found in one person. Knowledge to be acquired—facts, rules, and heuristics about a domain—is known to the domain expert, but its specification as needed for encoding into a knowledge-base requires an understanding of knowledge representation alternatives as well as a mastery of symbolic manipulation, which is the trade of yet another expert, the knowledge engineer. In a sense the knowledge engineer represents the end-user, who will likewise ask questions of the KBS and expect answers and solutions supported by explanations and clarifications. Such responses coming from domain experts must be based on their formal education and on-the-job experience. All this knowledge is organized, perhaps in *chunks*, which are groupings of interrelated information stored in long-term human memory. How many chunks relevant to a domain qualify a person to be a domain expert depends on the discipline of the domain, but could vary from 50 000 to 100 000. For a knowledge engineer who has a large number of chunks of professional information to master and use, such a quantity of information is difficult to absorb and retain.

The need for the separation of responsibilities between the knowledge engineer and the domain expert is better appreciated when we examine the process of knowledge elicitation.

KNOWLEDGE ELICITATION

Traditional psychologists, with their techniques of quizzing subjects followed by the statistical manipulation of the data so obtained, have been instrumental in developing new styles of KA interviews—although their preferred name for this is *knowledge elicitation*. There are many strategies for what a human expert should be asked and how the data should subsequently be manipulated and presented, and so all that we can do here is to dip into this rich sea of possibilities and describe one example in detail.

One technique that has been used is to generate a list of all the concepts used by the human expert within the chosen domain. In, say, a stock management system the relevant concepts might include *shelf life*, *wastage*, *seasonal demand*, etc. Then, in order to elicit their knowledge of stock management, human experts in this domain are asked to rate each pair of terms as to how related they are (on some scale, say, 1–10). Thus *shelf life* and *wastage* might be judged to be highly related (say, 9), while *shelf life* and *seasonal demand* might only be viewed as distantly related (perhaps 2). The mass of data on paired relatedness that is collected from a group of human experts is then subjected to various mathematical and statistical manipulations in order to construct a representation of the knowledge that would support all the individual judgements recorded.

These empirical techniques for knowledge elicitation are many, varied, and still largely experimental. The common factor is that they present a more subtle approach to the problem of acquiring knowledge from a human expert. Instead of just asking the expert to describe the reasoning used, the experts are asked to make simple judgements about features of their expertise, and, from this primitive judgemental data, the task is to construct a representation of knowledge that accounts for the responses obtained and can provide a foundation for mechanized expert reasoning.

Donald Michie, the doyen of AI in the United Kingdom, presents a rather different scheme for KA, but one that also addresses the problem that direct acquisition via a knowledge engineer is singularly unsuccessful on many occasions. Michie presents the following characterization of the

Table 7.1 Two views of an expert's repertoire of skills

	Power to recognize examples of key concepts	Power to describe these	Power to identify key primitives	Power to generate good tutorial examples
As seen by the expert	Good	Excellent	Excellent	Good
As seen by the analyst	Excellent	Very poor	Moderate	Excellent

From D. Michie (ed.), *Introductory Readings in Expert Systems.* © 1982 Gordon & Breach, New York.

ability of human experts to articulate their expertise, as seen by themselves, and as seen by the knowledge engineer (see Table 7.1).

Given that the analyst has the more accurate assessment of the situation *vis-à-vis* the expert's performance, classical KA techniques (column 2) are to be avoided, and the expert's skill with key concepts and tutorial examples should be exploited. This is what Michie does. He aims to elicit a comprehensive set of tutorial examples in the domain of interest, and you would expect an expert to be very good at dealing with such specific examples—after all, that is what expertise essentially is.

So, in the earlier stock management domain, he would gather together a set of specific examples of stocking plans and strategies. Given, say, a valuable (i.e. high-priced) but perishable (e.g. shelf life of two weeks) commodity with a good profit margin that is always in demand (i.e. not seasonal) and can be obtained from suppliers at short notice, what stocking strategy should be adopted for this particular commodity? When faced with such a specific example, human experts will deliver an accurate and high-quality judgement—for this is what their expertise is.

From a large and comprehensive collection of such examples it is possible to extract the general strategy that the human experts appear to be using. More precisely, it is possible to extract this general strategy (i.e. the knowledge that underlies the human expertise) as a decision tree. Even better, *inductive generalization algorithms* are available that will accept a set of such examples and automatically generate the decision tree.

Michie's scheme for KA thus boils down to using the domain expert to generate and adjudicate on a comprehensive set of specific example problems in the domain, and then to apply an inductive generalization algorithm to this set, which will yield a generalized representation of the knowledge required. The resultant ES is then based upon this decision tree rather than on the more traditional knowledge-base of facts and rules.

This radically different approach to the KA problem has had some impressive successes. It was, for example, used in Illinois to construct an ES for the diagnosis of diseases in the soya bean crop. Much to everyone's surprise, the ES turned out to be more accurate than the human experts upon whose tutorial-example decisions it was based.

The major limitation of this method stems from the limitations of current algorithms for inductive generalization. They can only process efficiently and accurately certain forms of examples of expertise. But there is much current research aimed at improving these algorithms, and we can confidently expect to see significant extensions to their domains of applicability in the near future.

In sum, knowledge is thought to be the key to manifestations of human expertise, but it is not clear how we can best elicit it from the human experts. A number of different approaches are being explored, and at the moment it is not clear which will turn out to be most efficacious.

The basic interactions in KA can be summarized graphically, as shown in Fig. 7.4. The knowledge engineer asks questions, makes queries, and states problems based on what expert advice is required from the KBS by the end-user and manager of the target system. In response the domain expert, as a result of experience and known information, responds with answers, explanations, solutions, cases, and then states facts, beliefs and suggests new concepts and heuristics for the domain problems at hand. The process is very interactive with one explanation leading to another question and yet another answer and even another heuristic.

A tricky problem for the knowledge engineer is to ensure that knowledge, especially the rules expressed by the domain expert's natural language, are transformed within the constraints of the knowledge representation environment and in the context of problem solving without losing, distorting, or misinterpreting the knowledge acquired. This may not

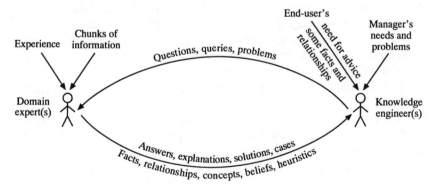

Figure 7.4 Consultation between domain expert(s) and knowledge engineer(s).

always be possible but this must be the objective. Despite the relevant and adequate background of an expert, the process of acquiring knowledge is not always fast or easy. The experience and operational knowledge of the domain expert has to be transformed into heuristic rules for arriving at inferences and conclusions. Sometimes the domain expert is shy or protective of the domain knowledge. The domain expert then has to be drawn out, which may require the knowledge engineer to establish a personal relationship with the domain expert to earn the domain expert's confidence. The knowledge engineer may even need to earn the domain expert's professional respect, which may require the knowledge engineer to learn more about the domain, understand its basics, learn its jargon and acronyms, and appreciate the domain's contributions to society. This process may take a few weeks or months, depending on the domain and the knowledge engineer. The knowledge engineer must then move from the listening phase to one of greater interaction in which the knowledge engineer controls the dialogue and directs questions that elicit relevant knowledge and heuristics based on domain facts and experience.

There are many formal techniques for deriving and acquiring knowledge. Diaper (1989) has a discussion of 12 such techniques; we offer a different list in Fig. 7.5. Many of these techniques are well known to the behavioural scientist and even the analyst of a transactional system or DSS would use these techniques in the user-specification stage. The difference is that in KA the interactions are much more intensive, and the sessions may each be long in duration as well as spread over a long period of time. There is also, however, a preference for having many short sessions rather than a few long ones. This is partly determined by the availability of time and the small attention span that most humans possess, but also because recorders are not used in short sessions. The knowledge engineer can rush from a session and quickly record the sayings and wisdom of the domain expert. This is not a sly manoeuvre: experience has shown that a recorder makes many domain experts 'freeze' and become cautious and inhibited. After all, domain experts are humans and have all the hang-ups and inhibitions of many a human. Extracting knowledge then becomes an exercise in psychology and group dynamics. Some of this work can be automated, eliminating the human interaction with a knowledge engineer. One such approach to automation are text-understanding computer programs that interpret statements written by the domain expert. Other programs engage the domain expert in a dialogue by asking questions prompted by a previous answer à la Weizenbaum's ELIZA. Such programs have been used successfully for eliciting data from hospital patients. It has been found that humans responding to questions posed by a computer often exhibit few, if any, of the inhibitions present in a human–human dialogue. Such systems used in KA can result in the domain expert being much more outspoken in expressing opinions and advice.

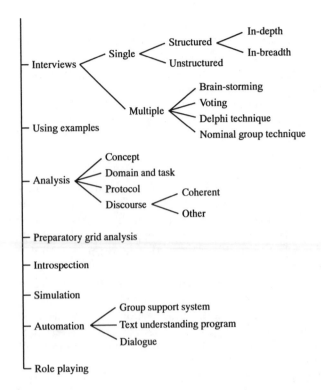

Figure 7.5 Techniques of knowledge acquisition.

INSTRUMENTS USED FOR KNOWLEDGE ELICITATION

Instruments such as specially designed forms could be used to document the knowledge acquired and to formulate it ready for coding into a knowledge-base. Many of these instruments are not new to computer science nor to the necessary processing for transactions of a DSS. They include a rich picture where everything related is recorded; or an influence diagram (Shachter and Heckerman, 1987) where every input or variable affecting decisions is recorded; or a flow diagram as in the case of Checkland's soft methodology; or a flowchart where the flow of logic and control is important.

The instrument chosen will depend on the knowledge representation schema selected. If the representation is a frame, then a form appropriate for frames will be used. If, however, a rule-based system is chosen, then a decision tree or a decision table will be chosen. The choice depends on the preference of the domain expert who may come from a managerial background with great familiarity with decision trees. Such trees can be readily transformed into decision tables. Since the rule-based system is the most commonly used approach to a KBS, we shall say a little about these two approaches. Decision-table theory has an axiomatic foundation. There are many ways to consolidate large tables and ways to break them up and have tables within tables—a process known as *parsing*. There are also formal ways to check for contradiction, redundancy, and duplication of rules. But we shall be brief in order to give the reader a flavour of the techniques used in knowledge acquisition.

Decision Trees

A *decision tree* is a structure in which each branch from a node to one of its successors is a decision point, i.e. at each node there is an explicit question to answer, and the actual answer given determines which of the alternative subsequent tree nodes is selected as the next decision point. A path through the tree from the root to a leaf (or terminal node) thus represents a complex decision made up of many smaller decisions. Thus the full scope of a complex decision-making situation can be represented in a decision tree in terms of alternative sequences of much smaller decision tasks.

A decision tree, like a decision table (next section), can be used in decision analysis. This technique helps a system analyst study the relationships between conditions and actions, and concepts that are common to all decisions.

Figure 7.6 is a sample decision tree that describes the conditions and actions involved in an ordering application in business. This technique of decision analysis does not work well for complex systems, because the size of the tree quickly becomes unwieldy. But for problems with few combinations of conditions and actions, the tree is useful as an analysis

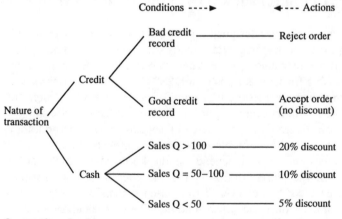

Q = quantity ordered

Figure 7.6 Decision tree for determining action on cash or credit transactions.

tool. Use of such trees appeals to people who like graphic representations. Decision trees are easy to read, and all the implications of choices are immediately apparent.

The decision tree facilitates the writing of code in a programming language. Figure 7.6 shows the code for the top path of the transaction decision tree, written in a generic notation, often called *pseudocode*, which is intermediate between a natural language, like English, and programming languages such as Pascal. Use of pseudocode avoids the ambiguities of natural language by exploiting the basic logic of a programming language while, at the same time, keeping a lot of the clarity of expression found in natural languages. The pseudocode for the top path of our decision tree is an IF–THEN rule:

IF on credit AND a bad credit record
THEN reject order

One problem with decision trees as representational structures is that one wrong decision, which may be somewhat equivocal anyway, can send the processor off down a completely wrong branch of the tree. In other words, in intelligent decision making we cannot always expect to be able to make clear-cut decisions on every subproblem. Sometimes we need to reason probabilistically, i.e. we need to leave specific minor decision points without doing more than preferring one possible outcome slightly more than another; one answer is probably true but the other is also possibly true.

Certain types of decision tree are being developed to deal with this problem. The probabilistic decision tree described below provides us with a first example of a structure for probabilistic reasoning—a fundamental and important AI problem which is being attacked from many different directions, and we shall see a number of them in this book.

Figure 7.7 is a decision tree for the diagnosis of certain aspects of thyroid disease. The diagnoses, such as hyperthyroid, goitre, or negative (i.e. no hyperthyroid condition), occur at the leaves. Diagnosis of a specific case involves starting at the tree root (far left), applying the test there (i.e. in this particular case is the FTI attribute less than or equal to 155?), and moving through the tree as determined by the answer to the question (i.e. take 'f' branch if answer is 'no', and 't' branch if answer is 'yes'). Clearly a case to be diagnosed must be characterized in terms of the attributes used in the decision tree. Such movement through the tree will eventually terminate at a leaf node. Hence we have a diagnosis for the case in hand.

This tree was automatically generated from a training set of 2800 cases. The numerical annotation associated with leaf, i.e. (n) or (n/e), captures the accuracy of that leaf in classifying the training set, and it is used to estimate the reliability of a decision arising from that leaf. The number n is the

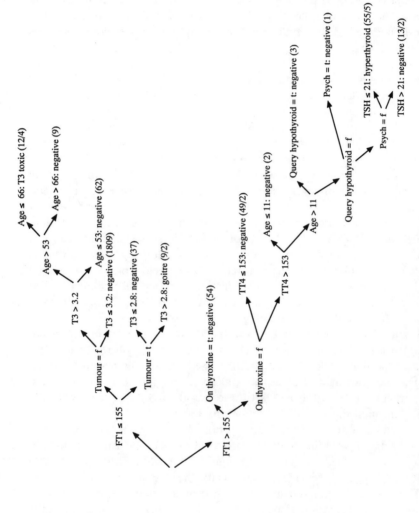

Figure 7.7 A decision tree to support probabilistic reasoning. (From J. R. Quinlan, 1987, Proceedings of 4th International Workshop on Machine Learning, this version reprinted with the permission of Intellect Books, Oxford.

number of cases in the training set that terminated at that leaf, and the number e, if it appears, is the number of cases that were misclassified. Thus for the T3 toxic diagnosis following the test age $\leqslant 66$, the annotation (12/4) means that 12 of the training set cases ended here but only 8 of them were correct diagnoses. In this way noisy training data can be accommodated by an automatic mechanism that delivers a compact and manageable, but probabilistic, decision tree. It is an approach to a style of diagnosis in which the system can diagnose a 'sort of' goitre rather than just goitre or not goitre. In addition, the extra statistical information available can be used to alleviate the bad effects of several other important problems.

The designer of this probabilistic decision tree, Ross Quinlan, suggests dealing with the lack of the necessary information at a choice point (e.g. no FTI value would stop us even starting the diagnosis process) by following multiple paths (i.e. do not make the decision). He presents a scheme for then combining the relative probabilities associated with each of the final diagnoses that are eventually produced.

For the problem of the brittleness produced by sharp thresholds he introduces the notion of *soft thresholds*, and sketches out several ways of using them. The basic idea is to use the misclassification information available in order to assign a probability component to the overall result that is dependent upon how close a given case is to a vague threshold.

DECISION TABLES AND PRODUCTION RULES

A *decision table* is a tool for expressing logical relationships in an understandable manner. A matrix containing rows and columns is used to represent the following:

1. Conditions (events or facts that determine a course of action to be taken).
2. Actions (processes or operations to be performed under certain conditions).
3. Decision rules (the relationship between combinations of conditions and actions).

The conceptual model of a decision table is shown in Fig. 7.8.

Conditions	Decision rule
Condition stubs	Condition entries
Action stubs	Action entries

Figure 7.8 The decision table matrix.

	Rule 1	Rule 2	Rule 3	Rule 4	Rule 5	Else
Is it cash?	Y	Y	Y	N	N	
Is sales Q > 100?	Y	N	N	–		
Is sales Q ≥ 50?	Y	Y	N	–		
Is sales Q < 50?	N	N	Y	–		
Is credit record good?	–	–	–	Y	N	
Give 20% discount	X					
Give 10% discount		X				
Accept order but no discount			X	X		
Reject order					X	
Make 'exception' report						X

Figure 7.9 A decision table for determining action on cash or credit transactions.

Note that each table has four parts: *condition stubs, condition entries, action stubs,* and *action entries.* According to convention, double horizontal and vertical lines separate these four components. Condition stubs are those criteria that are relevant to an action or decision. (The phrasing in a condition stub is equivalent to an IF statement.) Action stubs contain actions to be taken when specified conditions are satisfied. (The phrasing in an action stub is equivalent to a THEN part of the statement.)

Decision rules (i.e. IF these conditions exist, THEN perform these actions) are expressed as follows:

1. Conditions are identified by a Y or N in the Condition Entries sector of the table: Y = YES, N = NO, the condition does not apply. A dash means that the condition is irrelevant to the decision.
2. Actions are identified by an X in the Action Entries sector of the table: X = activate course of action. A blank action cell means that the action is not taken.
3. Each decision rule is represented by a vertical column of condition and action entries (i.e. combinations of Y, N, –, and X).

A decision table incorporating the features discussed above is shown in Fig. 7.9. Note that it is the equivalent of the decision tree in Fig. 7.6.

Advantages of Decision Tables

1. A decision table has a standard format for problem definition in which each set of conditions and its set of actions are clearly and unambiguously identified.
2. A decision table is concerned with the logic of decision rules and is, therefore, problem oriented. (In contrast, a flowchart is procedurally or

programming oriented. It does specify the necessary logic, but in a less clear way, because the logic is intertwined with the procedural steps for applying the logic in a mechanical way—after all, flowcharts are primarily used as a representation for programming.)

3. There is little danger that a program based on a decision table will have incomplete or inconsistent logic, since the structure of a decision table promotes a logically complete and consistent problem definition.

4. In some programming packages (e.g. DETAB II), a decision table can be directly converted into a COBOL computer program, thereby reducing programming costs.

5. Decision tables facilitate checking for redundancies and contradictions.

6. The format of decision tables facilitates expansion, contraction, or revision of logic.

7. Decision tables are an effective means of communication between members of the system development team, users, and managers.

8. Decision trees and also flowcharts can be readily transformed into decision tables.

TESTING THE KNOWLEDGE-BASE

Once the knowledge-base is formulated according to the planned data-representation scheme, it is ready for coding (a subject to be discussed in later chapters). Once coded, the knowledge-base is ready for testing.

The testing of a knowledge-base is shown in Fig. 7.10. The first five boxes in the diagram are similar to those in Fig. 7.1, our overview of the creation of a knowledge-base. Testing corresponds to box 6 in Fig. 7.1 and is expanded in Fig. 7.10. It is shown to be done in two phases: first is *verification* (box 6a), a process of checking for errors. This is done with inputs from both the knowledge engineer and the domain expert. The knowledge engineer looks for errors that could have crept into the knowledge formulation or knowledge coding. For example, boundary conditions will be checked to ensure that they are interpreted correctly as these are often a cause of errors. Likewise, the domain expert will check for accuracy but from a conceptual viewpoint to ensure that the rules are accurate or, at worst, a reasonable approximation. Cases with known solutions from a case library could be used for testing purposes. If no relevant cases are available or if the local conditions demand, then cases are specially designed for purposes of testing.

Validation is also part of testing (box 6b). This is the process of ensuring that specified conditions are met. These specifications are formulated in the user specification stage or even in the stage of planning of the knowledge-base (box 1). The main source for the desired specification is, of course, the user specification, and the knowledge engineer is keen to see that these specs are fulfilled. The end-user is also concerned with the fulfilment of the user specification document, but may wish to wait for the acceptance testing of the entire system. End-users are interested in the testing of the knowledge-base depending largely on their level of appreciation and understanding of the knowledge-base.

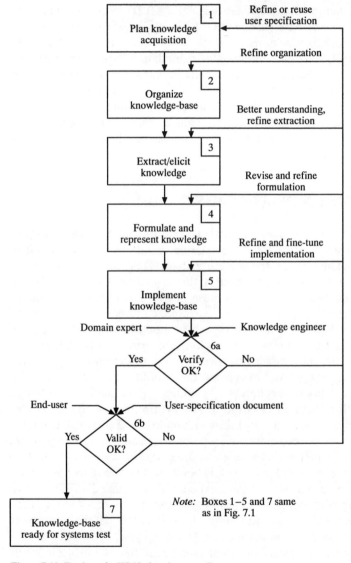

Figure 7.10 Testing of a KBIS showing recycling.

Validation and verification unfortunately have different meanings for different authors in the literature; moreover they may not even be separated, as in our discussion, but instead treated as one process. We separate them to emphasize the conceptual distinction and also the fact that different functions are performed by different personnel. Whether done together or separately, once tested satisfactorily, the knowledge-base is ready for systems testing with other subsystems (box 7 and 'yes' exit from box 6). If the test is unsatisfactory, then there is a loopback to the relevant point in the development as shown in Fig. 7.10.

Testing of the knowledge-base is sometimes left until the systems test. This is not recommended even for small and simple-looking systems. The reason is that interactive development for a knowledge-base is needed more often than not and isolating an error in a subsystem of a knowledge-base is far easier than identifying errors in a large system, especially one with many subsystems. Errors in one test for the entire system also presents the problem of pinpointing the blame, i.e. when a large system malfunctions, which subsystem is to blame?

DISTRIBUTION OF RESPONSIBILITY AND EFFORT

We have mentioned many persons involved in different stages of knowledge-base creation. They have responsibilities in different stages, as shown in Fig. 7.11. We start with the planning stage, which is the major responsibility of management, notably the project manager, the project sponsor, or management responsible for the project once it is ready for operations. These personnel appoint the knowledge engineer and the domain expert, who are largely responsible for organizing the knowledge sources and for working very closely together for KA. Once knowledge is formulated, it is ready to be coded and this is the responsibility of the knowledge engineer or the programmer working for the knowledge engineer. Once the knowledge-base is ready in machine-readable form, it is ready for testing. Here the responsibilities depend on the type of testing performed. The verification is done by both the knowledge engineer and the domain expert, each looking for different types of problems—technological and conceptual, respectively. Validation is the checking of the product, in this case the knowledge-base, with the user specifications or/and the specifications made by the planning group for the knowledge-base. This checking should be done by the knowledge engineer and the domain expert for their respective areas of expertise, but the final responsibility lies with the end-user who may designate the project manager to perform this task.

The knowledge engineer and the domain expert take most of the responsibility and certainly put in most of the effort. Their effort is,

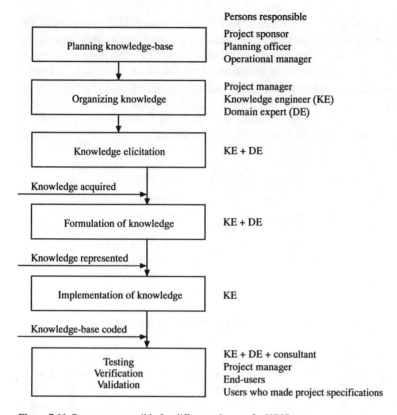

Figure 7.11 Persons responsible for different phases of a KBIS.

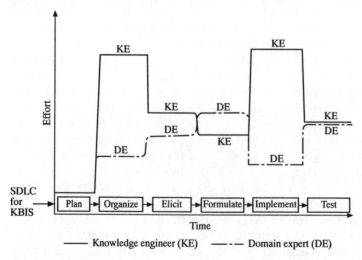

Figure 7.12 Distribution of effort between knowledge engineer and domain expert.

however, distributed over time and the different stages of development of the knowledge-base. This is shown in an approximate distribution curve for a typical knowledge-based project in Fig. 7.12. We see that knowledge engineers and the domain experts spend different proportions of their time on the project. Neither work full time on any one stage, except perhaps in the stage of implementation. Both mostly work part time, staggered throughout the project, allowing them to do other jobs; knowledge engineers would most likely be working on another knowledge-based project while the domain experts have an on-going job and work on the project only when released from their permanent tasks.

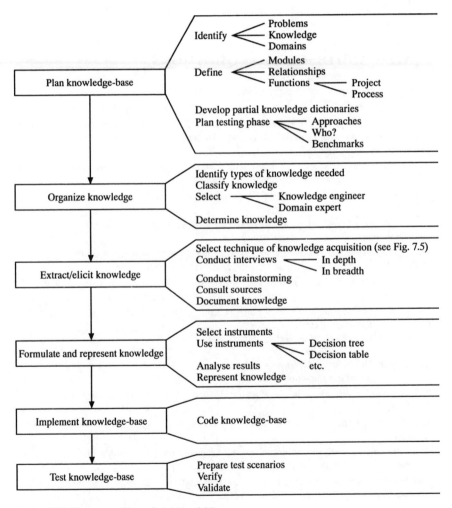

Figure 7.13 Summary of knowledge acquisition.

SUMMARY AND CONCLUSIONS

A summary of the activities and their functions in developing a knowledge-base, including the activities of knowledge acquisition, are shown in Fig. 7.13. Not shown in Fig. 7.13 are the feedback loops resulting from unsatisfactory testing. These loops are shown in Fig. 7.10.

A knowledge-base can be quite large and not easy to access, whether this be for development, modification, or preventive maintenance. To facilitate access, a development interface is needed. This interface along with other interfaces for a KBIS is the subject of our next chapter.

REVIEW AND DISCUSSION QUESTIONS

7.1 'Knowledge acquisition is central to any KBIS.' Comment.

7.2 'Knowledge acquisition is a highly creative and interactive activity.' Comment.

7.3 What are the prime characteristics of a good domain expert? Can these qualities be acquired by approaches like education and training or must one be born with these qualities?

7.4 Need the domain expert be of a compatible temperament with the knowledge engineer for knowledge acquisition to be (*a*) efficient or (*b*) effective?

7.5 Need the temperaments of multiple experts be compatible for a successful knowledge acquisition? Explain.

7.6 If multiple domain experts are used, should their knowledge be different or complementary? Explain.

7.7 'The most essential element in a good knowledge acquisition process is group dynamics by all those involved.' Do you agree or disagree? In either case, explain your position.

7.8 Should a domain expert have a voice in choosing a knowledge engineer or should the knowledge engineer have a voice in choosing a domain expert? Explain.

7.9 What is the best strategy for knowledge acquisition? Does it depend on the following?
  (*a*) Size of project.
  (*b*) Complexity of project.
  (*c*) Need for efficiency.
  (*d*) Desire for effectiveness.
  (*e*) Speed in completion of project.

7.10 'Knowledge elicitation is more an art than a science, and will always remain so.' Comment.

7.11 'Knowledge elicitation is the biggest bottleneck in the creation of a knowledge-base.' Comment.

7.12 'The current state of the art in natural language processing holds great promise for automating the knowledge elicitation process.' Comment.

7.13 Which decision comes first: knowledge representation or knowledge acquisition? Which comes first in implementation? Explain the reasons for the dependency.

7.14 What is the role of encoding in development of a KBIS?

7.15 'Having too many people responsible for the testing process makes the process longer and more confusing than necessary.' Comment.

7.16 Does the separation of validation and verification help conceptually in development as well as operationally in implementation? Who and how does it help

    (*a*) The knowledge engineer?
    (*b*) The domain expert?
    (*c*) The end-user?
    (*d*) The project manager?

7.17 'The division of labour and responsibility in creating a knowledge-base is too diffused and compartmentalized to encourage efficiency.' Comment.

7.18 How are the personnel involved in knowledge acquisition different from those in a data-processing system?

7.19 Why and how does the knowledge acquisition process differ from, say, the data acquisition process in traditional data processing?

7.20 What roles do the following play in knowledge acquisition:

    (*a*) End-user?
    (*b*) Operations manager of the KBIS?
    (*c*) Project manager?
    (*d*) Project sponsor?
    (*e*) Librarian at processing centre?

CASE 7.1 MANUFACTURING IN MEXICO— 2: KNOWLEDGE ACQUISITION

In 1987, CYDSA, a chemical and textile corporation with annual sales of $600 m., was persuaded by the CAI (Center for Artificial Intelligence) to develop KBISs for their manufacturing and repair plants.

Two to three months were required to train analysts from CYDSA as knowledge engineers with production processes and equipment and with the terminology and vocabulary relevant to the problem.

Knowledge acquisition was done through intensive working sessions among domain experts and knowledge engineers, and their sources of knowledge were as follows:

1. Interviews with experts.
2. Observation of experts solving real problems.
3. Observation of production processes and machines.
4. Document history of problems and solutions found.
5. Trouble-shooting manuals from equipment manufacturers.
6. Simulation of problems and their solutions.

Source: J. Cantu-Ortiz (1991) 'Expert systems in manufacturing: an experience in Mexico', *Expert Systems with Applications*, **3**, 445–455.

Questions

1. Critique the process of knowledge acquisition as a generic process for knowledge acquisition.
2. Is the methodology of knowledge acquisition appropriate for functional applications other than manufacturing within Mexico and in countries outside Mexico? In the case of other countries, does it matter whether the country is a developed country or a developing country?
3. What is the point of 'documenting history of problems and solutions found'? Is it worth all the paperwork and effort?
4. What are the limitations (if any) of training local analysts in manufacturing selected to become knowledge engineers for a KBIS?
5. Is the 2–3 months required for training in KA sufficient and adequate? Explain.

CASE 7.2 R1/XCON—2: KNOWLEDGE ACQUISITION

There were four reasons why knowledge was added to R1:

1. To make minor refinements (adding knowledge to improve R1's performance on an existing subtask) (10 per cent of total knowledge).
2. To make major refinements (adding the knowledge required for R1 to perform a new task, 40 per cent).
3. To provide additional functionality needed to deal with new system types (35 per cent).
4. To extend the definition of the task in significant ways (15 per cent).

The knowledge addition needed to result in a major refinement can be made in two kinds of situations:

• When R1 does not have any knowledge about how to perform some subtask.
• When its knowledge of how to perform some subtask becomes so tangled that ways need to be found of representing the knowledge more generally.

Source: Bachant, J. and J. McDermott (1988) 'Four years in the trenches', in R. Englemore (ed.), *Readings from the AI Magazine*, American Association of Artificial Intelligence, Menlo Park, CA, pp. 177–188.

Questions

1. Is the type of knowledge required for R1 typical for all KBISs? Or for certain industries? Or only for large systems? Explain.
2. Is the knowledge required for major refinements unique for R1?
3. How would you distinguish between a major and a minor refinement? Or do we perhaps need to define a 'refinement' first?
4. Who determines when additional knowledge is needed?
5. Would you perform a cost–benefit analysis before making determinations of collecting additional knowledge? Or would it be left to the discretion and judgement of an individual? Which individual?
6. Is the percentage distribution of the reasons for adding knowledge of any significance? If so, how?

CASE 7.3 SPELLING DUTCH NAMES—1

Unlike many European languages, the Dutch language lacks cedillas, circumflexes, accents, and umlauts. However, thousands of Dutch family names are spelled with such diacritical marks. Should Dutch databases be designed to store such marks?

To many people, the spelling of a family name is a matter of personal pride. No wonder the decision by some 700 Dutch municipalities and the tax office to omit storing and processing diacritical marks in computer processing has caused offence. Richard Gütlich claims that his brother was buried under a name not his own, because the town registrar could not deal with the umlaut. A woman whose name is Hör (pronounced like the French word fleur) objects that her name is officially Hoer (pronounced whore), because the umlaut was replaced with an oe, as in the German usage.

An organization called the 'Up and Down' has been formed in the Netherlands of activists who want Dutch names processed by computer to be spelled as families write them. The group is planning a lawsuit to force modification of the name field in government databases.

Source: 'Spell that name again, please', *Time* (23 January 1989), p. 19.

Questions

1. The above application can be implemented as a transactional system. Would it be better implemented as a KBIS? If yes, why? If not, why not?

2. Assuming a KBIS system is needed, how would you acquire knowledge for it?
3. If you were responsible for selecting the domain experts for this application, how would you go about it?
4. Would you select more than one domain expert? If so, what professions would they come from? Would they include members from the 'Up and Down' organization solely because of their devotion to the concept of the project? Would the domain experts include laypeople?

BIBLIOGRAPHY AND REFERENCES

Byrd, T. A., K. L. Cossick and R. W. Zmud (1992) 'A synthesis of research on requirements analysis and knowledge acquisition techniques', *MIS Quarterly*, **16** (2), 117–138.
   The authors compare RA (requirements analysis) with KA and found them almost identical in entities and processes involved. The authors compare (on p. 128) 18 different methods in terms of informational information, process understanding, behaviour understanding and problem frame understanding (p. 128).
Chan, C. and I. Benbasat (1991) 'Case research on knowledge acquisition', *Knowledge Engineering Review*, **6** (2), 96–120.
   A CASE research methodology is used to examine the variables that include problem domain, domain expert, KE, KA process, potential users, organizational setting and the expert system construction process.
Diaper, D. (ed.) (1989) *Knowledge Elicitation*, Ellis Horwood, Chichester.
   This book has a list of 12 techniques of knowledge elicitation followed by 40 pages of explanation of terms and concepts. There are 18 pages of references.
Easterbrook, S. (1991) 'Handling conflict between domain descriptions with computer-supported negotiations', *Knowledge Acquisition*, **3** (3), 255–290.
   A technique still in its early stages of application but worth watching.
Eriksson, H. (1992) 'A survey of knowledge acquisition techniques and tools and their relationship to software engineering', *Journal of Systems Software*, **19** (1), 97–107.
   The author argues that many KA 'techniques and approaches to tool support are relevant to software engineering, especially in complex domains and during early analysis stages'.
Gaines, B. R. and M. L. G. Shaw (1993) 'Eliciting knowledge and transferring it effectively to a knowledge-based system', *IEEE Transactions on Knowledge and Data Engineering*, **5** (1), 4–13.
   The sample given is 'simple enough to be completely analyzed but exhibits enough real-world characteristics to give significant insights into the process and problems of knowledge engineering'.
Hart, A. (1986) *Knowledge Acquisition for Expert Systems*, Kogan Page, London.
   Hart takes a broad view of KA and discusses interviews, reasoning (fuzziness too!), machine induction, and the repertory grid. She also has two case studies.
Hoffman, R. R. (1987) 'The problem of extracting the knowledge of experts', *AI Magazine*, **8** (2), 53–68.
   The perspective of experimental psychology is used to extract knowledge from experts.
Johnson, P. E. (ed.) (1987) *Expert Systems*, **4** (3), 144–207.
   This issue is dedicated to the nature of expertise. Included are useful articles on the

subjects of consultant expertise, making expert systems more like experts, and ways to extract expertise from experts.

Liou, Y. I. (1992) 'Knowledge acquisition: issues, techniques and methodology', *DataBase*, **23** (1), 59–63.

A good tutorial on the subject.

Liou, Y. I. (1992) 'Collaborative knowledge acquisition', *Expert Systems with Applications*, **5** (1), 1–13.

Techniques of collaborative KA discussed include 'brainstorming, Nominal Group Technique, Delphi technique, focus group interviews, group repertory grid analysis, and voting'.

McGraw, K. L. and K. Harbison-Briggs (1989) *Knowledge Acquisition: Principles and Guidelines*, Prentice Hall, Englewood Cliffs, NJ.

An excellent book. Well written and thorough.

Moore, C. J. and J. C. Miles (1991) 'Knowledge elicitation using more than one expert to cover the same domain', *Artificial Intelligence Review*, **5** (4), 255–271.

Based on personal experience, the authors argue that 'more than one expert throughout the knowledge elicitation process can improve both the efficiency of the approach and the quality of the knowledge acquired'.

Reich, Y. (1991) 'Design knowledge acquisition: task analysis and partial implementation', *Knowledge Acquisition*, **3** (3), 237–254.

Does what the title suggests.

Santamarina, C. and G. Salvendy (1991) 'Fuzzy sets based knowledge systems and knowledge elicitation', *Behaviour and Information Technology*, **10** (1), 23–40.

Discusses knowledge elicitation for fuzzy set representations.

Shachter, R. D. and D. E. Heckerman (1987) 'Thinking backward for knowledge acquisition', *AI Magazine*, **8** (3), 55–60.

A good discussion of the use of influence diagrams in knowledge acquisition.

Subramanian, G. H., J. Nosek, S. Raghunathan and S. S. Kanitar (1992) 'A comparison of the decision table and the decision tree'. *Communications of the ACM*, **35** (1), 89–104.

The authors state many research propositions and then critique them.

8

DATA AND KNOWLEDGE REPRESENTATION

Abstraction is a crucial feature . . . of knowledge, because in order to
compare and to classify the immense variety of shapes, structures, and
phenomena around us we cannot take all their features into account,
but have to select a few significant ones. Thus, we construct an
intellectual map of reality.

Fritjof Capra, *The Tao of Physics*

INTRODUCTION

Knowledge-bases require special representations for knowledge. But
organizations that are likely to need a knowledge-base are also likely
already to have a common database and a database management system
(DBMS). This represents a large investment. One may well then ask: why
cannot my existing database incorporate a knowledge-base, and why cannot
my DBMS manage my knowledge-base also? To answer this question we
need to examine the different models of data representation used with
existing DBMSs and their ability to handle knowledge-bases. This is what
we propose to do in this chapter. We examine the three common data
representation models: hierarchical, network, and relational. In analysing
these databases, we will soon conclude that while the DBMS and its data
models are appropriate for transactional applications and even some DSSs
(i.e. situations where data and algorithms are used to solve problems), they
are not adequate for AI applications where knowledge is used to make
inferences. For such applications, we need knowledge databases. We need
special data representations for knowledge and special management systems

for knowledge-bases. We next examine representations for knowledge-bases like the rule, the frame, the semantic network, logic, the object–attribute–value triplet, and the object-orientated approach. We also indulge in some prediction-making and discuss future intelligent systems.

Knowledge representation and knowledge bases do not replace data representation and databases. Instead, they all coexist. Databases are used extensively for the processing of transactions and as a basis for computation with algorithms for purposes of control and planning in business and in commerce. Databases are also used in some KBSs and hence it is not surprising that we start our discussion of knowledge representation with the representation of data in databases.

Level of fit.

FROM FILES TO KNOWLEDGE-BASES

The earliest common data representation was the *file*—also called a *flat file* because when laid out flat, it was a string of sets of data, each being a *record* of logically related data elements. This organization was appropriate for sequential processing of transactional data. However, as demands grew for random access, which required storage that was more flexible than sequential storage on a tape, so new random-access storage was developed. But the file representation persisted, though it did increase in complexity. Soon there were too many interrelationships between records within a file and relationships between different files. This led to great redundancy and inconsistencies, resulting in inefficiencies and ineffectiveness. The solution was to have a common database and a *DBMS* to manage the operations of the complex set of data. The DBMS is a software package that is the interface between the stored data and the end-user. A DBMS offered powerful facilities for accessing, modifying, and making queries of the data. Each DBMS was designed around one type of data representation. The ones commonly used, taken historically, are: hierarchical, network (CODASYL), and relational. Each will now be discussed briefly.

Hierarchical Data Model

A typical business organization chart is an inverted tree structure with branches and nodes representing the business organization structure. An example is illustrated in Fig. 8.1. In this model, a node representing a file, record, or data element with dependent nodes is called a *parent* (or owner), while each subordinate node is called a *child* (or member). To illustrate, each node in level 3 is a child of a node in level 2 in Fig. 8.1, but at the same time may be a parent of nodes in level 4.

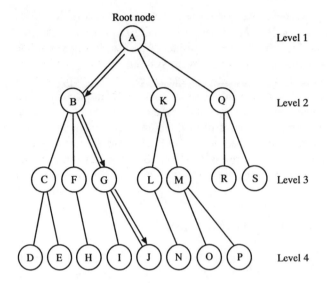

Node C is the child of B, but the parent of D and E. Node J can
only be reached through the path A to B to G to J.

Figure 8.1 Hierarchical data model.

A database organized in this hierarchical structure is shown in Fig. 8.2.
Note that every node has to be accessed through its parent (except, of
course, the root.) A DBMS that supports this logical organization of data
follows established paths under program control in searching for an item—
it does not have to search randomly the entire population of data items.

The problem with this model is that analysts must spend much time
working out data relationships when the logical structure of the database is
being designed. With a poorly structured database, some of the data may be
difficult to access. Another problem is that new links must be forged when
new kinds of data are added to the database. Care must be taken to ensure
that these new links do not invalidate or corrupt existing connections.

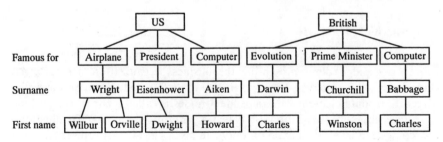

Figure 8.2 Hierarchical database.

Network Data Model

The network data model resembles the hierarchical data model with one important exception—a child can have more than one parent. In Fig. 8.3, which structures the data in Fig. 8.2, you will note that there are lateral connections as well as top-down connections within the database. This structure complicates database design and modification, but the model offers flexibility in searching for data without much loss of speed.

The network data model was developed in 1971 by a working committee of CODASYL (Conference on Data System Languages), the group that developed the language standards for COBOL. But the reception of the model has been lukewarm despite the authoritative source of its design. One reason is that the model is complex and somewhat incohesive. Complaints have been made that decisions regarding the model's design were often based on group politics, not technical merit. Because agreement could not always be obtained in the CODASYL committee, there are many variants of core concepts that create confusion among those who try to use the model.

Relational Data Model

The relational data model, first proposed in the early 1970s by Dr E. F. Codd of IBM but not fully developed until the 1980s, is based on the mathematical theory of sets and relations. In this model, data relationships are represented in tables. (Although the relational database can be conceptualized as a collection of related tables, it is formally a mathematical set of tables. A table entry is a relation in mathematics.) Each horizontal row describes a record (tuple) and each column describes one of the attributes (data fields) of the record, as illustrated in Fig. 8.4. (Note that the data in this table are the same as those in the hierarchical database in Fig. 8.2 and the network database in Fig. 8.3.) The simple structure of the

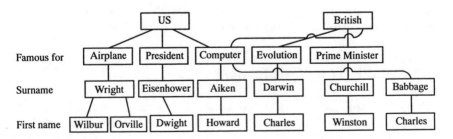

Figure 8.3 Network database.

Nationality	Fame category	Surname	First name
US	Airplane	Wright	Wilbur
US	Airplane	Wright	Orville
US	President	Eisenhower	Dwight
US	Computer	Aiken	Howard
British	Computer	Babbage	Charles
British	Evolution	Darwin	Charles
British	Prime Minister	Churchill	Winston

Figure 8.4 Relational database.

relational model has widespread appeal and has drawn supporters from computer users unhappy with the hierarchical and network data models.

With the relational model, data can be entered into a database without too much thought about how they will be used. To add new data is like adding a new column of attributes or a new row at the bottom of the table. Programs can be written to manipulate or extract data from the database using relational algebraic operations such as AND, OR, NOT, JOIN, and PROJECT. For example, the JOIN command will combine two tables to produce a third. PROJECT will extract columns from one table and combine them into a new table. The power of relational systems is ascribed to this flexibility.

However, to find a particular item, a search of all the tables may have to be made by the computer system. In effect, each row in each table is searched sequentially until the item is found. Clearly this search process will be slow when databases are large. Moreover, every time that information is needed, the same search path takes place even though the same data may be needed hundreds of times a day in the processing of applications programs.

Although fast hardware may reduce search time, the cost of such hardware may raise the cost of processing. Speed may also be gained through programming effort. For example, an index can be prepared of common search paths with index pointers to frequently sought items. Then the computer can be programmed to scan this index as the first step of any search. The disadvantage is that this will lengthen search time for non-indexed items. Also, an index uses up computer storage space.

DATABASE OR KNOWLEDGE-BASE?

Databases are adequate for transactional processing and the DBMSs provide interactive dialogue languages (like the fourth-generation languages) for accessing and querying the database. But all processing involves the arithmetic manipulation of data. What is also needed is the ability to make inferences such as those made by a human expert to generate new data from old, i.e. logical manipulation of data. To do this, what is needed are programming languages that can efficiently and effectively implement a mechanism of inference. To facilitate such inferencing we need knowledge that is more than just straight data items. Knowledge includes facts, theories, heuristics, relationships, attributes, observations, definitions, and other types of information about a problem area gleaned from one or more experts in a given field, and supported by the literature, such as books and manuals, in that field of study. Such knowledge is represented in a way that facilitates reaching an inference or a conclusion based on the knowledge available. These representations of knowledge can take the form of either rules, frames, semantic networks, O–A–V triplets, logic, or objects. Each of these representations will now be discussed.

KNOWLEDGE CODING AND REPRESENTATION METHODS

Rules

The *rule* is a knowledge representation for use in making inferences as a human expert does. It is used extensively in ESs where the *rule* is applied to knowledge to reach a conclusion (or activate an action). These rules can be stated in an IF–THEN (or IF–THEN–ELSE) format and included in the knowledge-base. For example, a rule in an ES to diagnose engine failure might look like this:

IF   the engine is idle, and the fuel pressure is less than 38 p.s.i., and the gauge is accurate,
THEN   there is a fuel systems fault.

To facilitate the implementation of these rules for reaching a conclusion or activating an action, we need knowledge that must be represented such that it can be easily used by a programming language. In the case of detecting a systems fault the rule is of the form:

IF   condition(s) exist
THEN   take specific actions (or reach specific conclusions)

The above format of relating conditions to a conclusion (or action) is referred to as a *production rule*. It is extensively used in rule-based ESs, and has the great advantage of being readily understood by domain experts as well as end-users.

Basically, a production rule has an antecedent and a consequent. The *antecedent* is the set of conditions. The *consequent* could be an action, in

Q: Is it a mammal?	*A:* Yes
Q: Does it live in a jungle?	*A:* Yes
Q: Does it have four feet?	*A:* Yes
Q: Is it a carnivore?	*A:* What is a carnivore?
Q: Does it eat meat?	*A:* No
Q: Is it feline?	*A:* No
Q: Is it herbivorous?	*A:* Yes
Q: Does it have a trunk?	*A:* Yes
Q: Does it have tusk(s)?	*A:* Yes
Q: Does it have large teeth of ivory?	*A:* Yes, two of them

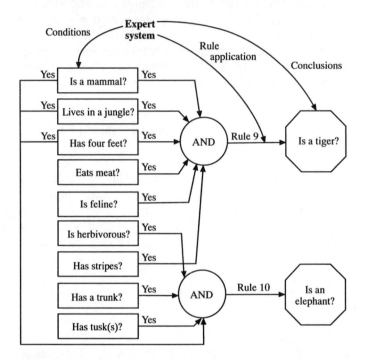

Figure 8.5 Dialogue with an expert system and rules to identify an elephant and a tiger.

which case the satisfaction of the antecedent is equivalent to scheduling an action for execution. Alternatively, the consequent could be a conclusion, in which case the satisfaction of the antecedent would lead to a conclusion such as an expert's opinion in an ES.

This form of statement is easily programmed in many a procedural third-generation language like FORTRAN, PL/1, Pascal or other languages inheriting the ALGOL IF–THEN–ELSE structure. The rules can be expressed in a set of questions or answers as expressed schematically in Fig. 8.5 determining whether an animal is an elephant or a tiger. This may seem a very trivial problem but in structure it is similar to a decision tree commonly used in decision making for a DSS. It can be expressed as an equivalent in a decision table as shown in a partial decision table in Fig. 8.6. The conditional stubs that are relevant to an action or decision, the equivalent of an IF part of the statement, appear in the left-hand upper quadrant; action stubs, the equivalent to the THEN part of the statement, appear in the lower left-hand quadrant. Each decision rule is a column to the right of the vertical double line. Thus rule 10 in Fig. 8.6 says that IF the object being examined is a mammal, and lives in a jungle, and has four feet, and is not a carnivore, and is not feline, and is herbivorous, and does not have stripes, and has a trunk, and has tusks, THEN that object is an elephant.

Rules have the advantage of being able readily to *capture* problem-solving knowledge in a standardized representation format which facilitates checking and coding. The great disadvantage of rules is that they cannot be modified incrementally without unpredictable interactions with other rules. Also, with a large number of rules, the system becomes unwieldy to validate and difficult to maintain—the structure is too flat and diverse.

The rule representation is often appropriate for an ES, and a third-generation language can be used for programming it. However, some ESs and many other AI applications use another form of representation. One such early data representation was the frame, which will now be discussed.

	...	Rule 9	Rule 10
Is it a mammal?		Y	Y
Lives in a jungle?		Y	Y
How many feet?	.	4	4
Does it eat meat?	.	Y	N
Is it feline?	:	Y	N
Is it herbivorous?	.	N	Y
Does it have stripes?		Y	N
Does it have a trunk?		N	Y
Does it have tusks?		N	Y
It is a tiger	...	X	
It is an elephant			X

Y = yes, N = no, X = conclusion.
Although the above rules seem adequate at first glance, baby elephants lack tusks as do some mature female elephants, while some male elephants lose their tusks in fights. Therefore, the identification of an elephant should not depend on the presence of tusks as rule 10 states. In many subject domains, only experts have the necessary knowledge and knowledge engineers have the experience to state complete, unambiguous and unique rules.

Figure 8.6 A partial decision table showing rules 9 and 10 for the elephant and tiger example.

Frames

A frame is a knowledge representation proposed specifically for work in AI by one of its pioneers, Marvin Minsky. Similar structures are found in cognitive psychology as models of human memory.

A *frame* is a data structure for representing a stereotyped situation. Attached to each frame are several types of information, including information on how to use the frame. This information 'attached to each frame' is in a *slot*, which is an extension of a field in a record or file in that it goes beyond merely holding a value. These slots define an event or a concept at each *node* (a point where an item links to another item or branch). A slot can contain information on rules, pointers to other frames, default values, as well as procedures. The procedures could be of many kinds, like the IF-added procedure to be executed when new information is placed in the slot, or the IF-remove procedure to be executed if information is deleted from the slot. These procedural attachments are incorporated in what would otherwise be a declarative representation. Frames can also allow inheritance by appropriate linking.

Ideally, a frame is a small chunk of information that is easy to understand as well as easy to modify. This latter characteristic is important because a frame is a dynamic representation in short-term memory, memory actively used during a problem-solving session. As the system acquires more facts or there is a changed environment, the frame changes accordingly.

Frames are very useful when the content of information is important in problem solving as in pattern recognition of speech or visual screens of pictorial representations, where changes in slots may cause a change in a pictorial representation, called *'active value' slots*. Thus, frames allow for a very rich representation, but they have the disadvantage of being difficult to maintain because the interactions between frames are often not clearly defined. Also, there are many relationships between frames preventing modularity in a frame system.

Figure 8.7 is a sample frame containing descriptive information about an elephant. It would facilitate a knowledge-base search for rules and relevant data necessary to answer the user queries of Fig. 8.5 since all relevant information on an elephant is organized in a logical grouping. This frame has a default value of two tusks. Since some elephants may not have two tusks (because of deformity or loss of tusk in battle), two tusks are a default value. Specifying a default allows us to assume the most obvious value unless otherwise specified. We also have (in Fig. 8.7) an upward pointer to a superclass, a mammal, which makes an elephant a mammal by inheritance and gives it all the characteristics of a mammal. There is also a downward pointer to a special case, a circus elephant, which has a frame of

```
Frame: Elephant
Superclass: Mammal
Subclass: Circus elephant

Value slot
    Habitat: Jungle
    Colour: Grey
    Size: Very large
    Feet: Four
    Tusks: Default: two
    Food: Vegetation
    Rule slot: If a herbivorous mammal has a trunk and tusks, then
        it is an elephant
```

Figure 8.7 Example of a frame.

its own with the peculiarities of a circus elephant stated there. Thus the frame structure allows linking in an inheritance hierarchy as well as a representation of a concept in isolation with respect to class of objects or individual instances which are components of objects.

Semantic Networks

Another option is to organize knowledge using semantic networks. Here we need to define the two terms: semantic and network. *Semantic* refers to 'meaning' and *network* is a structure with 'connections'. A *semantic network*, then, is a structure of interconnected nodes that represent some desired meanings. The *nodes* represent objects, events, or activities as well as descriptors that further describe the nodes, much like adjectives describe a noun. The interconnections are links referred to as *arcs*, which represent relationships between objects. The arcs can be one of many kinds:

1. *Is-a link*, short for 'is a', as in 'an elephant is an animal'.
2. *Has-a link*, short for 'has a', as in 'an elephant has a trunk'.
3. *Definition link*, as in 'an elephant is a very large, herbivorous animal'. A definitional link may be found in a specialized dictionary.
4. *Heuristic link*, captures heuristic information, as in 'an elephant normally lives in a jungle because it must eat large quantities of leaves'.

An example of a semantic network for an elephant is shown in Fig. 8.8, which contains information about an elephant that would facilitate a knowledge-base search for the type of questions raised in Fig. 8.5 since all the information relating to an elephant is organized into a logical grouping.

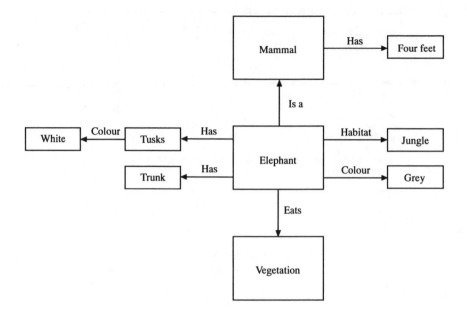

Figure 8.8 Semantic network representation of an elephant.

We have persisted with the elephant case in order to provide some continuity and comparison with the examples for other representation structures. But let us consider another example, that of an automobile, as shown in Fig. 8.9. In this example an automobile has an engine, needs gasoline, and needs one driver only. We have an 'is-a' link connecting a Ford and a Chevrolet to an automobile, and the Ford and the Chevrolet thus inherit all the characteristics of the automobile (has an engine, etc.). We do not need to repeat these characteristics. We merely add an 'is-a' link from the new object to the object class and the new object inherits the characteristics of its parent object class.

One problem with semantic nets is that the 'is-a' relationship can represent a class relation, or instance, leading to multiple interpretations and hence confusion. Another problem is the variety of relations that can be represented by the links. There are no widely accepted standards and hence very little portability of semantic network representations. Everyone devises their own network.

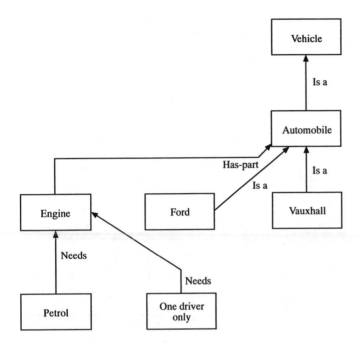

Figure 8.9 Semantic network example.

Object–Attribute–Value Triplets

Object–attribute–value triplets, also known by the acronyms *OAV* or *O–A–V*, are a special case of semantic nets and are often used in knowledge representation of physical objects. An example for selecting a dog as a pet is shown in Fig. 8.10. The bottom row is the set of attributes that are the input, the higher levels are attributes that are inferred. When all attributes are inferred according to the rules of what values of attributes are acceptable, then the final goal (in this case, the selection of a pet dog) is reached. Thus it may be necessary to associate values to attributes by giving an OAV triplet of information. Using the dog pet example, suppose that the criterion of selection was a dog that had to be brown, a cocker spaniel, less than 1 ft. high, between 1 and 2 years old, and had to cost less than £100. When constrained values are violated, they are rejected. A dog with attributes satisfying all conditions on its values is accepted. But what if more than one candidate satisfied all the conditions? This problem is discussed later in Chapter 9, 'Making Inferences'.

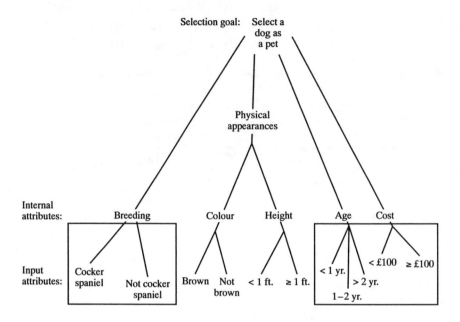

Figure 8.10 Object–attribute–value triplet for selecting a dog.

The OAV method is more structured than semantic nets, but as the number of objects increases, the attributes associated with the objects also increases, making the OAV method conceptually complex. This is often the case with large organizations of knowledge.

Logic

One type of logic is *propositional logic*, where a statement as a proposition may be either true or false. Statements can be linked together into compound statements by the connectives AND, OR, or NOT. A truth table will give the true or false value of a compound statement. Thus if X is true and Y is false, then X AND Y is false but X OR Y is true.

A more complex type of logic is *predicate calculus*, where statements or assertions about objects are called predicates. Thus 'is-animal (elephant)' is an assertion that the 'is-animal' predicate is true of the object 'elephant', i.e. it is stating that an elephant is an animal. A specific assertion is then a fact used by a model, while a general assertion is a rule and may be part of a theory. Both model and theory are part of a logic representation (see Fig. 8.11).

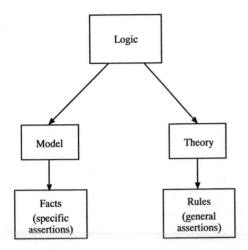

Figure 8.11 Rules, facts, and logic.

An example of the use of logic in a query situation in order to arrive at an answer is shown in Fig. 8.12. Note the possible ambiguity in the example of a pumpkin being larger than a pea. In it there was an assertion that a pumpkin is larger than a pea. But is it possible that a small pumpkin is smaller than a large apple? If so, then the ambiguity must be resolved by making assertions about small pumpkins and not just any pumpkin; otherwise the knowledge-base using logic will not arrive at an answer that is always true.

DATABASES AND KNOWLEDGE-BASES

We stated earlier that databases are not usually appropriate for situations where we need to make inferences. Having just discussed knowledge-bases, we can now confirm that statement and appreciate the differences between conventional databases and KBSs. Although there are many differences in terminology there are also many equivalencies, and these are listed in Table 8.1. There are also differences in content, as listed in Table 8.2. One important distinction is that conventional databases support procedural programming languages, while KBSs are typically *declarative* (if A is true then B is true) and are supported by AI languages like LISP and PROLOG to be discussed in a later chapter.

Question: Is a pumpkin smaller than a pea?

Premise: Greater than (x, y) AND greater than (y, z)
⟶ greater than (x, z)

Facts: Greater than (pea, apple)
Greater than (apple, pumpkin)

Answer: Yes
where x = pea
y = apple
z = pumpkin

Explanation:
Given the rule ⟋ , and given the two facts | | ,
it can be deduced that greater than (pea, pumpkin)
is true.

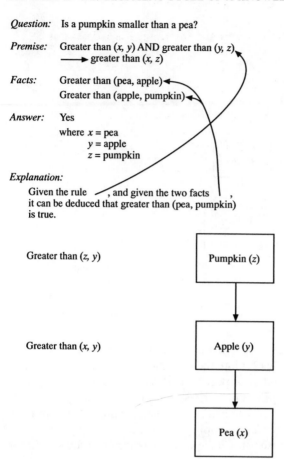

Greater than (z, y) ☐ Pumpkin (z)

Greater than (x, y) ☐ Apple (y)

☐ Pea (x)

Figure 8.12 Logic example.

Table 8.1 Similarity mappings of a database to a knowledge-base

Databases	Knowledge-bases
Data	Knowledge
Input preparation	Knowledge acquisition
Output devices	Presentation module
Data representation	Knowledge representation
—File	—Rule
—Hierarchical	—Frame
—CODASYL	—Semantic network
—Relational	—Logic
	—Object–attribute–value
Database management system	Knowledge-based management system

Table 8.2 Comparison of conventional and knowledge-based databases

	Conventional	Knowledge based
Structure	Hierarchical	Frames, rules, logic
	Network	Semantic models
	Relational	Object-orientation
Capture	Transactional facts	Knowledge
		Inferential relationships
Manipulation of	Data/character strings	Knowledge
Concerned with	Facts	Rules
		Meaning
Purpose	Store	Representation
	Manipulate	Reasoning/inferencing
	Retrieve	Explanation
Programming language	Procedural	Declarative
		Logic-based
	3GLs as host	LISP/PROLOG
	Query languages	Object-oriented languages
Orientation	General purpose	Specialized
Environment	Certainty	Uncertainty
Perspective	Values of data	Chunks of knowledge
Personnel		
Collection	Clerks	Domain expert
Data organization	Systems analysts	Knowledge engineer
	Database specialists	
Discipline	Data processing	Artificial intelligence

The conventional and knowledge-based databases are distinct but they may well come together. In fact there are currently many attempts at extending the heavily logic-oriented relational model to include knowledge-bases. There is the advantage that a standard for the relational query language, SQL, already exists. Other attempts favour the use of object-oriented databases, our next topic, though there is some controversy over whether these should be grafted on top of the relational model or developed entirely separately.

OBJECT-ORIENTED DATABASES

Our last type of representation is that of the object-oriented model. It claims to have both a database orientation and a knowledge-based orientation. The object-oriented databases are like frame-based databases in the sense that they represent both the static and the dynamic characteristics of the real world. But there are many differences. Object-oriented databases have chunks that are not just passively stored, manipulated, and retrieved but are active objects. The stored objects have declarative and procedural knowledge. Objects have properties and *behaviour* (ways to trigger the properties) and rules giving meaning. Objects also hold complex and unconventional data such as picture images, voice, and multimedia, which are very useful in complex problem environments such as computer-aided design (CAD). The object-oriented database has properties of hierarchy and encapsulation (mechanisms whereby the specification of an operation and its implementation are separated). An object is identified and a message sent to it with the selector in the message specifying the operation to be performed. The object-oriented database has its own programming language, object-oriented programming (OOP), and its own object-oriented DBMS, OODBMS. It needs its own design and implementation. It also has its own methodology of design and implementation and it even has its own environment of supporting software. It requires a chapter to itself and is thus discussed elsewhere.

FUTURE INTELLIGENT SYSTEMS

The future may not bring us what we want, but perhaps we know what we want. End-users want the ability to move easily and seamlessly between multiple databases without obstacles raised by using media from a number of vendors and multiple locations. The last requirement of location transparency implies interconnectivity, which may well come from integrated distributed network databases which integrate heterogeneous sources of data and heterogeneous databases and are accessible also through intelligent interfaces. These interfaces will not only accept input in a variety of media but also check for incorrect input, detect and adapt to patterns of end-user behaviour, and accept inexact queries with algorithms for optimizing distributed queries.

Future databases may well be very large, around 10^{12} bits, i.e. *terabits* in size. And they will be more complex, especially with the database needs of AI. Before we can cope with such very large and complex databases, we need to learn a great deal more about concurrency, crash control, fast maintenance, higher performance as well as easy and quick accessibility. These problems will not yield to brute-force solutions of faster hardware and larger memories. What we will get is perhaps some representation models as 'add-ons' to existing representation models that coexist and perhaps lead to an intelligent database.

One prediction for the future is that of an intelligent database that will include a knowledge-base. One view of such an intelligent database is shown in Fig. 8.13. It has as inputs the conventional databases as well as knowledge-bases coming from ESs and an object orientation as well as additional inputs of new knowledge. There must also be tools like the data

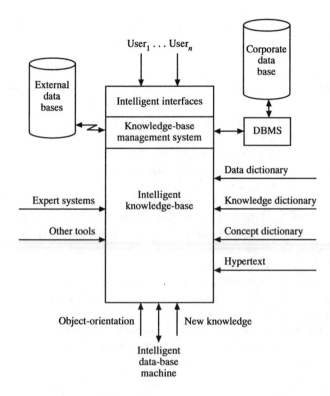

Figure 8.13 Intelligent knowledge-bases/databases.

dictionary as well as a *concept dictionary* which allows users to associate values with terms, e.g. 'tall' is between 6 ft. and 6 ft. 4 in., 'very tall' is above 6 ft. 4 in. We need a *Hypertext system* to provide a sophisticated capability for linking pieces of discrete information together. Finally, the intelligent database is connected to an intelligent database machine and accessed through an intelligent interface to which queries can be made in any media (even natural language, handwriting, or voice) and in most commonly spoken natural languages.

Intelligent databases involve a combination of database systems and KBS technology. This new class of database system attempts to provide the user with an optimal (or near-optimal) combination of query evaluation search as found in the traditional DBMS, together with the inferential search that is characteristic of KBSs (and ESs). Query evaluation search is usually more efficient than inferential search, but not as powerful. So the general idea may be to keep as much as possible of the search capability within the traditional DBMS component and use the knowledge-based technology only when necessary. The price to be paid may be poor overall operating characteristics but that is a trade-off often worth making.

SUMMARY AND CONCLUSIONS

In this chapter we examined the three important representation schemas for a database: hierarchical, network, and relational. These models are still important to transactional systems and even some DSSs but not to many AI applications. Hence the need for knowledge-based representations (rules, frames, semantic nets, O–A–V, and logic) and object-oriented systems arises. One view of the evolution of these databases is shown in Fig. 8.14. Not shown is the possible evolution of an intelligent database that will not only be able to process the complex transactional and DSS environment but also knowledge in varying input media, and do so intelligently much as human beings think and process information.

In this chapter we have examined the selection of a knowledge representation schema. Once this is determined, the knowledge must be coded to create a knowledge-base that is accessible to the inference engine. Such coding will not be necessary if one has decided on a shell or an environment. Alternatively, if we decided on a programming language, then its selection will largely depend on the inference engine, the subject of our next chapter.

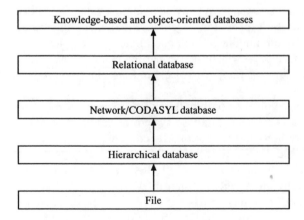

Figure 8.14 The evolution and hierarchy of databases and knowledge-bases.

CASE 8.1 SURVEY ON METHODS OF KNOWLEDGE REPRESENTATION

A survey was conducted by the University of Loughborough (UK) in 1987/88. One objective was to determine the methods used in making inferences in a KBIS. Fifty producers of an ES from academia, industry, and commerce were interviewed in depth. The results for methodologies used in knowledge representation were as follows:

Form of representation	%
Rules	56
Everything	17
Frames	10
Semantic nets	7
Decision trees	5
Object-oriented programming	5

Source: M. O'Neill and A. Morris (1989) 'Expert systems in the United Kingdom: an evaluation of development methodologies', *Expert Systems*, **6** (2), 90–91.

Questions
1. Are the results what you expected? Explain.
2. Do you expect the results to be very different now compared to 1987/88? Explain.
3. Would you expect the results to be different in countries other than the UK? If yes, why? If not, why not?
4. Do you expect the percentage of use to change much in the future? Explain your reasons for thinking so.
5. Would you expect the percentage to be different if the survey were done exclusively for large firms and complex projects as opposed to small firms and simple projects? Explain your position.

DISCUSSION AND REVIEW QUESTIONS

8.1 Under what problem environmental conditions would you recommend using one of the following?
(*a*) Frames.
(*b*) Objects.

(c) Rules.

(d) A DBMS database representation?

8.2 'A rule is a very friendly and easy to understand approach to data representation.' Comment.

8.3 'A frame is an orderly and neat way to represent data for all purposes.' Comment.

8.4 'A DBMS data representation in a DBMS is good for data representation but not suited to a knowledge representation.' Comment.

8.5 Why does knowledge require a different representation model than does data?

8.6 Can a KBS efficiently use data available in a common database organized in a hierarchical network?

8.7 In what model(s) can heuristics and hypothesis be best represented?

8.8 What is the contribution of a frame to data representation? What are its limitations, if any?

8.9 Can a KBS be consistent with an institutional database system? Explain.

8.10 'A knowledge-base is a logical evolution of a database.' Comment.

8.11 'Knowledge-bases can incorporate and encompass a database.' Comment.

8.12 What problems of (a) security and (b) privacy does a knowledge-base create? How are they different from those in a database system?

8.13 What is the difference between a knowledge-based management system and the management of a knowledge-base? Who should be responsible for it? Should this management be in 'breadth' or in 'depth'?

8.14 Can a KBS be efficiently integrated with other database systems? Explain.

8.15 'A knowledge-based system is an infrastructure of data and knowledge that can be used by all levels of management and end-users and by all functional departments of an organization.' Comment.

8.16 'A knowledge-base can efficiently and effectively replace an institutional database with a DBMS.' Comment.

BIBLIOGRAPHY AND REFERENCES

Brachman, R. J. and H. J. Levesque (eds.) (1985) *Readings in Knowledge Representation*, Morgan Kaufmann, Los Altos, CA.
An excellent collection of papers on virtually all main issues of data representations, including Marvin Minsky's classic article on frames (pp. 245–262).

Kellogg, C. (1986) 'From data management to knowledge management'. *Computer*, **19** (1) 75–83.
An excellent article on knowledge management including a discussion of a large-scale knowledge-management system: KM-1.

Parasaye, K., M. Chignell, S. Khoshafian and H. Wong (1990) 'Intelligent database', *AI Expert*, **5** (3) 38–47.
Discusses the evolution and merger of several technologies like intelligent search, hypermedia, automatic discovery, automatic error detection, flexible query processing, intelligent inferencing, and intelligent interfaces.

Robinson, A. E. (1990) 'Current ideas in knowledge-based management systems', *Information and Software Technology*, **32** (4), 266–273.
This article is a good overview of a KBMS: a definition of a KBMS, historical roots, functionality, and future directions.

Silberschatz, M. S. and J. Ulman (1991) 'Database systems: achievements and opportunities', *Communications of the ACM*, **34** (10), 110–120.
An excellent discussion of the subtopics as stated in the subtitle.
Szolovits, P. (1986) 'Knowledge-based system: a survey', in M. L. Bodie and J. Mylopoulus (eds), *On Knowledge Base Management Systems*. Springer-Verlag, Heidelberg.
An excellent survey.
Thuraisingham, B. (1989) 'From rules to frames and frames to rules', *AI Expert*, **4** (10), 30–39.
The author discusses how one can reconcile contrasting needs and allow for a variety in knowledge-bases by moving from a rule to a frame representation and vice versa.
Yoon, Y. and T. Guimaraes (1992) 'Developing knowledge-based systems: an object-oriented organizational approach', *Information Resource Management Journal*, **5** (3) 15–32.
An excellent article. In justifying the need for an object-oriented approach, the authors critique the other approaches to knowledge representation. The authors then illustrate the need for an object-oriented approach to knowledge-based systems and illustrate its development process with a case study.

9

MAKING INFERENCES

There are two equally dangerous extremes—to shut reason out and to let nothing else in.

Pascal, 1670

WHY INFERENCES?

Making inferences from available data is common and important for many decision-making situations. It is crucial and central to ESs, where the subsystem that makes the inferences is known as the *inference engine*. The term 'engine' is used perhaps because it performs all the important calculations as in the analytical engine, the first calculating device designed by Charles Babbage. In addition, it can be seen as the mechanism that 'drives' the actions of the ES.

The inference engine is essentially a logic-based mechanism implemented as software. It uses declarative knowledge together with procedural rules for drawing inferences and reaching conclusions. In analysing the rules, it has two strategies of *reasoning*: it could reason from the front of a rule, i.e. the facts and conditions to the back, i.e. conclusions; or it could start from the end of the rule and search backwards for the facts and conditions that could cause the conclusion which is perhaps guessed or desired. In either case, in situations with a large number of rules and large problem space, the line of reasoning must be guided by some strategy of *search*. The two most common basic approaches are breadth-first or depth-first searches, which we encountered in Chapter 4, 'Problem Solving'. Thus

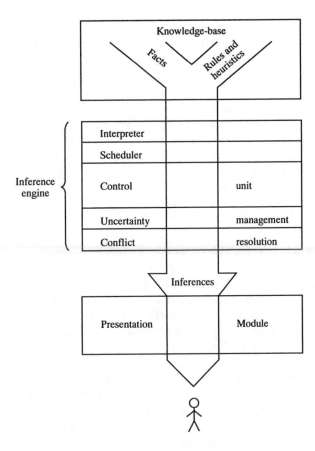

Figure 9.1 Overview of an inference engine.

there are at least four common combinations of strategies of reasoning and search. There are also other strategies, but whichever one is selected, and rules interpreted, there is a need for a control mechanism that in a rule-based system would make decisions such as which rule to start with and when to stop, as well as the sequencing and ordering of rules. And if there are conflicts in making the choices, then we need ways of *conflict resolution*. We examine this in the framework of a rule-based production system. It is these topics that are the subject of this chapter. An overview is shown in Fig. 9.1.

There are some topics that we will discuss only very briefly, such as the problem of *uncertainty management* which results from the need to manage fuzzy values of the variables involved. This is too important and complex a subject to be discussed as just one subtopic in a chapter. It needs a chapter of its own, and it will be the subject of our next chapter.

There are some topics that we will not discuss at all. For example, we shall say nothing about how to communicate the results of drawing inferences, a process that needs to be user-friendly. The communication systems must also offer facilities for the user to question the inferences and demand elaborations. This subject is discussed in Chapter 11 on interfaces. Finally, there is the entire set of questions regarding the nature of the software of an inference engine. Would it be a shell, an environment, or a programming language? The selection problem was discussed in the chapter on systems design. The details are the topics of two later chapters.

Despite all the exclusions, there is still much of substance and importance in this chapter. We will discuss them in the order of the topics highlighted above.

STRATEGIES FOR REASONING

Consider the following problem. You are a doctor whose patient has specific symptoms. How would you diagnose the disease that is causing the symptoms? You may want to match the symptoms with those for different diseases. This would be difficult even for a computer system because there are over 1000 diseases in the database. This is what happened in the case of the medical expert system, INTERNIST. The solution, of course, was to adopt a systematic line of reasoning to reduce the search space. This was done in INTERNIST I, which started with the symptoms and manifestations and traced the node (disease) that accounted for the set of symptoms and manifestations. This is the *forward reasoning* approach. But what if the number of terminal nodes (i.e. diseases) were enormous? Then you take another approach, as used by INTERNIST II. It started with the set of most likely diseases and traced back to match the manifestations that could cause each of the selected diseases with the given symptoms. This is simplifying the reasoning process, and it illustrates the concept of working backwards, i.e. *backward reasoning*, or *backward chaining*. As it was driven by the goal (a likely disease), it is called *goal driven* or *consequent driven*, and because it starts at the top, it is also called the *top-down* approach. The *forward-reasoning* approach also has other sensible names, like the *forward-chaining*, the *data/knowledge-driven*, the *antecedent-driven* and the *bottom-up approach*. These approaches are shown graphically in Fig. 9.2.

There are many other strategies of reasoning. One suggested by forward and backward reasoning is a hybrid approach combining the two and referred to as the *bidirectional* approach. Then there is *monotonic reasoning* where once a fact has been established it cannot be altered. In contrast, *non-monotonic reasoning* is where facts can be altered once established, thus facilitating the inference of tentative conclusions which may later be

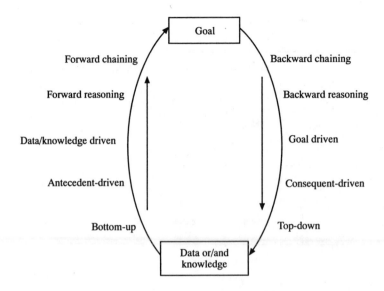

Figure 9.2 Approaches to reasoning.

abandoned as a result of, for example, new conflicting information. Another way to contrast approaches is *deductive reasoning*, which reaches conclusions from the general to the specific but monotonically; while *inductive reasoning* concludes from the special to the general and must be tentative.

Other reasoning strategies include *common-sense reasoning*, which infers with 'little overhead from a lot of knowledge'; *default reasoning*, which concludes from standard or expected values for lack of better knowledge; *example-driven reasoning*, which builds a decision tree from a knowledge-base containing representative case studies; and *expectation-driven reasoning*, where the number of valid facts increases monotonically, i.e. no facts become invalid (Altenkrueger, 1990: 5). These reasoning strategies are summarized in Fig. 9.3.

Having selected the best approach for reasoning, there may still be a problem with a large search space. If this is the case, one selects a search strategy such as those discussed in Chapter 4, 'Problem Solving'. The two most popular used in KBS are the breadth-first and depth-first methods and, each of these search techniques is combined with the two approaches to reasoning. These combinations will now be discussed.

Forward Chaining

In forward chaining one starts with an initial set of facts and rules and proceeds forwards towards decomposed subgoals and eventually to the

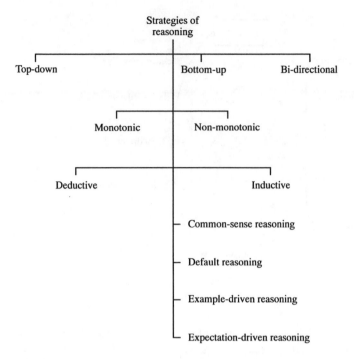

Figure 9.3 Strategies of reasoning.

goal. This approach is good when the search space leads towards the goal state with few if any dead-ends that may require back-tracking.

The forward-chaining strategy is efficient where a set of data, conditions, or events must exist in order to perform a task such as the selection of the configuration of components required for a particular computer system (as in XCON at Digital Equipment Corporation, which was the first commercially successful large ES). Another example would be the selection of a candidate for hiring given a set of qualification requirements.

Within the forward reasoning there is a search strategy, which could be breadth-first as illustrated in Fig. 9.4. Here each fact is represented by a node and a set of links leading to the goal. Sometimes, one path or rule may lead to another and then the selection and *firing* (execution) of the rule is repeated. Here the broader view of the search space is taken before it becomes necessary to look deep into the search space. The other search strategy is the depth-first approach as illustrated in Fig. 9.5, where one looks deep before taking a broader view. Which approach is best depends partly on the structure of the problem and partly on the philosophy of the designers of search strategies, i.e. the knowledge engineer and perhaps the domain expert. If a specialist view reigns, then the problem is defined and

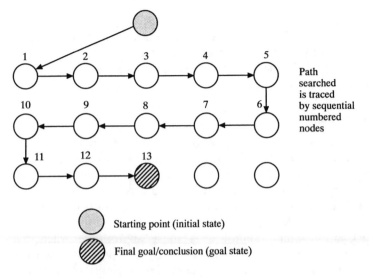

Path
searched
is traced
by sequential
numbered
nodes

Figure 9.4 Forward chaining: breadth first.

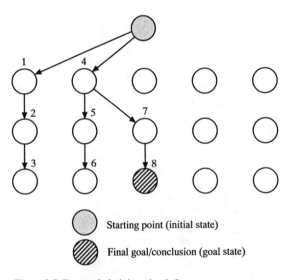

Figure 9.5 Forward chaining: depth first.

an in-depth search is pursued. This is analogous to what happens in the office of a medical specialist, or a dentist or dermatologist. On the other hand, if the designers are generalists, then a breadth-first approach may suggest making a general search before a specific search plan is pursued. Taking the medical environment again for our example, the generalist approach would be akin to the general practitioner who takes the temperature and blood pressure, etc., before making a diagnosis and reaching a conclusion. A broad-based global approach is appropriate in complex problems of planning, design in industry, and pattern recognition (speech and vision) in AI, where broad but 'shallow' levels of knowledge are quite adequate.

Backward Chaining

This is the more common approach taken not only in AI including KBSs and ESs but also in a DSS for business and commerce. In this approach, one starts from the goal and searches for the antecedent—the facts, rules, and heuristics that led to the goal and the desired conclusion. Here we are interested in knowing whether the known facts are consistent with a hypothesis that is plausible

The backward-chaining approach is most appropriate when the outcomes are reasonably small in number. It is only possible when the system is given, or has some way to hypothesize, a plausible goal. The approach is also appropriate for systems where the user seeks to select an outcome or goal from a set of possible states of knowledge, which will be symptoms and manifestations in the case of a medical diagnostic ES (as in MYCIN, which was the earliest diagnostic medical ES implemented). Another example would be detecting faults in a repair shop where the knowledge of a set of symptoms and heuristics can provide an educated guess as to where the fault may reside. We have a defective subsystem and we wish to identify which part is causing the fault.

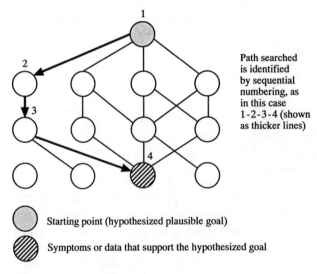

Path searched is identified by sequential numbering, as in this case 1-2-3-4 (shown as thicker lines)

Starting point (hypothesized plausible goal)

Symptoms or data that support the hypothesized goal

Figure 9.6 Backward chaining: depth first.

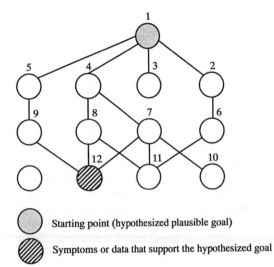

Starting point (hypothesized plausible goal)

Symptoms or data that support the hypothesized goal

Figure 9.7 Backward chaining: breadth first.

In backward chaining, as with the forward chaining, we have two possible combinations of depth-first and breadth-first search, as shown in Figs. 9.6 and 9.7, respectively.

Given a forward- or backward-chaining approach, there is sometimes a hardware factor to be considered in selecting a search strategy. The selection of a breadth-first search strategy is very memory-intensive because data on all the parallel paths in the breadth-search must be stored.

STRATEGIES FOR SEARCHING

We have just discussed two strategies for searching and discussed others in Chapter 4. There are still others which are important to KBSs and to other applications in business, commerce, and industry, and it is these that we will now consider. Before doing so, we will review our understanding of the term strategy and its relationship to an algorithm, whether this be in AI or OR. An *algorithm* is an effective organization of information for solving a problem, while a *strategy* is concerned with how to use this information in reaching a solution. We will now examine a few strategies of search.

Generate and Test

Generate and test, also referred to as *model-directed search* is a general strategy that involves generating a solution and then testing it, but keeping the two roles completely independent of each other. The generation of all possible solutions may require considerable searching. For example, it has been estimated that the possible combinations of opening a safe with five digits between 1 and 100 is around 10 billion. One solution to this problem of combinatorial explosion is to solve partial solutions 'so that, hopefully, entire subtrees can be pruned or ruled out from further search' (Dym and Levitt, 1991: 47).

This strategy, as well as the breadth-first and depth-first strategies discussed earlier, are said to be *weak* methods because they are very general and do not have the power associated with strategies that are 'knowledge-guided' and do not make use of domain knowledge. In contrast, the *strong methods* do use domain knowledge. We will now consider some of these strong methods, of which hill climbing is the most interesting as well as very useful.

Hill Climbing

Hill climbing is much like the depth-first strategy but with heuristics to determine the choices between possible paths. It is a recommended approach when there is a natural measure of goal distance and thus a likelihood of making a good choice at each choice point (Winston, 1984: 94). But hill climbing has the danger that one can get 'stuck' along the path. This may be the *plateau problem*, where there is mostly a flat area separating the peaks; the *ridge problem*, where you are stuck in a part of the search space that is higher than surrounding areas but cannot be traversed in any direction by single moves; and the *foothill problem* where there are many peaks and you find the local optima but not the global optima. (This was the case in the inventory simulation model in Chapter 4 and as we saw there are solutions to this type of problem.) The hill-climbing method is not suitable for rough and irregular terrain.

Best-first Search

The best-first approach, a popular form of 'hill climbing', always moves forward from the node that seems to be closest to the node that is the final goal. It is appropriate when

> there is a natural measure of goal distance and a path may look bad at shallow levels . . . this method would tend to be nearer the optimal than those found by pure depth-first or breadth-first searches which move slavishly without regard to the problem. (Winston, 1984: 99)

Winston offers the following analogy:

It works like a team of cooperating mountaineers seeking out the highest point in a mountain range: they maintain radio contact, move the highest subteam forward at all times, and divide subteams into subteams at path junctions.   (Winston, 1984: 99)

Branch and Bound

The search technique of *branch and bound*

generates complete reasoning paths and keeps track of the shortest path found so far. When the length of a path being explored becomes greater than the shortest path so far, it gives up and continues on the shortest path.   (Stylianou *et al.*, 1992: 42–43)

Thus termination occurs only when the shortest complete path is shorter than the shortest incomplete path.

Backtracking

There are a whole set of strategies that use back-tracking, which involves taking a step backward before going forward again. *Chronological backtracking* is coming back to the last choice point to undo an inference chain and to try another one; *dependency backtracking* is where one wipes out the effects of wrong assumptions and continues from there; and finally, *selective*

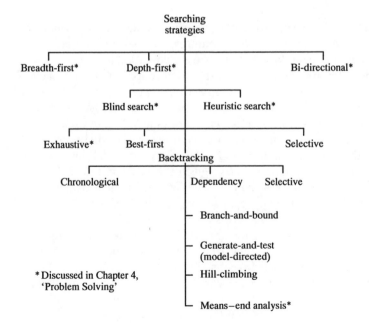

Figure 9.8 Searching strategies.

backtracking is where selection according to some criterion returns you to a previous choice point, not necessarily the last choice point (Altenkrueger, 1990: 5).

The strategies of searching discussed above and those discussed in Chapter 4 but also applicable to an inference engine are shown in Fig. 9.8.

CONTROL

Whatever strategy of search (and reasoning) is chosen, it is necessary to control the process of making inferences much like the control unit in a computer's CPU. The actions to be taken are listed, prioritized, and the one on the top is then scheduled. In an inference engine, control is needed to determine which production rules are to be used and fired (activated); what data is needed; what questions of a user are to be answered; how the questions are to be answered, and the reasoning explained for operations to be performed. The control unit is also responsible for starting and ending the reasoning and search process. And in between, there may be cause for conflict such as when two or more rules are ready to be fired. Which one must go first? This must be resolved and is the subject of our next section.

CONFLICT RESOLUTION

The bare bones of the architecture of a production system are shown in Fig. 9.9, where $C_n \rightarrow A_n$ represents a production rule consisting of a condition (C_n) and an action to be followed (A_n) when the condition is true.

The major components, as you can see, are a collection of rules, each of which is composed of a condition and an action, a working memory (WM), which contains information that defines the current state of the system, and a control loop, which cycles continually from rules to WM and back again.

The operation of a production system is to match the conditions of the rules against the information in the WM and to fire a rule that matches, i.e. a rule whose condition evaluates as true given the values in the WM. What if more than one rule matches the current WM? The typical strategy is to select just one of the rules that can be fired from the subset that could possibly be fired. This selection process is called *conflict resolution*. Conflict resolution usually involves heuristic strategies and is thus a major focus of the AI in the production system (the other such focus is the rules themselves). It is time for an example.

A knowledge-base might be represented by the following productions:

R1: (UNCLEOF X Y) → (NEPHEWOF Y X)
R2: (UNCLEOF X Y) AND (HOBBIT Y) → (HOBBIT X)

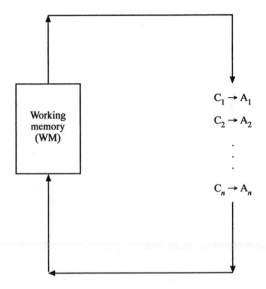

$C_1 \rightarrow A_1$
$C_2 \rightarrow A_2$
.
.
.
$C_n \rightarrow A_n$

Working
memory
(WM)

Figure 9.9 The skeleton of a production system.

and the current state, or working memory, which is given by the facts:

F1: (HOBBIT BILBO)
F2: (UNCLEOF FRODO BILBO)

The first rule, R1, states that, if X is the uncle of Y, then Y is the nephew of X, where the values of the variables X and Y are expected to be people's names. The second rule, R2, which is marginally more complex, states that if X is the uncle of Y and Y is a Hobbit, then X is also a Hobbit. The current state of the WM—i.e. the two facts F1 and F2—provides us with some specific names associated with two of the relations that comprise the rules. Fact F1 states that Bilbo is a Hobbit, and fact F2 states that Bilbo is the uncle of Frodo.

With this somewhat less than awe-inspiring example, we would find that the condition parts of both R1 and R2 will match the WM. We have run straight into a situation that requires a strategy for conflict resolution. In keeping with the general level of this example, we will set up a similarly trivial strategy for conflict resolution: assuming that the control regime attempts to match rule conditions against the WM sequentially from top to bottom in the list of rules, fire the first rule that matches. It does not exactly take your breath away, but it does the job.

Thus, in the current situation, rule R1 will fire, although we have not yet told you what execution of the action part is meant to achieve.

Typically, execution of the action part of a rule (i.e. firing the rule) changes the state of the WM by adding and/or deleting information. In addition, the action part may generate some information that is external to the production system proper. Thus an action part may output a message, for example. So, in the current example, the firing of R1 causes the fact (NEPHEWOF BILBO FRODO) to be added to the WM.

Now, although our trivial conflict resolution strategy contains no heuristics and is painfully simple, several non-obvious features about the production system follow. Control structure is now contained in the ordering of the rules. Different rule orders will give different results on exactly the same problem. We have added hidden constraints to the condition parts of the rules. This is obvious if you consider that the second rule can only fire if its condition part matches the WM *and the condition of the first rule does not match*. This brings us onto a second piece of bad news about this particular system.

The second rule can *never* fire. Any state of the WM that matches R2 will also match R1, which will thus be fired in preference under the conflict resolution scheme we proposed. The second rule is in effect:

R2: (UNCLEOF X Y) AND (HOBBIT Y) AND (NOT(UNCLEOF X Y))
   → (HOBBIT X)

Just in case you are wondering: this is not a sensible rule. If you were not wondering, then take another look at the effective condition and do not proceed until the penny drops. Clearly, this condition can never be met. The point that we want to make is that the problem is not a problem with rule R2 itself, but a problem that is generated by our conflict resolution strategy and a rule that precedes R2—to wit, R1. So even with the ludicrously simple example we already see problems arising that are due to the interaction of several elements of the system. The production system architecture has proven its worth in many diverse models in AI, (besides the ES) but the construction of a major production-system-based model is not without its headaches.

Building control information into the set of production rules can facilitate efficient searching of the rule base. But the introduction of these context dependencies does, of course, aggravate the problem of understanding and modifying production systems. The general trade-off here is between searching context-free representations and providing guidance at the cost of introducing context dependencies.

One final point concerns stopping these systems. The skeletal architecture in Fig. 9.9 was an infinite loop. The system can be stopped by an external agent when some desired information appears in the WM—information like the answer to the specific problem that the system happens to be working on. Alternatively, it will grind to a halt whenever no rule matches information in the current WM—clearly, no further progress can be made without the introduction of external information.

RULE-BASED SYSTEMS

In discussing conflict resolution we used a rule-based system as our frame of reference. Why a rule-based system? Because it is the most common type of KBS. Again, why? Because it has many advantages. But first, an overview of the inference engine for a rule-based system, as shown in Fig. 9.10. The first step in Fig. 9.10 is to examine the relevant knowledge-base (the facts, rules, and heuristics), and, with the help of one or more facts from the WM, select rules that seem relevant and promising. Once a rule is selected, it is checked along with the relevant knowledge for the semantics of the rule condition and the desired relationship and state of condition. If all checks out, the rule is interpreted by the rule interpreter and executed, except when the rules are non-procedural. The interpretation may involve pattern recognition of similar rules that are stored in working memory.

There are many advantages to a rule-based system. Rules are easy to formulate and check. All persons familiar with a flowchart, and its equivalent, the decision table, seem to be able to follow rules easily. The rule structures an analytical formulation of imperative knowledge in a way that is easily understandable by the end-user and the domain expert. It helps that the decision table has fairly rigid standards of format that make it easy to

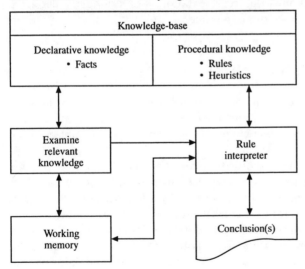

Figure 9.10 A rule-based inference engine.

follow even across professions and organizations. And the decision table does have a theoretical and axiomatic foundation for testing for completeness, redundancy, and consistency. Maes and Van Dijk make the following observation.

> the modeller's knowledge and insight may be incomplete, inconsistent or at least crumbled and unclear. We have shown that the systematic elimination of these regularities via the 'life cycle' concept can be a thought-provoking exercise, leading to a consistent and description of the decision situation. (Maes and Van Dijk, 1988: 419)

Another advantage of a rule is that it has an IF–THEN structure that corresponds to the structure of many procedural third-generation programming languages. Hence a rule-based system is quick and easy to program in most computing facilities without the need for a specialized compiler or programmer. The production rule is structured, simple, and homogeneous. The rules are independent of each other, which allows for incremental learning as productions are added or deleted.

There are limitations to the production rule system. Control structures are contained in the ordering of the rules, resulting in loss of flexibility. Different rule ordering will give different results on exactly the same problem and there is no optimal order for the firing of rules. It is difficult sometimes to assign confidence ratings to rules. With a large number of rules the system gets too cumbersome to maintain. And there is always the danger that knowledge is forced into rules when other knowledge representations would be better. There is, however, the possibility of using rules within another knowledge representation. For example, rules have been used successfully in the slot of a frame.

UNCERTAINTY MANAGEMENT

One last important function of an inference engine is to manage uncertainty. As mentioned in the introduction, this is a complex and important subject. It deserves a chapter of its own, and is the subject of the next chapter.

However, to provide a motivation for that chapter and to provide completeness to this chapter on inference engines (and just in case you decide not to read the next chapter), we will say a few words on the role of uncertainty and the need for its management in an inference engine.

Inference engines must manipulate data and knowledge that is either incomplete, inexact, or uncertain. Thus is the result of the unreliability of the source of data and information; incomplete data and information; disagreement and conflicting opinions among the sources of data especially when there are multiple domain experts; multiple uncertain premises; uncertainty in the conclusions being reached; and an imprecision in the interpretation and manipulation of data and information received and processed. To be able to cope with these needs or uncertainty, we require a system that manages uncertainty.

Our business world is dominated by rules that are 'usually true', or 'often true', or 'typically true' rather than rules that are 'always and absolutely true'. And while the mechanism of logical inference works perfectly in domains of absolute certainty, there are problems to be faced when constructing an inference engine for reasoning with uncertainty.

The fundamental problem concerns the combination of probabilistic rules and facts to infer probabilistic conclusions. The inference engine has to combine probabilities to generate a probability measure to associate with the inferences it draws. Consider the following example, if the lights are quite dim, say 0.8 dim, and the engine is turning over quite slowly, say 0.7 slowly, then what is the number to be associated with the inference that the battery is flat? Is it 0.75 of 0.9 (i.e. average of conditions as a proportion of the probability given for totally true conditions)? The answer is: no one knows. The usual strategy in ES development is to explore several different techniques and see which one performs best.

There are well-defined formalisms for combining probabilities (e.g. Bayes' theorem and fuzzy logic), but often they do not result in the desired ES behaviour (i.e. behaviour that is similar to that of a human expert). Nevertheless, both of these schemes for reasoning with uncertainty have been used successfully in ESs. Another popular scheme, reasoning with *certainty factors*, was developed as part of the MYCIN system (and is described in outline in an earlier section). It is a scheme that has no formal underpinning but it does seem to support the right sort of reasoning in the domain of medical diagnosis and many others.

The mechanism that a rule-based system for reasoning with uncertain knowledge is known as an *uncertainty management system* (UMS). UMSs based on fuzzy logic, which was invented by Dr Zadeh in the United States, are most commonly found in Japanese software technology, though one US company, Togai Infralogic, Inc., based in California, is devoted to developing systems based on fuzzy logic.

Fuzzy logic is a formal system that expands the traditional notion of set membership—e.g. every object is a member of the set of human beings or not. But many real-world phenomena are not that easily classified. Is a 6 ft. man in the set of tall men or not? We tend to feel more comfortable not making such yes/no decisions, but saying that he probably is, or something like that. Fuzzy logic allows us to extend the simple traditional, yes/no notion of set membership to a probabilistic one. Thus a 6 ft. man might have a 0.8 chance of being in the set of tall men, where 0 is not a member and 1.0 is definitely a member, whereas a 5ft. 6in. man may be associated with only a 0.5 chanced of membership in the set of tall men. The well-developed mechanisms of fuzzy logic provide a clear-cut and consistent way of combining these numerical values in order to support reasoning with uncertainty.

SUMMARY AND CONCLUSIONS

An inference engine sounds like a piece of hardware but is not. It is a set of software routines that reach conclusions after using one or more strategies of reasoning and search on a knowledge-base designed specifically for a particular problem domain. The inference engine is also able to state its conclusions in a format that is understandable and friendly to the end-user. This is usually done through the presentation and explanation module.

Depending on the structure of the knowledge-base, one uses different programming languages: a rule-based interpreter for knowledge stated in rules, frames, or object–attribute–value triples; and declarative languages and logic programming for a knowledge-base stated in predicate calculus. Instead of a flexible but low-level programming language, a language environment or perhaps a shell can be used. If a programming language is used for the inference engine we may need specialized hardware. But aside from the problem of hardware and software, there is still a great need for a better understanding of heuristics and how they can be adapted to computer performance and human behaviour.

The inference engine is discussed separately from the knowledge-base, not primarily for pedagogical reasons but because they need to be treated as two separate units. They are purposely designed to be isolated from each other so that the two units can be developed, modified, evaluated, and maintained separately. Changes to one unit—such as the knowledge-base, which must grow and be continuously updated—should not affect how knowledge is processed in the inference engine. And conversely different inference engines, embodying radically different strategies of search, may be applied to the same knowledge-base (at different times, of course).

One set of strategies relate to the management of uncertainty in the problem environment. This is the subject of our next chapter.

Case 9.1 AUTOMATED COMMERCIAL UNDERWRITING

In 1988, Bristol Polytechnic and Clerical Medical, a major insurance company in the United Kingdom, developed an ES for life under-writing.

The eventual system had 600 rules and was implemented on the company's PCs. There were 'extensive explanation screens used to enhance the training function of the system, giving the rationale behind the system's design'.

The developers found that deciding 'the level at which to automate can be problematic, since it is often unclear how to capture complex judgements as a thorough-going set of rules. Furthermore, for complex applications, such as attempting to model the medical aspect of life underwriting, it is clearly unrealistic to fully automate decision-making: the law of diminishing returns applies. A decision-support system aiding rather than replacing the expert is the usual compromise, such as the Underwriter's Aid developed by Nippon Life and CSK Research Institute, and the Tarex system cooperatively built by Swiss Reinsurance Co. and Coopers and Lybrand.'

Source: J. Gammack and G. Rowe (1991) 'Expert systems: the future is assured', *Computer Bulletin*, **3** (7), 20–21.

Questions
1. Is this an application primarily for a DSS and secondarily for a KBIS or vice versa?
2. Is this an application that is a good candidate for an integrated application? If so, integrated with a DSS or a transactional system or both?
3. Why does the 'law of diminishing returns' apply? How can its adverse affects be avoided or at least minimized?
4. Is the application of a KBIS for automatic decision-making unrealistic or is it a viable option? Explain.

Case 9.2   R1/XCON—3: INFERENCE MECHANISM

The inference-making mechanism of R1 can be gauged by the following description:

> The average conditional part of R1's rules has 6.1 elements (the range being 1–11). The action part of an average rule has 2.9 elements (range 1–10). Each element in the conditional part 'has a pattern that can be instantiated by an object defined by as many as 150 attributes'. Each element in the action part 'either creates a new element or modifies or deletes an existing object. A rule is applied when all of its condition elements are instantiated.'

The growth of the number of rules showed almost a straight-line growth path. In early 1979 there were 250 rules; by the end of 1980, there were 850; by early 1982 there were about 1750, and in early 1984, there were 3303.

More statistics on growth from 1980 to 1984 are as follows:

	1980	1984
Average rules per subtask	7.6	10.3
Average rule firings	1056	1064
Percentage of knowledge frequently used (%)	44	47
Number of parts in the database	420	5481

Source: J. Bachant and J. McDermott (1988) 'RI revisited: four years in the trenches', in R. Englemore (ed.), *Readings from the AI Magazine, Volumes 1–5, 1980–1985*, American Association for Artificial Intelligence, Menlo Park, CA, pp. 177–188.

Questions

1. Is the growth rate what you would expect from a very successful KBIS.
2. Is the growth in the number of rules and the number of parts in the knowledge-base significant? Why?
3. There is hardly any growth in the average number of firings. How do you explain that?
4. Do you think the percentage of knowledge frequently used is low or would you expect it to be below 50 per cent? Would this depend on the nature of the application?

Note: If you are interested to know the answers to the above questions from the designers of XCON, then read the source article.

REVIEW AND DISCUSSION QUESTIONS

9.1 What is the difference (if any) between an inference engine and a computer program that makes inferences in, say, a problem in business or industry?

9.2 What is the role of an inference engine in a KBS?

9.3 Can or should the inference engine be integrated with the unit succeeding or preceding it? If yes, why? If no, why not?

9.4 Can the inference engine be changed without changing the knowledge-base accordingly? Explain.

9.5 Should the presentation module be separate from the inference engine? Explain.

9.6 Should the inference engine be a 'black box' to the user? Explain.

9.7 Is the inference engine in a shell different from an inference engine when a programming language is used?

9.8 Is forward chaining better than backward chaining? Explain.

9.9 Give at least two examples from business and industry (preferably not those mentioned in the text above) where the following has the comparative advantage:
- (*a*) Forward chaining.
- (*b*) Backward chaining.
- (*c*) Breadth-first.
- (*d*) Depth-first.

9.10 For each example from the previous question, when would you use each of the strategies of search? Give at least one example of its use.

9.11 Can an inference engine make proper and correct inferences on all types and sizes of problems? What types and size of problems makes a knowledge system an undesirable alternative to a human expert?

9.12 'Inference engines in knowledge-based systems can make almost any inference that a human can make.' Comment.

9.13 Should an inference engine be interactive? Can it be interactive? What would be the advantages and disadvantages of being interactive?

9.14 'Changes in the environment made interactively would enable one to simulate a desirable conclusion'. Comment. Is that feasible? If feasible, is it desirable?

9.15 How would the absence of a control unit affect conclusions from a KBS? Discuss.

9.16 Do you find the rule-based system to be difficult to understand conceptually? If yes, why? If not, why not?

9.17 Specify a situation where a conflict needs to be resolved in an inference engine. How would you resolve that particular conflict?

9.18 Do you think that rule-based systems are easy to formulate, understand, and check? Will your answer change if you were a knowledge engineer instead of a domain expert?

9.19 Which of the strategies of reasoning and search can be used in problems for OR, like the inventory problem examined in Chapter 4.

9.20 Should an inference engine be developed by an SDLC or should it be developed by prototyping? Explain your choice.

BIBLIOGRAPHY AND REFERENCES

Altenkrueger, D. E. (1990) 'KBMS: aspects, theory and implementation', *Information Systems*, **15** (1), 1–7.
A superb glossary of terms in reasoning, search, and control. It is a shame that the author was so brief especially on the theory of implementation of a KBIS. Maybe he will elaborate later. Unfortunately, the author is from Germany and may not write much in English-speaking journals. But it is worth keeping an eye on the *Siemens Review*, printed in Germany but in English.

Dym, C. L. and R. E. Levitt (1991) *Knowledge-based systems in Engineering*, McGraw-Hill, New York.
A thorough Chapter 2 on 'Problem Formulation and Search'.

Hayes-Roth, F. (1985) 'Rule-based systems', *Communications of the ACM*, **28** (9) 921–932.
An excellent article on rule-based systems and inference engines. The author is a co-editor of *Building Expert Systems*, Addison-Wesley, New York (1983).

Maes, R. and J. E. M. Van Dijk (1988) 'On the ambiguity and completeness in the design of decision tables and rule-based systems', *Computer Journal*, **31** (6), 481–489.

A good discussion of seven types of problems that arise and how they can be overcome.

Parsaye, K. and M. Chignell (1988) *Expert Systems for Experts*, Wiley, New York.

There are many books on ES and KBSs but none has detailed discussions on all the main topics of this chapter. Thus Chapter 6 is on uncertainty management; chapter 7 on inference engines; Appendix A on search; and Appendix B on reasoning.

Stylianou, A. C., G. R. Madey and R. D. Smith (1992) 'Selection criteria for expert systems shells: a socio-technical framework', *Communications of the ACM*, **35** (10), 30–48.

The title does not suggest much on inference engines but this article has perhaps the best two and a half page summary on inference engines. Also a good but brief discussion on search strategies.

Winston, P. H. (1977) *Artificial Intelligence*, Addison-Wesley, New York.

Chapter 4 is a standard assignment for search strategies in academia.

10

MANAGING UNCERTAINTY

> There is nothing fuzzy about fuzzy logic
> Earl Cox

INTRODUCTION

We as human decision-makers are comfortable with certainty and un-comfortable with its absence, i.e. uncertainty. Why? Perhaps because we like the simplicity that certainty involves. Something either exists, or it does not. There is a yes/no answer to the question of its existence. It is either true or it is false. This binary logic is also appealing to a programmer who is very well versed in the IF–THEN–ELSE binary choice programming statement. But long before the computer, there was unhappiness with the simplicity of certainty. Earlier in this century, Bertrand Russell commented: 'All traditional logic habitually assumes that precise symbols are being employed. It is therefore not applicable to this terrestrial life, but only to a celestial existence.' And indeed our life, especially our business and industrial life, could not be represented in precise symbols or in precise values for symbolic variables. On the contrary, we are much accustomed to expressing ourselves in linguistic variables often modified by value adjectives. To handle such situations, Lofti Zadeh suggested the notion of fuzzy sets which provides

sets, but is more general . . . such a framework provides a natural way of dealing with problems in which the source of imprecision is the absence of sharply defined criteria of class membership rather than the presence of random variables.   (Zadeh, 1965: 339)

Zadeh's fuzzy and multivalued logic for his fuzzy sets led to a precise and exact logic but with the capability of capturing approximation. Zadeh predicted wide applicability of his fuzzy sets in the fields of 'pattern recognition and information processing'. He did not predict other applications that have also been very successful, such as those in the areas of natural language processing, KBSs and smart products.

We do not wish the reader to get the impression that fuzzy sets and fuzzy logic is the only way to handle uncertainty and we will discuss a few other approaches like certainty factors, the Dempster–Shafer theory of belief and plausibility, and Baysian probability. Only then will we discuss fuzzy logic—its nature, its transformation of linguistic to numerical values, its implementation, its applications, and its limitations. First, however, we need to discuss the situations that lead to uncertainty in a business and in a KBS environment.

WHY UNCERTAINTY?

There is uncertainty all around us in our daily lives, and also in business and industry. One cause for such uncertainties was implied earlier, i.e. a lack of sufficiently accurate instruments. There may also be uncertainty resulting from the aggregation of data. Uncertainty also arises from the fuzziness and vagueness with which we make many of our descriptions and classifications. Uncertainty may also arise from the fuzziness inherent in the information and knowledge being used.

All this results in unreliability of data or information especially if it is based on observations. Also, we tend to round-off and approximate in our daily activities and transactions. How often does one buy exactly 3.86 lb. of groceries or state one's age in months let alone in days or hours? In the case of groceries we may ask for 'around' or 'roughly' 4 lb., willing to round upwards or downwards. In the case of age, we are not so willing to round upwards but often purposefully round downwards. Sometimes one may want to round age upwards, say in an establishment with a minimum age limit, and then we hedge with modifiers like 'almost', 'nearly', or even 'roughly'. The time and energy required for exactness is either not desirable or simply not worth the trouble.

There is uncertainty arising from the design of ESs and KBSs. The use of heuristics is inherently an acceptance of uncertainty. There may be uncertainties in the existence and description of parameters and conditions as well as the resulting conclusions. And the rule connecting the conditions with a conclusion (or action) may be weak and hence raise the level of uncertainty in the conclusion or inference arrived at. And there is uncertainty resulting from the aggregation and propagation of uncertain data for many conditions and the compounding of such uncertainties in the premise through to the conclusion.

Uncertainty can also arise when domain experts do not agree. Missing or incomplete data or information can cause uncertainty; this situation may arise because the necessary data are not available, or because collection or possession of the information is illegal.

APPROACHES TO UNCERTAINTY MANAGEMENT

How do we cope with all these uncertain data and information resources? Many approaches have been suggested and tried; these include Rescher's plausibility theory (1976); Doyle's reasoned assumption approach (1982); Rollinger's evidence space (1983); and Bundy's incidence calculus (1984). We shall not discuss these many approaches but instead the four most commonly used approaches in KBSs: certainty factors, Dempster–Shafer's theory of belief and evidence, Bayesian probabilities, and fuzzy sets.

Certainty Factors

It is ironic that we use the term 'certainty' as in 'certainty factors' to represent 'uncertainty'. But it does make some sense if you consider that the absence of certainty is uncertainty. And so we use a certainty factor (CF) to represent uncertainty. Its value typically ranges from -1, which indicates no certainty, i.e. complete uncertainty, to 1 which indicates complete certainty, i.e. no uncertainty, and 0 which represents no information, either certain or uncertain. We can now represent uncertainty in, say, a rule for an ES with a CF = 0.9 for its conclusion as in:

IF   condition 1 AND condition 2 exist
THEN   conclusion: X exists (0.9)

The CF here represents the strength and degree of belief and confidence. The CFs could be assigned to each condition as well, in which case we need CF algebra to combine the two CFs.

Formally, a *certainty factor*, CF(h, e), is the degree of confirmation of the hypothesis h based on evidence e. It is a numerical measure between -1 and 1 that measures belief in the validity of a fact or rule.

Certainty factors can be combined by arithmetic operators. Let us consider an example with two conditions A and B with an AND conjunction in between:

Let CF(CA) = CF for condition A = 0.7
     CF(CB) = CF for condition B = 0.4

For the AND conjunction, we use the formulae:

$$CF(CA,CB) = CF(CA) + CF(CB) \times [1 - CF(CA)]$$

Substituting the numeric values, we have:

$$CF(CA,CB) = 0.7 + 0.4 \times (1 - 0.7)$$
$$= 0.7 + D.12 \qquad = 0.82$$

Note that the greater the first CF, the less the CF added by the second. Also note that combining low levels of confidence produces a measure with a higher level of confidence than the CF for either of the conditions considered.

The actual CF algebra used may vary with implementations of the system. In the case of MYCIN, when facts are ANDed together to reach a conclusion, MYCIN associates the minimum CF of its premises with the conclusion it derives. However, if the facts are ORed together to give a conclusion, the conclusion is given the maximum CF of its ORed premises. The final CF given to a rule-based conclusion is the product of the maximum or minimum value (derived as described) and the CF of the rule itself (remember, the rules are likely to be heuristic and thus probabilistically true themselves). This final CF is only computed (and the conclusion produced) if the maximum or minimum certainty factor is greater than 0.2—anything below that threshold is considered too uncertain to be worth pursuing. This can happen when a single assertion with a high measure of disbelief can overwhelm several measures of belief, resulting in counter-intuitive behaviour under certain circumstances.

EMYCIN is a shell of MYCIN and has many users. It seems to give good results in a variety of problem domains.

MYCIN incorporated CFs but this ES was never implemented in practice for medical diagnostics, though it did serve as a spur to countless subsequent ES projects. MYCIN tackled a difficult problem domain, and did well enough to convince enough people that practically useful ESs were buildable for less ambitious problem domains. This indeed turned out to be the case. Expert systems using the CF approach include EXSYSM, INSIGHT, Goldworks, Humble, Guru, and Personal Consultant.

One problem still to be confronted is that of determining the CFs. Who determines them? The domain expert. However, even if the domain expert is very experienced and knowledgeable of the domain, the expert's opinion is still subjective. Even though the CF is a scalar and has a numeric value, it is still subjective and inexact. However, sometimes adding subjective/judgemental and intuitive approaches to the decision process can be helpful to the modelling process. The problem is determining when it is useful and when it is not.

Certainty factors are often overrated. CF uncertainty management is used because it is available in a shell, or it is a concept well known to the domain expert or the knowledge engineer. However, unless there is a specific advantage in using the CF approach and there is also a good understanding of how uncertainty is viewed in calculating the CF, it should not be used, or used with caution and care.

Dempster-Shafer's Theory of Belief and Evidence

In 1967 Dempster suggested that there were upper and lower probabilities induced by a multivariable mapping. In 1976 Shafer proposed a belief function within the Dempster framework. Together, Dempster and Shafer argued that there was a lower probability associated with a degree of belief and that the upper probabilities were associated with a degree of plausibility. Their theory

> allows the decomposition of a set of evidence into separate, unrelated sets of evidence; a probability judgment can be separately assigned to each set of evidence. This approach, however, involves many numerical computations, and in the case of a long inference chain the structure of the resulting belief function would be very complex.   (Leung and Lam, 1988: 44)

There was also the problem of the presence of normalization, which was shown to produce incorrect and counter-intuitive results. Thus the Dempster–Shafer approach did not become popular but did add to our understanding of the process of reasoning under uncertainty.

Bayesian Probabilities

Probability is a concept known to all of us. There is no culture shock in having to use it. Probabilities can be computed and have the aura of being the result of a neat mathematical concept. But probability has some limitations. First, you need relevant and often considerable data to compute probabilities and this can be time and energy consuming (as in queuing and waiting-line problems) even when this be possible. Which brings us to the second difficulty: the necessary data are either not available or are totally irrelevant. For example, we have had many wars in the past. Can we calculate the probability of a war in the future? Similarly, can you tell us the probability of the inflation rate increasing by 50 per cent in the next 10 years or the probability of there being a depression in our lifetime? The answer is that one has to be very cautious in doing so. This does not mean that we must ignore the past or not learn from it. Actually, we can and should supplement objective probabilities with other relevant information to better our estimates of probabilities. Bayes argued that preceding events and experiences should influence the probability of our conclusions. Opinions on preceding events and the interpretation of past experiences are, of course, subjective. That is why *Bayesian probabilities* are often referred to as *subjective* probabilities.

There are, however, some limitations to Bayesian probabilities.

1. It is difficult to obtain all the necessary prior and conditional probabilities.
2. Bayes' law holds only if all possible outcomes are independent.
3. As the knowledge-base grows, it becomes difficult and almost impossible to make a change in one probability without causing a ripple effect that incorrectly changes other probabilities.

Despite these difficulties, it should be used where the evidence and information, however subjective, is relevant and important. Bayesian probabilities are used in ESs such as PROSPECTOR.

FUZZY LOGIC

Why Fuzziness?

We start our discussion on fuzziness by discussing what we all agree is not fuzzy. Take, for example, a decision rule announced by an instructor of an introductory computer science course, say CS100, that all average final scores between 60 and 80 inclusive will be given a B grade. This set of scores is called a *crisp set*, because the values on the boundaries are clear and crisp. There is no ambiguity or doubt as to who has *membership* in the group of B students. The set includes Danielle who scored 60.2, Tahira who got 70, and Misha who scored 79.6—all of them get a B. This set of scores in a *membership function* is shown in Fig. 10.1. Figure 10.1 has an *X*-axis of scores and a *Y*-axis that represents the existence of truth, with a value of 1 representing certainty of truth and 0 representing no existence of truth at all.

Is this a good way to grade? Danielle is extremely happy. She just managed to squeak a B and her grade sheet shows a grade point of 3.0 even though she almost did not make it. Tahira got an average score. She is definitely and without a doubt quite satisfied. Misha, however, is not happy. She is positively very unhappy. She just missed an A. She was more unhappy when she heard that her fierce competitor Marilyn got an A by scoring 80.2, a difference of only 0.6 per cent. Misha also resented being put

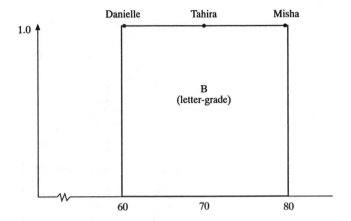

Figure 10.1 Membership function for scores for letter grade B.

into the same group as Danielle, who scored roughly 20 points less. But poor Misha can do nothing about it since the instructor has over 200 students and cannot attend to the many special cases. The instructor has a computer program that calculates the average score and assigns letter grades with no appeals and no questions asked.

The same instructor has another class, an upper division class with only around 30 students. Here the instructor has time to look at marginal cases and so the distribution is different, as shown in Fig. 10.2. Here we have some scores that have membership in more than one letter class of grade. This is the grey area, known as the fuzzy area or overlap set. If this distribution were used for CS100, then Misha (with 79.6 points) would be in the fuzzy area of overlapping and *partial membership* of both sets A and B, while Danielle is now in the partial and overlapping membership of B and C with a possible C and no longer an undisputed B. The instructor must now examine other relevant information or reassess existing information to assign letter grades. The reasoning process is now different: its crisp exactness has been replaced by inexactness. There is an area of uncertainty and all relevant data must be used to reduce the uncertainty. The truth of who gets what letter grade is no longer a binary 0 or 1 but is now *multivalued*. Decision making with multivalued logic is not crisp and exact but makes a lot of sense.

A few observations of the curves in Fig. 10.2. Note that they need not be symmetrical (or even linear). Also, not all the distributions need to be fuzzy; some can be crisp—e.g. 100 is an A. The sets shown in Fig. 10.2 are *fuzzy sets*, which are collections of elements having varying *degrees of membership*, from non-membership of a *grade* category of 0 to full membership of a grade category of 1; like $M(A) = 0.48$ for Misha in the set

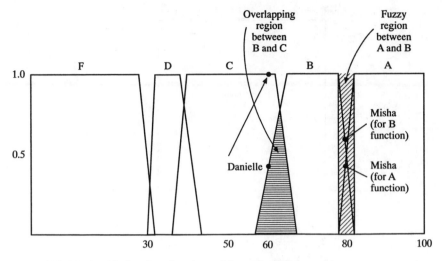

Figure 10.2 Membership functions for crisp and fuzzy sets of letter grades.

of A scores and M(B) = 0.55 in the set of B scores, with Danielle dropping from a M(B) = 1 to M(B) = 0.4. In contrast, in conventional set theory there is a binary choice: an object is either a member M(A) = 1 say, or not a member, M(A) = 0. Thus the fuzzy set can be considered to be a label attached to a class of linguistically expressed entities with no precise boundary. However, with no vagueness as per our opening quote, the fuzzy set idea transforms uncertainty to a precise notion; whether it is a 'correct' or useful transformation is still to be decided.

The Y-axis of Fig. 10.2 represents the *truth values*, with 1 representing absolute truth and 0 representing absolute falsity. The truth values are part of *fuzzy logic* or *fuzzy truth* where inexact adjectives are used to describe the object. Fuzzy logic is a kind of logic that uses

> graded or qualified statements rather than ones that are strictly true or false. The results of fuzzy reasoning are not as definite as those derived by formal logic, but they cover a larger field of discourse.   (Zadeh, 1984: 26)

Fuzzy logic is a general multivalued theory, with two-valued logic and set theory being a subset of it. Fuzzy logic, then, offers the knowledge engineer an alternative way to represent knowledge and reduce uncertainty. Attributes that add to the degree of clarity can now be measured on a fuzzy scale to contribute a meaningful value.

The qualifiers referred to in Zadeh's definition are the adjectives that we so generously use in our daily language. They are referred to in fuzzy logic parlance as *hedge*, and a list of these is shown in Table 10.1. We have used

Table 10.1 Examples of hedges and their meanings

Hedge	Meaning
Very Much Extremely	Intensification of fuzzy region
Almost Definitely Positively	Intensification contrasted
Just Quite Rather Somewhat	Dilution of fuzzy region
Not	Negation or complement
Above	Broaden a fuzzy region
Below	Restrict a fuzzy region
About Around Nearly Roughly	Approximating a scalar value

many of these above, especially in our discussion of the grades for CS100 above. We quite casually used hedges and fuzzy quantifiers such as *just, not, almost, very, quite, definitely positively, roughly, about, below*, and *extremely*. In another context we could have used hedges such as *generally, usually, somewhat, rather, sort of, rather*, and *around*. Such linguistic hedges can be modelled as set theoretic operations so as to modify a membership function. This allows definitions to remain subjective but their operations consistent.

Fuzzy set truth (or membership) functions can be represented by a vector of real numbers. They can then be coded in a high-level language (for an example, see Cox, 1992a: 31). This ability would certainly make Misha happy for she might get an A. However, Danielle could now well end up with a C, and Tahira gets a B. The grey area of marginal grades is no longer an area of uncertainty but has now been empowered with greater meaning and, in the case of Misha, equity. And the grading is still all automated.

Linguistic to Numeric Values

We have discussed the truth diagrams in Figs 10.1 and 10.2. We should discuss how one derives such curves, and who and what determines such curves. We shall answer the second question first. The domain expert, with perhaps some data collected by the knowledge engineer and in some cases from the experience of the operational manager, determines the curves. What is done in the case of our CS100 example by the course instructor is illustrated in Fig. 10.3 where we have a trapezoidal-shaped membership function curve for assignment of a B grade. The domain expert—in this case the instructor (with perhaps help from his or her department head who has recommended distributions in mind)—decides that scores of 65–78 are solid B grades. There are then two sloped segments of the trapezoidal figure, one increasing monotonically from ordinates (57,0) to (65,1.0), and the other decreasing from (78,1.0) to (82,0) as shown in Fig. 10.3. Now for a score of, say, 80, we can use the curve to find the *grade membership* value as 0.5.

The membership grade of Misha and Danielle have both dropped from 1.0 to around 0.55 and 0.4, respectively, since both now have partial membership in other sets. Misha has membership in the A set and may improve her letter grade from the high B in the crisp scoring method to a low A. Meanwhile, Danielle has a partial membership in the set C and may well end up with the lower grade. Tahira is unaffected.

The 'grade of membership is very subjective in nature; it is a matter of definition rather than measurement' (Zadeh, 1984: 26). Another way of looking at it is to say that the *Y*-axis of grade membership represents *possibility values*; fuzzy theory can then be referred to as *possibility theory*.

We have considered scores as our variable measured in numerical values. They could also be stated in linguistic values such as average, below average, above average, excellent, etc. Another variable that can take on linguistic values is age, which can be stated in numerical values of years or even correct to the day and also in linguistic values such as old, very old, young, etc. Some variables can take only linguistic values such as happy,

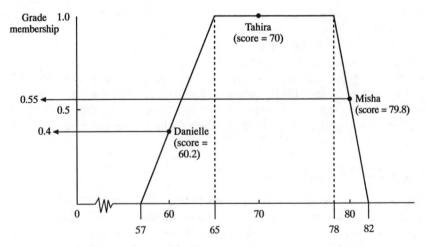

Figure 10.3 Fuzzy membership functions for letter grade B.

success, stable, busy, liquidity, etc.—with hedges and attributes to qualify them. These are known as *linguistic variables* and are part of the daily vocabulary we use to represent a particular fuzzy set in a given problem, such as 'large', 'small', 'medium', or 'OK' (Zadeh, 1984: 26). Linguistic variables take on words or phrases from natural language, as distinct from traditional variables that take on numeric values.

The fuzziness membership distribution discussed in Figs 10.2 and 10.3 is trapezoidal. The distribution could approach a bell-shaped curve, but we have purposely avoided the bell-shape for our membership distribution lest it be mistaken for the classic probability distribution. It is time to make the distinction. Probability is an after-the-fact measurement, while fuzziness is a continuous on-the-fact measurement. Probability is concerned with undecidability in the outcome of the event, while fuzzy logic is concerned with the ambiguity or undecidability inherent in events. Probability typically measures the frequency of occurrence, while fuzziness captures the vagueness and undecidability of the event. Also, probabilities of alternative independent events must add up to 1.0, but truth values for a variable with partial memberships need not add up to 1.0.

The membership and possibility distribution need not be trapezoidal or bell-shaped. It could be a long tilted (to the right) S-curve as one would get when one considers a person who is 'tall' or 'short' or 'young' or 'old'. Modifiers like 'very' or 'quite' could then be used with arithmetic operators that could represent the fuzzy concept of say 'very tall' and 'quite tall'. Or,

> . . . given the sets 'young' and 'old' one can construct other sets, such as 'very young', by squaring the membership function for 'young', or 'more or less old', by taking the square root of the membership function of 'old'. 'Not very young' is obtained by squaring the function for 'young', as in very 'young', and then subtracting the result from one, to represent 'not'. (Zadeh, 1984: 28).

To illustrate some of the operators implied above, consider the linguistic variable 'overdue'. This is measured in days and could be the overdue of an accounts receivable or the delay in production or a delay in delivery to a warehouse. But one may need a membership function of overdue that are 'just' or 'quite' overdue as well as those that are 'very' or 'much' overdue. The membership functions of the modified variable can be derived by using the *intensification* or *dilution operator* on the base variable, i.e. overdue which we call $F(O)$. We now have the operations as follows:

$$INT\ (O) = [F(O)]^2 \qquad \text{(long overdue)}$$
$$DEL(O) = [F(O)]^{1/2} = \sqrt{F(O)} \qquad \text{(just overdue)}$$

These operations are illustrated graphically in Fig. 10.4. Note that the

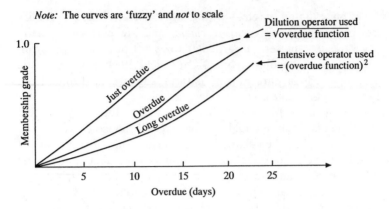

Figure 10.4 Membership functions for overdue with intensive and dilution operations used.

results are very intuitive. Thus if you draw a vertical line across the base function for 'overdue', you will find the function 'just overdue' with a higher membership value (because of the square-root operation) and a corresponding lower membership value (because of the square operation) for those that are 'much' or 'greatly' or 'long' overdue. Such membership values and functions are often useful; in the case of accounts receivable being overdue, for example, whether they are just overdue or long overdue can trigger different administrative procedures in the accounting and accounts receivable office.

To represent degrees of uncertainty, one could use fuzzy intervals instead of scalar values. Bonissone and Tong (1985: 242–243) state it well:

> The degree of necessity is represented by the lower bound of the fuzzy interval and the degree of possibility by its upper bound. *Necessity* and *possibility* respectively represent the amount of support for the hypothesis, and the amount of failure to refute the hypothesis provided by the evidence. Unlike lower and upper probabilities, necessity and possibility do not require normalization. The value of the necessity of an hypothesis is always smaller than or equal to the value of the possibility. Violation of this constraint during aggregation of conclusions from different experts suggests rule inconsistencies among the knowledge sources.

(The words in italics are provided by the authors to indicate a definition of an important concept.)

Implementation of Fuzzy Logic

Once we have a symbolic representation of uncertainty, we are ready for the necessary set operations. These were first stated by Zadeh (1965: 339–353):

The notions of inclusion, union, intersection, complement, relation, convexity, etc. [together with] . . . a separation theorem for convex fuzzy sets is provided without requiring that the fuzzy sets be disjoint.

Since this early statement of the mathematical and theoretical foundations, much work has been done (mostly by Zadeh) on the refinement of the arithmetical operation on fuzzy sets. But it is not necessary for the knowledge engineer much less the end-user manager to master all this set theory. To them this need only be a black box, though it would be helpful for the knowledge engineer to appreciate the theoretical foundations of fuzzy set theory. Fortunately, fuzzy sets have been incorporated in many shells, and a few are programmed to facilitate the incorporation of fuzzy logic in KBS (see Silverman, 1987, for details). For business applications, these include PRICE for a small rule-based DSS; FANFARES a financial accounting application that assesses a firm's overall liquidity position and compares causes for any deficiencies in liquidity; FAULT diagnoses problems in financial accounting networks; and STRATASSIST is for strategic business planning.

There are hardware implications of implementing fuzzy sets in a KBS. Implementation requires three main components: one is *fuzzification*, where the real-time input is combined with information on input membership functions to produce fuzzy inputs. The second stage is the *rule evaluation*, where rules are interpreted for the fuzzy inputs, producing fuzzy outputs. These fuzzy outputs are the inputs to the final and third stage of *defuzzification*, where the output membership functions are combined with the fuzzy outputs to produce the desired system outputs. These stages of hardware implementation are shown in Fig. 10.5.

Applications of Fuzzy Logic

Some applications to KBSs in business were listed in the discussion of implementation of fuzzy logic above. There are numerous successful applications in almost all functional areas of business, including asset and

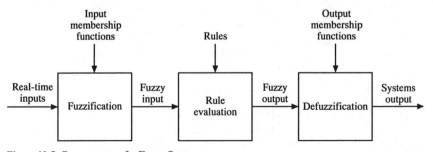

Figure 10.5 Components of a Fuzzy System.

liability management, auditing, cash-flow analysis, credit checking, financial control and planning, insurance industry management, portfolio management, savings and loan management, securities management, and venture capital assessment. For details see Levy *et al.* (1991: 651–669).

There will undoubtedly be more applications in business as managers, especially top managers, realize that fuzzy logic allows them (to some extent) to state their objectives and requirements in their everyday style of talking and not have to be restricted to the jargon and constraints of the computer systems analyst. The manager can now talk in terms of linguistic variables and provide linguistic data as input. This can be very useful in corporate planning because fuzzy systems are well suited for just such an environment and will allow vagueness and lack of specificity of input, which can be duly recognized and systematically handled. Planners and top managers should love this flexibility, especially when the approach is refined.

Then there are the industrial applications and signal analysis where it all started with Zadeh, the control engineer. In 1989 there were already over 120 successful applications of fuzzy logic in control engineering. The traditional proportional integral differential (PID) approach to control is now being rapidly replaced by fuzzy controllers. A diagrammatic representation of fuzzy control systems is shown in Fig. 10.6.

Industry is still a fertile environment for fuzzy logic applications,

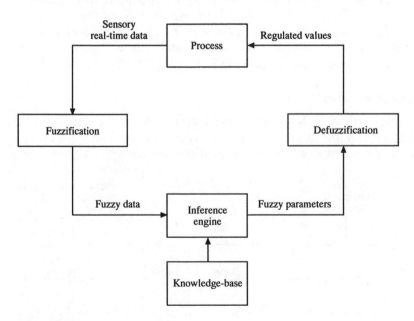

Figure 10.6 Fuzzy systems control.

especially as systems get more complex and as input get more varied and fuzzy. It should be recognized, however, that fuzzy concepts are used in control systems even if the input is not fuzzy, for fuzzy control concepts are used for processing of data, both fuzzy and not fuzzy. Typically, an industrial fuzzy control system would consist of 20–100 such rules that are run through in a loop. Although controlling real-time physical systems is difficult enough, it is much more difficult to control real-time human–machine systems such as the control of a train. Here one needs fuzzy logic to represent the qualitative variables in the technical system and also to model the fuzzy manner in which the process controller acts and the train driver behaves.

There are numerous other applications of fuzzy logic, both current and potential, outside the mainstream of business and industry. These would include agriculture, especially agricultural planning; medical diagnosis, which has been the first area for applications of KBSs and will continue to be a rich area of application because of the fuzzy nature of some of the real-time systems inputs; weather prediction, which is both difficult but extremely valuable since it could save many human lives all over the world as well as save vast amounts of money in farming, etc.

There are applications in the computer industry especially in the areas of pattern recognition of voice and image processing; vision systems; biometrics systems (identification of physical attributes) for security; robotics; and in natural language processing, especially natural language understanding where the real-time inputs can indeed be very fuzzy.

Since fuzzy logic is based on the idea of linguistic variables—linguistic concepts that can be represented as fuzzy sets—it appears likely that fuzzy sets can help with the great difficulties of natural-language communications with computers . . . it seems probable that in the next decade fuzzy logic will become routinely applied in many areas of artificial intelligence where communication with people or imitation of the thought process is involved. This may help to bridge the gap between the analog and flexible thinking of humans and the rigid framework of present computers.   (Zadeh, 1984: 32)

Finally on applications of fuzzy logic, we shall discuss smart products. These microprocessor-based products came of age in the 1980s. Later, with the continual miniaturization of microprocessors coupled with the maturing of fuzzy logic, smart products became much smarter and more accessible. Fuzzy logic is now embedded in video cameras, controlling their movement; in gearboxes to determine the optimum time to change gear; in braking systems to determine when to start applying the brakes; in vacuum cleaners to determine the optimum suction to use; in washing machines, air-conditioners, and a host of consumer and industrial goods. Panasonic, a Japanese manufacturer, estimates that it alone will soon fuzzify over 200 of its products. This includes a smart shower-head controller to adjust the temperature of the water in the shower for different members of the family at all times of the day and in different seasons.

Why Is Fuzzy Logic Not More Popular?

The terms 'fuzzy logic', 'fuzzy sets', and 'fuzzy theory' have two types of negative reactions from a typical business manager. The terms 'logic', 'sets', and 'theory' are all very mathematical and intimidating. Many managers do not have the time or inclination to learn another logic or set formalism. And when these terms are coupled with the prefix 'fuzzy', then the issue sounds distinctly fishy. True, all managers work with uncertainty and inexact information all the time but they do not always wish to admit it, especially when it is argued that a mathematical method is going to help them with what they conceive as essentially a qualitative matter. But this attitude will change as fuzzy systems make their way into society and in the home just as microcomputers did.

It was once believed that fuzzy systems would be too complex to develop and too computer intensive to implement. This has changed. Fuzzy systems are now being implemented on microcomputers and their complexity is hidden in the black box of a shell.

Fuzzy sets can be a great boon to the development of information systems. One of the biggest problems in development as conceived by both developers and end-users (including corporate managers) is the specification of the user's needs, objectives, and constraints. The systems analyst and the computer programmer demand that these be specified in operational and quantitative terms. Many an hour has been spent by computer specialists and practitioners of OR/MS in assigning weights for objective functions or in devising criteria to be used in the selection of equipment and other resources. This comes hard for the corporate manager. With fuzzy sets, these managers can now talk, as they prefer to, in terms of linguistic variables. Of course, there is the problem of stating the membership functions but that is not of concern to the manager. Also, the fuzzy system helps in constructing some membership functions (remember the intensification and dilution factors?). Thus fuzzy sets may result not just in relieving the manager of a chore but of actually improving communication between management and the technicians.

We discussed earlier how fuzzy systems have been used extensively in KBS and ES. They have not, however, been used to any extent in OR/MS where they could be very useful in modelling the decision-making process for a corporate manager. This too will change. As knowledge engineers interact with OR/MS personnel (either on a personal or organizational level) there will be a transfer of technology from the knowledge engineer and from other AI personnel. We will then see many applications of fuzzy systems in all business functions and at all levels.

SUMMARY AND CONCLUSIONS

In our daily life and in the business world we have data that are either crisp or fuzzy or both. We saw in the example of grading for a course, trivial maybe but quite realistic, how grading could be either crisp or fuzzy. The two types of membership functions are superimposed in Fig. 10.7 (superimposition of Figs. 10.1 and 10.3). The resolution provided by the fuzzy function can be important to both the student and the instructor. We could get greater resolution than the trapezoidal membership function if desired, for theoretically fuzzy sets do provide a continuous interpolation between the high and low ends of the domain.

Fuzzy logic is just one of the many approaches to uncertainty. There is also the use of certainty factors, the Dempster–Shafer approach and the Bayesian approach. These are summarized in Table 10.2. But fuzzy logic has many attractions. Fuzzy logic provides a sound numerical foundation for handling fuzzy inputs of linguistic variables that are imprecise and inexact. It is a general-purpose and powerful tool for reasoning under uncertainty. Fuzzy logic enables us to represent and process a conceptual framework at a high level of abstraction and represent complex decision spaces to enable decision making based on evidence.

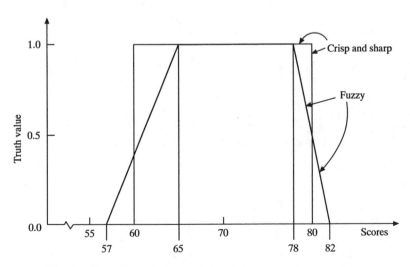

Figure 10.7 Superimposition of crisp and fuzzy sets for scores of letter grade B.

Table 10.2 Comparison of approaches to uncertainty

	Example	Foundation	How Determined	Advantages	Disadvantages
Certainty factors	MYCIN EMYCIN Guru EXSYSM INSIGHT Goldworks Personal Consultant	Belief	Arbitrary and subjective	Gives good results over wide range of domains	Being subjectively assigned, the CF may lead to incorrect results
Dempster–Shafer	None commercially	Belief and evidence	Subjective	Allows for subjective belief and evidence	Produces inaccurate and counterintuitive results
Bayesian probabilities	Crystal EXSYS	Probability theory	Subjective probability association	Accurate Allows for subjective opinions and data	Difficult to obtain and check prior probabilities and ripple effects on large databases
Fuzzy logic	EXSYS Guru OPS-2000 Shells PRICE FANFARES FAULT	Logic and set theory	Through using set operations on membership functions	Accurate Allows for linguistic variables with hedges and inexactness	Has bad image: —Too mathematical —Too complex —Difficult to develop —Need to generate membership sets

There are dangers that must not be overlooked. For example, the danger in translating from linguistic to a calculus (which is often guesswork) and then assuming that the output is exactly correct.

Despite the dangers, fuzzy logic has many applications in conducting business, especially in production. It also has many applications when embedded in products to make them smart, and has been used extensively in constructing ES and KBS. The great potential of fuzzy logic, however, lies in its use in DSSs where we are often faced with uncertainty and where the variables that managers are most comfortable with are linguistic variables. This is an environment in which fuzzy logic will be useful once we overcome the resistance in applying the fuzzy-logic technique. Until then, fuzzy logic has an image problem: the technique has an undeservedly bad reputation for being too mathematical and complex, and hence difficult to implement.

Looking into the future, it seems likely that fuzzy logic will not be used alone but in conjunction with other techniques such as neural nets and probabilistic reasoning. The components of fuzzy logic, neural nets, and probabilistic reasoning are referred to as *soft computing* as shown in Fig. 10.8. Soft computing subsumes belief networks, genetic algorithms, parts of learning theory, some of the reasoning approaches, management of uncertainty, and chaotic systems. Fuzzy logic, neural nets, and probabilistic reasoning are complementary rather than competitive; together, they exploit the tolerance of imprecision, uncertainty, and partial truths.

Software increases the *machine intelligence quotient* (MIQ), and mimics 'the ability of the human mind to effectively employ modes of reasoning that are approximate rather than exact' (Zadeh, 1994: 77).

Concluding our discussion of uncertainty management and hence the discussion on inference engines, we are now ready to examine the interfaces necessary to access the conclusions and recommendations of the inference engine. This is the subject of our next chapter.

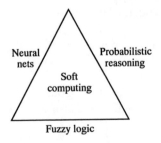

Figure 10.8 Soft computing and its components.

CASE 10.1 SOME EXAMPLES OF FUZZY SYSTEMS

Below are listed some applications of fuzzy sets:

- 'Since 1987, the Japanese city of Sendai has had a driverless subway system that is automatically operated by a so-called fuzzy controller. . . . Typically, a fuzzy controller consists of 20 to 100 . . . rules that are run through a loop. . . . Both the gradual decision-making functions and the rules and their execution are coupled to very elementary operations, which provides the basis for specific software and hardware support (fuzzy chips), and thus permits efficient, real-time-capable solutions.'
- Washing machines that make do with 4-bit processors, whereas conventional controls require 8-bit processors.
- Panasonic is aiming for the 'fuzzification' of some 200 products including the regulation of water temperature.
- A review in 1989 revealed over 200 successful industrial applications of fuzzy control, mostly in Japan.
- Sanyo is using a fuzzy-system focusing mechanism in their single-lens reflex camera.
- Yamachi Securities uses a 800-rule fuzzy system for financial planning.
- The automobile industry is using fuzzy automatic braking systems.

Sources: M. Reinfrank (1991) 'Fuzzy control systems: clear advantages', *Siemens Review*, **6**, 28–32; T. J. Schwartz (1990) 'Fuzzy systems in the real world', *AI Expert*, **5** (8), 29–36.

Questions
1. From the above list of applications can one extrapolate the extent of the use of fuzzy systems in the future? Would you care to try?
2. What are the main limitations of such fuzzy systems?
3. Are you likely to see fuzzy systems embedded in home products or industrial products or both?
4. What are the constraints in the greater popular use of fuzzy systems?
5. Why do you suppose that the application of fuzzy systems is to be found mostly in Japan when it originated in America. Could fuzzy systems be used just as extensively in the US and in Europe? Why the lag?

CASE 10.2 FUZZY LOGIC FOR LOAN ANALYSIS

Fuzzy logic has been used for commercial loan analysis. Using company-specific and industrial financial data, systems appraise a company's credit, capital, and capacity performance.

The fuzzy logic evaluation system consists of three major components: two utility programs; specific fuzzy sets and edit rules (used by systems developers); plus the Evaluator, which applies fuzzy logic to financial data about the problem. The system uses TurboPascal and can be run on a IBM PC on MS-DOS.

> A typical rule has a single linguistic variable for its consequent, while its antecedent consists of those variables branching immediately beneath it . . . for each credit rule, depending on whether Efficiency, Liquidity and Profitability are either Poor, Weak, Normal or Strong, fuzzification embeds the vector of scalars into the corresponding triple of membership grades. Then evaluation and defuzzification follow . . . the system combines efficiency with liquidity and profitability to draw a conclusion about credit.

Source: J. Ley, E. Mallach and P. Duchessi (1991) 'A fuzzy logic evaluation system for commercial loan analysis', *OMEGA: International Journal of Management Science,* **19** (6), 651–669.

Questions

1. Do you think that the principles of the logic system for the loan analysis system described above are applicable to many other business problems. (Ley *et al.* think so, p. 666.)
2. We have considered above only the credit variable which includes profitability, efficiency, and liquidity. Could fuzzy sets be applied to the other variables in a loan decision such as capital, capacity, collateral, and general business trends?
3. In determining whether or not to use fuzzy sets, would you perform a cost–benefit analysis? If so, how will you determine the benefits of a fuzzy system?

REVIEW AND DISCUSSION QUESTIONS

10.1 'Certainty factors must be reliable because they have a mathematical foundation and were calculated by a computer.' Comment.

10.2 Most of the approaches to uncertainty are subjective, so which one of these is reliable and why?

10.3 Some approaches to uncertainty depend on one's belief. Why should I trust the belief of the knowledge engineer or the domain expert?

10.4 Identify some linguistic variables in any type of business activity you may know of. If you cannot think of any, consider shopping for an automobile.

10.5 How does a linguistic variable vary from the traditional variables used in decision-making? How does either make you better off or worse off?

10.6 List hedges that could be used in any business you know (other than those discussed in the text). If you do not know a business, then consider your department head as a business person.

10.7 Explain why a membership function can be confused with a probability distribution and why are they different?

10.8 What is the difference between certainty factors, fuzzy logic, and Bayesian probabilities?

10.9 What are the potential sources for the following?
  (*a*) Subjective probabilities.
  (*b*) Certainty factors.
  (*c*) Membership functions.

10.10 Why not use probabilities for managing uncertainty? Some use Bayesian probabilities, why not just probabilities?

10.11 How can fuzzy logic in smart products affect the following?
  (*a*) Standard of living.
  (*b*) Style of living.
  (*c*) Other.

10.12 For a business, how will smart products using fuzzy logic affect the following?
  (*a*) Productivity.
  (*b*) Competitiveness.
  (*c*) Profit.

10.13 It is argued by some that fuzzy logic is the best approach to uncertainty. Do you agree? If you do not, explain. If you do, why then has fuzzy logic not replaced other approaches to uncertainty? Do you think that fuzzy logic eventually will replace other approaches to uncertainty?

10.14 Is fuzzy logic a satisfactory approach to uncertainty so that we should concentrate on refining it? Or should we try an entirely different approach?

10.15 How can fuzzy logic affect a business manager in terms of the following aspects?
  (*a*) Style of management.
  (*b*) Effectiveness of decision making.
  (*c*) Modelling the real world.

10.16 Does the term 'fuzzy logic' intimidate you? If so, why?

10.17 Do you think fuzzy logic is fuzzy?

EXERCISES

10.1 Suppose that you are an instructor (for a course taken previously) and your students requested a membership function for grading that was not trapezoidal. Construct such a membership function with a justification of important points of the curve.

10.2 Draw a membership function for a linguistic variable 'tall'. Then derive and draw the membership functions for 'quite tall' and 'very tall'.

BIBLIOGRAPHY AND REFERENCES

Bonissone, P. P. and R. M. Tong (1985) 'Editorial: reasoning with uncertainty in expert systems', *J. ManMachine Studies*, **22** (3), 241–250.
> Old by some AI literature standards but still very relevant. It is fairly comprehensive and well written.

Cox, E. (1992a) 'Solving problems with fuzzy logic', *AI Expert*, **7** (3), 31–36.
> Cox is a frequent writer on fuzzy systems and often in the same journal. He has a wide range of interests and expertise including neural systems and expert systems. This article discusses hardware and programming code, and has membership diagrams—all very readable.

Cox, E. (1992b) 'Applications of fuzzy systems models', *AI Expert*, **7** (10), 34–39.
> Cox argues that approximate reasoning is a process and 'not a paradigm: applying it to business problems provides a high level of abstraction in problem representation'.

Klir, G. J. and T. A. Folger (1988) *Fuzzy Sets, Uncertainty, and Information*, Prentice Hall, Hemel Hempstead.
> This is a good self-contained text designed for the post-graduate or upper undergraduate level student.

Leung, K. S. and W. Lam (1988) 'Fuzzy concepts in expert systems', *Computer*, **21** (9), 43–56.
> This article has a very short but excellent overview of the approaches to reasoning under uncertainty. Most of the article, however, discusses the hardware details of the implementation of a shell, System Z II.

Levy, J., E. Mallach and P. Duchessi (1991) 'A fuzzy logic evaluation system for commercial loan analysis', *Omega*, **19** (6), 651–669.
> An excellent survey of the applications of fuzzy systems in business followed by details on one implementation including a discussion of the specification of fuzzy sets, edit rules, and evaluation.

Ng, K.-C. and B. Abramson (1990) 'Uncertainty management in expert systems', *IEEE Expert*, **5** (2), 29–45.
> If you want a mathematical treatment of this subject (including the Dempster–Shafer theory), then this is for you.

Munakata, T. and Y. Jani (1994) 'Fuzzy systems: an overview', *Communications of the ACM*, **37** (3), 69–76.
> An excellent short tutorial of the theory, applications, and literature on fuzzy systems.

Rothman, P. (1989) 'Selecting on uncertainty management', *AI Expert*, **4** (7), 56–62.
> An excellent overview of the subject with a judicious sprinkling of codes, tables, and membership functions.

Sibigtroth, J. M. (1992) 'Implementing fuzzy expert rules in hardware', *AI Expert*, **7** (4), 25–31.
> This article has no surprises on content. It offers what the title advertises and does it well.

Silverman, Barry G. (ed.) (1987) *Expert Systems for Business*, Addison Wesley, Reading MA.
> Chapter 5 is on 'Fuzzy Knowledge in Rule-based Systems' and discusses five systems designed for a decision support system.

Ton, B. E., R. Goeltz and C. Travis (1992) 'Eliciting reliable uncertainty estimates', *Expert Systems*, **9** (1), 25–33.
> A study which suggests that knowledge engineers 'should endeavour to have experts express their uncertainty estimates using consistent modalities'.

Whinston, A. B. and C. W. Holsapple (1987) *Business Expert Systems*, Richard D. Irwin, Homewood, IL.
> This book is an introduction to ESs but has some excellent technical material in it like Chapter 11 on 'Manipulating Fuzzy Variables'.

Zadeh, L. A. (1965) 'Fuzzy sets', *Information and Control*, **8** (3), 338–353.

This article has about a page and a half of prose and the rest is set notation. You are not expected to read let alone absorb the text but it is recommended that you hold the article and feel its import.

Zadeh, L. A. (1984) 'Making computers think like people', *IEEE Spectrum*, **21** (8), 26–32.
This article was written for an engineering journal but is addressed to the layman and is an excellent survey of fuzzy systems including predictions of future uses for fuzzy systems.

Zadeh, L. A. (1992) *Fuzzy Logic for the Management of Uncertainty*. Wiley, New York.
This book was written some three decades after the author wrote his seminal paper on fuzzy logic. It is no longer addressed to the mathematician or the engineer but to the end-user. It certainly does not lack authority or clarity.

Zadeh, L. A. (1994) 'Fuzzy logic, neural networks, and soft computing', *Communications of the ACM*, **37** (3), 77–86.
Only for the reader comfortable with mathematics.

11

INTERFACES

Computers have promised us a fountain of wisdom but delivered a
flood of data.
A frustrated management executive

The user is always right. . . . Know thy user, for he is not thyself.
Richard Rubenstein and Harry Hersh

INTRODUCTION

Besides a knowledge-base and the inference engine, we need two sets
of interfaces: one at the front end to access the knowledge-base and
the other at the back end to access the inference engine. The
interfaces are software packages. The front-end interface is for the
developer and the back-end interface is for the end-user who may not
only wish to get expert advice but may demand explanations and
justifications interactively. The end-user may even want to specify the
format of the output and other facilities expected of a user-friendly
system. But both the front-end and the back-end interfaces go
through the systems interface, one that facilitates access to other
software and to the system hardware (CPU and knowledge-base). The
systems interface may also include considerations of security. These
interfaces are shown in the overview of the system in Fig. 11.1 and
are the subject of this chapter.

We will also discuss the need to humanize interfaces and the development methodologies for the different interfaces.

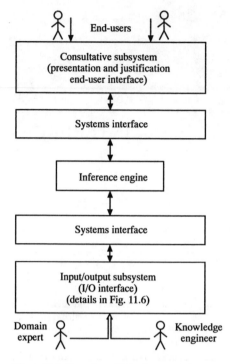

Figure 11.1 Overview of interfaces.

DEVELOPMENT INTERFACE

In the development phase, both the knowledge engineer and the expert can be helped by aids that edit, debug, and structure the knowledge presented. These aids are listed in Fig. 11.2. Some non-obvious ones are discussed below.

An editor is a recognized aid for database construction. It is called an editor, but often it also validates syntax and the general format of the rules being entered or manipulated. For a knowledge-base there is another facility called *automatic bookkeeping* which automatically keeps a record of the new entries and changes made to the facts and rules that constitute the knowledge-base. The record-keeper identifies the person making the changes and records his or her name, together with the date and the changes he or she made. This is a log that is useful for future reference, when, say, we wish to determine the rationale behind a particular change that was made in the past.

Another editing facility is the screen editor. This, however, is activated by the user interface or controls the user's screen format and contents. The

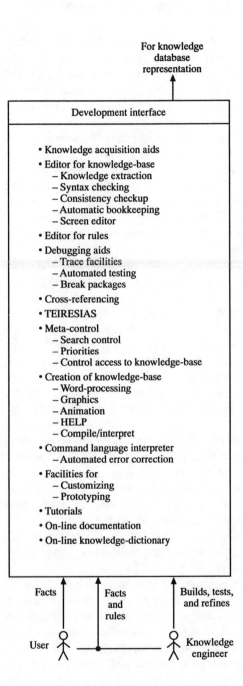

Figure 11.2 Development of interface aids.

program for controlling the screen layout is constructed in the developmental phase, as are the programs for the knowledge-base and the inference engine. These programs for the editing, debugging, and I/O facilities are a major component of the *programming environment*. We shall examine some specific, but general-purpose, programming environments in Chapter 15.

Another developmental interface function is checking for consistency in the knowledge-base (e.g. does an inference from one rule contradict an inference from another?). A new addition to the knowledge-base is checked against the existing knowledge. Typically, this checking is a heuristic strategy, as exhaustive checking of all possible inconsistencies is not possible for large knowledge-bases. The checking facility may simply report a detected inconsistency or indicate the reason it occurs, or even suggest what might be done to correct the problem.

In general, this is a difficult, but important problem, and the more ambitious checking facilities are state-of-the-art AI systems in their own right. One of the more ambitious attacks on this problem was the TEIRESIAS system. It contained and exploited *metaknowledge*—i.e. knowledge about the knowledge-base being developed. It knew, for example, the usual 'pattern' of certain classes of rule, and so it could check the structure of a new rule against these 'patterns'. When it found a mismatch, it would then query the user to ensure that the structure of the new rule was indeed correct. But a robust and reliable facility, with the power of TEIRESIAS, is still a future event for which the practising ES developer will have to wait.

There are other debugging facilities for assisting in the development of a knowledge-base. One is *tracing*, which identifies an action that has been initiated by a rule and displays it on the screen. A *break package* can stop the program at specified points so that the crucial values can be examined before continuing (general facilities to support this sort of exploratory system development are described and illustrated in Chapter 15, in the context of the particular programming environments in which they occur). *Automated testing* of rules, against some benchmark problems, can also be provided by certain developmental facilities.

Other features of a *development interface* should include facilities for creating a knowledge-base which includes capabilities of word-processing, graphics, and even a HELP routine for a new developer or an old developer who has forgotten the features of this KBS. The ability to compile or interpret a program will be part of the command language with automated error corrections. At the developers' level it is not crucial that the command structure be very high-level and close to the human language, as it is in the presentation module, but familiarity with the language used will be important not only in the development phase but also in the maintenance stages. Furthermore, the command structure should have basic capabilities, including predicates like IF, THEN, AND, OR, ELSE, and some of their combinations.

One is not restricted in the level of the programming language in the development interface as one is in the presentation module. The user of the development interface is often a computer professional and may actually prefer a third-generation language as opposed to a fourth-generation language which is likely to be preferred by a expert non-computer end-user. We will have more to say about programming languages and programming environments in later chapters.

Facilities for prototyping become important, especially in interactive systems, as does the need for customizing. Again, these are more important in the presentation module but the problems are different. For example, *customizing* in the presentation module may be important at the personal level, such as addressing the user by name, but in the development stage customizing may mean using terminology and acronyms familiar to the client organization and in the industry. Such customization will not only make the system more accurate and relevant but will also help to win over the end-user.

Tutorials and *documentation* are important in a KBS as in any computer system but again the problems are somewhat unique. The developer is a knowledge engineer, a computer professional well versed in AI and KBSs and may find it a waste of time if not an insult to be tutored on simple computer concepts which may be important in a presentation module. But tutoring on the domain could be both useful and important to the knowledge engineer. Documentation will be important for maintenance and refinement of the system not just by another engineer but also for the knowledge engineer who has designed the system but has designed other systems meanwhile and may need to refer back to the documentation even if it is his or her own. The importance of documentation cannot be overemphasized: countless software systems have had to be abandoned or redeveloped because the documentation was inadequate (incomplete, or complete but badly written) to support the system.

An *on-line knowledge dictionary* is very useful especially in large knowledge-bases. It could be made more accessible and useful with indexes (KWIC or KWOC, key-word-in or out-of-context) and Hypertext. A rule-variable (or condition) and variable-rule index as well as the identification of associations and dependencies can also be most helpful not just in tracing paths to conclusions but in the testing, debugging, and maintenance phases of the system. Some systems provide a graphic representation of the inferencing paths, as in a tree representation which can be a very important complement to textual explanations.

A summary of aids and features of a development interface is shown in Fig. 11.2.

END-USER INTERFACE

There are two important components of the user interface software:

- Input/output facilities.
- Explanation and justification.

Input/Output Facilities

The input/output facility allows the user to:

1. Ask questions.
2. Change the knowledge-base.

Changing the knowledge-base while on-line may be necessary, depending on what current information is available to the user. The MYCIN system allowed this and even encouraged it through a menu subsystem.

Asking questions may be simple, one-way communication. Alternatively, it may be part of a continuing sequence of interaction, where the answers and expert advice for one question may lead on to others. Thus, the output leads to more input (questions) until the user is satisfied.

The system may give prompts or ask for more information. The user need not be intimidated; if he or she feels imposed upon, the user may demand to know why the particular prompt has appeared or why the system needs further information. Such questions on prompts and input (as with output) can be asked during the consultations or afterwards.

Besides straightforward textual questions there may be questions that need to be intermixed with graphics or spreadsheets or even results from some DSS model. Also, the graphics may be straightforward high-resolution display images or they be moving results from a simulation. The output facility should be able to cope with such non-standard modes of enquiry.

The output needs to be controlled for standard procedures, or for pruning purposes, or for security purposes. Control for security can be at the level of the data type or type of access, or could be at a much lower and deeper level such as the data-element level. This is technologically possible but causes an increase in processing time and response time. The cost may be worth paying because in some KBSs the output can be very valuable to a competitor who may well attempt some industrial espionage and try to penetrate the system. Hence unauthorized access or misuse of output must be controlled and even audited. Security control may be the responsibility of the systems interface or the end-user interface or both.

An interface for input should allow for on-line and sometimes even real-time run input. Keeping such input within the bounds of format constraints is not as difficult as it is for input entered by a human. The human may need a great deal of hand-holding compared to an input clerk in a transaction system. In contrast to the transactional input clerk, the person providing input for a KBS is not trained in input preparation and is also perhaps a professional though casual user of computers. Such a person needs assistance through HELP routines, cases, examples, and tutorials. The importance of tutorials and documentation has been mentioned earlier in connection with the development interface; these areas are just as valid and important for the input interfaces and a shade less important for output interfaces.

There are some requirements for interfaces that apply to both input and output with equal importance. One is the word-processing and editing capabilities of the interface. With the increasing popularity of PCs, almost everyone is now acquainted with, and even addicted to, WIMP capability (windows, icons, menus and pointers, e.g. mouse). Without WIMP capability an interface will almost certainly be considered 'unfriendly' by many end-users of a KBS. And even within the WIMP configuration there will be additional demands such as not just menus but pull-down and pop-up menus. For windowing systems there may be demands for colour as well as for a specific number of windows.

Screen editing is also necessary along with default options as well as error-checking facilities. Screen design for various I/O format options may also be desirable and the designer should try and keep the soft image format and procedures similar to and consistent with those for the hard copy to which the end-user is accustomed. In this way the shock caused to end-users from having to adapt to too many changes is reduced.

The software for responding to I/O needs or explanations is accessed through an interface unit. There are four basic methods for interfacing:

1. Menu driven (where the user makes a choice from a set of alternatives presented in a menu).
2. Command oriented (where the user enters a programming command or instruction to elicit a desired computer response).
3. Natural-language based (where the commands are in a natural language, not a programming language).
4. Customized (where the interface structure and details are specifically designed for a particular user, or small class of users)

The choice of which method to adopt is determined by the type and the sophistication of the user (not to mention the budget and commercial importance of the system). The interfaces that are command or menu driven, or that handle natural language, often come as part of an ES

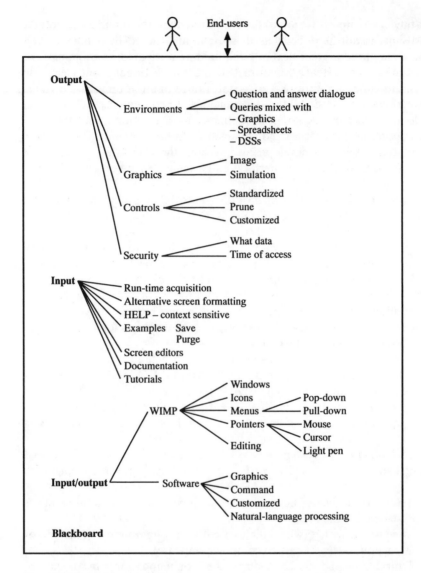

Figure 11.3 Input/output interfaces.

package. If this is not the case, the system must be customized to meet the user's needs, which provides the opportunity to meet any special needs of the particular user group under consideration.

Most I/O facilities are concerned with presenting output that is easy to comprehend and assimilate. These facilities are outlined in Fig. 11.3. The options offered vary greatly with different systems. The ES GURU supports over 100 environmental variables (i.e. values that can be set by a specific user to customize the resultant system); each such variable has a default value, so that the user need only explicitly set those of particular interest. In addition to such options, systems typically offer utilities, e.g. for formatting output or testing individual rules. GURU offers 50 such utilities. The utilities and environmental variables offer the user a high level of control in tailoring and monitoring the user environment.

Another feature of the I/O interface, one that is not visible to the developer but essential to the working of the system, is the *blackboard*. It is much like a blackboard in the office of a knowledge engineer who keeps a list of things to be done and the priorities for each task identified. Such a blackboard needs to be internal to the system for tasks to be scheduled and performed. These tasks are then assigned to different units to be performed, as for example, the following;

1. *The plan*—This lists goals and objectives that must be achieved and strategies for achieving them.
2. The agenda—A record of actions that need to be taken. In a rule-based system, it would be the production rules and actions awaiting execution.
3. The solutions—Intermediate results of decisions, answers, and conclusions that have been completed but await other decisions or actions.

Features of the I/O interfaces are summarized in Fig. 11.3.

Explanation and Justification

One of the most useful features of ES technology for the business manager (or any non-computer expert) is that such systems can be instructed to explain their reasoning at any time. Many ESs are said to exhibit a *self-explanation capability*, i.e. when asked to do so, they can generate an explanation of the chain of reasoning employed on a specific problem. It is typically possible for the user to ask both '*how?*' and '*why?*' in appropriate circumstances.

It is appropriate to ask a '*how?*' question after the system has generated some result. The system response will be to show you the specific rules which led to that result. Thus, if the stock management system says that commodity X should be stocked in quantities not exceeding 500 and restocked when the stocked quantity falls below 50, you can ask 'How was this conclusion reached?' The system might then begin its explanation with:

Rule 677 says that
IF the commodity is perishable AND sells in low volume AND is a medium profit commodity
THEN maximum stock should be 500

This begins to explain part of the system's stock management decision, but you might be curious why the system concluded that commodity X 'sells in low volume' and what this actually means. Then you might ask the further question:

WHY sells in low volume?

which causes the response:

Rule 45 says that
IF the commodity is priced at less than £50 per unit AND average weekly sales are less than 100
THEN it sells in low volume

And this sort of dialogue can continue, allowing the user to probe the reasoning behind a specific decision.

In addition to the 'why?' (for relevance) and 'how?' (for reasoning path) question, there is also the 'what?' question (for paraphrasing). Example 'what?' questions occur where the end-user asks for a clarification such as 'What is the meaning of the question being asked?' or 'What are the facts for this rule?' Note that the 'what?' and 'how?' questions are for explanation while the 'why?' question is for *justification*. This module, then, is for both explanation and justification but more for explanations, and hence for brevity it will be referred to as just the 'explanation interface'.

Other questions that may well be asked are the 'what if?' question for *simulation* where one may change a whole set of parameters, variables, or relationships; or questions for *sensitivity analysis* where one is concerned with the sensitivity of one parameter or variable.

One interesting feature that is often desirable is the ability to change previous decisions and answers without having to rerun the entire problem all over again and then compare the results before and after the changes. In such cases as well as situations of simulation and sensitivity analysis it is important to have the ability to *save* results.

In receiving results, explanations, or justifications, it is desirable that the responses are *customized*. This will help somewhat to reduce the alienation caused by the perception that computer systems are impersonal. The customized response is greatly appreciated by end-users, especially the casual user. We discussed customizing for the development interface. Here the customizing can be more personal. For example, the name of the end-user when the user logs-on is recognized by the system and its responses are addressed to the user by name. A good profile of the end-user stored as part of the dictionary would tell the title and sex of user, which would make the personal addressing acceptable if not flattering. Also the text may be personalized to meet the end-user's preferences and even idiosyncrasies. For example, the mathematically oriented person may not want the words 'greater than' spelled out and would prefer the mathematical symbol '>', likewise this end-user may well wish to use the symbol in all input instead of having to spell out the corresponding words. The mathematical symbols, however, if used for all end-users may make the system appear too formal, and thus unfriendly and annoying.

It is important to recognize that for a presentation interface, unlike the development interface, the user will not always be a technical person. The end-users will often be a mix of professionals with a strong mathematical and computer background as well as persons who are novices in mathematics and computers, and perhaps casual users of the system.

This mix of capabilities (and even attitudes) is important when using word-processing capabilities. The users of the presentation interface (end-users of the system) are a far more heterogeneous group than, say, the users of the development interface. Some of these end-users want default values and detailed menus at many levels, while other end-users will object to too many defaults and long menus unless they have the ability to jump around in the menu. Thus the needs and preferences of the end-user can vary greatly and any interface for such end-users must be very flexible in the demands made by and on the end-user. The same problem applies to HELP routines, which must anticipate the need for help on all sorts of problems, technical as well as mundane. A really friendly system will only assume that you know how to switch the system on, and thereafter will size you up and respond at your level for your needs.

Tutorials and documentation are important, as they are for the development interface. The difference is that the needs of the end-user are more varied. The documentation must be at a level that does not insult or bore the professional and yet is comprehensible and interesting to the lay person.

A summary of the capabilities of an explanation and justification interface is shown in Fig. 11.4. Listed but not discussed is the natural-language processing (NLP) capability. NLP is not yet a common capability for the presentation interface but has great potential There is a great need for a natural-language interface for any KBS. Natural-language processing is not so important for the development interface but it is of great importance for the end-user who may be a highly trained and educated in the domain but has not the appropriate attitude for computers, especially in preparing inputs. An NLP interface for natural language input, also called the *natural-language interface (NLI)*, is not as sophisticated as some would like but it is making great strides forward in applications other than KBISs. NLI has great potential for any KBIS and hence it will be discussed briefly below.

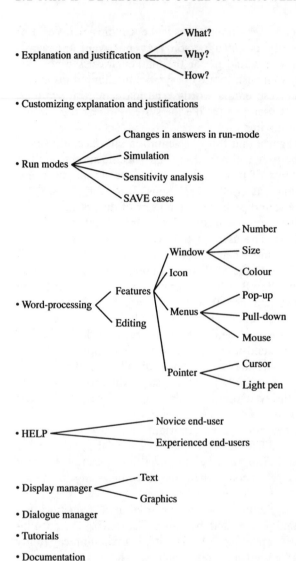

Figure 11.4 Explanation and justification facilities.

Natural-language interfaces

An NLI system is a module that is positioned between the computer, which is capable of performing some useful task (e.g. an accounting task) by virtue of the existence of another piece of software also resident inside the machine, and a human being who wishes to utilize the machine's capability without having first to learn a special language. An NLI system makes the computer appear to be capable of communicating in a human language, usually English.

These systems typically recognize some very restricted subset of English and generate more or less prepackaged responses. So the potential user of such a system has to learn to use only a small and well-defined subset of English, which appears to be a very acceptable substitute for many people. If you know what information some database contains and what sort of service it was designed to give, then the scope of reasonable questions is quite limited (when compared to all the things that can be said in English).

Nevertheless, the current reality is that many companies are developing NLI systems, and there is no shortage of prospective purchasers. It may be that the crudity of current NLI systems is such that they quickly destroy any conception that a user might have that communication can proceed in a human way. As NLI systems become more sophisticated, we may well see the problems of misinterpretation grow to challenge the simplistic view of NLI system design.

As an example, we can consider the INTELLECT system. INTELLECT, developed by Artificial Intelligence Corporation (AIC) of Waltham, Massachusetts, is a program that allows a manager to get information from a computer without having to ask a computer expert for help. People who work with computers every day quickly master the rules for using a computer. That is, they learn the codes they need, how to program commands, how to work through menus, and so forth. Managers who are occasional computer users, however, seldom know how to get information they want from a computer. INTELLECT, a product of extensive AI research, is programmed for them.

INTELLECT takes an English-language request typed in by the user and translates this request into a form that the computer can process, taking into account the peculiarities of the database being queried. This may sounds easy, but it isn't. The computer must have knowledge about the user's intention and background in order to make this translation. For example, if a manager types, 'What is the average earnings of the salesmen in New York?' the program must be able to determine from the database that New York has two meanings, city and state. It must, then respond by asking the manager which one he or she is referring to.

Each time INTELLECT is sold for a commercial application, a dictionary of appropriate vocabulary is developed by AIC and added to the program. This may even include corporate slang. Ford Motor Co. uses INTELLECT to handle questions about which cars have met which environmental rules. Du Pont uses it to handle questions about sales and production of polymers and resins. INTELLECT is successful because it operates in a limited domain. It cannot understand natural language outside that domain.

Back to the basics of the presentation and justification interface. Whether there is an NLI or not, the presentation and justification interface does perform many important functions. It does offer definitions on terms and concepts besides clarifications and elaborations through the HELP routine. On request, it identifies facts and heuristics and paths of reasoning that lead to each set of conclusions, thereby increasing the confidence of the end-user in the integrity of the system and the soundness in its reasoning strategies and capabilities. This increase of confidence in KBSs is important if such systems are to be accepted and commonly used.

The presentation interface also keeps the end-user informed, when requested, of the status of the system at all times, including where the system is in its computation sequence. The knowledge of the status and the ability of end-users to question the system for explanations and justifications on any question that they may have gives the perception that the end-users are in command. This feeling of self assurance can be very important to many end-users.

Another function of the presentation interface is to transfer information about the system; this is why it can be used very successfully for the training of both a new end-user and a knowledge engineer who is new to the system. The interface has been found to be surprisingly helpful during maintenance, especially when enhancing the system.

These functions of the presentation and justification interface are summarized in Table 11.1. The need and justification for having to

Table 11.1 Functions performed by the presentation and justification interface

- Through HELP routine, provides definitions on
  —Terms
  —Concepts
- Identifies facts, heuristics, and strategies that led to conclusions
- Identifies reasoning paths
- Helps understanding by proving examples
- Increases confidence in the integrity of the system and the soundness of reasoning capabilities
- Increases confidence in the use of KBSs
- Increases acceptance of the system
- Informs end-user of current status of systems operations
- Gives end-user the perception of being in control of the system
- Used for transferring information about the system, i.e. used for training of
  —End-user
  —Knowledge engineer
- Facilitates maintenance of the system

humanize interfaces and make them user-friendly will now be discussed, followed by a discussion of the systems interface.

JUSTIFICATION FOR HUMANIZING INTERFACES

In the early days of computing, users had to do what the computer system required; this was often very demanding, inconvenient, and sometimes even seemed like harassment. There were many occasions when the user did not have the option of taking what seemed an easier way to navigate through the system because the system just would not allow it. All that is changing and changing fast. Perhaps it was the backlash from the user, perhaps it was the increasing capability and flexibility of computer systems, but partly it is due to a change in the attitude of the computer industry. The industry now recognizes that systems should be developed for the user and not require that the end-user mould to the computer system. Information systems must now be 'user-friendly' and must be tolerant of user-errors. Systems must also be physically convenient and comfortable to use, which leads to ergonomically designed systems. They should also be psychologically easy to use, which has led to the discipline of *human factors*. *Ergonomics* and human factors are converging in their practices and the objective is the same: to make computer systems easy to use, and eliminate or at least reduce *computer anxiety* and technostress for the user. This anxiety and technostress can be partially reduced by making the work environment and equipment safe, comfortable, and not contributing to fatigue. The height of the chair, the angle of the computer screen, the distance of the screen from the chair, and the level of the arm when entering data can all be adjusted ergonomically to make the work area comfortable and less exhausting.

An extension to the definition of a user-friendly and *humanized* information system is that there must be fun and pleasure in using it. The system should not be just a way to save time and money and do required tasks, but instead should give the user control and power over the system. Why should an end-user not feel the power and derive pleasure as do those who play computer games? Developers must learn to ratchet the level of difficulty incrementally upwards, ensuring that the user is always challenged but never overwhelmed. The user must be encouraged to experiment and explore without the terrifying fear of losing data or not knowing what is happening. The user must enjoy using the system, each step forward being greeted, say, with colourful screen displays. The end-user, as in a computer game, must be posed with new challenges, hard enough to keep the processing interesting without it becoming unpalatable. This can bring pleasure and even excitement by supplementing the human mind. The potential for computer-induced enjoyment—like that for human creativity—is essentially boundless.

Ben Shneiderman (1987) suggests eight underlying principles that should govern all interface design:

1. Strive for consistency of format, terminology, and commands.
2. Enable frequent users to use short cuts such as abbreviations, function keys, and macro facilities.
3. Provide feedback to the user of effects of actions initiated.
4. Design dialogues to yield closure.
5. Offer simple error handling.
6. Permit easy reversal of actions
7. Give users the sense of control.
8. Design displays with short-term memory load in mind.

One could add to Shneiderman's list of design considerations for interfaces such as the following:

- Design messages carefully.
- Design menus that are not too detailed or too short.
- Provide appropriate defaults.
- Design systems procedures that are tolerant.
- Design response times that will not annoy the end-user.
- Design dialogues that are user-friendly.

Each of the above suggestions for design needs elaboration but that would take us beyond the scope of this book. However, to give the reader a flavour of the details involved, we list a few guidelines for the design of user-friendly dialogues in Table 11.2.

SYSTEMS INTERFACES

Besides interfacing with humans, both developers and end-users, there is the problem of interfacing with the system itself. This involves software that facilitates the interface with hardware, knowledge and databases, and other software.

We will discuss the hardware needed for a knowledge-base in the next chapter, including a disscussion of the specialized CPU hardware needed. Not all CPU needs will be examined for much is almost in the public domain as is the personal computer. The PC, and more generally the microcomputer, is a very important platform for a KBS as evidenced by a survey done in 1992 which showed that over 70 per cent of the reported ES

Table 11.2 Guidelines for user-friendly interactive dialogues

• Offer flexibility in the formatting of input	• Report errors without opinions attached
• Allow abbreviations and acronyms for frequently used data	• Report errors in context and with clues to errors
• Provide examples of input options	• Report errors politely
• Explain any interpretations of data	• Avoid using error codes or references to manual of codes
• Allow use of pointer instead of keys	• Offer on-line HELP routines
• Allow 'jumping' in menus	• Integrate HELP routines with error processing
• Allow short-cuts in processing and navigating	• Use examples to illustrate HELP
• Minimize conceptual load	• Provide clearly marked EXITS
• Avoid clutter of information	• HELP should not interfere with accomplishing current task
• Information content should be confirmed	• Do not ever criticize user
• Defaults used should be identified	• Do not ever blame user
• Use feedback when welcomed	• Delay time should be minimized
• Spring no surprises on user	• Responses should not take more than 5–10 seconds
• Use colours but do not go overboard	• Delays should be predicted when possible
• Select colours judiciously	• Delays should be explained
• Use graphics to supplant and supplement text	• Provide examples, provide more examples
• Use voice only in highly structured environments	• Test dialogues with peers of user, and test again and again
• Select 'friendly' voices	• Screen must always indicate what is happening

used microcomputers (Stylianou *et al.*, 1992: 40). However, for larger systems we will need a more powerful hardware base, such as a minicomputer, a mainframe, a specialized LISP machine, or a workstation.

In selecting software for the systems interface, the following choices need to be made: customizing the software with a programming language of choice, using a programming environment, or using a shell. These choices are discussed in a later chapter, which is followed by a chapter on the selection of available programming languages.

The next problem is the selection of hook-ups to other systems, which may be other programming languages, knowledge-bases (internal or external to the organization), or a conventional corporate information system in which the KBS is to be embedded.

Finally, we have the considerations of security in the systems interface. These were mentioned in the discussion of the presentation interface, but security is such an important issue that it requires consideration at the systems level, especially when the knowledge involved is of a sensitive and propriety nature.

A considerable measure towards keeping users from inspecting the knowledge base can be achieved by allowing them access to a compiled version of the knowledge base. Several other forms of protection can also be available such as encryption, passwords and read/write privileges. The availability of multiple-level passwords is important in cases where various classes of users with different authorizations and privileges exist.   (Stylianou *et al.*, 1992: 41)

A summary of considerations for systems interfaces is shown in Fig. 11.5.

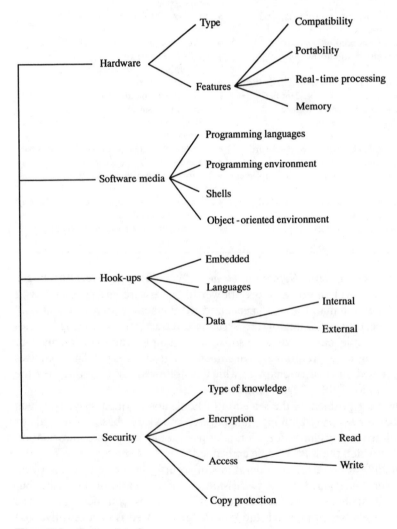

Figure 11.5   Systems Interface.

DEVELOPMENT METHODOLOGY

The development methodology used, whether it be the systems development lifecycle (SDLC) or prototyping or some automated approach, will depend on the type of problem being coded and developed. Thus far in a KBIS we have encountered at least four types of problems that need to be coded: the knowledge-base, the inference mechanism, or the inference engine; the I/O interface; the end-user interface; and the systems interface. The knowledge-base coding is typically part of the development of the subsystem of creating the knowledge-base, which includes knowledge acquisition and representation. Thus could be a set of activities that need to be scheduled and controlled through an SDLC. An SDLC could also be used for the inference engine and the I/O interface and the systems interface. In each of these cases, it is software that has to be developed and each has its own lifecycle for software development. However, in the case of the inference engine prototyping may well be used. Why? Because the inference engine is not always a structured situation where you 'design before you begin to implement' as in a knowledge-base or systems interface development. Instead, it is a situation where you are representing someone else's knowledge, which may not be fully understood or appreciated before you have to begin. You have to design and implement at the same time and to do so interactively. This is where prototyping becomes desirable.

Prototyping is also desirable for the end-user interface, but for a very different reason. Here, it is the end-user who is not known or not understood adequately. The end-user's needs and preferences for an interface are not known to the end-user let alone the knowledge engineer who is designing and implementing systems. This is an excellent application for prototyping where a solution is designed and implemented with the active involvement of the end-user(s) who would accept or reject the solution. If rejected, as often happens in *rapid* and *throw-away prototyping*, then the solution is thrown away and another implemented through intensive involvement and interaction between the knowledge engineer and the end-user(s). However, evolutionary prototyping is usually more productive. In this style of development certain aspects of the prototype are rejected, and the reasons for rejection form a basis for 'evolving' the next prototype.

SUMMARY AND CONCLUSIONS

A summary of the interface considerations for a KBIS are shown in Fig. 11.6.

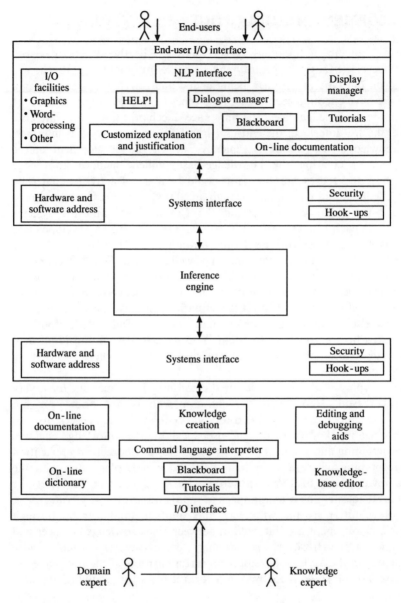

Figure 11.6 Summary of Interfaces.

The importance of interfaces can be gauged by looking at a survey ranking some 86 factors considered in the selection of shells. Those criteria related to interfaces are listed in Table 11.3. We assume that the criteria for shells are also appropriate for a KBIS. Nineteen of these 86 criteria (around

Table 11.3 Ranking of topics relating to interfaces among criteria for selecting shells

Criteria	Ranking
Embeddability	1
Rapid prototyping	2
Explanation facility	4
Linking to databases	5
Ability to customize explanations	6
Documentation	7
Linking to languages	12
Customizable features	15
Colour/windows/menus	18
Compatibility with existing systems	19
Linkage to special software	24
Tutorial/sample KBS	29
Access to underlying software	31
Mouse/icons support	55
Blackboard system	69
Sensitivity analysis	74
Natural-language interface (NLI)	75
Access to special hardware	81
Speech I/O	86

Notes: The total number of criteria considered was 86.
  ~ Ninety per cent of the sample of 631 were taken from the subscription list of *AI Expert*.
  The source of this table is Stylianou *et al.* (1992: 36).

22 per cent) are related to interfaces and include the two extremes: the most important (embeddability) and the least important (speech I/O). The low ranking of speech and voice processing is understandable because voice is not crucial as it is for input in the case of some assembly operations where both hands are occupied. The low ranking of NLIs is surprising but understandable if one recognizes that the sample for this survey were mostly AI personnel. If this survey had included end-users, then the ranking of NLI would most likely have been higher. Its importance will increase as more end-users and managers demand NLP for most of their interactions with computers, be they for a KBIS or any other information system.

Another change in the future will be that systems will have to be humanized and end-user friendly. Yet another change will be the demand for more explanation and justification interfaces. This type of interface engineered by AI through its development of ES technology is very important in that it has increased the credibility of AI products in particular and problem solving in general. In conventional systems, like a DSS, and even in transactional systems the system was treated as a black box either because the modeller was unable to explain or justify the model and its assumptions, or because the end-user was unable (or perceived to be unable) to understand what was being explained. Now all this has changed. The end-user is now encouraged to ask any question of the system and demand any explanation or justification, and to do so without any inhibitions or pressures from the overbearing technical analyst. The tracing routine has given the end-user the ability to trace the path of a solution and see the results as they develop. This capability is especially useful in simulation models where more than one variable or parameter can be changed and the consequences cannot otherwise be easily isolated.

Systems of problem solving, even a technical ES or a KBS, can now be explained and justified. This will greatly increase confidence in such systems; remove much of the mystique surrounding them; decrease the alienation of such systems; increase the chances of acceptance of the system; and increase the comfort level of the end-user not just for a KBIS but for all problem-solving systems.

Concluding the discussion of interfaces, we have examined the detailed design and implementation of the last subsystem of a KBIS. Once these subsystems are tested satisfactorily, they are ready for the systems test, the subject of our next chapter.

CASE 11.1 A FINNISH BANKING EXPERT SYSTEM— 2: INTERFACES

Matias is an ES developed by the Okobank in Finland to provide fast service for farmers in need of long-term, low-interest loans. The traditional wait of 2–3 weeks of processing a loan application was reduced to 15 minutes and the quality of decisions was also improved.

The Matias system consists of 350 rules divided into approximately 40 knowledge-bases and runs on MS-DOS with 60 kbytes of memory. A shell, Xi Plus, was used but since this was 1987/88, the shell was new and a large number of bugs were discovered which were fixed quickly with the help of the shell's vendor.

The development required 3 man-years of effort. The schedule for the project was as follows:

First prototype developing inference rules	4 months
Evaluation of prototype and detailed project planning	4 months
Knowledge acquisition, knowledge-base design, and implementation	4 months
Interface design and implementation and systems testing	6 months

Source: J. Konito (1991) 'Matias: development and maintenance of a large but well defined application', *Expert Systems with Applications*, **3** 241–248.

Questions

1. There is no development interface in this application. Why do you think this is the case? Would you recommend a development interface, and if so, explain why.
2. The end-user interface is developed (designed and implemented) in parallel with the systems test. Do you think that systems testing should be de-coupled from interfaces? Explain why.
3. Should the interfaces (for development and for end-users) be tested before the systems test. Why?
4. What should be the components of the interface for the following?
   (*a*) Development.
   (*b*) End-user.
5. Should the interfaces be developed (and tested) separately or together?
6. How long do you think it would take and what effort (in human-hours) would be required for the development of the two interfaces.

REVIEW AND DISCUSSION QUESTIONS

11.1 Is the development interface crucial to a KBIS? If, yes, why? If no, why again?

11.2 What aids in the development interface do you consider crucial? Why and to whom?

11.3 Would you use TIERESIAS? Why? When?

11.4 What is the relevance of the following tools to a KBS?
   (*a*) Tracing.
   (*b*) Break package.
   (*c*) Automated testing.

11.5 How would you use meta-knowledge? Give an example.

11.6 Who uses a development interface? When and why in each case? Is it used only in initial development of a system? If not, when is it also used?

11.7 Who is a user and an end-user in a KBS?

11.8 What is the best end-user interface? Why?

11.9 Why is a NLI not common for a KBIS? What is its potential use for a KBIS?

11.10 Should a NLI be used for input or output or both? Explain.

11.11 Is voice processing relevant to a KBIS? Explain.

11.12 How is the presentation and justification interface different from the following?
   (*a*) Conventional data-processing systems.
   (*b*) Decision support systems.

11.13 What is the difference between the presentation and the justification functions. How does it affect the efficiency or effectiveness of a KBIS?

11.14 In which interface should prototyping be used and why?

11.15 Does a presentation and justification interface make the KBIS a user-friendly system? Why?

11.16 Identify the five most important features that make a system end-user friendly? Explain.

11.17 Is the system's interface important? Should it be customized or should it be what the hardware manufacturer offers?

11.18 Rank the five most important features of interfaces. Explain your rankings.

11.19 Can a presentation interface be designed to make it end-user friendly to one type of end-user or all types of end-users? Explain the problems involved? Give examples. What are the dangers and limitations in designing a system that is of general relevance to all end-users?

11.20 Why should a KBIS explain the why, how, and what of its inference-making process? What are the limitations of such explanations?

11.21 What do you think of the results (other than the extreme values) of the survey for selecting shells as they affect interfaces?

EXERCISE

Look at the book *Information Anxiety* by Richard Saul Wurman (Doubleday, New York 1989). Comment on whether you think the conventional end-user interface in a KIBS contributes to the reduction of computer anxiety. How can computer anxiety be reduced in a KBIS?

Wurman defines 'anxiety' as being 'the black hole between data and knowledge, and it happens when information doesn't tell us what we want to need to know'. Do you agree with Wurman's definitions of knowledge and 'information anxiety'? Would you like to extend the definition of 'information anxiety' as seen from the point of view of the end-user of a KBIS?

BIBLIOGRAPHY AND REFERENCES

Benbasat, I., F. J. Lim and P. Todd (1992) 'The user-interface in systems design', *Informatica*, **1** (1) 62–95.
   A superb tutorial on graphic, iconic, and direct manipulation interfaces. Has an extensive bibliography.

Berry, D. C. and D. E. Broadbent (1987) 'Expert systems and man–machine interface. Part two: the user interface', *Expert Systems*, **4** (1), 18–27.
   Looks at the 'cognitive aspects of user interface, including dialogue control, explanation facilities, user models, natural language processing and the effects of new technology'.

Berry, D. C. and A. Hart (1991) 'User interface standards for expert systems: are they appropriate?', *Expert Systems with Applications*, **2** (4), 245–250.
   The authors discuss both sides of an important and controversial topic.

Cleal, D. M. and N. O. Heaton (1988) *Knowledge-based Systems: Implications for Human–Computer Interfaces*, Ellis Horwood, Chichester.
   A good discussion of human–machine interactions.

Ellis, C. (ed.) (1989) *Expert Knowledge and Explanation*, Ellis Horwood, Chichester.
   This is a set of 12 papers 'concerned with the communication of knowledge and of explanations in the context of intelligent knowledge-based information systems'.

Hartson, H. R and D. Hix (1989) 'Human–computer interface development: concepts and systems for its management', *ACM Computing Surveys*, **21** (1), 5–92.
   This is long and old but a thorough and still relevant survey of human–computer interface management. Written from the computer science point of view, the article focuses on the

'process of developing quality human–computer interfaces, design, implementation, execution, evaluation and maintenance'. Also discussed are concepts of dialogue independence, structural modelling, interactive tools, rapid prototyping, and development methodologies and control structures.

Hartson, H. R. and D. Boehm-Davis (1993) 'User interface development processes and methodologies, *Behaviour and Information Technology*, **12** (2), 98–114.

The authors discuss ways in which one produces interfaces with increased usability.

Hendler, J. A. (ed.) (1988) *Expert Systems: The User Interface*, Ablex, Norwood, N.J.

A set of 13 contributions covering both general and specific topics. An 'old' book but still very relevant.

Hollsapple, C. W. and A. B. Whinston (1987) *Business Expert Systems*, Richard Irwin, Homewood, IL.

A good discussion of end-user interface in the chapter 'Invoking an Inference Engine'. The authors have also written a book on GURU.

Ishikawa, H., Y. Izumida, T. Yoshino, T. Hoshiai and A. Makinouchi (1987) 'KID: designing a knowledge-based natural language interface', *IEEE Expert*, **2** (2), 57–70.

The five co-authors are from the Fujitsu Laboratories in Japan and give some insights into NLI developments in Japan. The reader needs to be very comfortable with programming languages in order to enjoy this article.

Lamberti, D. M. and W. A. Wallace (1990) 'Intelligent interface design: an empirical assessment of knowledge presentation in expert systems', *MIS Quarterly*, **14** (3), 279–311.

Employee expertise, knowledge presentation format, question type, and task uncertainty 'are examined for employee problem solving and decision-making performance (speed and accuracy)'.

Preece, J. and L. Keller (eds) (1990) *Human–Computer Interaction*, Prentice Hall, Hemel Hempstead.

The collection is rather general and covers a wide area of human–computer interaction. The book is very functional for academicians as well as for practitioners.

Shneiderman, B. (1987) *Designing the User Interface: Strategies of Effective Human–Computer Interaction*, Addison-Wesley, Reading, MA.

The author has written many articles and books on the subject. He writes well and authoritatively so. This 1987 edition book is not the latest edition but currently the most accessible.

Southwick, R. W. (1991) 'Explaining reasoning: an overview of explanation in knowledge-based systems', *Knowledge Engineering Review*, **6** (1), 1–12.

Included is a discussion of theories of human discourse and explanation as well as issues that may well be 'increasingly important for future explanation systems'.

Stylianou, A. C., G. R. Madey and R. D. Smith (1992) 'Selection criteria for expert systems shells: a socio-technical framework', *Communications of the ACM*, **35** (10), 30–48.

The title does not do justice to the contents of this article. It not only has a good technical survey of the selection of shells but an excellent tutorial on KBSs.

Wexelblat, R. L. (1989) 'On interface requirements for expert systems', *AI Magazine*, **10**(3), 66–71.

The author discusses 'significant aspects of behaviour and user expectations are peculiar to expert systems and their users'.

12

THE DEVELOPMENT CYCLE—CONTINUED

Testing shows the presence, not the absence of bugs.
Dijkstra

WHEN DOES DEVELOPMENT END?

We have discussed the activities that led up to the implementation of the subsystems of a KBIS. But the implementation of this set of subsystems does not imply that the system is complete, even if the subsystems are tested satisfactorily. Certain activities that concern all subsystems must be designed and implemented. These activities are shown in the overview diagram in Fig. 12.1, discussed earlier but now extended to show the activity of documentation (100–890) (890–900 is a dummy activity).

The most important of these activities not yet discussed is that of organizational changes, which includes the activities of orientation and training. All these activities and subsystems then need to be tested as a system (700–800). Only when the system receives a satisfactory acceptance test by the end-user is it ready for final documentation, conversion (800–900), and operation (900-1000). Only then can the system development process be considered finished. Meanwhile, all these activities must be coordinated and managed by some project manager technique (300–900), which must be documented as part of the final documentation of the system. It is these topics that finish the project which are the subject of this chapter. We start with the organizational changes (300–700) necessary for implementing and operating a KBIS.

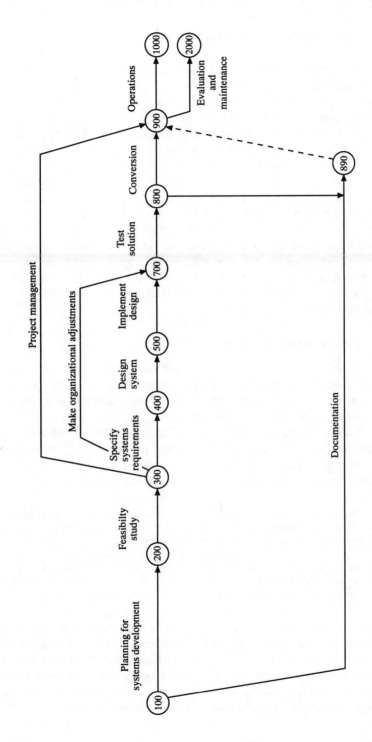

Figure 12.1 Development of a KBIS.

ORGANIZATIONAL CHANGES

The organizational changes required for a KBIS (activity 300–700 in Fig. 12.1) are similar to those faced by a transactional system or a DSS, except that they are more severe—e.g. there may be resistance from those who are non-mathematical and those who have anti-computer attitudes. But with an ES or a KBIS there may be an additional bias against AI—or just ignorance about it. One survey in the early 1990s in North America found that 94 per cent of chief executive officers had not heard of AI or consider it infeasible. This attitude has to be changed if a KBS is to be successfully accepted by an organization. Here we have a problem of education, which is in addition to the problem of training. Training for an ES and a KBS is more difficult and time consuming than for conventional information systems partly because there are now concepts of knowledge databases and knowledge-engineering methodology, new languages (e.g. LISP and object-oriented languages), and different hardware (e.g. specialized workstations and LISP processors). But all this is not insurmountable, especially if the difficulty is properly recognized and sensibly dealt with.

Organizational alternatives

One of the first acts of a project manager, in a large project such as a KBIS is to structure the project development teams. Several approaches to the organization of such teams are possible: organization by function, project organization, and matrix organization.

Functional organization generally keeps traditional line–staff relationships, with a vertical flow of authority and responsibility. For some projects this type of organization does not work well, because the projects require the cooperation and use of resources from many line units.

> The essence of project management is that it cuts across and, in a sense, conflicts with the natural organizational structure. . . . Because a project usually requires decisions and actions from a number of functional areas at once, the main interdependencies and the main flow of information in a project are not vertical but lateral. . . . Projects are characterized by exceptionally strong lateral relationships, requiring closely related activity and decisions by many individuals in different functional departments.   (Stewart, 1969: 295–296)

Project organization is the creation of a unit with responsibility for all aspects of project development. In this schema, professional, technical, and administrative staff are hired for the duration of the project. When systems development projects are organized in this manner, serious problems can arise in attracting competent personnel. Many AI personnel, domain experts, and computer professionals are unwilling to join projects of an AI type that offer no job security, and they dislike jobs of this nature because of the fluctuating workload.

A matrix organization combines functional and project approaches to project management. The staff is 'borrowed' from functional divisions. In the case of a KBIS development team, members might be drawn from operations research, management service including AI, and data-processing departments and end-users. Which employees are borrowed is negotiated by the project manager with functional department heads. The choice is usually based on the availability of personnel and the qualifications demanded by the project. Sometimes department heads are reluctant to release competent personnel. However, most recognize that having staff members assigned to the development team can be advantageous to them. Departmental interests are protected by having staff representatives on the team, and staff experience in the development process will be beneficial when future information systems for that department are planned.

One problem with matrix organization is that project members have two bosses. They are responsible to the project manager for work assignments, yet their permanent supervisors retain jurisdiction over personnel matters such as salary and promotions. The two bosses may clash in values and objectives, with the project member caught in between. Such potentially explosive situations can be defused if, before the team is constituted, ground rules are negotiated between the project manager and functional heads regarding shared authority and responsibility over project members.

In summary, a matrix organization is advantageous because it:

- Allows a project manager to cut across vertical organizational divisions.
- Involves functional departments and is responsive to their needs because of representatives are on the project staff.
- Has access to the resources in all functional departments (on a negotiated basis).
- Provides a 'home' for project personnel after the completion of the project.
- Does not permanently disrupt organizational subgroupings or the continuity of seniority, fringe benefits, and so on.

An example of matrix organization is shown in Table 12.1; it illustrates the concept that both individuals and departments may be assigned to development teams and may participate in several projects simultaneously.

Management style may be one factor in the choice of project organization. As shown in Fig. 12.2, a functional organization is appropriate when people are the primary concern of a project manager. Project organization is appropriate when more importance is placed on

Table 12.1 A project matrix for a KBIS system

	B19	B22	P35	P41
Management	A. Brown	D. Capron		
End-user		S. Power	S. Rich	S. Finch
OR/MS	W. Smith	W. Smith	OR/MS Dept.	R. Campbell
Systems analyst	A. Rogers	A. Rogers	J. Small	
Programmer	U. Hyder	D. Able		J. Maple
	B. Jones			
Knowledge engineer	F. Williams	L. Samuel	J. Wilks	
Domain expert	J. Adams	W. Hall		
DBA	E. Jones			
LISP programmer		B. Karshmer	J. M. Adams	
Telecom	R. Sullivan	B. Squires		

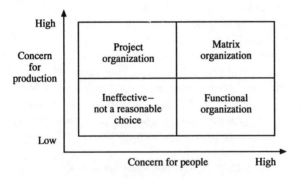

Figure 12.2 Choice of project organization.

production than on people. A matrix organization balances high concern for both people and production.

There is much anecdotal material on teams but little hard data identifying environmental variables that affect team performance, especially in an AI systems environment. This section has suggested some factors in team structure that affect development efforts, but wide disagreement exists on what makes projects, especially AI projects, successful.

Training and Education of Personnel

The process of education and training includes various media such as programmed instruction, computer-aided instruction, and diploma and degree programmes. It also uses lectures and seminars and approaches like in-house versus on-the-job training. And, of course, incentives like payment for courses taken, or salary and rank rises, are also typically used. However, training and education are very important if we are to plan and implement career paths so that the professional is not only motivated and happy as a result of the training, but in addition the firm gets higher productivity by enabling professionals working with AI technology to achieve their full potential.

The training matrix is instrumental in helping plan career paths and matching educational approaches and media to individual needs. The matrix shows which content should be covered, by what media, and when—for each person or group of persons.

Career paths may sometimes specify certain courses or academic programmes as prerequisite for advancement along the career path. Firms differ in their policies regarding released time or financial support for additional studies done in parallel with the normal workload. But all firms should offer advice and encouragement to employees willing to make the educational commitment in order to advance their careers in a prescribed and orderly progression. Indeed, management should encourage job mobility, since it is in the interests of a firm to have an experienced core of employees who know the organization and can provide backup for a number of jobs. And since career development is a key to job satisfaction, advancement within the firm should help foster company loyalty and reduce job hopping to other companies.

Although an employee should theoretically be able to cross over and move up career ladders to reach any desired position in computing by gaining qualifications and experience, openings must be available and management must be willing to promote or transfer the employee. Sometimes, however, managers turn down requests for promotion or transfer, and for quite valid, but not immediately obvious, reasons. For example, programmers who wish to switch to the more prestigious career ladder of the systems analyst or knowledge engineer may lack the requisite temperament, though they have the required technical competence. Programmers tend to be loners who shun interpersonal relationships, whereas analysts and knowledge engineers need to be perceptive of group dynamics and at ease when dealing with people. So our programmer might find a certain career path or choice blocked in some organizations, even though jobs have been designed to allow for vertical or lateral movement.

Many computer departments sponsor training programmes to provide employees with the background knowledge, skills, and up-to-date information needed to support the firm's hardware and software systems. The programmes may also be designed to promote career development of the personnel. The justification for the expense of the career programme is that they help reduce turnover, improve productivity, instil cooperation and loyalty to the firm, attract applicants, and also help retrain at a lower cost than hiring and firing when new computer systems upset the job structure of the firm.

The approaches used by corporations in training computer personnel are much the same as those used to train employees in other departments of a firm. Programmes range from on-the-job training, briefings, and seminars to coursework that rivals the degree programme of many universities.

Many software houses and manufacturers of hardware provide training materials, such as programmed instructions in manuals or as a software package for a terminal. The primary advantages of computer-based training over formal classwork is that the course is self-paced and can be scheduled at the employee's convenience. (But it is a sad fact that many people lack the self-discipline to successfully take a course of this type.) Vendors may also sponsor training programmes of their own at reasonable cost for their corporate clients.

Some firms organize training by setting up an educational matrix that identifies groups of employees and the courses needed by those groups, scheduling courses on the basis of the matrix. Other firms build courses around jobs, scheduling courses needed for becoming a programmer or manager, for example. Still others provide counselling to employees, customizing the training for individual career development. Figure 12.3 shows part of a sample training matrix for employees within such a programme. The company draws up a list of training needs prepared from the status reports and then plans and schedules courses accordingly.

Although training based on individual needs is expensive, it may prove to be the solution for firms otherwise unable to fill openings due to the low supply of, and high demand for, qualified computer personnel. Additionally, such training may be the only way to get the needed specialists—e.g. employees trained in ES design, or in the use of the specialized programming languages that AI technology tends to use.

Career paths and education/training to achieve career development are important factors in attracting and retaining professional personnel for AI systems. Other factors, certainly not unique to this domain, are attractive benefit packages, sharing rewards, and grievance procedures. Factors for

	J. Small	S. Rich	B. Karshmer
Courses			
Linguistics	X		
Software engineering	X	X	
Human–machine interface	X		X
LISP programming	X		
Introduction to OR/MS		X	
Knowledge acquisition		X	
Seminars			
Advances in AI	X	X	X
AI system design			X

Figure 12.3 A partial training matrix.

making the work environment a 'great place to work', and again not unique but certainly relevant to AI systems personnel, are those that enrich the job and affect employees' physical and psychological behaviour positively. The result is improved employee output represented in higher productivity, improved motivation, as well as lower absenteeism and staff turnover. We discussed a number of these factors in an earlier section when we endeavoured to distinguish the needs of computer (and particularly AI) personnel from those of the other employees that must be managed effectively. A general summary of all these factors, together with their interrelationships, is illustrated in Fig. 12.4.

TESTING

Testing performed on a component, function, or a subsystem as a unit is referred to as *unit testing*. In a small system components and functions and sometimes even some of the subsystems are treated as a unit for the purposes of testing. Such unit testing is performed by the domain expert or the knowledge engineer either separately or in sequence. Once the subsystem is satisfactorily tested and all other subsystems are satisfactorily tested, then they are ready for the systems test. This test is performed by the technical personnel and later by the end-user and management. Once they are satisfied, the system is accepted and made ready for operations. Such testing is referred to as *acceptance testing*.

Once the acceptance test has been completed, the system is ready for conversion (800–900 in Fig. 12.1). It is then that old knowledge, programs, and procedures must be purged from the system and new ones instituted.

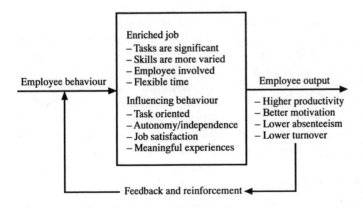

Figure 12.4 Factors in improved work environment.

This is also a period of danger in the sense that everyone is relaxed and a potential intruder can, for example, slip-in a code that allows unauthorized access later on. Some-end-users therefore lock-up the source code after the acceptance test until such time as it is used. We will have more to say about the acceptance test later in this chapter.

In testing, we see quite a difference between testing in conventional software systems development and testing in the context of KBIS development. In the conventional setting, we test that the implemented system exhibits exactly the behaviour stipulated in the system specification. And, assuming that the implementor did not blunder, we might find a few minor problems which are corrected, and the software is finished, ready for delivery to the customer.

For an ES, and for any AI system, we are likely to have only a loose and patchy specification. It will be loose in the sense that it will state what sorts of behaviour are expected without specifying precisely what this expectation is— e.g. a financial planning system may be specified in terms of producing the same sorts of plans as a human expert in the field. The specification is likely to be patchy in that precision of specification will be possible in some places (and it should, of course, be exploited whenever possible), but not in others.

All this means that testing cannot always be the classical form of testing in which the program's behaviour is clearly right or wrong with respect to some specific input data. As Hayes-Roth *et al.* put it, one final time, *testing*

> involves evaluating the performance of the prototype program and revising it to conform to standards of excellence defined by experts in the problem domain. Typically the expert evaluates the program's performance and assists the knowledge engineer in the forthcoming revisions. (1983: 24)

Another problem is: once we have an ES whose behaviour the domain experts assess as good enough, how can we validate it in a general sense? If the KBIS is to be used in an application that is not constantly monitored by human domain experts, then the KBIS user has to have some confidence in the reliability of the KBIS. Validation of KBISs is a problem area that is still quite open at the present time. The consensus seems to be that validation of these systems must be a long-term, in-use procedure that involves human domain experts continually monitoring system performance, which many would claim is no different from the accepted methods of 'validating' a human expert. Although it is by no means ideal, it is not too heavy a price to pay for very sophisticated software systems.

Verification and Validation

A KBIS has to be validated (and sometimes verified according to the more ambitious practitioners—hence V&V) before it is fit for public use, or any real use, even an in-house application. Validation is a process that determines that a particular version of the software system has attained (or has not attained) an adequate level of performance with a reliability and efficiency that is satisfactory for the proposed application. We shall concentrate on adequate level of performance but we should not lose sight of the fact that a useful practical system must simultaneously satisfy a web of constraints.

So, validation is a stopping test. Successful validation is not necessarily the cue for a full stop on the development cycle, it is more the sanctioning of a move from experimental to real-world application. The incremental development of the system may well continue within the system's application niche (in fact, it almost has to), for AI software is never finished: it is always possible to evolve a more adequate system from the current version.

The reason that incremental development is almost certain to continue within the application niche is that validation cannot be a one-step procedure: it must be a long-term, in-use procedure. So we cannot expect to validate our AI system completely in an abstract test harness. We need cautious use of the system, and then validation will be attained as we build confidence in the system by assessing its performance repeatedly in the work environment. As is sometimes pointed out, this is exactly the way that we assess a human candidate for expert qualification.

There are, at least, two rather different views of the notion of validation with respect to AI software systems. The view presented above expresses the idea that validation and verification are two different processes. The latter is usually associated with the formal notions of proof of correctness, leaving the former term to cover the more down-to-earth, workman-like activities of checking that the system satisfies the operational need. This view is summed up neatly as follows:

- Verification confirms 'We have built the system right'.
- Validation confirms 'We have built the right system'.

Verification is used to determine that the system is composed of modules correctly implementing the desired functionality. If, for example, you have determined that a sorting procedure is needed, then the implementation of that sort can be verified (in some sense). Thus you can be assured that the sorting function does indeed sort correctly. Validation is concerned with the problem of whether a sorting function applied in this particular context will contribute to an adequate solution to the problem, i.e. is sorting the right thing to be doing?

Another view of the relationship between validation and verification is found in the VALID project (Vaudet and Kerdiles, 1989) which aims to produce generic validation tools for knowledge-based systems. They have designed VETA, a meta-language for validation. Figure 12.5 illustrates their validation.

As you can see, verification is no longer seen as a different sort of checking procedure to validation, but as a component of the validation process—a major subdivision contrasted with *evaluation*. Vaudet and Kerdiles describe their two major kinds of validation as follows:

> By *verification* is meant 'proving that the KB or the KBS is in accordance with specifications or expectations'.

> By *evaluation* is meant 'judging or measuring the KB or the KBS characteristics'   (1989: 4)

These two views can be brought together if we call validation in the first scheme evaluation. Then given this renaming, you can see that determining that we have built the right system (i.e. validation in the first scheme) seems to closely fit judging the KBS characteristics (i.e. evaluation in the second scheme—the one illustrated).

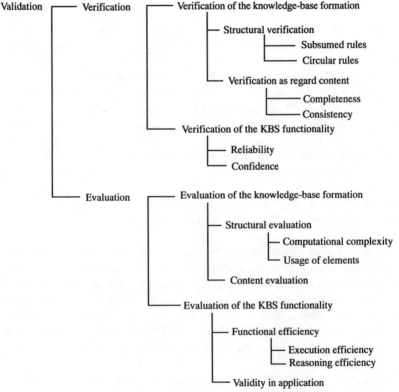

Figure 12.5 The validation structure used in the VALID project. (*From Vaudet and Kerdiles, 1989: 4.*)

An important validity-checking technique that has arisen in AI is that of the self-explanation by the system of the reasoning behind its behaviour. Using this technique, the software system actually presents to the observer a rationale—a justification for the validity—of its specific output. This is a technique that has been pioneered in KBS because it is particularly easy to implement in conjunction with the basic architecture of an ES, i.e. a set of facts and rules together with a mechanism of logical inference. Nevertheless, it is an idea that has potential in all types of software systems, but it is yet to be thoroughly exploited outside (or inside for that matter) the domain of KBISs.

An objection to this approach to software validation is that just because a software system tells us this is how it is computing a result, that is no reason to believe it. The point is not that software systems tell lies (mostly they do not), but that any programmer will tell you how easy it is to tailor a system to output totally misleading information. So can we put any credence in the system's explanation of its behaviour? Clearly, we must be careful, but, given safeguards about the generality of the underlying mechanism and the independent random checking of some explanations, this technique can be reliable and useful. We cannot guarantee that the explanation-generating module is correct and never generates spurious explanations, but then this sort of guarantee is never possible in the real world anyway. How do we verify the verifying system? The answer is: we cannot, but we can generate sufficient confidence and use the results in conjunction with other information to minimize reliance on any one source.

Interestingly, Michie and Johnston (1984) elevate this ES feature of AI (often viewed as no more than a minor spin-off from ES technology) to *a* (perhaps *the*) fundamental goal. They see the rise of technology as increasing the complexity of the environment which the human race must learn to comprehend and control if it is to continue to develop and prosper. From the software viewpoint, they believe that we must strive to construct programs that are understandable, and this means that the programs must be built

'in the image of the human mind. . . . No longer can they be built with the central aim of maximizing performance and making the best of machine resources. Instead they will have to be . . . designed to be anthropocentric'.   (Michie and Johnston, 1984: 60)

So, for Michie and Johnston, the important question seems to be not whether the algorithm is a correct implementation of the specification but whether an applied software system is transparent to its users, i.e. can the user readily 'see' why and how the system is doing what it is observed to be doing? As examples of this problem, they cite the Three Mile Island nuclear power station disaster as well as numerous other instances of problems caused by the inscrutability of high-technology systems. As a path to the solution of this problem, they offer us AI. 'What AI is about is . . . making machines *more* fathomable and *more* under the control of human beings, not less' (p. 214). And what they mean is that we need 'rule-based systems' for they 'are specifically designed to operate with human concepts, both accepting them from the domain specialist and displaying them to the user as explanations' (p. 72).

So far, we have concentrated on the nature of individual elements of a validation strategy, but what about the overall strategy? Testing for correctness has its problems as we noted in the earlier chapters. But a given software system either succeeds on a suite of test data or it fails. Adequacy, as opposed to correctness, is a very different phenomenon. Experts will argue about adequacy of system performance with respect to a suite of test data, and there is no well-defined way to adjudicate.

This raises a question more properly considered earlier (perhaps) of how should we best proceed from one inadequate version of the system to the next. If the system is clearly in error, then we know that the error is to be removed in order to progress to the next version, but if the system is fairly adequate, what should we do to generate a more adequate version?

The scheme that we like to invoke in this awkward situation first came to our attention through the architectural design work of Alexander in his influential little book *Notes on the Synthesis of Form* (1964). There has been much subsequent research on design methodology, and his simple linear scheme is undoubtedly much too simple. Nevertheless, his basic idea is still valid and can be used to seed systems development in the AI domain, especially a KBIS.

His core idea is to approach adequacy through the elimination of major inadequacies. We do not say 'Is this system adequate?', but 'Does it exhibit any major inadequacies?' If so, it is not adequate. This may seem like a trivial shuffling of the words that leave the problem much the same. It is not. If you can say that a system contains no major inadequacies, that system is adequate.

The implication of this approach to the problem of incremental system development is that the direction of successive modifications of the system should be towards eliminating major behavioural inadequacies of the system. This may be a non-trivial strategy, but it is by no means a solution to the fundamental problem either. In fact, we will leave this topic as a largely unsolved problem, which is what it is in reality.

Approaches to Testing

There are many approaches to testing: pilot testing, parallel testing, simulation, systems testing, and functional testing. Each approach is appropriate in a specific problem environment. For a **KBIS**, especially a large complex system, it is often best to consider functional testing where each function is tested before each set of functions in a subsystem is tested. In a complex environment one may go one step further and test for each component and then the set of components in a function. This schema is represented in Fig. 12.6. The important rationale for this type of testing at different levels of aggregation is that it is much easier to detect and correct an error at (or close to) its point of origin before it propagates through the system, which is likely to happen if we go straight to the system test. The other advantage is that at each level it is possible to bring the relevant expertise to check for errors and correct them.

Consistent with Fig. 12.6 for a **KBIS**, one can see the different levels of testing for one subsystem, the knowledge-base subsystem, back through to its components. This is shown in Fig. 12.7. Here each component is an instrument in the collection of knowledge used in the knowledge-acquisition function. This level of detail may seem trivial but it need not be. Testing of the instrument (or form for collecting data) could be very important. This happened in one case of a university information system that calculated the

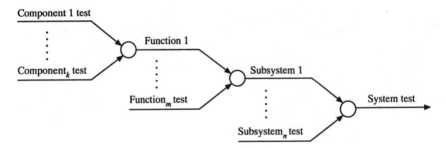

Figure 12.6 Levels of testing.

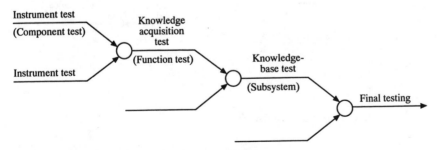

Figure 12.7 Examples of levels of testing for the subsystem.

average age of graduates. The calculated average seemed all very normal and very credible because it was generated by a computer. But one faculty member was suspicious that the age of a particular graduate was too high and so the computation was checked. It was in error. Why? Because of the instrument used for input. It asked the applicant the name of his or her father (innocent enough!) and then the year of birth. The date of birth was supposed to be the date of birth of the applicant but in some cases the applicant assumed it to be the date of birth of the father and so the program subtracted the date of birth of the father from the graduation date. The average age of the graduates was thus higher than it should have been, and all because the instrument of data collection was bad and hence misinterpreted. The instrument was not checked at the component level. In our case study, the institution was small and one individual insisted on his instinct, but that is not always possible in large and complex problem environments.

Testing as represented in Fig. 12.7 is shown in detail for one subsystem. A more generalized representation of testing for a KBIS, especially in its final stages, is shown in Fig. 12.8. Here each of the subsystems is implemented and tested separately before the final stage of integrated testing.

Final testing is often performed in two stages. First comes the systems test, which is concerned with verification and validation and is performed by the technical personnel such as the knowledge engineer and the domain expert. Sometimes a knowledge engineer who is not responsible for the

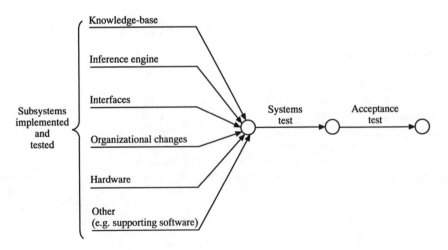

Figure 12.8 Final testing of a KBIS.

KBIS also participates in the final testing in order to provide some objectivity by not making assumptions. Such cross-project testing also provides back-up training for each project. More objectivity of the final testing can also come from a consultant who could bring in knowledge and experience not available in the organization.

Once the systems test is performed successfully, the system is now ready for testing by the end-user(s), who may be joined by the project manager and the project sponsor and any manager assigned to the task of testing by top corporate management. A consultant may also be used to provide objectivity, knowledge, and experience in representing the end-user's viewpoint. Once this group approves of the project, however, then the development team is absolved of further responsibility since the system has now implicitly been 'accepted'. Hence the term *acceptance test*.

Interaction in Testing

The discussion thus far and the diagrams showing the development activities may give the impression that all these activities are neatly sequential. This is not, however, generally the case, especially for testing. Seldom is the first test satisfactory, and much repetition is needed. This is shown in Fig. 12.9, which is consistent with Fig. 12.1. Only the main interactive activities are shown, however, and the design activity is disaggregated into the overall design and the detailed design.

Another view of interaction in testing is given by using a flowchart as in Fig. 12.10. Here we can see explicitly what triggers the repetition. In this case, the interactive loop goes back to the design stage, which may be the overall design or the detailed design stage.

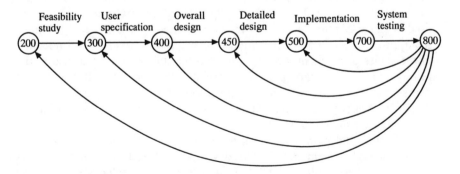

Figure 12.9 Backtracking after systems testing.

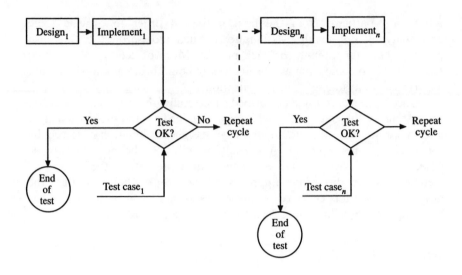

Figure 12.10 Recycling in testing.

PROJECT CONTROL AND MANAGEMENT OF A KNOWLEDGE-BASED SYSTEM

A discussion of the techniques of project management and control are beyond the scope of this book. There are, however, some special considerations for project control and management of the development of KBISs that we need to identify and briefly discuss. One is the unique configuration of personnel involved. There are technical personnel like the knowledge engineers and the AI programming-language programmers. Then there may be many human domain experts involved not just in the knowledge acquisition but also in testing. In the study done by O'Neill and Morris (1989: 93) on ESs in the United Kingdom, multiple experts were used in 22 per cent and a varied number were used by another 15 per cent of the approximately 300 systems studied. Consultants are also used not only in the stages of problem identification and feasibility study, but also in the testing phase. The main players in the development of a KBIS are, of course, the domain expert and the knowledge engineer. They bring different resources, background, and perspectives to development. Some of these differences are shown in Fig. 12.11.

The time and money spent on developing ESs have decreased over the years. The early system DRENDAL developed in 1965 took around 12 years and many million dollars. XCON took a few million dollars but only five years to develop. Some systems in the 1990s have taken even less money and

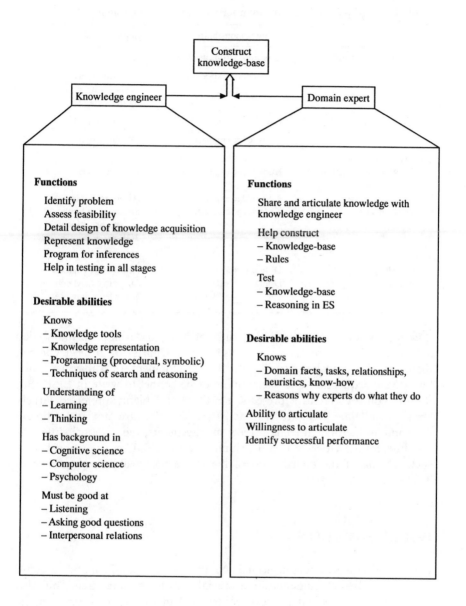

Figure 12.11 Domain expert and knowledge engineer.

Table 12.2 Responsibilities during a KBIS project development

Phase	Prime responsibility	Support staff
Problem identification	User and corporate staff	Consultant(?)
Feasibility study	Management appointee	Domain expert Consultant Systems staff
User specification	User	Domain expert
Design	Knowledge engineer	Domain expert
Implementation		
Knowledge acquisition subsystem	Knowledge engineer	Domain expert
Inference engine	Knowledge engineer	AI programmer
Interface user	Knowledge engineer	Specialist in human factors and psychology 3GL programmer
Testing		
Knowledge	Domain expert	Knowledge engineer
System	Domain expert	Domain expert consultant Knowledge engineer

time to develop, especially if they did not have to develop all the needed software in-house. Many systems use Gannt Charts for project control; these can be used extensively for the development of subsystems like knowledge acquisition and the training of personnel to write in LISP. But for the control of entire projects, PERT is still highly preferred largely because the time estimates for activities involved are not the ultimate determining factors. In some project managements, the responsibilities for the different activities can be distributed between different personnel. One such schema of the distribution of the prime responsibilities is shown in Table 12.2.

DOCUMENTATION

Documentation is a most neglected activity in many an information system, not just a KBIS. Documentation is crucial not just to maintenance but also during the development process, as depicted in Fig. 12.12. For example, documentation of systems specifications are used in the overall design process, and documentation of the overall design is used for the detailed design and implementation activities. In a small system, such documenta-tion is replaced by word of mouth but in a complex system, and one that involves many people, this can be hazardous. People do not always say

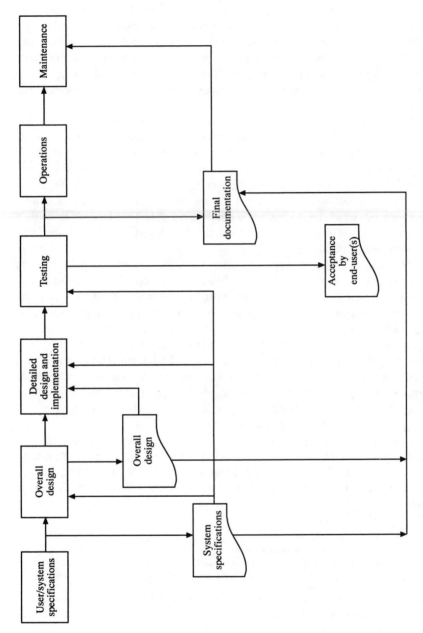

Figure 12.12 Flow of documentation in different stages of development

305

what they mean; people do not always remember what they have said; people change their minds. It is in the best interests of both the knowledge engineer and the end-users to document all commitments, explicit or implicit. It is sometimes necessary to document not only actions but intentions such as what would have been done if specific resources had been available or certain constraints had not been imposed. Documentation can be particularly useful during maintenance and enhancement of the system.

Documentation should include a formal acceptance after the acceptance test by the end-users and perhaps even management that sponsored the project. Documentation should be progressive and not left to the end; otherwise it may never be completed or available when needed during the development process. Finalizing documentation is perhaps the very last activity in the life of a project. At this stage the project itself should also be documented, which could include a description of lessons learned in project management and even a record of the history of individuals at estimating times for project activities.

Because it is not a popular activity among analysts and knowledge engineers, documentation is sometimes contracted to a consulting or specialist company. The problem with contracting outside is that the knowledge acquired by documenting is lost to the organization. This loss is especially important when the documentation could have been done by someone other than the knowledge engineer responsible for the job who is then available for evaluation, maintenance, and back-up. The problem with documentation is that it tends to become bulky. There is too much paperwork involved. Werner von Braun, a famous space scientist, once said: 'Our two greatest problems are gravity and paperwork. We can lick gravity, but sometimes the paperwork is overwhelming.'

The importance of documentation can be judged by the following case study: a knowledge engineer was being interviewed. After an intensive discussion of the technology and financing involved there seemed to be a good understanding that the candidate was well liked. The following dialogue then ensued:

Employer:	How soon can you join us?
KE:	Not till at least three months.
Employer:	Can't you come sooner? We prefer not to wait that long.
KE:	No, I can't come any earlier. I need to document a project I have just completed.
Employer:	If that is how strongly you feel about documentation, I shall be happy to wait three months.

Perhaps we can indulge in another anecdote, this being the last chapter in this part of the book. It occurred at an international conference with directors of computer centers on a panel. A question from the floor was: 'What is your greatest problem: hardware, software, people-ware, money or something else?' 'Something else' was the answer. 'It is documentation. Analysts often consider documentation as not being a creative activity and hence tend not do it. They tend to procrastinate. Or they do not adhere to documentation standards. We know of many projects—elsewhere—that had to be redeveloped because of a lack of complete and usable documentation.'

Many such anecdotes are from conventional information systems but we strongly suspect that they apply to KBISs.

SUMMARY AND CONCLUSIONS

Documentation, as with organizational changes, is an activity that must be performed throughout the lifecycle of systems development, culminating in testing. Testing is done at different levels of subsystems. These activities have a spiral lifecycle such as the spiral of an SDLC as discussed in an earlier chapter. There is also a spiral within an SDLC and even in part of an SDLC such as software, especially when one is using prototyping. The spiral model of such a software process is represented in Fig. 12.13 (Partridge, 1992: 75); it has some new activities and some new terms but these activities are not inconsistent with those discussed elsewhere in this book. The difference in activities and terminology is not to be unexpected in the evolving life of systems methodology and we shall not protect the reader from the different terminologies.

The completion of testing is part of project management. Projects as complex as a KBIS need project management and such management is punctuated with surprises. Empirical evidence shows that we have consistently underestimated the difficulty of eliciting and transferring knowledge from the human expert. Here the knowledge engineer has to get inside the head and thinking process of a human expert, which is a time-consuming and difficult process. We have also underestimated the lengthy learning curve of programming in languages like LISP and the use of its memory hungry and specialized hardware. We are still very much on the upward learning curve for developing a KBIS and will perhaps stay there for a while. We face the problems of integrating a KBIS with conventional information systems, of end-users of a KBIS become more demanding, and of the systems consequently becoming more complex.

In discussing the development of a KBIS in Part II of this book we made passing references to the resources needed for a KBIS, namely hardware, software, and personnel resources. These are the topics of Part III, the next part of our discourse.

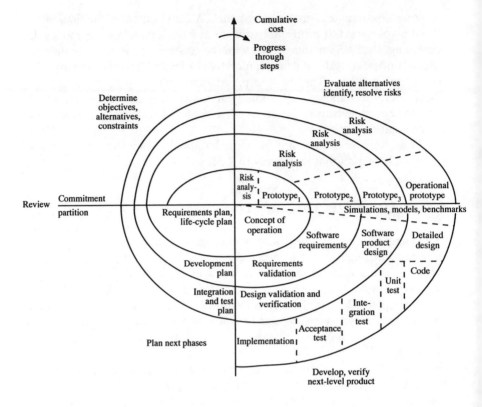

Figure 12.13 The spiral model of the software process. (From B. W. Boehm, 1976, *IEEE Computer*, May, 61–72. © 1976 IEEE.)

CASE 12.1 OBJECT ORIENTATION FOR THE US AIRFORCE

The Air Logistics Command of the US Airforce in Utah had problems of constant maintenance on its 3000-node network. Frequent changes in personnel and a bad mix of old and modern equipment were the underlying reason for this continual problem. The Airforce wanted a system that would monitor their network and automate the fixing of problems as they arose.

TRW Inc. was given the contract and chose object-oriented technology because of the flexibility and the suitability of object orientation to the task. Specifically, this technology made the job more manageable, and made the software development cycle 20–30 times faster than if an object orientation were not employed.

> When the network was modeled, classes of objects were set up to represent each type of device and network component. For example, a class of objects was established for network interface units, bridges and routers, and each type of host device. Each class includes a set of slots, which defines the attributes and behavior for the objects within that class, and a set of slot relationships, which define how these objects relate to each other.

Now if the network configuration changes, such as the inclusion or modification of a device, then the operator needs to define that changed device only once, as a particular object. All the specifics about that device such as its location, type, address, and behaviour, would then be automatically inherited by all objects to which knowledge of that changed device was relevant.

Bill Green, the project manager, comments: 'As long as you have defined your object relationships correctly, you only need to enter a new device one time.'

Source: D. Baum (1993) 'TRW puts Airforce network on automatic pilot', *Computerworld*, **15** (40), 80.

Questions

1. Who should select the project leader for such a project: TRW, the Airforce, or the project sponsor?
2. If you were the project leader, what professionals would you assemble for the project team? Explain your reasoning.
3. Would you classify this project as involving mostly software, or hardware, or both?
4. Give your ranking for the objectives for this project.
5. State your ranking for the advantages of an object orientation for this project.
6. Do you think that this project arose from a bad design of the original project? Could this project have been avoided? How?
7. Why do you think that the Airforce would contract this project to TRW, a firm specializing in credit reporting, instead of using its computing staff in the Airforce and the Defense Department? What are the costs and benefits of this decision?

CASE 12.2 MANUFACTURING IN MEXICO—3: TESTING

In 1987, CYDSA, a chemical and textile corporation with annual sales of $600 million, were persuaded by the CAI (Center for Artificial Intelligence) to develop KBISs for their manufacturing and repairing plants. Four problems were selected, all on diagnosis, and one for each plant. Each system required prototyping that took approximately 120 person-hours per system.

After implementation, each system was 'tested against test cases designed by external people and revised by experts and knowledge engineers'. Although they had 'six years of experience in testing software using structured techniques', project personnel 'could not apply these techniques to testing production because they rely on different control mechanisms than conventional code. We are starting a research project at CAI to develop methods for validating rule-based system, based on our experience with structured techniques for conventional software and ad hoc testing of expert systems.'

Source: J. Cantu-Oritz (1991) 'Expert systems in manufacturing: an experience in Mexico', *Expert Systems with Applications*, **3**, 455–455.

Questions

1. Do you believe that the experience stated above can be applied to the following?
   (*a*) Other functions in the same firm.
   (*b*) Other firms in the same country.
   (*c*) Other countries.
   Explain your reasoning.
2. To what extent is the experience in testing conventional software portable across to a KBIS and to what extent is this not possible? Explain
3. Is the testing of a rule-base system different from other knowledge-based structures for a KBIS? How is it different?

CASE 12.3 THE INNOVATOR FOR FINANCIAL PLANNING

The Innovator is an ES used to give advice on managing the mix of a financial portfolio. The system contains 24 rules; runs on a IBM 4381 using the VM for its operating system; and interfaces with the DBMS using SQL statements.

The system was tested using the Turing test by providing a set of test scenarios to the system and then comparing its recommendations with 'inter-experts' (experts who were not involved in the development of the systems) and 'intra-experts' (those helped in the development of the system).

> Financial planners and finance professors developed 25 scenarios, taking into account recent product and service developments in the financial-services industry. Each scenario involved a new product service that had to be evaluated.

Each expert was assigned nine scenarios at random but controlled for learning effects. For ten scenarios, the advice of the systems and the experts was identical. In five scenarios, there were differences, and the rules and the parameters used were then examined to explain the discrepancies and to make adjustments.

Source: S. Ram and S. Ram (1990) 'Screening financial innovations: an expert systems approach', *IEEE Expert*, **5** (4), 20–7.

Questions
1. Why do you think that the Turing test was used in this case? Under what circumstances would a Turing test be most appropriate?
2. Does it matter if a 'senior' domain expert differs from a 'junior' domain expert and if a domain expert differs from an end-user? How does one weigh the opinions of the participants?
3. How does one decide on the sample size for the test?
4. Is there a methodology for tracing a discrepancy in the test results to the cause of the discrepancy?
5. What comments do you have about the design of the scenarios and their designers?

CASE 12.4 R1/XCON—4: TESTING

R1/XCON is an ES that configures parts and components for computer systems at Digital Equipment Corporation (for details see Case 6.3).

The validation process of R1 'consisted of giving R1 the 50 most recently booked orders and having a group of six experts carefully examine R1's output for correctness. The experts were given orders in groups of 10; they spent 8 hours on the first order, 2 hours on the second, and then 1 hour on each of the other 48. After checking the group of 10 orders, they forwarded errors' to different personnel depending on the nature of the cause of the error (due to incorrect configuration knowledge or due to inaccurate description in the component database). The 'problems were fixed and the incorrect orders were rerun with the next group of ten'.

R1 made 12 mistakes (all of which were quickly fixed) in configuring the 50 orders. All but two of the mistakes were at a level below that at which humans responsible for configuring systems work out the configurations.

Source: J. McDermott (1981) 'R1: the formative years', *AI Magazine*, **2** (2), 21–9.

Questions
1. Is the testing approach used for R1 not the same as the Turing test? Are they equivalent or just alike? Or are they different? In each case, explain how and why.
2. Since R1 and its successor has been successfully operational for over a decade, is it legitimate to say that the testing methodology used for R1 is 'good' or just viable?
3. In 'learning' from successful experiences such as XCON, is there a danger that we follow its techniques blindly and therefore inhibit other innovative approaches that may be better? Is this true just of the testing techniques or of the other techniques used successfully in XCON?
4. Is there much that we can learn further than the XCON experience especially as it pertains to the 'experiment design' of sample size and sampling methodology for testing.
5. How has testing methodology changed since the days of R1? How is it better?

REVIEW AND DISCUSSION QUESTIONS

12.1 What organizational changes are necessary for a KBIS?

12.2 How are the organizational changes necessary for a KBIS different from say a transactional system or a DSS?

12.3 Who should initiate, implement, and approve changes resulting from a KBIS?

12.4 Are the changes resulting from the integration of a KBIS with other subsystems organizational or only technological? If organizational, how can they be overcome?

12.5 'Resistance to a KBIS is the most serious organizational problem resulting from the installation of a KBIS.' Comment.

12.6 How could resistance to a KBIS manifest itself? What determines its intensity? How can it be overcome, or at least reduced?

12.7 Compare the unit-testing approach with approaches to testing as being appropriate for a KBIS?

12.8 Is validation and verification more important or more difficult for a KBIS than for other information systems? Explain your position.

12.9 Identify the different testing to be performed in a complex KBIS. In each case, identify who should perform the testing.

12.10 What is the relevance of 'acceptance testing'? Who should perform it, how, and at what stage of development?

12.11 'The acceptance test is the bottom-line for any KBIS.' Comment.

12.12 Explain the relevance of project management to a KBIS.

12.13 Is project managment of a KBIS more or less difficult than for a conventional information system?

12.14 How are the project teams different in size or composition for a KBIS than for other systems?

12.15 Is project management for a KBIS different from other information systems? If so, why? How?

12.16 What is the role of documentation in the following phases?
  (*a*) User specification.
  (*b*) Design?
When should it be performed? Who is responsible for the documentation?

12.17 List the different modules of documentation desirable or essential for a KBIS. In each case who should be responsible for the documentation?

12.18 What are the advantages and disadvantages of contracting the documentation activity to an outside vendor?

12.19 'Documentation is crucial to any KBIS.' Comment.

BIBLIOGRAPHY AND REFERENCES

Alexander, C. (1964) *Notes on the Synthesis of Form*, Harvard University Press, Cambridge, MA.

Cupello, J. M. and D. J. Mishelevich (1988) 'Managing prototype knowledge/expert systems projects', *Communications of the ACM*, **31** (5), 534–545.
'Fundamental issues of technology transfer, training, problem selection, staffing, corporate politics, and more, are explored.'

Hamilton, D., K. Kelley and C. Culbert (1991) 'State-of-the-practice in knowledge-based systems verification and validation', *Expert Systems with Applications*, **3** (4), 403–410.
The authors used the survey instrument to examine validation and verification practices in use by ES developers. The authors recommend addressing readability and modularity issues and developing requirements for validification and verification.

Hayes-Roth, F. P., D. A. Waterman and D. B. Lenat (1983) *Building Expert Systems*, Addison-Wesley, Reading, MA.

Huws, H., M. Wintrub and N. Martin (1992) 'Knowledge-based systems development', *Journal of Information Systems Management*, **9** (3), 51–56.
The authors describe methodology and offer solutions to many of the management problems confronting those responsible for KBS development and implementation efforts.

Knowledge Engineering Review, **7** (2) (1992), 143-146 is 'Verifying Knowledge-Bases: A Bibliography'.

An invaluable source for research on the subjects of knowledge-bases and verification with 89 entries.

Lydiard, T. J. (1992) 'Overview of current practices and research initiation for the verification and validation of KBS', *Knowledge Engineering Review*, **7** (2), 101–113.

McTear, M. F. and T. J. Anderson (eds) (1990) *Understanding Knowledge Engineering*, Ellis Horwood, Chichester.

Eleven authors, many from the University of Ulster in Northern Ireland give an excellent coverage of the development of a KBIS including its project management.

Michie D. and R. Johnston (1984) *The Creative Computer*, Viking, London.

Mengshoel, O. J. and S. Delab (1993) 'Knowledge validation: principles and practice', *IEEE Expert*, **8** (5), 62–88.

The tool KVAT is claimed to address the question of how should knowledge validation be integrated into the knowledge acquisition cycle.

Morris, P. W. G. (1990) 'The strategic management of projects', *Technology in Society*, **12**, 197–215.

O'Neill, M. and A. Morris (1989) 'Expert systems in the United Kingdom: an evaluation of development methodologies', *Expert Systems*, **6** (2), 90–91.

Partridge, D. (1992) *Engineering Artificial Intelligence Software*, Intellect, Oxford.

Plant, R. T. (1992) 'Expert systems development and testing: a knowledge engineer's perspective', *J. Systems Software*, **19**, 141–146.

Sprague, D. D. and R. Greenwell (1992) 'Project management: are employees trained to work in project teams?' *Project Management Journal*, **XXIII** (1), 22–26.

Stewart, M. (1969) 'Making project management work', in D. I. Cleland and W. R. King (eds), *Systems Organization, Analysis Management: A Book of Readings*, McGraw-Hill, New York, pp. 295–296.

Vaudet, J. and P. F. Kerdiles (1989) 'VALID: a proposition to advance capabilities for knowledge-based systems validation', *ESPRIT Conference*, Brussels.

Williams, I. (1990) 'Project management software', *Which Computer?*, **13** (4), 81–93.

Yunus, N. B., D. L. Babcock and C. O. Benjamin (1990) 'Development of a knowledge-based schedule planning system', *Project Management Journal*, **XXI** (4), 39–48.

Discusses time, cost, and performance in the different project management activities of planning, scheduling, monitoring, and control.

Part III

Resources Needed for a Knowledge-based System

This part of the book concentrates on the resources needed to support a KBIS. An overview of the chapters in Part III is shown in Fig. III.1. The chapters are all stand-alone so that the reader knowledgeable about any one or more resource may wish to skip over selected chapters. The chapters can be read in any order.

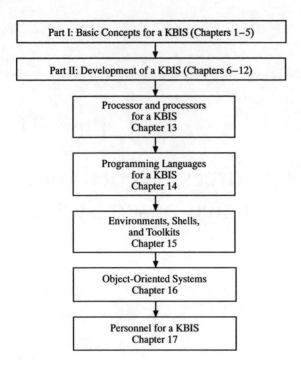

Figure III.1 An overview of the chapters in Part III.

13

PROCESSOR AND PROCESSORS

This is a Man Age. The machines are simply tools which man has devised to help him do a better job.

Thomas J. Watson (of IBM fame)

I don't think the mind was made to do logical operations all day long.

Patrice

INTRODUCTION

In later chapters we shall explore the major options with respect to the programming languages and software environments available for programming in the field of KBISs and AI. In this chapter we shall look at the special-purpose hardware that is available to support KBISs and AI with particular attention to the possibilities that stem from parallel processing— both human and software options. In addition, we shall examine the remaining features of computer technology (i.e. hardware–software combinations and neural computing) and its recent advances, paying particular attention to its importance with respect to business, engineering, management, and the promises of AI.

Will minicomputers and mainframes be the dinosaurs of the 1990s? If so, what will be the implications for both computing power availability and the locus of control for management?

The IBM PC, PC compatibles, and more recently the IBM PS/2 have posed a challenge to mainframes in a wide range of applications, including operating systems, user interfacing, and networking. The concept that mainframes are synonymous with serious computing is under threat. The mainframe paradigm is being seriously challenged in the area of large-scale processing of broad-based problems, and in terms of general performance reliability, capacity planning, the practice of 'charging back' for services, and the danger of start-up paralysis. However, 'the mainframe is not just an object of technology. It is a corporate information processing paradigm' for solving serious commercial problems in computing. It is part of corporate culture and relates to the control that centralization with a mainframe can achieve. Mainframes are needed for power and for control. The mainframe crisis has been accelerating strongly since the late 1970s, but 'mainframe computing is a cultural pillar sunk deep into 30-year-old data processing bedrock' (Viskovich, 1987).

The demise of mainframe computing will not be tomorrow, but IBM, the 'lord of the mainframes', is now threatened by its own PS/2, and not only in terms of processor speed, memory, and control, but also throughput. It is also threatened by companies that are smaller but more nimble and adaptable to changing technology and manufacturing methods.

Machines of other vendors, as well as departmental machines, workstations, and PCs, will form the basis of high-performance computer systems as parts of networks of machines, none of which are mainframes. Such systems will readily support serious business applications as well as AI and integrated systems in an office or factory. But all this will require planning for 'a technology architecture, that is, a model of future information processing hardware, software, and data communications infrastructure' (Viskovich, 1987).

PROCESSORS

First, let us look at some of the major options for special-purpose hardware to support AI. We have processors optimized for LISP, computer systems designed for maximum computational power, and hardware to support parallel processing in a variety of different ways.

LISP Machines

The 1980s have seen the emergence of single-person workstations (the notion of 'workstation' is dealt with, in-depth, below) optimized for system development using the LISP language. This general class of computer as known as a *LISP machine*.

The advent of LISP machines represents a significant break with prevailing trends in computer hardware design for a number of reasons. Firstly, an expensive and powerful computer system has been designed with one, very specific, programming language in mind—LISP. The trend had hitherto been towards general-purpose computers that can be configured quickly and easily to run a wide variety of languages. And, although a typical LISP machine may also be used to run, say, FORTRAN or Ada, the majority of hardware design decisions were taken on the basis of what would best support the LISP language. They are thus very fast and efficient LISP processors, and other languages are implemented via LISP— a FORTRAN compiler written in LISP is a somewhat strange notion at first.

Another way in which LISP machines bucked the trend of the times was in the move to single-user machines. A significant feature in the development of computer systems up to the 1980s was the increased sophistication of successive generations of multi-user computer systems, i.e. one large computer system could be used by many different people at once, and this made for efficient utilization of an expensive resource. In addition, much of the time the population of simultaneous users on a large computer would hardly notice that they were sharing the computer system—because computers are very fast and humans are slow entering data, etc. LISP machine technology, by way of contrast, has returned to the earlier idea of one person, one computer—i.e. single-user, standalone computers. The reasons behind this move are obvious when you consider both the nature of AI programming languages (i.e. highly flexible) and the incremental nature of AI system development.

The language flexibility (e.g. variables do not have to be 'declared', and lists may be automatically extended and contracted as any particular run of the program demands) means that an efficient and powerful implementation of, say, LISP must include a sophisticated memory management component. This component of the implementation will keep track of all unused (i.e. unused by the particular user program that is running) memory in order to make suitably configured chunks available to the program on demand—e.g. when a new item is added to a list, a portion of unused memory, appropriately structured to be able to store the particular list element, must be linked to the end of the list and removed from the pool of unused memory. In addition, when a list is reduced in size by the user program, the memory management system must be able to retrieve the unrequired memory space and return it to the pool of unused memory.

Clearly, such a memory management system component will take up space in the computer, but more importantly, it will take up time on the CPU *at the same time* as the user program is running. There are a number of other components of a LISP system that will similarly be competing with the user program for computational resources in order to provide maximum support for the user program. So the single-user machine philosophy found in the LISP machine technology is necessary in order to concentrate computer power to efficiently support the many facets of running a LISP program.

The second reason for single-user LISP machines is similar to the above but may be considered external to the language being used rather than internal to it. Incremental software system development is considerably enhanced if the programmer has a sophisticated support environment at his or her disposal (as we learned in the previous chapter). The provision of tracing, debugging, etc., support systems to augment the programming language is again the inclusion of competing subsystems, and thus there is a further degradation of computational resources that are available for simply executing the user's program.

The latter half of the 1980s saw the rise of LISP-machine technology. In general, these machines are expensive, special purpose, and it takes both considerable time and dedication to learn to use them to full effect. It remains to be seen whether they will be the model for AI hardware of the future, or whether they will just be vaguely remembered as a short-lived innovation that did not catch on.

One glimpse of what the future may hold, with respect to LISP machines, is provided by Texas Instruments Inc., which has brought out a LISP chip: 550 000 transistors (i.e. 60 per cent of the circuitry of their LISP machines) are packed onto a thumbnail-sized chip. Such innovations will make the special features of a LISP machine available at a much lower cost than a LISP machine itself.

Supercomputers

Another growth area in computer hardware technology has been that of so-called supercomputers. A *supercomputer* is the name given to computers that are optimized for speed of execution of central-processor instructions (as opposed to say, I/O operations), and are based on a conventional serial-processor architecture (in contrast to, say, parallel architectures). They are large and expensive computers: about 50 000 times more powerful and about 1000 times more expensive than a PC.

Supercomputers are typically associated with massive numerical computations (commonly known as *number crunching*), which are commonly required in, for example, nuclear physics. Business applications, by way of contrast, are typically characterized by large amounts of input and output activity (e.g. entering large data files and generating many long reports) and relatively little numerical computations. Supercomputers are therefore not usually associated with computation in business and management applications.

But when we begin to consider the possibility of AI software, whatever application area we choose, we run into the problems of massive computation which typically swamps a conventional computer system. AI applications are not characterized by a demand for large quantities of numeric computation, it is true, but the searching and pattern matching operations (i.e. the necessary symbolic computation) puts similarly excessive demands on the central processor. It makes little difference whether the central processor is called upon to execute vast numbers of simple numerical or simple pattern-matching operations—the end result is the same: the computer system has too slow a response time.

Problem solving in AI is typically represented as searching a space of possibilities, and what makes the problem an AI problem is that there are too many possibilities to explore. Thus a manager, when faced with a decision task, cannot explore all the possible options. The human manager will typically focus on just a few of the most likely options and perhaps consider the consequences of this small set of choices. Computer systems, when applied to AI problems, and in the absence of the sophisticated human expertise that a good manager possesses, have to search and explore many more options in order to stand a chance of eventually finding a high-quality decision. What all this means is that a lot of computation is involved, and thus supercomputers, which are high-speed computational devices, may well be found to have applicability in the business world when AI software is widely used.

PARALLEL PROCESSING

A second avenue of approach to this demand, by AI systems, for raw computational power is to move to parallel architectures, i.e. hardware that can use more than one processing unit on a given problem *at the same time* (in other words, processors working in parallel). So, if the AI system has to search many options in order to find a 'good enough' one, then perhaps it can search more than one option at once, i.e. the search can be executed in parallel. This is the sort of promise that parallel processing hardware offers for AI. But, at a finer level of detail, there are several rather different styles of parallel architectures, and there are a number of very different ways to exploit parallelism in AI programming.

To begin with, there are both coarse- and fine-grain parallelism to be found in AI problems. At the so-called coarse-grain level a problem is composed of a small number of significant subproblems that can be processed in parallel. Thus, at the top level of the management decision-making task, there will be a number of quite distinct alternative possible decisions that could be made. A coarse-grained parallel implementation of such a problem may be able to use a small number of processors all working in parallel, each one processing a different alternative decision. At some point each independent processor must then report its findings as to the worth of the specific decision it processed (this might be in terms of how well it solves the original problem, its cost and side-effects, etc.) to a central processor, which will then choose the best decision to make.

Notice that there is always a need for some processor in the system to assume exclusive control from time to time. In the case of our simple example, this centralization of control was only necessary at the end of the task (and presumably at the beginning in order to decide how and what alternative decisions to explore initially). But, in general, there is a continuing need for this sort of processor intercommunication throughout the process of complex problem solving. In addition, it is often hard to predict, in advance, exactly when and what will need to be communicated between the processors working in parallel.

Hence the difficulty in designing systems to exploit such coarse-grained parallelism. It is relatively easy to construct computer hardware composed of a number of processors that are both capable of working independently in parallel and of intercommunication. But it is very difficult to structure programs so that they can effectively exploit the coarse-grained parallelism inherent in a given problem. The construction of accurate and efficient simple sequential programs (i.e. conventional programs) is in itself a very demanding task. To construct parallel programs appears to be much more difficult. So, in this class of parallel system's work, the hardware is well in advance of ability to use it effectively.

The answer is, of course, for the computer system itself to detect and exploit the parallelism inherent in a problem as and when it occurs. Then the programmer's task would reduce to the conventional one of providing a correct sequential algorithm (with perhaps some indications of parallel possibilities), and the computer system would, according to its sophistication, parallelize the algorithm for more efficient computation. It is quite conceivable that an operating system could exercise this sort of judgement on a program that it is running, and, although there are a number of system-development projects working towards this sort of goal, such systems are still largely a future event.

Coarse-grained parallelism, with its relatively small number of parallel processors, is sometimes known as *mere parallelism* to contrast with *massive parallelism*, which, as the name suggests, involves large numbers of parallel processes (also known as *fine-grained parallelism*—a term that emphasizes the elemental nature of the parallel processes). These are shown in Fig. 13.1. Computer hardware is available for directly supporting this fine-grained parallelism. These machines (such as the Connection Machine, see Waltz, 1987) offer the programmer a large number of quite primitive processors, as opposed to the previous category, which made a small number of powerful processors available for the programmer's use.

One step at a time:
traditional sequential
architecture

Several processors
operating simultaneously
and in parallel
(mere parallelism;
coarse-grained parallelism)

A network of processors
interwoven in complex and
flexible ways in massively
parallel systems
(fine-grained parallelism)

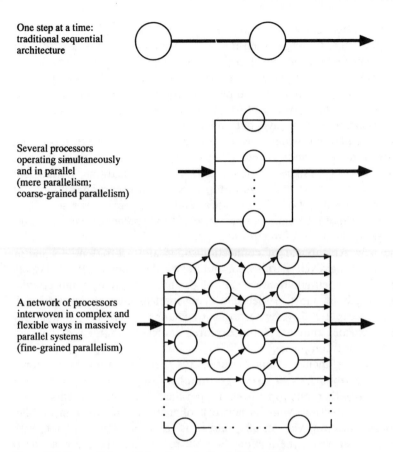

Figure 13.1 Sequential, parallel, and massively parallel processing.

A first point to clarify concerns the possibility of using such massive parallelism when we have just explained the great difficulties involved with the effective use of only a few parallel processors. In fact, these massive parallel machines are easier to use than the previous ones we have discussed. And this is because the primitive processors either do not need to communicate with each other while executing, or because the necessary intercommunication is simple and predictable in advance.

When does this type of parallelism arise? It actually occurs in a number of somewhat different ways in AI problems. It commonly occurs in vision systems and also in many different types of so-called neural-network models—the new *connectionism*.

You should know that computer processing of visual input amounts to the processing of thousands of simple data items known as *pixels*.

Furthermore, the early stages of this visual processing—e.g. the noise removal and edge finding—often involves a very simple computation that has to be repeated on each pixel in the image. And finally, the operation to be performed on each pixel typically only involves the few nearest-neighbour pixels. Each quite simple operation can then be performed independently of most of the other pixels in the visual image, and so we have an application of massive, but simple, parallelism.

Such parallel hardware is so important for efficient image processing (and pattern recognition in general) that there are a whole range of different hardware products designed for just these sorts of applications. We have, in the earlier chapters, seen the importance of visual or graphic input and output for applications of AI to business and management, and so we can confidently predict the coming importance of this type of parallel computer in business applications of the future.

The new AI subfield of connectionism is another potentially major application of massively parallel computers. At the moment, this is largely an unfulfilled potential, because, although there are many connectionist models being built, most of them are being implemented on conventional, sequential computers—we expect this to change. There are many, very different, schemes that are being explored under the banner of connec-tionism or neural computing.

The unifying theme in this AI subfield is that the main computational effort is distributed over a large number of primitive processors, networked together and operating in parallel. The analogy with brain structure and function, with its network of neurons operating in parallel and communicating via on/off pulses, is easy to see but not very productive. Currently, the analogy is only superficial; there are no deep similarities between human brains and so-called neural computers or connectionist models.

Nevertheless, neural-network models seem to offer problem-solving potential that is, in some significant ways, superior to that obtainable from more conventional implementations of AI problems. The neural computers themselves have proved to be powerful pattern-recognition devices.

A last category of parallel processing computer systems, which merits special mention, is the PROLOG-based parallel devices. In the next chapter we explain why the language PROLOG is particularly suitable for use with parallel systems as well as for KBSs. A number of PROLOG-based computers, offering varying degrees of parallelism, are now available, and there are likely to be many more in the near future. This approach to parallelism to support implementations of AI problems is one of the bases for the Japanese Fifth Generation project (about which we shall say more later).

INTELLIGENT WORKSTATIONS

Before we begin to discuss the nature and likely uses of intelligent workstations in the business world, we must spend some time on discussing the notion of a workstation itself.

Defining a *workstation* is like shooting at a moving target—difficult to hit squarely, because by the time your definition is disseminated the concept will have changed. Nevertheless, we must try to provide you with some characteristic features, and that we shall do.

The capabilities and performance of a workstation are improving in steps that are substantial and frequent. But then so is the PC, which is fast catching up with the workstation, while the workstation is catching up with the minicomputer and the mainframe. Thus, the boundaries are becoming more blurred, and there is much overlap. Nevertheless, it is possible to describe the workstation in terms of six important features:

- Speed
- Memory
- Multitasking
- Graphics
- Network interface
- Operating system

We shall examine each of these features in turn below.

The speed of a workstation in the early 1980s was sometimes faster than the mainframes of the day but always faster than the PCs. Processor speeds vary enormously from vendor to vendor, from machine type to machine type, and even between individual models of the same family of computers, for each may be operating in quite a different overall system configuration. A fast workstation processor speed is likely to be in the region of 10 million instructions per second (or 10 MIPS). A doubling of processor speed in each new generation of machine was common in the 1980s. Similar increases have been experienced in memory capacity, where 1 megabyte of *random access memory* (RAM) is now almost a minimum, as is a capability for virtual memory. Four megabytes are often available, depending on the operating system used. The popular operating system, UNIX, for example, is especially memory intensive.

But it must be said, in all fairness to the workstation, that the escalation of internal memory needs is not confined to workstations; the same story is true of minis, mainframes, and even PCs. As to external memory needs: 4 megabytes of RAM and 120–350 megabytes of hard-disk space are not uncommon.

The next feature, multitasking, is not new to mainframes or minis, but is unavailable in most PCs. The concept is not unknown to us in daily life: we multitask when we chew gum and drive a car, and, although not advisable for everyone, most of us can do both at the same time safely. More complex multitasking would be chewing gum while driving in traffic and reading the paper. Humans are not capable of this degree of multitasking. The sensible ones do not try it; the others usually die in the attempt. Multitasking in computers is usually not so dangerous, but it is complex because it requires scheduling of the tasks and intercommunication between the processors so that all the tasks are performed efficiently and effectively. This problem is one of the problems of parallelism that we discussed earlier.

Fortunately, more recent hardware, such as the 80326 chip, has built-in support for multitasking in addition to direct hardware support for paging and virtual memory requirements of workstation functionality. The hardware architectures of workstations vary in their support of multitasking performance, and some require cache memories (i.e. very high-speed buffer memory) for their central processor, with 8K bytes of cache being quite standard.

The graphics feature refers to the large graphic display capability that is characteristic of workstations. Screens 15 in. × 19 in. were quite common even in the early days. Large screens facilitate the use of *windows* (i.e. multiple views of a given computation or of a selection of simultaneous computations—there might be textual program code in one window, data in another, and graphical output in yet another), with screen resolutions reaching the megapixel range—a *pixel* is a single picture element, also known as a *pel*. Such screen sizes allow something like a 1024×1024 array of pixels to be displayed. This contrasts with screen displays on a PC, which tend to be more like 640×480 pixels. The workstation display screens can be either monochrome or colour, and high-performance graphics workstations offer many choices of colour together with high resolution.

The networking interface feature is powerful, because a workstation is seldom used as a stand-alone facility but more commonly as part of a computing environment with associated processors of varying capabilities and exotic or large peripherals. Accessing such hardware facilities and common databases requires a network capability. Hence workstations come with built-in and embedded modems, largely invisible to the user, and the resultant sharing and indirect access of facilities enables the workstation to become an integral part of a larger computing environment. This is an important characteristic of workstations.

Workstations vary as to their networking capabilities, but most use Ethernet with at least the TCP/IP family of telecommunications protocols.

The final workstation feature that we are to consider is its *operating system* (OS)—the heart of a computer system. An OS is the program that more or less permanently resides in the hardware and largely dictates the way the computer system behaves, i.e. what sort of human interface it offers, what language compilers it will accept, what application software can be run and how, etc.

The OS for most workstations is the UNIX system, the OS developed by AT&T and written in the C language. UNIX is a multitasking as well as a multiprocessing and a multiuser OS. It provides direct software support for networking, as well as direct support for virtual memory, giving each active task the illusion of a large amount of memory for that task while protecting each task from errors generated within the others. UNIX also supports a good graphics system.

Some end-users, however, are not enthusiastic about UNIX. One reason is that it is a complex system—understandable, given its many features and capabilities—and to run it, and use it effectively, often requires a UNIX expert, a role for which many a non-computer professional does not qualify. Also the UNIX system has not, as yet, attracted a large library of application programs, especially in the area of DSSs. But UNIX is popular among professionals in AI, partly because of its association with workstations.

The limits of UNIX, however, may well be overcome with the passage of time, especially as UNIX is being recognized and supported by the many computer vendors that constitute the Open Software Foundation (OSF). OSF members share UNIX and related technology with the common goal of developing a single UNIX-based system that all member companies will support. Even IBM, in its OS/2, has recognized UNIX and will offer most of the capabilities of UNIX, albeit in a different way. AT&T is also supporting the popularity of UNIX by licensing its service code and making it available on easy terms.

As there are so many features of a workstation, it will be very expensive to have all features available in one workstation, especially if the maximum capability of each feature is required and if a workstation is desired by each type of professional. Fortunately, not all maximum capabilities are required at one time by each user of a workstation. Also, each type of user has unique and specialized needs, in addition to the characteristics common to most workstations. In response to these needs, we have witnessed the growth of a series of workstations, each one designed for a particular type of user. Unfortunately, there is no one workstation which meets all the diverse needs of a user of an intelligent DSS, but instead a mix of workstations is necessary. This mix includes the engineering, the AI, the managerial, and a general-purpose workstation. It is the potential for intelligent workstations that we shall concentrate on.

In an engineering workstation speed of computation and multitasking capabilities are most important. This sort of power is necessary to give adequate support for the computationally intensive use that is likely of such a workstation—computations in say, fluid mechanics, product design, or flight-path simulation. Engineering-type computations may be done by a MS/OR practitioner. In linear programming, and especially dynamic programming, the computations are many and complex and may well involve matrix manipulations not easily done on a PC.

Software packages are particularly important to a manager who is an end-user of an intelligent DSS, i.e. a DSS with AI capability. Unlike the DSS practitioner, the end-user manager may not be knowledgeable about programming languages, except perhaps a DBMS query language or a fourth-generation language. The higher-level or the more English-like the language, the better as far as most managers are concerned. Menu-driven systems and those with prompts are preferable to command-driven systems.

Interactive computing and multitasking are desirable, but speed is not that critical for the end-user of a DSS with AI. The faster the better, but a second delay in computations, or a fractional second of a delay in response time, is not that critical. What is critical is connectivity. For the end-user of AI, connectivity to a more powerful system, such as the corporate mainframe, is necessary. The end-user manager requires such connectivity to access the corporate database and to use the DBMS query language to obtain information as well as to create *ad hoc* reports.

In a transaction mode, one window monitors transactions while another handles *ad hoc* enquiries. Once the display screen is finalized, the manager may wish to communicate this material to a remote node (say, the Pacific coast or European office), or use it in teleconferencing mode (e.g. when many users are simultaneously using the computer system and seeing the same screen image).

Another important requirement of a managerial workstation is that it must be user friendly. But what is user friendly to one user may not be so to another. Generally speaking, however, one can say that most managers are not computer people; they may not like or understand computer jargon and acronyms; they will not tolerate a pedantic computer system; they may even resist (actively or passively) the use of computers and hence ignore their workstation. In contrast, a technologically oriented DSS practitioner is typically neither fearful of, nor antagonistic to computers. He or she is likely to be quite comfortable with the usual command-language jargon, e.g. may perfer symbols like ' > ' rather than the phrase *greater than*, and may even like the 'company' of computers and not simply acknowledge them as important tools.

Thus there is a big difference between different categories of workstation users in a company. The manager end-user has neither the time nor the inclination to learn about computers for more than, say 2–3 days. For such a person it is important that a workstation gives at least the perception of being user friendly and highly tolerant of end-user errors. And this is where AI technology has a role to play.

FIFTH-GENERATION COMPUTER SYSTEMS

It is desirable to have an intelligent processor in a workstation, but what would be even more desirable and meaningful is a computing system in which all the main components contribute to the intelligence of the system—giving a broad-based and highly effective form of machine intelligence. This holistic approach has been taken in Japan's Fifth Generation Project, and we shall consider this important phenomenon as a whole in this chapter. But to begin with we can just look at their proposals, as they are probably the most comprehensive ones outlining an intelligent workstation (see Fig. 13.2).

Starting from the basic hardware, we have extensive use of very large-scale integrated (VLSI) circuitry for a logical inferencing machine that exploits non-Von Neumann (i.e. parallel) architectural organization. The use of an innovative parallel architecture is expected to support processing speeds (measured in *logical inferences per second*, or LIPS) several orders of magnitude greater than that available of the machines of the early 1980s (i.e. when the project was launched.).

The workstation is designed to use a knowledge-base, a relational database, and intelligent interfaces which can accept input in graphical form (i.e. tables, graphs, or diagrams), and even free-form (such as disciplined handwriting) and spoken instructions as well as the customary textual input. It is proposed that natural languages (Japanese and English) will be a major medium of communication, which should of course be of great interest to management and to non-computer-programming end-users in general.

The core programming language chosen is PROLOG (described in Chapter 14) which has excited many potential users as a refreshingly new approach, but has also sharpened the arguments among AI programmers around the world, and especially the ardent supporters of LISP in the United States.

How much of this very ambitious plan is realizable in the near future remains to be seen (and we shall take up this point in this section of the book). But perhaps the fact that some of the grander goals will not be achieved immediately does not matter much, for we are guaranteed the appearance of some sort of intelligent workstations in the near future just because computer technologists around the world are allocating a lot of resources to this general goal. And the advent of these machines will be of great significance to decision-makers in the business world.

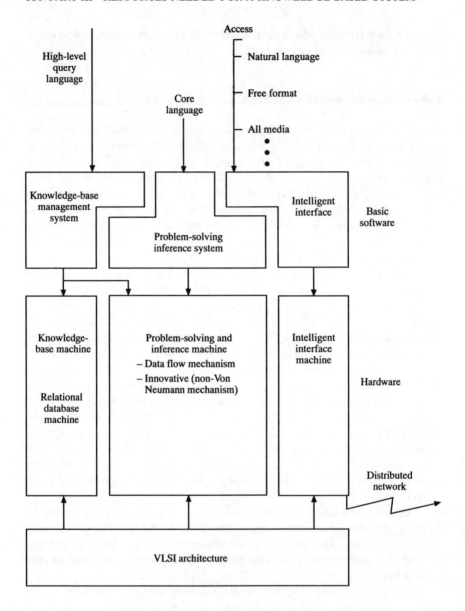

Figure 13.2 The structure of a fifth-generation workstation.

Nowadays the term 'fifth generation' is in general use, even if most users do not really know what it means. In addition, the Fifth Generation initiative, and the many projects that it caused to come into being outside

Japan, have had time to produce their first results. We shall thus look at what the Fifth Generation project aimed at, and what it has so far achieved.

In April 1982, Japan's Ministry of International Trade and Administration (MITI), in cooperation with eight computer companies, launched the Fifth Generation project. The proposed research would span more than a decade and would, it was hoped, result in a leap forward in computer technology (both hardware, software, and database) to the *Fifth Generation Computer System* (5GCS).

Prior to this formal announcement, the Japan Information Processing Center had outlined the 'image of the fifth-generation computer'. This outline emphasized four points:

- There would be a considerable diversity of application encompassed in the project—from high-speed processing on large computer systems to specialized tasks on personal computers.
- However, there would be a general move away from more general-purpose systems and towards specialized ones.
- There would also be a move away from the dominant hardware architecture—the so-called Von Neumann computers, with their sequential access to global memory—to develop non-Von Neumann machines with fundamental capabilities for parallelism.
- Increased emphasis was to be placed on new micro architectures, generated by combining processors, hardware, software, and firmware modules. The importance of the underlying architecture was to grow.

In addition, the possibilities for human–computer interaction were to be drastically expanded. Human input to computers should encompass natural language, pictures, handwritten characters, and speech. A genuine intelligent dialogue capability was proposed, with the computer extracting meaning from the human input and responding with prompts for more or missing information, suggestions, queries, etc. Clearly, a major excursion into the field of AI was envisaged right from the outset.

The Institute for New Generation Computer Technology (ICOT) was set up to run the project. ICOT was divided into three research laboratories: one for hardware, one for basic software, and one for applications software. In addition, there were five, mostly university-staffed, longer-term research groups. They were to work in the following areas:

- Parallel processing mechanisms
- Higher-order inference and kernal language
- Natural-language processing
- Consultation systems
- Basic theory

In more general terms the 5GCS project was aimed at developing 'knowledge information processing systems'. And much to everyone's surprise they identified PROLOG and logic programming as the basic tools, rather than the much more widely used LISP language. The very fact that PROLOG is as well known today as it is, is in large measure due to this decision by the Japanese. Another direct consequence of this choice is that, with fifth-generation systems, we typically rate hardware speed in terms of LIPS, which replaced the previously more common term MIPS. You should recall from Chapter 10 that the execution of a PROLOG program is a series of logical inferences—thus the LIPS measure is a good guide to the speed of execution of logic programs in general.

So what has come out of it all? Certainly we now have available all manner of new computer technology as a direct result of the Japanese project, but will this (or any of the competitive US or European responses) give us fifth-generation systems in the near future? It is hard to answer this question directly.

Once the shock and sense of emergency to respond to the Japanese initiative had abated, people began to take a cooler look at what the goals of the project were. In general, they cover a wide range of possibilities. Natural-language interfaces with computers, for example, have a wide range of interpretations—as you will have gathered, we hope, from your reading of Chapter 11. At one level, we can claim to have natural-language interfaces. There are, for example, robust, reliable, and very useful natural-language interfaces to databases now commercially available. So we might be tempted to say that this goal has been reached. On the other hand, intelligent dialogue in terms of unrestricted (or even anything much better than drastically restricted) natural language between man and machine will not be possible in the foreseeable future. So maybe we should feel inclined to say that the goals of the Fifth Generation project were much too ambitious, given the announced 10-year span of the project. From this perspective, we would be tempted to say that fifth-generation systems will not be available by 1995, or any time immediately thereafter.

If nothing else, the 5GCS project in Japan has aroused the Americans, British, and other Europeans into a friendly, competitive rivalry. There is now a goal to shoot at. The United States does not have a MITI to set targets and to provide seed money, and the US has antimonopolistic laws. But the US does have an industrial base in computers that is both inventive and innovative.

Whatever else does or does not eventually emerge from this global surge in search of radically new computer technology, one thing is assured: dramatic changes in the nature of industrial and commercial computer systems will occur in the near-term future, and the managerial sector will likewise have to sustain some radical reshaping of its functions.

NEURAL COMPUTING

Another rapidly emerging paradigm, which is intimately bound up with the notion of parallel processing, is neural computing (NC). Neural computing was developed initially as a way of computing that mimicked the way the human brain appears to compute, i.e. to compute with a large number of small and primitive processors that are highly interconnected. Partly because we have very little idea how, in detail, the brain does compute, and partly because technologists have their own agenda for what they want their nets to compute, the field of NC (despite its name) has matured as a technological innovation quite divorced, in most cases, from research in neurobiology and brain modelling.

An *NC system* is a network of primitive processing elements, nodes, or units. There are many very different varieties of NC system, and so all we can do is to present a flavour of the idea with a representative example—the feed-forward network.

Each network has input, output, and internal (or 'hidden') neuron-like processing units. Each network also has a 'weight' associated with each connection (or 'link') between processing units. These weights express the relative strengths of the connections between the various processing units. It is these weights that are repeatedly adjusted, leading to 'learning' or training of a neural net. Neural nets with connection weights that specify decision-making criteria can be used to make inferences. Neural nets are a viable and an important alternative in a KBIS when the human domain expert is not able to explain his or her line of reasoning, or may explain or interpret it incorrectly. Neural nets are also an alternative when rules for decision making and problem solving are not known, or the problem is too complex, where the flow of information is interrupted, or where a human domain expert is not available. In this sense it is the automation of a KBIS, also referred to as an *expert network* (Caudill, 1990: 41).

Neural computing is becoming popular partly because of advances in neuroscience and computing technology and partly because of a better understanding and interest of the mechanisms of the brain and of the thinking process, but primarily because network technology, such as training algorithms, is becoming better understood. The feed-forward type of net, for example, is typically trained with the *back-propagation algorithm*.

Figure 13.3 is an illustration of a very small feed-forward neural network. It contains four input units, two units in a hidden layer, and one output unit. Each of the 10 links is associated with a numeric weight. The net computes by processing input information through to the output unit. As a more specific example, let us say that this net has been designed to compute with four input integers and to tell us whether they are all even or not.

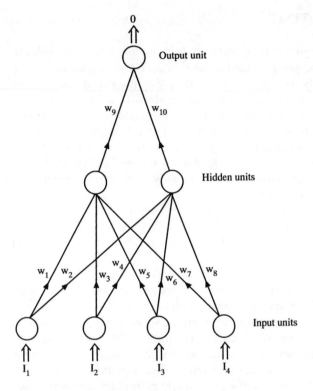

Figure 13.3 A simple feed-forward network.

Several preliminary decisions must be made: first, the four input integers must be coded into the input units; secondly, the output node must be decoded into the desired result (i.e. even or not-even); and thirdly, the links must be assigned appropriate weights in order for the net to compute what we desire. The input problem is easily solved: we feed one input integer into each input node as a numerical activation value. After a computation the output node will exhibit a similar numerical activation value; we must decide how to decode this into possible answers. Before we do this we will add a 'squash' function to this node, which will transform the total of its inputs from links 9 and 10 to a value between 0 and 1.0. Then let us choose a value in the range 0–0.2 as the result 'even', 0.8–1.0 as the result 'not-even', and intervening values as not 'meaningful'. Finally, we assign small random values as the link weights (usually values close to 0). The basic computational ability of this net is quite simple: each node sums its input values and passes this sum (possibly 'squashed' or thresholded) to each of its outgoing links. The value received by each link is multiplied by the weight associated with the link, and the resultant value passed into the node at the end of the link.

With our small net can we now compute our desired function? It seems unlikely. What with randomly assigned link weights, there seems to be no good reason to think that our net might succeed—and in fact it does not. All we have done in this initial setup is to build a net with the *potential* to compute the desired function. Now we must train it to do so.

We generate a training set of input–output pairs. Here is such a set, composed of four teaching examples:

1. (2 4 6 8)   (even)
2. (16 2 2 3)   (not-even)
3. (3 3 3 1)   (not-even)
4. (8 2 8 2)   (even)

Each of these training examples consists of a valid input paired with the correct answer for the function that we wish our net to learn. We now use this training set (in reality we would need a much bigger set) together with the back-propagation algorithm to train our net automatically. The basic training cycle is to put into the net one of our training inputs, say (2 4 6 8), process it throughout the net, and read off the output—let us say 0.5. This is not correct. A correct answer would be a value between 0 and 0.2. From this the back-propagation algorithm computes the error in the calculation (i.e. $0.5 - 0.2$) and uses this to alter the weights of all the links in the net (layer by layer from output back to input—hence *back*-propagation algorithm). When the modified net is presented with the same input, its computation will be closer to the correct answer. This is guaranteed by the back-propagation algorithm. So by repeating this cycle many times the net can be successively adjusted (just by changing the weights) to eventually compute the desired function correctly, though this may take many training examples and perhaps many thousands of iterations with each one. This task can be time consuming but it is done automatically and so consumes computer time rather than person time.

There are, however, some significant limitations of NC, namely that large amounts of data and long periods of learning time are required properly to train a complex system.

Some of the unsolved problems with this new technology are as follows:

1. How do we configure a net with the potential to learn a given function—e.g. how many units do we put in a hidden layer?
2. How do we construct a training set that is sufficient to train the net adequately?
3. How do we determine that the net has learned the desired function?

4. What do we do about acceptance test failure—train some more; retrain from scratch?
5. What do we do if our net does not seem to be learning to compute the training set?

Another persistent problem is that neural-net implementations do not automatically explain their decisions and justify them, which is now an expected feature of all KBISs. The inability to explain or justify decisions in neural nets arises from the fact that the connection weights do not always have an obvious interpretation. A comparison of neural nets with a KBIS is shown in Table 13.1.

There are many unresolved issues in neural-net technology, e.g. can we train nets to have human performance levels? Another issue and problem is that of integrating a neural net with a KBIS.

Table 13.1 Comparison of a neural net with a KBIS

	Neural nets	KBIS
Objective	To be trained to exhibit the desired behaviour	To be built to replicate human decision making and to transform expertise
Type of task	Analyse data after previous training or learning sets	Analysis with conventional and KBIS approaches
Driver	Numeric data	Knowledge and symbols
Scope	Self-organizing (largely unknown)	Narrow domain and closed
Nature of task	Semi-structured (in order to provide learning sets)	Semi-, ill- and well-defined and structured
When invoked	For pattern classification	Sequential, logic-based, repetitive symbolic manipulation
Interface	Not so friendly	Very friendly
Reasoning	Associative	Logical
Testing	Fast and easy	Slow and difficult
Mother discipline	Biological science Neuroscience	Artificial intelligence
Personnel involved	Neurocomputing engineer	Domain expert Knowledge engineer
Computer	Parallel processors (ideally)	PC to mainframe + LISP computer
Programming	C	Third-generation and AI languages

There are, however, some important advantages of NC. In knowledge acquisition, for example, it has always proved very difficult to specify in the abstract what a domain expert knows. By way of contrast, it is typically easy to get examples of the expert's expertise. So while the basis of a conventional, programming-type, implementation of the expert's expertise is hard to obtain, the basis for net training, the heart of an NC implementation, is readily available.

Table 13.2 summarizes the differences between NC and conventional programming.

It is too early to predict accurately where and how NC will most usefully contribute to the future of KBIS development. The main point is that it offers an entirely new option, and one that exhibits strategic strengths to cover for the weaknesses of more conventional approaches.

Finally, this chapter has been concerned mainly with hardware issues as well as parallelism. Currently, most neural nets which are inherently parallel computations, are simulated on conventional sequential machines. There are two reasons for this. First, conventional sequential-processing computers are more generally available than parallel computers; and second, at this early stage in NC, when many different options are being employed, it makes sense to explore with software simulations before any commitment to a specific parallel hardware is made.

Table 13.2 A comparison of neural computing and conventional computing

Neural computing	Conventional computing
Macro-engineering How many layers? How many nodes per layer?	Micro-engineering What specific statements? What specific order?
Automatic training	Manual algorithm design
Test failure → more training	Test failure → analyse algorithm
Maintenance More training Retrain from scratch	Maintenance analyze algorithm and devise changes
Robustness Behaviour relatively immune to random error	Robustness Fragile: one small failure can crash whole system
Accuracy Computes approximations	Accuracy Computes precisely
Specification Need only a set of examples	Specification Need a complete, abstract specification

NETWORKING

Whatever technology emerges for the future processor, there is great certainty that it will not be merely a stand-alone system. In a KBIS environment, there will be a need for the interconnecting of processors, not only to gain access to a more powerful processor but also to gain access to another knowledge-base or even another peripheral. One such interlinking for a workstation to other processors is shown in Fig. 13.4. In the real world the other processors may also be interconnected, though this is not shown in Fig. 13.4 in order to keep the diagram simple. Also, the strategy for networking used in Fig. 13.4 is a bus, and of course there are other strategies of networking. Networking and telecommunications are one of the fastest growing sectors of the computing industry. One factor that is holding back a greater acceptance and use of networking is a lack of standards—standards that range from architecture to the format of a message. Once standards, and preferably international standards, are adopted, networking will offer the access necessary for a KBIS.

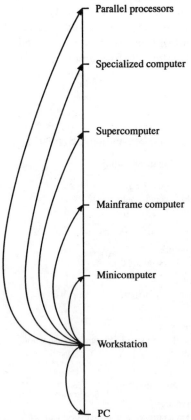

Figure 13.4 Interconnections of a works#tation to other processors.

SUMMARY AND CONCLUSIONS

In this chapter we have focused on the variety of computer systems that are available for use in business by managers for running a KBIS. We deal with programming languages in the next chapter and we will consider the people in a subsequent one. In addition to the hardware technology (LISP machines, parallel architectures, etc.), we compared and contrasted the major options open to managers who intend to computerize some aspects of their businesses. We explored the general notion of parallelism and saw that it is a complex issue in its own right. Subsequently, we reviewed an important emergent option in parallelism—neural computing. So the decision to exploit parallelism can be implemented in many different ways, each with its own advantages and disadvantages.

A historical view of the evolution of processors and processing, especially as they relate to a KBS, is shown in Fig. 13.5.

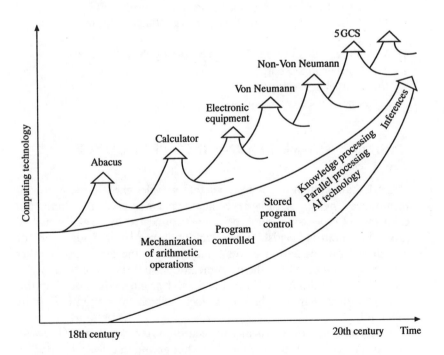

Figure 13.5 Evolution of computing.

CASE 13.1 SURVEY OF PROCESSORS

In a recent extensive survey in the United Kingdom, over 65 per cent of the interviewees favoured the PC approach to ESs. A rationale of this state of the use of processors is given by Richard Forsyth:

> I think one of the advantages we had in early days was the smaller budgets for developing expert systems than the Americans. We were forced to take the technology down to the PC level and build systems that ran on PCs and that gave us a strong UK market and a lot of development work going on at that level. . . . We have certainly managed to date not to be swamped by imported products on the small machines. So most of the work that goes on at the lower end of the market is home-grown. . . . The PC approach is giving way to a networked (or integrated) systems approach.

Source: R. Rada (1990) 'Expert systems in the UK: from AI to KBS', *IEEE Expert,* **5** (4), 12–17.

Questions
1. Is the PC a good processor for a KBIS—but only initially? Explain.
2. What are the advantages and limitations of using a PC?
3. Is the use of a PC dictated by the availability of suitable PCs in a country?
4. When and why should a PC be replaced by the following?
    (*a*) A larger processor.
    (*b*) Parallel processing.
    (*c*) A network of processors.

CASE 13.2 NETtalk: LEARNING TO PRONOUNCE ENGLISH

The NETtalk system is a neural net that was designed to learn how to pronounce English. A three-layer neural net was used; it contained a total of 309 processing units (or nodes) connected by 18 629 weighted links. The input is English text (a window seven letters wide), and the output is a pronunciation of the middle letter—the three letters either side provide a context for the pronunciation. So if the word 'roughly' is input, then the output should be the correct pronunciation of 'g' in this context rather than say 'g' in 'it goes', which is pronounced quite differently.

NETtalk was automatically trained on 50 000 words together with all the correct pronunciations, and though not perfect, learned to pronounce 95 per cent of all tests accurately. In only 55 per cent of further tests, however, was the system's pronunciation judged to be perfect.

Source: T. J. Sejnowski and C. R. Rosenberg (1986) 'NETtalk: a parallel network that learns to read aloud', Technical Report JHU/EECS-86/01, Department of Electrical Engineering and Computer Science, John Hopkins University, Baltimore, MD.

Questions

1. Pronunciation of English is typically characterized by about 300 pronunciation rules. All efforts to 'find' these rules within the trained network have failed. Why do you think this is so? Why do you think that researchers expected to 'find' these rules within the trained network?
2. NETtalk pronounced English with an American accent. What determined the accent learned by the neural net? What do you think needs to be done to change the system's accent to say a British-English accent?
3. What are the theoretical and practical implications of NETtalk?
4. What are the applications of NETtalk for business operations and for business management?

REVIEW AND DISCUSSION QUESTIONS

13.1 Why is there a need for special hardware for a KBIS?

13.2 LISP machines are special-purpose AI computers. Explain why they need to be large and powerful, yet only single-user machines.

13.3 'Parallel processing has always been viewed as a potential saviour of AI systems.' Give an account of the reasoning behind this statement, and indicate, in general terms, what opportunities exist to satisfy the AI demand for parallel processing.

13.4 'Parallel computers are usually much easier to build than to use effectively in AI.' Explain and discuss this statement.

13.5 Supercomputers are very powerful machines, but they are not widely used for AI programming. Explain why this is so, and give reasons why this may (or may not) change in the future.

13.6 Substantial success with the endeavours of automatic programming will open up new possibilities for computer usage by non-programming personnel, such as managers. Explain what is meant by automatic programming, hence suggest some of the new possibilities that might be open to, say, a manager, when automatic programming becomes a reality.

13.7 Automatic programming is a subfield of AI. Why is this so?

13.8 Computers that can learn will revolutionize computer usage in most businesses. Explain, with some specific examples, why this statement is true.

BIBLIOGRAPHY AND REFERENCES

Andersen, J. A. and E. Rosenfeld (eds) (1988) *Neurocomputing*, MIT Press, Cambridge MA.
An encyclopaedic discussion of neurocomputing with an emphasis on the use of neurocomputing for research.

Antonoff, M. (1989) 'Building the CEO workstation', *Personal Computing*, **13** (4), 90–92.
A good discussion of the needs of a top manager for a workstation.

Barron, N. (1989) 'The ever-shrinking, ever-expanding lap tops', *Byte*, **14** (8), 90–96; *Byte*, **14** (5).
This is a special issue on 'PC-Priced Workstations', Nick Barron authors 'Two Powerful Systems from SUN', pp. 108–112 and Ben Smith discusses 'The UNIX Connection', pp. 245–252.

Caudill, M. (1990) 'Using neural nets: making an expert network, part 4', *AI Expert*, **5** (7), 41–45.
This is the fourth in an informative series of articles on neural nets. In this fourth article, the author shows how 'expert networks can work for problems that require network solutions without the benefit of a domain expert's contributions'.

Coleman, K. G. and S. Watenpool (1992) 'Neural networks in knowledge acquisition', *AI Expert*, **7** (1), 36–39.
Discusses how neural nets can help in knowledge acquisition.

Duggal, S. M. and P. R. Popovich (1992–93) 'Practical applications of neural networks in business', *Journal of Computer Information Systems*, **XXXIII** (2), 8–12.
Against a background of excellent and profuse statistics, the authors discuss applications of neural nets in business.

Fisher, E. M. (1986) 'Building AI behind closed doors', *Datamation*, **32** (15), 46–48.
There is discussion of research techniques that are designed to go beyond the limitations of implementing AI problems as simple rule-based systems. In particular, the author reports discussions with several leading researchers on the potential for massively parallel architectures.

Gallant, S. I. (1988) 'Connectionist Expert Systems', *Communications of the ACM*, **31** (2), 152–169.
'Connectionist networks can be used as expert system knowledge bases. Furthermore, such networks can be constructed from training examples by machine learning techniques. This gives a way to automate the generation of expert systems for classification problems.'

Hillman, D. V. (1990) 'Integrating neural nets and expert systems'. *AI Expert*, **5** (6), 54–59.
'Flexibility, improved knowledge representation, and intelligence are just some advantages of these integrated systems.'

Horowitz, E., A. Kemper and B. Narasimhan (1985) 'A survey of application generators', *IEEE Software*, January, 40–54.
A good survey of this practical approach to automatic programming for business personnel. They cover the current state of the art in detail, with specific systems illustrated with detailed examples. Finally, they consider the possibilities of broadening the scope of AI technology, and they argue that its merger with conventional programming languages is both desirable and feasible.

Hwang, K., J. Ghosh and R. Chowkwanyum (1987) 'Computer architectures for artificial intelligence processing', *IEEE Computer*, January, 19–27.
The authors present a taxonomy of AI machines in which they first divide AI computer architectures in three categories: language-based machines, knowledge-based machines, and intelligent interface machines. The first category they further subdivide into LISP machines, PROLOG machines, and functional programming machines. Knowledge-based machines they further subdivide into semantic network architectures, rule-based, object-

based, and neural networks. The last category they subdivide into speech recognition systems, pattern-recognition/image-processing systems, and vision systems. Under each of these subcategories they list and provide further references to a number of specific example systems.

Their taxonomy is useful, and the full references to further details are very helpful, but the reader should not be too influenced by their categorization scheme—it makes for a tidy presentation, but it has a lot of debatable aspects, e.g. what is the justification for putting neural-network architectures as a subcategory of knowledge-based machines? Similarly, a number of their specific examples are software 'machines' (i.e. programs and not actual hardware computers).

Ingres, *News Relational*, 1/90 (1990) published by INGRES Limited, Anchor House, 15–19 Britten Street, London SW3 3TY.

A glossy magazine promoting the Ingres database products, but easy-to-read articles on the latest in relational database technology.

Kerschberg, L. (ed.) (1986) *Expert Database Systems*, Benjamin/Cummins, Menlo Park, CA.

This book is the edited proceedings from the First International Workshop on Expert Database Systems. The collection of papers it contains covers most aspects of expert database systems from 'theory of knowledge-bases' and the impacts of logic programming to concerns for the interfaces to these systems.

Lerman, S. R. (1988) 'UNIX workstations in academia: at the crossroads', *Academic Computing*, October, 16–18, 51–55.

This article is not confined to UNIX, nor to academia. It is an excellent tutorial on workstations.

Looney, C. G. (1993) 'Neural networks as expert systems', *Expert Systems with Applications*, **6** (2), 129–136.

A provocative article.

McCandles, H. (1989) 'Enter the business workstation', *Practical Computing*, June, 36–41.

A good discussion of 'a high performance assault on the office desk-top'.

Parks, C., C. M. Collins and G. R. Graves (1989) 'Parallel processing: a critical element in applying artificial intelligence to manufacturing', *Computers and Industrial Engineering*, **16** (1), 1–7.

The authors claim that the Japanese Fifth Generation project has spurred many researchers into investigating the potential benefits of parallel processing. They claim that 'much of this work is a result of the desire to apply artificial intelligence techniques in a real-time environment such as manufacturing'. They thus see parallel processing as a means simply to speed up AI systems which, they claim, tend to be inordinately slow.

Partridge, D. (1994) 'Neural networks in software engineering', in J. J. Marciniak (ed.), *Encyclopedia of Software Engineering*, Wiley-Interscience, New York.

An article outlining the potential of neural computing as a novel software engineering technology.

Robinson, P. (1987) 'A world of workstations', *Byte*, **13** (2), 251–260.

A detailed, but not too technical, discussion of price and performance curves of a workstation in comparison with a PC.

Rubin, C. (1988) 'Workstations: the personal computer alternative', *Personal Computing*, **12** (2), 124–131.

A very readable discussion of a workstation replacing the PC, from an author of books on PCs.

Schultz, B. (1988) 'Workstation graphics: blossoming for business', *Datamation*, **34** (5), 81.

Not only a good tutorial on the use of graphics, but also tips on selecting workstations for graphics.

Scientific American, Special Issue, **1** (1989).

This special issue is on 'Trends in Computing'. It has many articles relevant to this chapter. One is an overview of many trends in computing by Michael L. Dertouzos (pp. 8–15), a tutorial on 'The Connection Machine' by W. Daniel Hillis (pp. 16–23), and 'Networks for Advanced Computing' by Robert E. Kahn (pp. 34–43). There are also articles on advanced computer software and advanced computer chip manufacturing.

Six, G. (1987) 'When a micro can't hack it', *Computer Decisions*, **19** (3), 66–69.
A confrontational discussion of micros versus workstations with 'low-end technical workstations running rings around microcomputers'.

Stolfo, S. J. (1987) 'Initial performance of the DADO2 prototype', *IEEE Computer*, January, 75–82.
The DADO series of computers are special-purpose parallel computers that are designed to be attached to a conventional host processor and are used to speed up the processing in AI problems that are implemented as production systems. The basic idea is to search alternative possibilities in parallel. It is described as a 'medium-grain parallel machine'. The current prototype, DADO2, has 1023 8-bit processing elements and each element has 16K bytes of memory.

'Supercomputing', (1989) *IEEE Computer*, **22** (11), pp. 57–68.
This is a good survey of the growth of supercomputing with statistics on the number of American as well as Japanese supercomputers. There is also a detailed technical comparison of the Cray X-MP, Cray-2, Cray Y-MP, CD/ETA 10G, IBM 3909S, Fujitsu/Amdahl VP400E, Hitachi 820-80, and NEC SX-2.

Turban, E. (1992) *Expert Systems and Applied Artificial Intelligence*, Macmillan, New York.
Chapter 18, pp. 621–644, is on 'Neural Computing and AI'.

Uhr, L. (1987) *Multi-computer Architectures for Artificial Intelligence*, Wiley, New York.
The author provides an overview of both the present situation and future prospects for fast, robust, parallel systems. He pays particular attention to the special problems that AI introduces, but he also emphasizes approaches to solutions that show promise of handling complex real-world problems in real time. A useful and readable compendium of information on parallel architectures for AI problems.

Viskovich, F. (1987) 'What threatens mainframe computing?', *Computerworld*, **XXI** (42), 75–84.
The author presents the arguments for and against the demise of the mainframe computing in the face of technological innovations that have given rise to tremendous increases in computing power available in minis and PCs as well as networking possibilities—historical interest, if nothing else.

Waltz, D. L. (1987) 'Applications of the Connection Machine', *IEEE Computer*, January, 85–96.
An introduction to this specific parallel computer, and some discussion, with specific example applications, of the types of problems that it can be used to implement effectively.

Wasserman, P. D. and R. M. Oetzel (1990) *Neural Source*, Van Nostrand Reinhold, New York.
A good sourcebook.

Yoon, and L. L. Peterson (1992) 'Artificial neural networks: an emerging new technique', *Database*, **23** (1), 55–58.
Discusses characteristics and applications of artificial neural nets as well as a taxonomy of ANN learning algorithms.

Zahedi, F. (1993) *Intelligent Information Systems for Business: Expert Systems with Neural Networks*, Wadsworth, Belmont, CA.
There are three chapters and one appendix on neural nets.

14

PROGRAMMING FOR A KNOWLEDGE-BASED SYSTEM

> When someone says: 'I want a programming language in which I need
> only say what I wish done,' give him a lollipop.
> Alan Perlis, *Epigrams on Programming*

THE ROLE OF REPRESENTATIONS IN PROBLEM SOLVING

Most programming languages are equally powerful, i.e. what can be
programmed in one language can also be programmed in any other. Now, if
this is true (and it is!), the question that you should be puzzling over is:
'Why are there so many different programming languages?'

Part of the answer is that various groups of programmers have their
favourite language, for reasons historical, contextual, and totally idiosyn-
cratic. And part of the answer is the representational convenience that
certain languages offer for certain types of computation. It is one thing to
say that all programming languages are equally powerful; it is quite another
to say that they are all equally easy to use for a given problem.

So different languages facilitate programming in different problem
classes: FORTRAN is good for numeric computation; COBOL is
particularly useful for business applications that involve file processing and
report generating, etc. LISP is the favoured AI language, with PROLOG
emerging in recent years as the major alternative.

'What makes a language easy to program in?' This is a complex
question, but a large part of the answer is to be found in the quite simple

observation that, if the problem and the programming language contain similar structures for representing the essential data, then the programming task will be simplified. Thus, a business application such as payroll generation involves a large file of the company employees, some relatively simple calculations that must be repeated for every employee in the file, and the need to generate a report and pay-related information for each one. The language COBOL offers easy and efficient file structures and processing; it supports simple numerical computation; and it offers powerful, easy-to-use facilities for document generation. So the problem and the programming language fit together quite nicely. A problem in nuclear physics, on the other hand, is likely to involve matrices of numbers as input, huge and highly intricate calculations, and perhaps only a single number as output. For this sort of problem FORTRAN is ideal: it offers a straightforward representation for matrices of numbers and efficient mechanisms for processing them; it offers a very efficient numerical computation capability, in general; but its representational structures for document generation are both awkward and inefficient to use.

In sum, if the 'objects' in the problem statement (e.g. files or numerical matrices) are important representational features in a particular programming language, then that is the best language to use. But there is a further complication to this question. It concerns the objects in the problem statement—sometimes the necessary objects are obvious, but sometimes they are not. In fact, in AI applications the choice of objects (or, equivalently, the choice of representational scheme) can drastically affect the simplicity of adequate solutions to the problem. An initial part of AI problem solving is therefore an exploration of alternative representational schemes for the problem statement, and then, of course, both the representation scheme and the processing strategy selected will determine (to a large extent) the most appropriate programming language to use. Let us give a few examples.

The multilated chess-board is the popular example: remove a square from diagonally opposite corners of a chess-board; can the board, which now comprises only 62 squares, be covered with exactly 31 dominoes, given that each domino can cover two adjacent squares? The obvious and straightforward representation of the problem as a search space of partial coverings yields a vast search space which can, in principle, be explored exhaustively: choose a start square and generate a state for each possible placement of a domino on the chosen square and one of its neighbours; for each state place a second domino on an uncovered square, and for each of these placements generate the further set of alternative placements; and so on. ... In principle it is doable. You will either find a covering configuration or exhaust all possibilities. In practice, you will exhaust yourself, wear out the computer, and run into the heat death of the universe before the space has been thoroughly explored.

A better representation of the problem exploits the usual two-colour patterning (the two squares removed are of the same colour, and each domino must cover two differently coloured squares). Now the problem is trivial; the answer is obvious—isn't it? Enough clues.

Edward de Bono treats the reader to a number of such problems as part of his exposition of 'lateral thinking' (de Bono, 1969). For example, in the usual style of a knockout tennis tournament the winner of a match moves into the next round while the loser is out of the tournament. If in any round there is an odd number of players then one lucky person gets a bye into the next round while the rest have to slog it out in individual two-person matches. If 51 people enter a tournament, how many matches must be played to produce the tournament winner) Easy, the answer is just a sum of successive halvings of 51 with the minor complication byes when the halving results in an odd number, i.e. the answer is $25 + 13 + 6 + 3 + 2 + 1$. Most of us can formulate a computation to solve this problem, and within the envisaged computation the problem is represented as one of a summation of successive halvings with the added complication of byes when the number to be halved is odd. But if we do not jump to this obvious representation immediately, a little further exploration of the problem might enable us to see an alternative representation that simplifies the problem drastically. Instead of concentrating on the winners, spare a thought for the losers—you only lose once in a tournament, everybody loses except for the eventual winner, and every match played has one loser. So, from 51 entrants there must be 50 losers, hence, 50 matches.

HOW LANGUAGES AFFECT SOLUTIONS

From the above discussion it should be obvious that the choice of programming language can have profound effects on the computational solution developed—apart from easing the problem-solving process by a wise choice of language, the effect may be one of a bias to one type of solution rather than another (with no real grounds for saying that one is better than, or easier than, the other).

OVERCOMING THE LIMITATIONS OF PROGRAMMING LANGUAGES

As we shall see when we look at some of the details of AI programming languages below, the choice of a programming language necessarily introduces constraints and limitations on the possible computational solutions. The language PROLOG, for example, is a wonderful language for programming conventional knowledge-bases: rules and facts are the basic representational structures in the language, and logical deduction as a processing strategy is already built into the language. But if you want the knowledge-base to be processed using a scheme of probabilistic inference, or by combining forwards and backwards chaining, then you must eschew much of what PROLOG offers and build your desired processing strategy from scratch—you might be better advised to use LISP instead or an ES shell that directly supports the processing scheme that you want to use.

There is a general trade-off to be borne in mind that concerns the limitations imposed by the choice of programming language. A shell or tool is just a higher-level programming language, and, in general, the more customized a language is for a particular sort of application, the more awkward and inefficient it is to use it for a somewhat different task. This warning is especially important for managers, who are not computer experts themselves, when they contemplate which system (combination of actual computer and software shell or tool as described in Chapter 15) to purchase to support a move into ES technology, say. Efficiency and effectiveness suggests that a highly developed tool that directly supports, say, frames and certainty-factor reasoning, will be the best choice for a problem that seems to involve a frame-like representation of objects and a certainty-factor-like reasoning scheme. But if the problem also involves, say, extensive file processing, then that might be very awkward and slow to implement (as well as run, when it is finally implemented) in the particular tool selected. As these tools also tend to be high-priced pieces of software, considerable caution and forethought should be employed before a commitment is finally made.

LISP

LISP, one of the earliest high-level programming languages to emerge (McCarthy *et al.*, 1965), is still very much the vernacular of AI, although aficionados actually work with the extended dialects, such as MACLISP (Touretzky, 1982) or INTERLISP (Teitelman and Masinter, 1981)—dialects plus extras that constitute some of the finest program development environments available.

Flexibility

The nature of incremental system development, or exploratory programming, is such that you do not know quite where you are going to end up with your personal pile of code until you get there. An important characteristic of an AI program, then, is flexibility—keeping options open as long as possible. This can be contrasted with, say, FORTRAN, a programming language that typically offers minimal flexibility to the programmer, e.g. the names and maximum lengths of all array structures must be decided before a program can be compiled.

LISP embodies flexibility in a number of rather different respects. Program variables have neither to be declared before usage nor to be associated with any specific 'type' (e.g. integer or real, as in more conventional programming languages). No limits on data structure sizes (such as lengths of lists) need be specified—they are just grown and shrunk on demand during the running of a LISP program. Data structures can be converted to 'code' and executed at any time. And as a final example, the execution sequence can be halted, backed up, and restarted at any time, i.e. a programmer typically has the flexibility to explore alternative execution paths through a given program without having to rerun the complete program. But this leads us to programming environment support facilities; we will deal with them later.

So AI programming demands a myriad of flexibilities from the programming medium, flexibilities that are neither supplied nor required in more conventional programming, where the programming task is viewed more as a relatively mundane activity of coding a complete, verified, detailed design. In AI, programming is itself fundamentally a process of design. Conventional programming has its own varieties of flexibility: abstract data types, for example, are a minimum-prior-commitment device to aid the traditional process of algorithm design.

The Magic of Recursion

If you are a FORTRAN or a COBOL programmer, say, you would program the function to compute the length of a list as a loop with a counter variable that starts at zero and is incremented by one as each iteration of the loop causes a move to the next list element. When the loop reaches the last list element, it stops and the value of the counter variable is the length of the list. But the recursive thinker would not.

He or she would quickly observe that the length of a list is just the length of the list without its first element plus one (for the first element). And, of course, the length of an empty list is zero, i.e.

length(empty list) = 0
length(L) = length(headless L) + 1

'How true', you might be prepared to concede, 'but not much use'. It is like observing that the monthly sales figures are one plus the monthly sales figures minus one—i.e. a trivial restatement of the problem, and certainly not a solution.

But, you would be wrong. The analogy is false (as so many are these days). A complete, precise, and readily programmable definition of the list-length function is:

length (empty list) = 0
length (LIST) = length (LIST without first element) + 1

As an example of a LISP program we can specify a function that sums a list of values, say integers, and returns that sum as its result. Consider the following pseudocode specification of such a function:

function LISTSUM
    IF the list contains no values
    THEN return zero as the function value
    ELSE return the first list value added to
    the sum of the rest of the list values as
    the function value

The only slightly disturbing feature of this algorithm, especially to the non-recursive programmer, is the seeming circularity of the ELSE clause. The sum of a non-empty list is obtained by adding the value of the first element of the sum of the rest of the list. More disturbing still, perhaps, is the fact that this apparent circularity is real, but there are two reasons that together save the algorithm from endless circularity:

1. The rest of the list (i.e. the list without its first element) is always shorter than the list it derives from.
2. The THEN clause returns a result for the shortest possible list (i.e. the empty list).

Thus it is true that there is a circularity within the ELSE clause: the computation of the sum of a list of values is expressed in terms of the sum of a shorter list of values. But this circular self-referencing, known as *recursion*, will eventually terminate when the rest of the list is empty. The function will then automatically 'unwind'; it will compute the sum of the empty list, then the sum of the last list item, then the sum of the last two items, and so on, until it obtains and returns the sum of all items in the list.

In LISP the body of this function, LISTSUM would be:

```
(COND ((EMPTY LIST)                    O                    )
      (   T   (PLUS(HEADOF LIST)(LISTSUM(RESTOF LIST)))))
```

if we assume appropriate definitions for the functions EMPTY, PLUS, HEADOF, and RESTOF.

Recursion in LISP is the substitute for iteration in more conventional programming languages. (Although a conventional iteration mechanism is always also provided except in 'pure' LISP—a spiritual language that is theoretically capable of being all things to all programmers, but no one dares to sully it by actual usage for practical programming. A sobering thought for the FORTRAN or COBOL man is that 'pure' LISP also has no assignment statement!)

It may be some comfort to those readers who have been dazed by this first intrusion of recursion into their computational lives that normal people do experience great difficulty in mentally executing recursion: don't give up, you're just normal—though we hope to correct that before you reach the end of this book. This unfortunate human inability to think recursively in detail perhaps reflects a paucity of recursive structures in the natural world and a consequent absence of wetware (i.e. neuron-based) stack structures built into the architecture of the brain. So why do AI enthusiasts persist in pushing this obviously awkward mechanism as a central feature of their art?

The answer is that the machine-executable specifications of mechanisms (i.e. algorithms, but we do have an excuse for this specific circumlocution—'algorithm' is a particularly inept characterization of a PROLOG program, as you will see) for solving certain problems are most easily conceptualized and specified recursively, as opposed to iteratively with loop constructs. In fact, this ease of high-level conceptualization is one of the sources of disbelief and difficulty that the non-recursive thinker experiences when confronted with recursive solutions to problems—i.e. a recursive solution often appears to be obviously true, but little more than a restatement of the original problem and certainly not an algorithm for computing solutions.

For example, how can we compute whether some value X is a member of some list L?

```
function MEMBER(X,L)
    IF L is empty THEN return false
    ELSEIF X is the first element of L THEN return true
    ELSE return the result of applying the MEMBER function
    with X to the list L without its first element
```

There are three parts to this specification. If the list is empty then X cannot possibly be a member of it, right?—indubitably true. If X is the first list element, then X must be a member of the list—a similarly unassailable truth, I hope. Finally, if X is a member of the tail of L, then X is a member of L—true, but suspicious as a major component of the member function perhaps. Nevertheless, this specification can be translated directly into LISP code and will compute the membership function correctly. A number of similar examples follow in the PROLOG section of this chapter.

Code–Data Equivalence

Apart from choking on recursion, all of us reared on FORTRAN, BASIC, or COBOL know that code and data are totally different quantities. The program code specifies what is to be done (compute a function, generate a report, etc.), and the data are a set of values with which to do it. You now need to erase from memory this aberrant notion. It does not sit well with LISP, and is even worse as a cerebral companion to PROLOG.

One of the most important features of LISP for AI purposes is the equivalence between executable code and data. One reason for this can be found in the importance of adaptability in intelligent systems, and the consequent need to modify program statements of an AI system at run-time, i.e. to treat program statements like data structures.

In the above example we have a segment of executable code, the body of the function LISTSUM. It is also a list of items (note: a LISP list is delimited by one pair of parentheses).

(COND((EMPTY LIST) O) (T(PLUS(HEADOF LIST) (LISTSUM(RESTOF LIST)))))

This list is somewhat complex in that it contains sublists that themselves contain sublists. As it is a list, it is a valid LISP data item in which the list elements, say the atom COND or the sublist ((EMPTY LIST)O), can be manipulated by other LISP functions.

Although all lists can be treated as data structures, only certain lists can be executed, namely those lists whose first element identifies a function and the rest of whose elements provide appropriate values for the parameters of the particular function identified by the first element.

As you can see, the syntax of LISP is simple. For both executable code and data, the only structure is a list of objects delimited with parentheses. In fact the syntax of LISP is too simple; it is so uniform that the inherent structure of a LISP program tends to elude the human perceptual mechanism. What the programmer's eye tells the programmer's brain is that a LISP program is a collection of identifiers that has been liberally sprinkled with left and right parentheses in much the same apparent order as stars in the sky. Hence, the old joke that the name LISP is an acronym derived from Lost In Superfluous Parentheses. The real source of the name is reputed to be List Processing, and it could well be true. The reader should, at this point, be able to appreciate the wisdom of the choice of lists as the fundamental data structures for a language that uses recursion as a major control structure. Lists of lists can be used to represent trees, arrays, records, etc.— all the standard data structures of conventional languages— and yet most chunks of any of these fancy list structures are themselves lists. A recursive approach to computation thrives on data structures that can be successively whittled down to nothing, while all the time remaining as bona fide data structures of the original type. The simplest example is that a list without its first element is still a list (even if it had only one element to begin with).

But despite its perceptual opacity (or perhaps because of it) LISP is great for machines; that is to say, the syntactic simplicity and uniformity of program and data greatly simplify the implementation of program and data as interchangeable structures. And in addition, implementations of LISP are easily equipped with a more user-friendly syntactic face for human usage (e.g. the COND function given above can typically be programmed in terms of an IF–THEN–ELSE structure, which the system then immediately translates to LISPese).

The fact that LISP allows the manipulation of code-like lists as data structures is not too surprising. It is perhaps a little shocking to think that the sane system designer would contemplate such a thing, but, given that this is the objective of some misconceived project, we could do much the same thing in, say, FORTRAN: an input character string could have the form of an executable statement, and characters within it could be swapped around, etc. Suppose that you ended up with the character string 'GO TO 93', how would you execute this string of characters? Well, in FORTRAN you couldn't ('And quite right too', we can almost hear the non-AI enthusiasts murmur). But in LISP no holds are barred ('You are free to throttle yourself', the software engineer might add).

In all LISP systems we have available the function EVAL which, as its name suggests, evaluates (i.e. executes) the list that it is given. In fact, EVAL is virtually the LISP system itself. (The LISP system is just a three-function loop, READ–EVAL–PRINT. It reads in a list—which should be a reference to a function together with appropriate input values for that function—executes it, prints out the value returned by the function referenced, and then waits for another list to read, etc.) So EVAL turns a data structure into code. To move in the other direction (i.e. from code to data structure) the user can access the source code for a function that has been previously defined and simply change it. It can then be stored away again as the definition of the function for subsequent execution.

The Special Assignment

Pure LISP has no assignment statement—i.e. no statement for setting a variable to some value! This fact ought to elicit at least some raising of eyebrows for the traditional programmer who probably knows that about half of the statements in a conventional program are usually assignment statements. A large chunk of traditional programming consists in computing values and assigning them to variables, i.e. of programming assignment statements. But, as values can be computed and passed around using the parameter and function-result mechanisms, there is, in principle, no need for an assignment statement as such. In practice, however, it turns out to be a very handy thing to have available, despite the fact that it represents a blatant misuse of the functional philosophy. In most LISP systems, the function SETQ is used. So to set the variable X to the value 5, we type:

(SETQ X 5)

and the LISP system responds, quick as a flash, with

5

which is the value that this function returns. Functions always return a value; this is, in fact, the main function of a function: we send values to the function via the parameters, the function computes with these values, and it sends the result back—a function should not change the value of any of its parameters, as this would be a hidden change (it is hidden inside the function body), a generally undesirable *side-effect*.

But notice that in the case of the assignment function, SETQ, the whole point of the function is not to compute a value, but to change the value of its first parameter. Considering the statement involving SETQ given above: whatever the value of X was before SETQ was used, its value is 5 afterwards.

Assignment is thus a bad sort of function. Hence, pure LISP has no truck with it.

LISTS OF PROPERTIES

This section is not a diversion into the records of an estate agent, but a brief look at a second type of value that can be attached to LISP variables, and one that is particularly useful in AI. Associating objects, i.e. relating one object to another, is a key strategy in many knowledge-representation schemes. The property-list feature of LISP provides direct support for this requirement.

A *property list* is a list of (*attribute value*) pairs, such as (CONTENTS JEANS), (STYLE WESTERN), (COLOUR BLUE), (NUMBER 12). Such a property list may be associated with a variable, say CARTON_1.

We might write this total structure as:

(CARTON_1 ((CONTENTS JEANS) (STYLE WESTERN)
(COLOUR BLUE) (NUMBER 12))

Thus we can build complex structured objects for a program to manipulate in its efforts to display intelligent reasoning. The structure given above might be used by, say, an inventory management system.

Property-list items are associated with variables, referenced, and changed using primitive functions supplied by the LISP system. Property lists are a special feature of the LISP language, and that is useful in a KBIS.

LISP is an ancient language (not to be compared with Sanskrit, but on a par with FORTRAN) and consequently there are many varieties which have diverged so far from McCarthy's original vision that they are effectively different languages. In order to combat this diversification, a standard, Common LISP, has been defined (Steele, 1984). Most LISP systems now contain all of Common LISP as a subset (or at least claim that they do). Hence, programmers whose concern is portability can restrict themselves to just this subset of the goodies available.

PROLOG

The new boy on the block who has made a somewhat unexpected impact is PROLOG. It is a European language that provides a neatly defined and efficiently implemented theorem-proving capability; as an efficient inference engine it has a strong claim to be an appropriate language for the implementation of knowledge-bases in KBISs.

PROLOG (short for PROgramming in LOGic, its advocates claim; or PROtotype LOGic programming, as is rumoured by its detractors; or even PROgramation et LOGique, as the purists claim who note that, in the south of France, where PROLOG was born, English is definitely not the language of choice) is based on the predicate calculus—gruesome but true (we do not hide the truth, however unpalatable), yet mercifully quite unmemorable. All that you need at your synaptic fingertips, so to speak, is the knowledge that, given the rule that:

IF A is true THEN B is true.

and the fact:

A is true.

you are at liberty to conclude:

B is true.

But who in their right mind could do otherwise? Nevertheless, having mastered this mechanism (a mechanism of logical inference quite unbelievably called *modus ponens*), you are nearly a master of PROLOG.

Consider our earlier function LISTSUM. It is composed of two rules, one unfortunately but unavoidably recursive:

IF the list is empty   THEN the sum of its values is zero.
IF the list is not empty   THEN the sum of its values is the value
                                         of the first element plus the sum of
                                         the values in the list without its first
                                         element.

These two rules constitute a declaration of the logical relationships that hold between a list and the sum of its values, and as such they are almost a PROLOG program (all that needs to be added is the appropriate syntactic sugar). We have not specified, in a conventional programming sense, how to compute this function; we have just declared the relationships that must hold if the computation is correctly done, but that is all that you have to do in PROLOG programming. The PROLOG system takes care of how exactly these specified relationships are to be realized computationally. It is almost the programmer's dream come true, but as with all dreams it can turn into something more like a nightmare all too quickly.

The terms *procedural, functional, declarative, applicative,* as well as *symbolic* (one that we have already expressed our dissatisfaction with) are all commonly bandied about in descriptions of programming languages. Certainly these descriptors, which have emerged as accepted terminology in folk computer science, have some meaning, and some have some more meaning than others, but in general they are hazy terms. So treat with circumspection glib characterizations of programming languages presented in terms of these descriptors.

One of the less arguable uses of such descriptors is the categorization of PROLOG as a declarative language, or programming in PROLOG as declarative programming. The essence of this characterization is that programming in PROLOG is primarily a task of declaring the logical relationships upon which the desired computation rests. (Hence, the less defendable statement that programming in PROLOG *is* logic programming.)

The Independence of Declaration

In PROLOG the control structure and the declarative structure of a program are separated. A PROLOG program primarily specifies only the relationships that hold between the computational objects. How these relationships will be processed (i.e. what control structure will be used) is separate and part of the implementation of the language. This state of affairs can be contrasted with traditional programming, where the programmer has to work with a tangle of both declarations and control structure.

It is time for a concrete example of a PROLOG program, but first we must look at the data structure that we shall use in our program; we must see how PROLOG deals with lists.

A list in PROLOG is a sequence of objects separated by commas and delimited by square brackets. Thus [a,A,1] is a list of length three. The first element is the constant 'a' (denoted as a constant by the lower case used), the second element is a variable named 'A' (a variable is denoted by upper case), which would normally but not necessarily be associated with a value. The third and last element of this list is the numeric constant, the number 1.

An empty list contains no elements and looks like this [ ] —surprise, surprise. Finally, there is a list operator '|' which may be used to both behead and rehead lists (i.e. it can be used to remove the first list element or add a new head element to a list).

Now we are ready to translate our statements about lists and the sums of their values into PROLOG. The form of the 'listsum' procedure (or *predicate*, if you prefer technical nomenclature) that we have chosen uses two arguments, i.e. two quantities following the function name, enclosed in parentheses, and separated by commas. The first argument is a list, or the name of a list, and is the list whose sum is to be computed. The second argument is a numerical value, or a variable whose value will be numerical when the function is used properly, which will be the sum of the list elements when the listsum computation has been completed.

```
listsum([ ],0).
listsum([H|T], S):- listsum( T, Stail), S is Stail + H.
```

Let us read this for you in English. The first clause is a true fact, it states that the sum of the values of an empty list is zero (no problems with that, we hope). The second clause is an inference rule (note the inference operator ':-'), which states that S is the sum of the values of a list whose head is H and whose tail (i.e. the headless list) is T, if Stail is the sum of the values in the tail T, and (in PROLOG the 'and' is represented by a comma) S is the value of Stail plus the value of the first, or head, element H. This is also, if not equally, obviously true, isn't it?

The two clauses given above constitute a useful PROLOG program, and one moreover that either checks that a given value is the sum of a given list or alternatively can tell us the sum of a given list. How do we induce this program to compute? Well we ask it questions about lists and sums. For example, we could ask:

listsum([2,3,5], 10)?

and the response would be:

YES

Or we could ask:

listsum([5,2,1], X)?

In effect we are asking if there is a value for the variable 'X' that would make it the sum of the list [5,2,1]; again the response would be:

YES

and in addition it would tell us the value that makes the particular listsum relationship we asked about true, i.e. X = 10.

Loss of Control: Good or Bad?

Programming in PROLOG, a form of declarative programming, thus requires only that the programmer states the individual logical relationships that must be true if the desired computation is correctly done. The PROLOG interpreter then takes over the task of controlling the computation. It decides which rule to use and when. The programmer is freed from the burden of setting up loops and ensuring that they begin and end appropriately, etc. This must all seem like a very good thing. And it would be if it was entirely true, and if we did not care how long our computations took.

First, let us look at the truth of this claim that the programmer need not be concerned with issues of control sequencing in PROLOG programming—after all, it is almost true. One major result of this nearly true claim is that statement sequencing in PROLOG can almost be random. Readers with some years of wrestling with computers behind them will remember the days when a program was a deck of punched cards. If a PROLOG program were to be punched on such cards, one clause per card, it is almost true to say that we could shuffle the cards before each run and the resultant randomized version of the program would be just as correct as the original; it might take more or less time to execute after successive shuffles, but the results would be the same.

As we have said, this no-effect-statement-shuffling story is almost true. So when is it not true? Well, consider the following PROLOG program, which is designed to find a path between any two vertices in a network (a problem closely akin to the fundamental problem of traditional AI—finding paths from initial states to goal states):

```
path(V,V).
path(V1,V2):-transition(V1,V3),path(V3,V2).
```

The first clause states the fact that there is always a path from a vertex V to that same vertex V. You cannot argue with that, can you? The path is short, it is true, but it is also true that there is always a path nevertheless. The second clause states that there is a path from some vertex V1 to some vertex V2, if there is a transition from vertex V1 to some intermediate vertex V3, and there is a path from V3 to V2. This is also clearly true, but, as is the nature of recursive statements, it seems to be little more than a restatement of the problem, and certainly not an algorithm for computing paths. Yet it is.

Assuming that we have *transition* defined correctly (i.e. in terms of the set of possible moves between vertices for a given network), then the above program will search for a path between any two vertices in a network. Given the trivial network illustrated in Fig. 14.1, we can see how this program works.

This is not one of the more representative examples of a rich and complex search space, but one whose triviality has been marginally, but critically, reduced by linking the last vertex (numbered 4) back to vertex 1. Let me list the true facts about possible transitions in this network:

```
transition(1,2).
transition(2,3).
transition(3,4).
transition(4,1).
```

Thus the first fact listed above, i.e. transition(1,2), states that it is true that there is a path from vertex 1 to vertex 2. This set of all the possible transitions in the pathetic network illustrated in Fig. 14.1 states, in effect, that there is a clockwise circular path all around the network. And this is, of

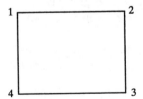

Figure 14.1 A trivial network.

course, a set of four **PROLOG** clauses, true facts that define the search space we have illustrated. Given these four facts and the two 'path' clauses, we can query this program.

path(1,2)?

Is there a path from vertex 1 to vertex 2, we might naïvely ask?

YES

is the firm response.

How did it do it? Well, the fact 'path(V,V)' was no help, because we were concerned about the possibility of a path between two different vertices, not about a path from a vertex to itself. But the second path rule states that there is a path from 1 to 2 if there is a transition from 1 to some other vertex, and a path from that other vertex to vertex 2 (i.e. when V1 = 1 and V2 = 2). The first transition fact states that there is a transition from vertex 1 to vertex 2, so 2 is tried as an intermediate vertex (i.e. V3 gets the value 2).

Now the first subclause of the right side of the rule is true when V3 = 2, so the problem reduces to determining the truth of the second subclause (path(V3,V2)) when V3 = 2 and V2 = 2, i.e. the system must prove that path(2,2) is true. And now we can see the worth of the apparently useless fact 'path(V,V)'. When the variable V is given the value 2, it states that path (2,2) is true, which is just what we wanted to know. Hence the PROLOG system can answer 'YES' to our query.

Declarations of recursive relationships are infinitely circular, e.g. path(V1,V2):-transition(V1,V3),path(V3,V2), and what gets us out of this not exactly vicious but definitely unhelpful circularity is the clause path(V,V). But in order for the PROLOG interpreter to cease chasing its own tail, so to speak, it must always encounter this stopping clause (i.e. there is always a path from any vertex to that same vertex) *before* it encounters the general case. PROLOG interpreters always work through the possible clauses sequentially from top to bottom. So, the upshot of all this is that, for the stopping clause to be considered before the general-case clause, the stopping clause must be higher in the list; it does not have to be directly above it, but the stopping clause does have to be somewhere above the general-case clause.

If you are not convinced, then consider a PROLOG program composed of the same set of seven clauses but with the clause path(V,V) placed at the bottom. Now you query this shuffled program:

path(1,2)?

You get no immediate answer. Some time goes by, and you tap keys randomly to determine if the computer has just died or not. Finally, you get the characteristically unenlightening message:

ENVIRONMENT STACK FULL

and the definite impression that the computer has abandoned its attempt to answer your apparently trivial query. Why? Stated succinctly: when the problem is reduced to determining the truth of path(2,2), the system uses the general clause again (it encounters it before the stopping clause, remember) and decides that there is a path from vertex 2 to vertex 2 if there is a transition from 2 to somewhere (and there is, namely transition(2,3)) and a path from that somewhere to 2. Hence, it 'reduces' the proof of path(1,2) to a proof of path(2,3), which 'reduces' to a proof of path(3,4), which 'reduces' to a proof of path(4,1), which in turn reduces to a proof of path(1,2), and there is no end—at least not until the environment stack is full, whatever that means.

The other effect of shuffling the program is a purely practical one: the program may take a lot longer to execute, and if there is more than one correct answer (i.e. more than one value for some variable that makes the question which you asked true), the correct values may be generated in a different order. The time-change feature is the one that we wish to focus on.

A change in program execution time may not seem like a problem to worry about, and certainly not something to have nightmares about in these days of cheap computer power and expensive AI-proficient persons. Gone are the bad old days of agonizing over pages of machine code in order to shave another microsecond or two off the program's running time.

But, at the other extreme, a whole subfield of computer science is occupied with analysing the run-time complexity of algorithms, because certain classes of algorithms are so slow that they are not practically useful. Many correct algorithms are known for a lot of awkward problems, but these algorithms are of absolutely no practical use because they take too much time to execute. As we shuffle the PROLOG deck, we may in so doing seriously undermine the practicality of our program.

An equally, or even more, serious time penalty can be generated by ignoring the sequence-control implications of alternative ways to declare the true relationships in our problem domain. A classic example is provided by sorting algorithms.

Suppose we wish to write a PROLOG program that sorts a randomly sequenced list of numbers into, say, ascending order. In the simplistic mode of PROLOG programming we need only declare the true relationships that must hold between a randomly ordered list, L, and the sorted version, S. Well, what can we say about L and S?

First, we know that, if the sorting is correct, then the list S will be ordered, but, in addition, S must contain all the same numbers as L contains, albeit in a different order most probably. That is to say, S must also be a permutation of L. Those two observations about the relationships between S and L constitute a complete logical definition of the notion of sorting a list. Let us translate these two logical relationships into a PROLOG clause:

sort(L,S):-permuted(L,S),ordered(S).

Let us state this clause for you in English. The sorted version of L is S, if S is a permutation of L, and S is ordered—again a true statement of the relationships between S and L that must hold if S is a sorted version of L. We can now execute this PROLOG program (assuming that we add the four clauses necessary to define *permuted* and *ordered*) by querying it with, say:

sort([3,2,4], X)?

We are asking if there is a value for the variable X such that the sort relationship is true for the list [3,2,4] and that value. The answer is:

YES
X = [2,3,4]

But how was this answer computed? Compactly stated: random permutations of L were generated and then tested to see if they happened to be ordered. At some point one such permutation was also ordered, and that gave us the answer. This is a terribly inefficient way to sort lists of numbers. More efficient sorting programs in PROLOG can be written, but to do so demands that the programmer both understands and exploits the control structure of the PROLOG interpreter. Sterling and Shapiro (1986) explore this question in their PROLOG book on advanced programming techniques.

Thus you may begin to see why some people would argue that this separating out of control has resulted in a loss of control.

Extra Logical Pollutants

Consider our earlier PROLOG 'sort' clause and reverse the order of the 'permuted' and 'ordered' subclauses. We get:

sort(L,S):-ordered(S),permuted(L,S).

Has this switch had any effect on the correctness of this clause? As a statement in logic is it just as true as it ever was, but as a clause in a PROLOG program it will no longer function correctly. If we query this clause (again assuming appropriate definitions of *permuted* and *ordered*) with:

sort([3,2,4],X)?

we will receive only a curt error message for our trouble. Why is this? Again it is because there is more to PROLOG than pure logic, and the user must be aware of this fact. The 'sorted' relation (as typically written) checks that a given list of values is in order. In the previous version of 'sort' a permuted version of the original list was passed to 'ordered' for checking. But in the current version 'ordered' has no list of numbers to check, so we get an error message. It is conceivable that the 'ordered' relation could be written to generate ordered lists of random numbers, and then 'permute' could check each such ordered list to see if it happened to be a permutation of the original list. This would be a correct PROLOG program, but has little else to recommend it. Its efficiency does not bear thinking about, let alone figuring out in detail.

What this example exposes is that the subclauses 'ordered' and 'permuted' are executed in left-to-right order. In logic there is no such notion; things are just true or not true. But in PROLOG some sequencing decisions had to be made, and left to right was the chosen order (we have already seen some repercussions of the top-to-bottom processing of complete clauses).

Another practically necessary piece of extralogical detritus in PROLOG is the 'cut' operator, '!'. The PROLOG interpreter is guaranteed to let you know that some input query is true, if indeed it is true with respect to the facts and rules that it has at its disposal at the time—its current database. A puzzling statement to the neophyte logician, perhaps; after all, that is the least you might expect it to do. But it turns out that providing this guarantee with reasonable efficiency was the great accomplishment of the PROLOG designers.

Searching for proof of the truth of a query with respect to a given database is a classic search-space problem (if this description means little or nothing to you, then you need to reread Chapter 4). The initial state is the initial database plus the query, intermediate states are generated by adding inferences to the database, and the goal state is attained when the query is proved true. The search space is usually portrayed as a proof tree. For example, the proof tree for the query, 'sort([3,2,4],Y)?', of our earlier, correct sort program is illustrated in Fig. 14.2.

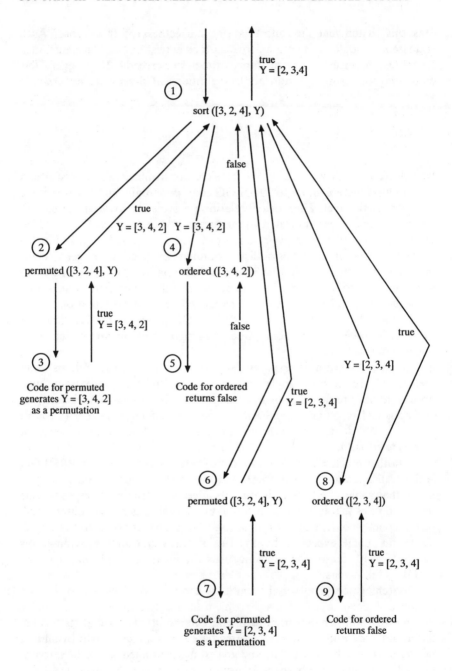

Figure 14.2 A proof tree for the query sort ([3,2,4],Y)?

In order to prove the truth of sort([3,2,4],Y) (node 1 in the proof tree), the system attempts to find a permutation of the list [3,2,4]. The clauses for 'permuted' (node 3) generate and return a true permutation: [3,4,2]. The system then determines if it is true that this generated list is 'ordered' (node 4). The clauses for 'ordered' (node 5) quite promptly and correctly disillusion the system about the current path to a proof' which it thinks that it is following. Node 5 returns 'false' to node 4, which hands the bad news up to node 1.

So this path to a proof of the query, which looked promising with the list [3,4,2], a true permutation of the original list, is in fact a dead end. What now? The PROLOG interpreter is not easily discouraged. It backtracks to an earlier state where there are other alternatives to try and tries one.

In this case it tries another permutation of [3,2,4] (node 6). The code for 'permuted' (node 7) returns a new true permutation, namely [2,3,4]. Hot on the trail of another potential proof path the system determines if this particular permuted list is 'ordered' (node 8), and it is (node 9). Node 9 then passes the good news up to node 8, which joyfully hands it on up with Y = [2,3,4] to node 1. Thus the proof is completed.

What is the significance of all this? Several things, we think. First the PROLOG interpreter has no intelligence (however, within reason, you define it, a PROLOG system has none); it exhaustively searches the space of possible proof trees until it finds a complete proof path (a depth-first search, in case you are interested). This means that the PROLOG interpreter must be able to backtrack—i.e. it must be able to go back to some earlier step in an apparent proof path, abandon all the results of the steps subsequent to the point it backs up to, and then continue forward again on the basis of a different alternative at the point it backed up to. Accurate backtracking requires complex, but well-defined, memorization and perfect recall, but, after all, that is what computers excel at.

Finally, we can get back to the 'cut' operator. If we place a cut operator to the right of the implication operator (i.e. the ':-') then once the system has, in pursuit of a proof path, crossed the cut, it cannot backtrack back over it. Let us illustrate this. Suppose we insert a cut in our 'sort' clause, like so:

sort(L,S):-permuted(L,S),!,ordered(S).

The system will no longer be able to backtrack and try the 'permuted' subclause more than once. So if it does not generate the 'ordered' permutation on the first try, then the 'sort' query will fail. Thus in our last example (in which 'permuted' came up with an 'ordered' version of the list [3,2,4] on the second attempt) the query 'sort([3,2,4],Y)?' would have failed.

Our new version of 'sort' is clearly not a great PROLOG program for sorting lists (we improved its efficiency, but at the cost of correctness; this is not usually considered to be an improvement). So why would you want to do this? You would not, at least not in the way that we have just used the cut operator. That was just a simple example. What we have not yet divulged about the PROLOG interpreter is that, not content with finding one proof of any given query, it slogs away blindly and explores all other possible proof paths!

Now we all know that there is only one sorted version of our old friend the list [3,2,4], but the PROLOG interpreter does not know this (you may recall our earlier statement about the absence of intelligence in these systems). If a list is large and you use our logically correct PROLOG 'sort' program, you may well find yourself spending large amounts of time hanging around the keyboard waiting for the program to finish back-tracking and looking for other (non-existent) ordered versions of your original list. The cut operator can prevent this logically impeccable but quite mindless exhaustive searching.

    sort(L,S):-permuted(L,S),ordered(S),!.

Having found one sorted value for S, the cut operator prevents back-tracking to try alternative permutations. So the cut operator is another PROLOG feature that is present for reasons of computational efficiency but has nothing to do with logic. It is purely a pollutant whose use is frowned upon by purists (but then they are frowned upon by everybody else).

Negation as Failure

The following question should be nagging at any reader who is not completely lost at this point: what happens when a query is actually false? Logic does not encompass the idea of explicitly proving things to be false. So the PROLOG interpreter has no option but to explore exhaustively all possible proof paths, and only when every one of them fails to lead to a proof is it in a position to conclude that the current query is false. Thus to conclude that something is false is the outcome of failing to prove that it is true. Hence, you may run across discussions of the pros and cons of negation as failure in PROLOG—not true, in a word, false, is the result of failure to prove truth.

This strategy seems quite appropriate, but it is in fact only appropriate if the PROLOG system has all relevant rules and facts in its database (i.e. if the 'closed world assumption' holds—to use more exotic terminology). This is typically not the case in much of AI, and hence the need to modify the action of inference engines in many applications of ES. It is not very often that a manager has available *all* the information necessary to make the perfect decision. More typically, some desirable information is missing, but a decision needs to be made, so a good manager makes the best decision possible on the information available at the time. Expert systems that are designed to function in any of the many similar decision-making situations that permeate all of business and industry will thus have to be based on a mechanism more sophisticated than simple logic.

Verify or Compute?

Another interesting feature of PROLOG is that we can, for example, 'drive' the declarative structure either backwards or forwards: either deducing the implications of our program, or checking if a given statement is true with respect to the program.

Thus the query 'sort([3,2,4],Y)?' is a case of computing a value for Y that makes the 'sort' relation true. In order words: is there an inference from the database such that the 'sort' relation is true when L = [3,2,4]?

A query from the class of verifications with the 'sort' program is 'sort([3,2,4],[1,2,3])?'. The system is in effect being asked to verify that the two given lists, [3,2,4] and [1,2,3], are associated by the 'sort' relation (in fact, they are not, but that just means the result of the attempted verification will, if all goes well, be 'NO'—PROLOG's way of saying that it failed to verify the truth of this relationship in this particular case).

There appear to be some interesting implications of these two modes—verify and compute—of using a PROLOG program. Analysis of these two modes may, for example, provide insight into the optimal use of forward- and backward-chaining strategies for knowledge-base inferencing in ESs (a subject that was explored in the previous chapters).

Bidirectionality

In the light of the knowledge that a PROLOG program can be used both to verify specific statements and compute results, it should not be too surprising that it is called a bidirectional language. A system of logic can be used to work backwards from a potential truth (i.e. that [1,2,3] is a sorted version of [3,2,4]) and verify or not, as the case may be, that the specific, potentially true statement is a valid inference from the database of facts and rules. Alternatively, such a collection of facts and rules can be driven forward in order to generate a set of statements that are true inferences. In the first case the system can work back from a specific statement to determine if the database supports it. In the second case the system works forward from the database to determine further true inferences.

So a given PROLOG program offers the promise of being usable in two rather different ways, and the extent to which the promise is realized is dependent upon the degree to which the programmer has resisted the inclusion of extra logical pollutants.

One attempt to exploit the potential bidirectionality of PROLOG in a significant manner that would find extensive application in the commercial world is in language translation systems (machine translation systems have been described in Chapter 3). A PROLOG program to recognize, say, English and translate it into Japanese would also (if it was fully bidirectional) be able to recognize Japanese and translate it into English.

Pattern Matching

Yet one more important aspect of PROLOG that we have been glossing over in this short introduction is the role of pattern matching—an operation that is central to much computing in AI, as we have illustrated in the previous chapters. The specific pattern-matching operation employed extensively in PROLOG is called *unification*.

In the earlier descriptions of how the PROLOG interpreter deals with specific queries, we wrote, for example, that the variable Y has the value [2,3,4]. In actuality what looks like simple assignment of a value to a variable is just a very simple case of unification. (Phrased more correctly: the variable Y unifies with the list [2,3,4], which results in the value of Y becoming instantiated with the value [2,3,4]—though do not waste time sweating over this sentence.)

The pattern matching of unification is seen more easily if we revert back to our PROLOG program for summing the values in a list, to wit:

listsum([ ],0).
listsum([H|T],S):-listsum(T,Stail), S is Stail + H.

The structure '[H|T]' in the 'listsum' rule is a pattern that will match (i.e. unify with, in PROLOG jargon) certain other patterns; in particular, it will match all non-empty-list patterns. And as a result of the matching, the variables H and T may obtain values. Thus when this program is queried with, say, 'listsum([1,2,3],S)?', the patterns '[H|T]' and '[1,2,3]' match, with the result that H = 1 and T = [2,3].

More trickily, '[H,a|T]' will match '[1,a,4]', with the result that H = 1 and T = [4], but the patterns 'H,a|T]' and '[1,2,4]' will not match. If you are beginning to grasp this, then try unifying '[H,2|T]' with '[3,2]'—it works.

Suffice it to say that there is a powerful pattern-matching operation at the heart of PROLOG, but it is beyond the scope of this book to delve further into its intricacies.

THE PROMISES OF PROLOG

As we intimated early on in this excursion into PROLOG, it was originally conceived as the first prototype of a mechanization of a logical proof procedure. So where might it be going once the prototype has been thoroughly explored and evaluated?

Parallelism

One future development of PROLOG that a number of groups of researchers are working on is some manifestation of a parallel PROLOG (e.g. PARLOG—Conlon, 1989). Logic itself contains no concept of sequentiality, i.e. that one inference be generated before another. Current computing systems are fundamentally serial, i.e. it is critical that the order of subprocesses be specified. This mismatch between the logical basis of PROLOG and its current implementations gives rise to many problems, as we have seen in this chapter. Thus for efficient computation PROLOG programmers must concern themselves with extra-logical problems, and the language must offer certain extra-logical features.

With a parallel implementation of PROLOG a number of these problems would go away (a certain number would not, and some new problems would emerge, which is why parallel PROLOGs are not yet commonly available). Nevertheless, the attractions of parallel PROLOG are clear. Consider the following two PROLOG rules (syntactic trivia: ';' is PROLOGese for 'or'): given below.

A:-B,C.
A:-D;E.

The first reads that A is true if B and C are true, and the second reads that A is true if D or E is true. In logic (but not in many PROLOG programs, e.g. the 'sort' program) A is true, if B and C are both true but the truths of B and C can be determined independently and in any order, or in parallel. Similarly, the truths of D and E can be investigated independently and in parallel. Thus, in a parallel PROLOG whose goal was to determine the truth of A, four processors could be set to work simultaneously and independently on the truths of B, C, D, and E (one proof-path search per processor, of course). Then the time taken to prove the truth of A (if it is true) will be the lesser of: the maximum time for proving either B or C, or the minimum time for proving D or E. This is hard to say unambiguously in English; after all it was not designed for saying such things was it? A more formal statement might be:

$$ttA = min(max(ttB,ttC),min(ttD,ttE))$$

where ttX means 'time for truth of X'. In a sequential system ttA might be as bad as (ttB + ttC + ttD + ttE). It is left as an exercise for the reader who must go into all this gruesome detail to justify our non-obvious claims.

As we stated in the previous chapter, the Japanese Fifth Generation project has cast both parallelism and PROLOG as essential components of their proposed new generation of computer systems. You will now be in a position to appreciate why this might be a wise choice of a language that had been only a minor European fad until the Japanese announcement.

A SPECIFICATION LANGUAGE

There is a school of PROLOG-oriented thought which espouses the view that, even though simple declarative programming leads to dreadfully inefficient programs, it does lead quickly and easily to correct ones. Thus PROLOG may develop into a machine-executable, problem-specification language. A specification can then be executed and checked for correctness and then compiled (i.e. automatically translated) into some more computationally efficient form.

But by this time we trust that you can see that PROLOG is a far-from-perfect (or even adequate) executable specification language (hint for readers who are not seeing this problem in sharp focus: recall the hidden sequence control in a PROLOG program, and do not forget that correctness loses a lot of its attraction if it is tied to an algorithm that is too inefficient ever to be usable).

Heuristic Controls

Given that a PROLOG interpreter blindly explores the complete proof tree associated with a particular query and database, the AI person is naturally tempted to try and prune the search with heuristics (the classic approach described in Chapter 2). It is not at all clear exactly how to do this, but one idea is to preface rules with a heuristic 'guard'. That is, a rule may be guarded by some prefixed expression that must evaluate to, say, true before the rule can be used. Thus, the programmer then has the opportunity to employ such prefixes to constrain the search of the proof tree. The prefixed expressions do not, of course, have to be heuristic in nature (i.e. rules of thumb that seem to work) but if they are formally valid constraints, then they could probably have been encoded into the rules in the first place.

As an example, recall the 'sort' program one last time. There is essentially only one sorted version of any list (especially if we exclude the possibility of duplicate list elements). Thus a smart version of 'sort' should quit as soon as it stumbles on a permutation that is ordered, but 'sort' without a cut operator does not. As an alternative to the cut operator we could use a 'guard' expression that was true until a solution was found and then evaluated to false, thus blocking the fruitless search for further solutions.

A major reason for the current prominence of PROLOG (as we mentioned earlier) is the Japanese connection. The Japanese are threatening to dominate computer technology with 'fifth-generation' machines (see Chapter 13), including a proposal that PROLOG might form the basis of the associated programming languages, also to be developed. It is not clear exactly how the Japanese intend to develop PROLOG, but it seems that they plan to use it as a core language on top of which they will layer the desired characteristics that PROLOG lacks. If they maintain PROLOG essentially intact and just bury it in a richer programming context, they will have developed an integrated programming environment—which just happens to be the subject of a major subsection of the next chapter. In Chapter 16, after examining such environments, we can take a brief look at object-oriented programming—a significant alternative to either LISP or PROLOG, but one whose exact status as a language subclass or a complete programming paradigm or a model for man–machine interfaces is a contentious issue.

PROCEDURAL LANGUAGES FOR A KNOWLEDGE-BASED SYSTEM

The discussion thus far has been on specialized programming languages of AI and for a KBIS. However, traditional programming languages like the procedural third-generation languages are often forgotten and yet may be most appropriate for many KBIS environments. Many a complex KBIS and ES has been implemented in a procedural language; these include ESE, Expert, KES, and Intellect.

When the knowledge structure is rule based, the IF–THEN structure of a procedural language can be very appropriate: IF certain conditions exist, THEN the following actions or conclusions should follow. The procedural language is also appropriate for many explanation-and-justification inter-faces. However, in designing and implementing the end-user interface, if there is much interaction between the designer and the end-user, then prototyping may be used and a fourth-generation language may be more appropriate.

The advantages of procedural languages are that they do not typically require special equipment like the LISP machine, nor do they demand the skills needed for programming in some AI languages. There is often no need for additional time or funds for training. The demands of a procedural language are typically already available for anyone considering a KBIS. The problem may arise that the prior experience with, and knowledge of, a procedural language outweighs the need for an AI language, and the effort required to learn and use it. Too often, in practice, unfortunately, one forgets the theoretical advantages of a programming language and succumbs to the ease and convenience of using what one knows well and is most comfortable with.

In comparing a procedural language with AI approaches to a KBIS, one can perhaps agree that both have their comparative advantage. The procedural language is appropriate for a rule-based logic and knowledge structure with a simple flow control and a problem environment of sequential and algorithmic processing, as in the case of uncertainty management with certainty factors and presentation and justifications in an interface module. The frame approach offers a way of conceptualizing the system and its relationships. The KBIS's logical constructs can be viewed as pop-up stacks, which are somewhat alien to the commercial programmer and user of procedural languages. All programming languages require time to learn and implement. That is why there is a trend towards shells and toolkits, to be discussed in the next chapter. But if there is a programming language that must be used, could it be one type of language in an integrated system easily accessible by all end-users? Some say that the object-oriented approach is an answer to that prayer, and we will examine that possibility in Chapter 16. Another approach to using one programming language for all problems including the KBIS is to use procedural languages, which are commonly used in most transactional systems and DSSs. The trend of embedding the KBS into the traditional system architecture has been perceived by Butler *et al.* (1988: 58) as follows:

> If successful integration is to occur, a tighter coupling with the procedural language environment is expected. One likely evolutionary strategy would favor attaching new logical structures to older views of languages. Yet to be determined is whether the traditional language approach or a specially designed syntax based on LISP and /or Prolog will be the prevalent strategy.

SUMMARY AND CONCLUSIONS

In this chapter we have looked in some detail at the major options for programming in an AI language. Despite the length of this chapter, we have not tried to provide you with enough detail to enable you to become say, a LISP programmer. Such was not our intent. Our goal was merely to introduce all of the major options to you, and yet provide you with enough detail that you gain some 'feel' for the basic similarities and important differences that exist between the various choices, information that may guide you more efficiently towards the selection of an appropriate language for your own particular purposes. Further detail on all of the options mentioned in the chapter can be found by reference to the works listed below in the Bibliography.

CASE 14.1 THE ADVISOR

The INTELLIPSE project was funded under the Alvey Directorate in the UK. It was a collaboration between Aston University and BIS Applied Systems, with British Steel involved when progress demanded. The project was to examine the design and implementation of a KBS, specifically the Structured Systems Development (SSD) methodology. Within this project there was ADVISOR, a 'more accessible version of the SSD training manual as well as presenting SSD in a more structured and logical manner than the manual'.

The ADVISOR is a passive, knowledge-based, question-answering system dealing with the SSD domain. The ADVISOR was implemented on IBM-compatible PCs running under DOS. A procedural language and a shell were considered but not chosen because they did not cope well with the proposed frame structure of the knowledge-base PROLOG was chosen over LISP largely because the development personnel 'preferred it'. However, it was possible that at the time, the PROLOG system for a PC was faster than its LISP equivalent.

> It was found during the development that PROLOG could not cope easily with the large amounts of text involved, and this problem was solved by interfacing with a word-processing package for text entry and editing. One or two of the shells would have avoided this problem, but had no facilities for over-riding their rule-based inference engines.

Source: J. S. Edwards (1991) *Building Knowledge-based Systems*, Pitman, London, pp. 148–178.

Questions
1. Do you think that LISP would have been chosen instead of PROLOG if the project personnel had had a LISP background?
2. Would the availability of a LISP machine instead of a PC have made LISP the preferred language?
3. Today, given the availability of some shells that do override 'their rule-based inference engines', would a shell have been used instead of an AI language?

4. Why was a word-processing interface so important in the selection of a language for implementing a KBS?

CASE 14.2 R1/XCON—5: PROGRAMMING LANGUAGES

The programming languages used for the different components of the XCON, the ES used for computer systems configuration at DEC, were:

BASIC	User interface and related mechanisms.
C	Component data base access.
BLISS	Component database access and creation.
Pascal	XCON batch control.
Macro	Transfer vectors.
SCAN	Pre-specified selection.
OPS5	Variety of tasks such as counting, sorting, and various numerical conversions, were performed by routines written in traditional languages and called by OPS5.

Source: V. E. Barker and D. E. O'Connor (1989) 'Expert systems for configuration at Digital: XCON and beyond', *Communications of the ACM*, **32** (3), 298–318.

Questions

1. If you had to select programming languages for an application like XCON, would you choose languages different from those chosen for XCON? Explain your choices.
2. What decision rule would you use in determining whether you could use the following?
   (*a*) Procedural language.
   (*b*) AI language.
   (*c*) Other language.
   In each case, justify your decision rule.
3. Why would you suppose BASIC was used?
4. Why do you suppose that Pascal was used instead of, say, FORTRAN or ALGOL?
5. When and why would you use a macro?

REVIEW AND DISCUSSION QUESTIONS

14.1 List some of the main limitations of programming languages, especially those used for a KBIS.

14.2 List some of the advantages of programming languages, specifically the specialized languages for a KBIS.

14.3 Identify problems that require the use of recursion in the following situations:

(a) In a KBIS environment.

(b) Outside a KBIS environment.

14.4 Identify problems that are most appropriate for symbolic programming. Is a KBIS appropriate for symbolic programming?

14.5 What is the importance of flow as opposed to control in programming languages?

14.6 What are the consequences of the loss of control on PROLOG?

14.7 Compare the assignment statement in LISP with that of another programming language(s) that you know. Which helps or hinders you?

14.8 Is the popularity of LISP largely linked to the greater (and earlier) availability of a LISP machine?

14.9 Compare LISP and PROLOG, from your experience, in terms of the following:

(a) Ease of understanding.

(b) Ease of use.

14.10 Explain the concept of logical pollutants. What are the implications for a programming solution?

14.11 Would you recommend LISP or PROLOG for pattern matching? Explain.

14.12 Is LISP or PROLOG better for heuristic problem solving? Explain with illustrations and examples.

14.13 Is PROLOG or LISP a better specification language? Explain.

14.14 'PROLOG got a great boost in popularity because it was adopted by the 5GCS (Fifth Generation Computer System). However, now that the 5GCS is all but abandoned, PROLOG will also decline.' Comment.

14.15 'Problems determine the choice of programming languages rather than programming languages determining solutions'. Comment.

14.16 'A computer without software is like a car without petrol, a camera without a film, a stereo without records.' Is this true of a KBIS?

14.17 Harlan Mills once said: '. . . computer programming has already posed the greatest intellectual challenge that mankind has faced in pure logic and complexity.' Comment. Has KBIS made matters worse or better? Explain.

14.18 'Programming languages are complex to understand and difficult to use. They will all be replaced by packaged software.' Comment.

BIBLIOGRAPHY AND REFERENCES

We thought that, in this chapter, it might be best to depart slightly from our usual alphabetized list of bibliographic references and present the material grouped in terms of the specific languages considered. But first, there are three general references.

Butler, C. W., E. D. Hodil and G. L. Richardson (1988) 'Building knowledge-based systems with procedural languages', *IEEE Expert*, 3 (2), 47–59.

de Bono, E. (1969) *The Mechanism of Mind*, Simon & Schuster, New York.
An intriguing book, nothing to do with programming but it does introduce and explain the workings of the 'jelly model' of the brain—as mentioned in this chapter.

Plant, R. T. (1991) 'Factors in software quality for knowledge-based systems,' *Information and Software Technology*, 33 (7), 527–536.

The author defines quality of knowledge-based software systems and discusses how to create such quality software including the specification and validation methodology involved.

LISP

There are a very large number of books on the LISP language. All we can do is list and comment on a few of them.

Charniak, E., C. K. Riesbeck and D. V. McDermott (1980) *Artificial Intelligence Programming*, Erlbaum, Hillsdale, NJ.

Not quite what its title might lead you to believe. It is a collection of LISP programming structures and techniques that an AI programmer (who knows LISP) will find useful.

Friedman, D. P. (1974) *The Little Lisper*, Science Research Associates.

A small, very easy-to-read, light-hearted tour of the LISP language.

McCarthy, J. (1965) *et al.*, *LISP 1.5 Programmer's Manual*, 2nd edn, MIT Press, Cambridge, MA.

The original LISP reference book by the man (plus many helpers) who invented the language. It is thus an interesting historical document, but has little else to recommend it, as it was constructed in the days when programming manuals were all equally indigestible to the normal human mind.

Steele, G. (1984) *Common LISP: The Language*, Digital Equipment Corporation, New York.

A good manual for the standardized LISP—Common LISP.

Teitelman, W. and L. Masinter (1981) 'The INTERLISP programming environment', *IEEE Transactions on Computers*, **C-14** (4), 25–35.

An introduction to one of the most comprehensive and well-developed environments within which the LISP language is embedded.

Touretzky, D. S. (1982) *A Summary of MACLISP Functions and Flags*, 4th edn, Computer Science Dept., Carnegie Mellon University, Pittsburgh, PA.

A technician's handbook for the MACLISP dialect of the LISP language.

Wilensky, R. (1986) *Common LISPcraft*, Norton, New York.

Another guide to standard LISP, of which the author says 'this book should be viewed more as a travel guide than a textbook', and that, 'without the accompanying exploration, real learning is not possible'. There are, of course, exercises and examples to guide your exploration, if that is what you want to do.

PROLOG

Clocksin, W. F., and C. S. Mellish (1981) *Programming in PROLOG*, Springer-Verlag, New York.

This book has been the standard, middle-of-the-road textbook of PROLOG. It introduces and presents the language in a straightforward and readable manner.

Conlon, T. (1989) *Programming in PARLOG*, Addison-Wesley, Reading, MA.

One example of the exploitation of parallelism using PROLOG. The promise of parallelism with respect to the PROLOG language is discussed in this chapter.

Sterling, L. and E. Shapiro (1986) *The Art of PROLOG*, MIT Press, Cambridge MA.

The advanced PROLOG book for those who want to go beyond the introductory texts.

15

ENVIRONMENTS, SHELLS, AND TOOLKITS

Give people the tools they need, and there is no limit to what they can achieve.

Anon

ALTERNATIVES TO ARTIFICIAL INTELLIGENCE LANGUAGES

Using programming languages demands a great deal of knowledge and discipline that many are not willing to devote to a problem. In that case there are alternatives: programming language environments, shells, or toolkits. A discussion of these topics is the subject of this chapter.

Yet another, more specific, possibility is to use an object-oriented environment, the subject of the next chapter. We start this chapter by examining programming environments in general.

PROGRAMMING ENVIRONMENTS

Artificial intelligence programming has pioneered the notion of a programming environment. This notion implies that it is not only (and perhaps not even primarily) the choice of a programming language that is important when considering implementation of an AI system. It is the programming environment as a whole that needs to be carefully considered.

AI programming is, as we hope that you have realized by now,

Table 15.1 Comparison of AI and Conventional Programming

Feature	AI programming	Conventional programming
Processing type	Symbolic	Numeric
Technique	Heuristic search	Algorithmic
Definition of solution steps	Not explicit	Precise
Answers sought	Satisfactory	Optimal
Control/data separation	Separate	Intermingled
Knowledge	Imprecise	Precise
Modification	Frequent	Rare

somewhat different from conventional programming. Ramamoorthy *et al.* (1987) presented a list of the differences shown in Table 15.1.

Clearly, a number of the entries in this table are somewhat debatable— e.g. heuristic search contrasted with algorithmic—but we hope that the reader is now sufficiently well informed on these issues to be able to take this tabulation as a starting point rather than as the last word on the subject. One indisputable conclusion to be drawn is that AI programming is more complex than conventional programming, and hence the need for supportive environments.

A *programming environment* is a programming language (or languages, as we shall see) and associated support software—support such as an editor, a debugger, etc. The quality of the integrated support system as a whole can have a profound effect on programmer productivity.

LISP Environments

LISP is a terrible language to program with: its basic structure is conceptually opaque, the flow of control through nested function calls rather than sequentially from one statement to the next is difficult to follow, etc. It is not the bare LISP language that is particularly useful; it is the language embedded in a support environment. This feature was one point of contrast between AI and non-AI languages: the latter were just programming languages to be judged as they stood, but the strengths of the former languages were only really evident when the language was embedded in an appropriate environment. This distinction is no longer so sharp: the thoroughly traditional language Ada, for example, has been developed together with a support environment.

Just as the neophyte LISPer is unlikely to be too impressed with bare LISP as a serious programming tool, he or she is quite likely to be equally cold about LISP within a sophisticated support environment. This is because the environment will appear to be extremely complicated to use. There will be too many options, too much to remember, and it will all seem excessive in the context of a small demonstration. And indeed it is; such environments only show their worth with large-scale problems and after a long, slow learning process. If you are going next door, then you might as well walk, but if you plan to cross the continent, then you had better learn to drive a car. And so it is with programming projects: you cannot play with a powerful support environment and a toy project and expect to get a feel for the situation where an expert user works on a large software system.

Extended dialects of LISP are one important manifestation of AI development environments, primarily because of the vast library of support subprograms that constitute an important part of these LISP extensions. The advantages of developing AI software on a LISP machine such as the SYMBOLICS 3670 are not chiefly due to the fact that it directly executes LISP, but to the support environment that comes with the machine; a major part of this environment is the 100 man-years of support functions.

Two of the important early LISP environments have already been mentioned, but at the risk of being repetitive, they are MACLISP and INTERLISP. The former has developed into a number of varieties such as ZETALISP, which is offered on the SYMBOLICS machines along with FLAVORS, an object-oriented system. INTERLISP is still widely used as INTERLISP-D, which is in fact the basis for the LOOPS environment, a description of which is next.

LOOPS

LOOPS is described as a 'knowledge programming system' that 'contains a number of integrated paradigms of programming' (Stefik *et al.* 1991). It is based on a LISP environment (INTERLISP-D) with the addition of other programming paradigms: a rule-based paradigm (i.e. rule-based inferencing as demanded by ES technology, and as provided by PROLOG), an object-oriented programming (OOP) paradigm, and an access-oriented programming paradigm. It is this latter component that is new to us, so we shall focus in on it.

Access-oriented programming (AOP) is presented as the dual to OOP. In OOP, the sending of a message from one object to another may cause the recipient object to change its data values, as well as cause other things to happen. In AOP, when a data value within an object is changed, it may cause a message to be sent.

AOP is centred on the notion of tying *annotations* to data. In LOOPS there are two manifestations of this idea:

- *Property annotations*—the association of a property list (a LISP feature, you may recall) with data items.
- *Active values*—the association of procedures with data items.

A program based on the AOP philosophy has two components: a traditional computation part, and a part that monitors the computations.

Ideally, the monitoring part—essentially the AOP contribution—does not interfere with the computational part. Thus adding and removing annotations should not cause a program to stop working, unless the program uses the annotations.

We shall focus down even further and describe *active-value programming* (AVP).

If a program variable is annotated with code for displaying on a screen a visual representation of the variable's value, we have a very powerful monitoring aid. Not only can we have a visual representation of the values of critical program variables, but these representations are active—i.e. when the program variable is changed by means of an internal computation, say, then the visual display is automatically changed to reflect this modification of the state of the computation. It is easy to appreciate how this behaviour could be achieved using AVP.

The screen display procedures are an AOP annotation to the program variable. Thus changing the value of the variable causes a message to be sent to execute the display procedures using the new value and thus displaying the new value on the screen.

Typically, some sort of dial or gauge is used as the visual representation of a variable's value. So a change of value in the annotated variable will be seen as the movement of a needle on a dial or a column of, say, red on a vertical scale—the choice of visualization details is up to the programmer; the AVP facility just provides the underlying mechanism for tying an internal change of value to a visual display of that change.

The mechanism can also function in the opposite direction: a modification of the visual representation (by means of, say, a mouse action) can be programmed to cause the appropriate change in the internal value of the variable being displayed.

Clearly, there are many possibilities to be explored for AOP, and perhaps for AVP in particular. It can certainly support a powerful facility for visualization of a computation, and as such can be considered as a mechanism to support the growing computer science subfield of program visualization (i.e. use of graphics to 'see' what is happening in a program). Clearly, developments that allow a manager to 'see' what is going on in a computer system could be of great value in the business world. It should also be apparent that AOP will readily support graphical simulation of processes. This notion of simulation is typically associated with OOP, and the LOOPS manifestation of AOP is based (you may recall) on the OOP paradigm.

POPLOG

PROLOG is also prominent in another AI programming languages venture: integrated multilanguage systems. POPLOG (Sloman and Hardy, 1983) is such a system, and it combines POP11 with LISP and PROLOG. The most important reason for having such a system is that different tasks in a single system can best be served by different languages. So, for example, in the implementation of a KBIS, the conventional control and computational algorithms may be best implemented in POP11, and the knowledge-base in PROLOG.

Sloman (1991) summarizes POPLOG as follows:

> POPLOG is a portable, integrated, environment for multi-paradigm software development using a rapid-prototyping methodology to speed up development and testing. It supports a range of languages: two procedural AI languages (COMMON LISP and POP-11), a logic language (PROLOG) and a functional language Standard ML. It runs under VMS(tm) and UNIX(tm) on a variety of minicomputers and workstations, with a common editor (VED), window manager and many hundreds of online teaching and help files and program library files.

To expand on this summary a little: the design of the basic POPLOG system is such that it can be tailored relatively easily to many new machines. All of the POPLOG languages have been integrated in such a way that setting up POPLOG on a new machine requires only implementation of the common high-level language (called high-level VM) on the target machine—i.e. you do not have to plough through the arduous process of implementing each of the component languages on the new machine.

The system is highly integrated in the sense that one can construct systems using just the desired features of each of the constituent languages, and the resultant system will be a coherent whole, not a loose farrago of a LISP program, and a PROLOG program, etc. What does this mean? Different languages can, for example, directly share a given data structure. And individual modules of a language can be compiled and recompiled (after modification), and are immediately automatically linked into the rest of the system. Systems that do offer this *incremental compilation* capability will require perhaps the complete language subsystem to be recompiled and relinked to the rest of the system whenever a module is altered—this would clearly be a serious drawback within an incremental development strategy (consider versioning (Chapter 6) if you are thinking that it is a basic mistake to be supporting this style of system development—the programmer ought not to be hacking the system in this way).

One further general feature that the closely integrated nature of the POPLOG system supports is the addition of new languages. Once a new language has been implemented in terms of POPLOG's common high-level language, it becomes an integral feature of the POPLOG system and enjoys all the benefits of the original constituent languages, i.e. full access to the editor, the development tools, all the POPLOG library facilities, and it runs on all machines that support POPLOG.

POPLOG is presented as a multiparadigm programming environment, but whereas LOOPS offer a variety of paradigms under the umbrella of a single language, POPLOG endeavours to supply the necessary choice by integrating a variety of languages. We would not be so rash as to try to order these two strategies, but it would seem that LOOPS could offer more efficiency at the cost of more difficulty in adding new paradigms.

After all the good news, there just has to be some not-so-good news—there always is. Clearly, in a large and highly integrated system development environment such as POPLOG, there are a lot of communication overheads. If the system is well designed, then the user is barely aware of all the behind-the-scenes communication (e.g. relinking a recompiled module to the overall system, and the checking that must be done in order to catch some of the many awkward problems that such an incremental development facility may have to face). But however well hidden these overheads are, the user will see one unfortunate effect—the system will respond rather slowly at times. Hardware advances, including exploiting parallelism, and powerful, single-user computers (such as LISP machines), will help to cancel out this time penalty, but it will probably always be noticeable, and with conventional, time-shared computers it can become a significant negative consideration. You seldom get something for nothing in this world, and it seems unlikely that you will ever get all the flexibility and generality that systems such as POPLOG offer without some time penalty. But, to finish on the bright side, how significant is a slightly slower system? A single high-level language may react to your commands a good deal faster than, say, the POPLOG environment, but will the overall system-development time be any shorter? And what about the comparative quality of the products of each system? There are many factors, and system-response time is by no means the critical one, but it is the one that makes itself immediately apparent to the new user trying out a system for the first time.

WHY NOT A SHELL?

The use of any programming language can be time consuming and requires the services of a programmer specializing in the language being used. It will deliver a custom-made solution, but is all the time and extra effort worth it? This is the oft-raised question of cost-effectiveness between a custom-made, *in-house developed* program and a *packaged program*, which in the case of a KBIS is called a *shell*.

In a shell, the logic structure and control mechanisms come pre-packaged, freeing knowledge engineers in the purchasing firm (or organization) from the burden of creating these. However, the knowledge-base must be added to the generic shell structure. That is to say, the KBIS has an

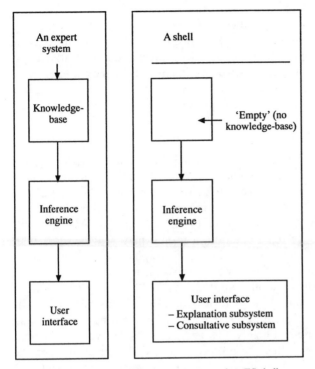

Figure 15.1 Comparison of an expert system and an ES shell.

inference engine and other support facilities so that it is capable of arriving at conclusions, but has no knowledge-base, as illustrated in Fig. 15.1. Following the purchase of a shell, a company's knowledge engineers will meet with the domain experts and raise questions to draw out facts, beliefs, concepts, relationships, and heuristics in the problem domain. This time spent by domain experts and knowledge engineers is greatly reduced when compared to building the KBIS from scratch. Typically, a shell shortens the development period by one-third to one-half.

The shell is typically quick and easy to use. It has been debugged and is available off the shelf. It will be cheaper than an in-house development and it may even be maintained by the vendor. It works and if it fits your problem it is certainly an attractive choice. But as often occurs with packaged software, it may not exactly fit your problem. The particular knowledge representation and the inference mechanism may not be totally appropriate, and worse, the full extent of this lack of fit may not be apparent until it is too late. Thus the shell may need to be modified, or the problem may need modification, or both. And the necessary representation modifications can be costly, time consuming and disruptive. The built-in knowledge representation may not be natural for the specific problem, which would make updating difficult for the knowledge engineer or the domain expert. Other disadvantages are that many shells have poor facilities for handling procedural tasks, lack graphics and good presentation facilities, and have an inflexibility in answering queries by the end-user.

TOOLKITS

One alternative to the shell is the *toolkit*, which has the advantages of a shell and, in addition, provides much greater flexibility than the shell for both the inference engine and data representation. For inferencing, the toolkit may provide the IF–THEN rule with chaining or a basic production system. Alternatively (or even additionally), the toolkit can provide AOP or OOP capability. In knowledge representation, a toolkit may provide more than one representation schema along with good graphics tools, making the work environment both user-friendly and user-comfortable.

The problem with the toolkit approach is that it is very expensive to acquire and maintain, and perhaps expensive also in terms of its demands on the hardware and operating system. But the resulting system could enable easy prototyping in a highly interactive and responsive environment. This is important when either the problem is not well defined or when the user is not experienced and needs prompting in a dialogue environment.

Toolkits are often discussed as synonymous with environments. They are similar in the sense that both have supporting software for helping the knowledge engineer in building, editing, debugging, and testing knowledge-based software. An environment (a *programming environment*), however, is basically a programming language that is surrounded and integrated with supporting software designed to produce a profound improvement in programmer productivity.

The costs of toolkits could drop as they become more popular. Currently, the number of toolkit sales is a very small fraction of sales of shells. In 1993, the popularity contest has the shell well at the top by a wide margin, with special-purpose languages, conventional languages, toolkits, and environments following in that order.

Because shells are the most popular, we shall examine the selection criteria for them. First, however, in Table 15.2, we present a summary of the discussion on comparisons thus far.

Selection of a Shell

If a shell is selected, there are large savings in time and money because the activities relating to knowledge representation and the inference engine are no longer necessary. But a new activity emerges in the design stage: that of

Table 15.2 Advantages and limitations of different types of tools for a KBIS

Tools	Advantages	Disadvantages and limitations
Languages	General purpose Very flexible Produces custom-made products High-performance product	Not easy to use Requires programming skills Time-consuming and slow to produce Product needs a lot of debugging and testing May need specialized hardware
Environments	High programmer productivity	Specialized mix of language and support software Needs debugging and testing May require specialized hardware May not 'fit' problem
Shells	Proven solutions (already debugged) Easy to use Available off-the-shelf Little (if any) new resources and training needed Often maintained and updated by vendor Shorter implementation period	Inflexible knowledge representation and inference mechanisms Poor for prototyping Good for 'special' purposes May not 'fit' problem well
Toolkits	Very flexible and powerful Good for rapid prototyping	Can be very expensive Can be difficult to use May need specialized hardware and operating system

selecting a shell, one of over 80 in the marketplace. This task may be left to the knowledge engineer in the implementation stage, but to avoid personal preferences from dominating any such decision and to provide the lead-time necessary for the acquisition of the shell, the decision on selecting the shell may well be taken in the overall system's design stage.

The criteria used for the selection of a shell are much the same as for any software package, especially those that relate to checking the vendor. Factors to be considered are the reliability of the vendor, age and maturity of the product, nature of any warranty available, possibilities of upgrading the product, and the support given by the vendor, both technical and educational. Then there are operational considerations such as the ease of use and the ease of maintenance, the flexibility in operations, a reasonably fast runtime, good documentation, the personnel and other resources needed, and finally the quality of the solution (correctness, integrity, portability, reusability and reliability). There are also criteria unique to the shell, such as having the appropriate knowledge-base and knowledge representation, the language and approaches used for inferencing, and finally, criteria for the interfaces (for the system, the developer, and the end-user).

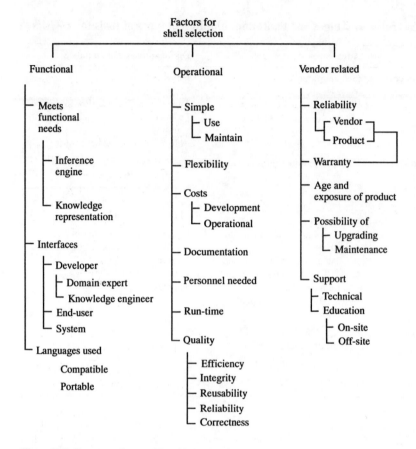

Figure 15.2 Factors to be considered in evaluating a shell.

A summary of all these criteria are presented as a theoretical list in Fig. 15.2. As in the case of the selection of languages, the reality is that personnel preferences are low cost (often the cheapest one) and far more important than what the checklist for the selection of a shell found in a textbook. Besides, a selection based on personal preference is a much faster route to take than computing all the many metrics that have been suggested and the benchmarks that are recommended in a textbook.

FUTURE ENVIRONMENTS

Ramamoorthy *et al.* (1987: 30–31) make the point that

> existing AI development environments support just the implementation phase, resulting in less reliable and hard-to-maintain programs. ... An ideal software development

environment should provide a powerful language for the application, as well as appropriate methodology and tools for program development.

In a phrase, an intelligent lifecycle support environment. They classify development environments as illustrated in Fig. 15.3.

As is apparent from Fig. 15.3, Ramamoorthy *et al.* (1985) see lifecycle support environments as a future event, although they do list three 'efforts in this direction': Genesis (their own work, see Ramamoorthy *et al.*, 1985), Gandalf (Haberman *et al.*, 1985), and SAGA (Kirlis *et al.*, 1985). But for the frontiers of the current state of the art they look towards ES building shells, such as Intellicorp's KEE system. These sorts of systems constitute their category called 'knowledge-based tools'. But there are others which are not wedded to ESs only, but which also tend to be less robust and therefore less usable in practice at the present time.

A major example here is the work of Rich and Waters on the 'Programmer's Apprentice' system. KBEmacs, their knowledge-based editor, provides 'plans' and 'clichés' to assist the system developer. They characterize 'the assistant approach' as illustrated in Fig. 15.4.

'The assistant interacts with the tools in the environment . . . in the same way as the programmer, and is capable of helping the programmer do what needs to be done' (Rich and Waters, 1986: 352). A 'cliché' is 'a standard method for dealing with a task' (p. 353). They are implemented as generic parameterized procedures, so all the system developer need do is to invoke a cliché and fill it with right parameter values in order to obtain a substantial chunk of program. A 'plan' is an abstract representation of a program. The 'plan formalism' is designed to represent two basic types of information: 'the structure of particular programs and knowledge about clichés' (p. 354).

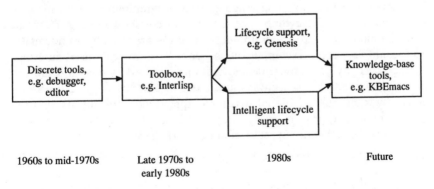

Figure 15.3 Classification of development environments. (From Ramamoorthy et al., 1987: 34.)

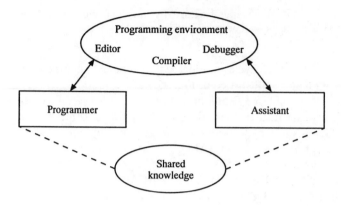

Figure 15.4 A programming assistant. *(From Rich and Waters, 1986: 353.)*

SUMMARY AND CONCLUSIONS

For most readers who have no intention of furthering their detailed knowledge of, say, PROLOG or LISP, we hope that this chapter has served to dispel much of the unnecessary mystery that habitually surrounds these esoteric programming tools. Informed decision making on programming languages does not necessarily require a detailed knowledge of the options; in fact, it is probably better to be merely acquainted with the major strengths and weaknesses of each possibility. And this level of acquaintance is what we hope that this chapter can foster, even in the totally non-computer-oriented manager.

In Table 15.2 we summarize the comparative advantages and disadvantages of environments, shells, and toolkits, and compare them to programming languages discussed in the previous chapter. We have seen that the alternative to a programming language is a programming environment, a shell, or a toolkit. The evolution of such software is shown in Fig. 15.5. But even the alternatives to programming languages are not always adequate. For example, complex applications with a graphical user interface characterized by pull-down menus, multiple windows, icons, and mouse-driven commands are not always adequate. It is in such applications and especially when our traditional structured approaches typically fail that the object-oriented approach excels (see Yourdon, 1990). It is these object-oriented systems that are the subject of our next chapter.

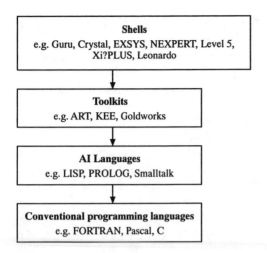

Figure 15.5 The programming language and software spectrum for a KBIS.

SUPPLEMENT 15.1 A SURVEY OF TOOLS USED IN JAPAN IN 1990

Eshell	10.2%
ES/Kernel	8.7%
KEE	4.7%
Sourgen	4.4%
OP83	4.4%
Brains	3.7%
Superbrains	2.2%
Other	61.7%

Source: H. Motada (1990) 'The current status of expert system development and related technologies in Japan', *IEEE Expert*, **5** (4), 5.

CASE 15.1 MANUFACTURING IN MEXICO—4: SELECTING A TOOL

In 1987, CYDSA, a chemical and textile corporation with annual sales of $600 million, was persuaded by the CAI (Center for Artificial Intelligence) to develop KBISs for their manufacturing and repair plants. Four problems were selected, all on diagnosis, one for each plant. Each system required prototyping that took approximately 120 person-hours per system. The systems were implemented on an IBM PS2/80 with 1 megabyte RAM under DOS.

In selecting tools, they looked for 'the following characteristics:

1. Represent heuristic and domain knowledge as structured rules.
2. Divide the knowledge-base into clusters of rules.
3. Does backward and forward reasoning.
4. Handles uncertainty in an ad hoc fashion.
5. Interfaces with databases and programming languages.
6. Interfaces with process control software and hardware.
7. Has a friendly user interface.
8. Contains debugging and tracing facilities.
9. Is supported by a stable company that can provide technical support, training, good documentation, and upgrading of new versions of the tool.
10. Has an acceptable performance in the following parameters: compilation time, execution time, launching time, knowledge-base loading, and saving time.
11. Is affordable.
12. Runs on personal computers.'

Source: F. J. Cantu-Orates (1991) 'Expert systems in manufacturing: an experience in Mexico', *Expert Systems with Applications*, **3**, 445–455.

Questions
1. Some of the characteristics listed above (e.g. 7, 9, and 10) are rather vague, without any generally accepted metrics to measure them. How do you overcome that problem?
2. Who does the evaluation of the presence or absence of the desired characteristics? Should it be one or more than one person? If more than one person, what happens should they disagree?
3. Some characteristics may be oversatisfied and some undersatisfied. Do they balance out? How are the characteristics weighted? Who does the weighting?
4. It is argued that the weighting approach has two subjective factors; one is the scoring and the other the weighting. Compounding two subjective factors can make this too subjective. Would the value-costing approach be better?

CASE 15.2 SHELLS IN A NUCLEAR PLANT IN JAPAN

KBISs are used extensively in heavy industries in Japan, and many applications use shells. An example is the Japanese nuclear power plants. The scheduling applications can be classified into three kinds of ES:

1. Maintenance scheduling.
2. Plant construction scheduling.
3. Job shop scheduling.

These applications are all implemented on a shell ES/Kernel. While all these applications involve planning problems, they differ slightly from one another. Maintenance scheduling and job shop scheduling can be formalized as the depth-first A* search method. Plant construction can be formalized as the branch-and-bound search method.

Users can build an expert system by:

1. Formalizing the problem as search, based on the classification tree.
2. Providing search strategies.
3. Generating a task-specific ES shell. (This can be done automatically.)
4. Providing domain-specific knowledge based on the shell's data structure.

Source: H. Motoda (1990) 'The current status of expert system development and related technologies in Japan', *IEEE Expert*, **5** (4), 3–10.

Questions
1. Does it surprise you that shells are used in organizations that do not necessarily have limited access to large computers or to programmers skilled in AI languages. Explain your answer?
2. Is the extensive use of shells in planning and scheduling problems an indication that ESs and KBISs will increasingly move into an area that was once the preserve of operations research and management science?
3. The techniques of search have been used intensively and extensively in the applications cited above. Is this unique to planning problems or can they be used in other applications in business and industry? Give examples.

REVIEW AND DISCUSSION QUESTIONS

15.1 Identify the problems in a knowledge-based environment as being appropriate for a programming language and each of its alternatives.

15.2 When would you use a shell as opposed to a toolkit?

15.3 What are the four most important factors in the selection of a shell? Order your selected factors or their importance. Explain your choices.

15.4 What are the advantages and limitations of developing a system in-house as opposed to using a shell or toolkit for a KBIS?

15.5 Draw up a table to compare an AI programming language relative to each of its alternatives for the following:
   (*a*) Ease of implementation.
   (*b*) Ease of use.
   (*c*) Cost.
   (*d*) Time of implementation.

15.6 What are the two most important differences between a traditional and an AI programming environment?

15.7 Does the selection of a shell, environment, or toolkit depend on the availability of the following?
   (*a*) Equipment.
   (*b*) Programming skills.
Explain.

15.8 'The final selection of a toolkit or shell or environment will not depend so much on the technological differences between them but on the bias of the knowledge engineer in charge.' Comment.

15.9 Using a table format, compare LOOPS with POPLOG. Include the problem environment in which each is most appropriate.

15.10 'Shells and toolkits often require adaptation to each problem environment. This is either painful or time consuming or both.' Comment.

15.11 What are the advantages and disadvantages of developing a system in-house as opposed to using a software package?

15.12 'Shells will eventually replace their competitive alternatives.' Comment.

15.13 'Many of the factors important in selecting a shell are also relevant in selecting a toolkit.' Comment.

15.14 'The vendor-related factors in selecting a shell or toolkit are intangible and difficult to assess.' Comment.

15.15 'The selection of a shell should be done by a consultant to eliminate bias among the in-house personnel.' Comment.

15.16 How do you see the future of
   (*a*) programming environments,
   (*b*) toolkits, and
   (*c*) shells in a KBIS?

15.17 'A shell or toolkit is dangerous to use unless you know all its assumptions and technology. And if you know all that, why not develop your own?' Comment.

15.18 Specify the requirements of a shell as if you were making the user-specifications.

15.19 What benchmarks would you use to test the suitability of a shell for your purposes?

15.20 Comment on the quote at the beginning of this chapter.

BIBLIOGRAPHY AND REFERENCES

Boley, H. (1990) 'Expert system shells: very-high-level languages for artificial intelligence', *Expert Systems*, **7** (1), pp. 2–8.

'The concept of expert systems shells is explained using seven classifications. A proposal for a shell-development policy is sketched.'

Gisolfi, A. and W. Balzano (1993) 'Constructing and consulting the knowledge base of an expert systems shell', *Expert Systems*, **10** (1), 29–35.
This paper presents an ES with a backward-chaining inference mechanism, uses Arity-PROLOG and runs on an IBM PC compatible.

Haberman, A. N. *et al.* (1985) 'Special issue on the Gandalf project', *Journal of Systems and Software*, **5**, (2).

Kirlis, P. A. *et al.* (1985) The SAGA approach to large program development in an integrated modular environment, Proceedings GTE Workshop on Software Engineering Environments for Programming-in-the-large, June.

Pedersen, K. (1989) *Expert Systems Programming*, Wiley, Chichester.
The book addresses the development of rule-based KBSs using a PC shell.

Price, C. J. (1990) *Knowledge Engineering Toolkits*, Ellis Horwood, Chichester.

Ramamoorthy, C. V. *et al.* (1985) Genesis—An integrated environment for development and evolution of software, Proceedings COMPSAC Conference.

Ramamoorthy, C. V., S. Shehkar and V. Garg (1987) 'Software development support for AI programs', *IEEE Computer*, **20** (1), 30–40.
The authors present the view that AI programming is radically different from conventional programming. They provide quick reviews of major programming languages as well as of commercially available shells for ES development.

Rich, C. and R. C. Waters (1986) *Readings in Artificial Intelligence and Software Engineering*, Morgan Kaufmann, Los Altos, CA.

Sloman, A. and S. Hardy (1983) 'POPLOG: a multi-purpose multi-language program development environment', *AISB Quarterly*, **47**, 26–34.
An introduction by the designers of POPLOG to this multilanguage system—readable and matter of fact.

Sloman, A. and POPLOG Development Team (1991) 'POPLOG: a portable interactive software development environment', in D. Partridge (ed.) *AI and Software Engineering*, Ablex, Norwood, NJ, pp. 203–231.

Stefik, M. J., D. G. Bobrow and K. M. Kahn (1991) 'Integrating access-oriented programming into a multiparadigm environment', in D. Partridge (ed.), *AI and Software Engineering*, Ablex, Norwood, NJ, pp. 183–200.
A fairly non-technical description of some of the more advanced features of an advanced multiparadigm programming environment—LOOPS.

Tannenbaum, A. (1990) 'Installing AI tools into corporate environments', *AI Expert*, **5** (5), pp. 54–59.
'Mainframe-based AI expert-system shells can be integrated into corporate data processing with a migration strategy.'

Yourdon, E. (1990) 'Auld Lang Syne', *Byte*, **15** (10), 257–263.
An introduction to object-oriented design, and a comparison with conventional design strategies.

16

OBJECT-ORIENTED SYSTEMS

My guess is that object-oriented systems programming will be in 1980s
what structured programming was in the 1970s. . . . And no one will
know just what it is.

                                                        Tim Rentsch (1982)

INTRODUCTION

Many predictions and claims have been made for object-oriented systems
(OOSs): their contribution to increased programmer productivity, a way to
implement complex programs, greater reusability of system components,
and lower maintenance costs. Criticisms of OOSs include the lack of
appropriate programming languages, the difficulty of integrating heterogeneous databases into an OOS, poor support, and the lack of standards for
OOSs. Such claims as to the advantages and limitations of OOSs are the
subject of this chapter.

It is tempting to discuss object-oriented databases in a general chapter
on databases; the development approaches to OOSs along with other
development approaches; and programming languages for OOSs in the
chapter on programming languages. However, that approach results in a
loss of continuity on the subject of OOSs; and besides, the components of
an OOS are not independent of each other and should not be discussed in
isolation. Thus all the components are best discussed in one chapter, and in
the context of a complete OOS.

We shall start by defining 'objects' and their properties in an object-oriented environment. We then discuss object-oriented databases followed by a discussion of the development of OOSs. We also discuss programming languages for OOSs and an object-oriented DBMS required for the operations of an OOS. Finally, we critique the object-oriented approach and examine its advantages and limitations.

Many terms and concepts will be introduced in this chapter. They will be defined explicitly or implicitly by their context. In either case, they will be highlighted in italics the first time they are used.

BASIC CONCEPTS

An *object* is an *abstraction* of parts of the real-world system as depicted in Fig. 16.1. An object models the composite units of activity and structure. Objects can be combinations of data and code. Objects are, from a very high-level view, any entities that exist uniquely in time and space. Objects could be chunks of code that range in size from a small subroutine to a large application. Such objects, not algorithms, are the fundamental building blocks of an OOS.

Each object has a set of *instance* attributes. The attribute's values represent the object's *status*. The status is accessed or modified by a *message* to the object to invoke a *method*—the way in which an object is manipulated in the database, or executes an action such as displaying or printing data.

Objects sharing the same characteristics (of, say, attributes and methods) are grouped into classes, where a *class* represents the commonalities in the group of objects. A class defined as a special case of a more general class is a *subclass* and inherits characteristics from a class that is its *superclass*. The property of inheritance permits a subclass to behave as if it has all the attributes of its superclass. Classes are related to one another via a hierarchy of inheritance relationships. The hierarchy in which operations are implemented at upper hierarchical levels can be automatically recognized at lower levels. 'The inheritance mechanism represents an important form of abstraction, since the detailed difference of several class descriptions are

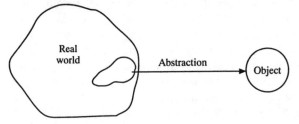

Figure 16.1 Object extracted from the real world.

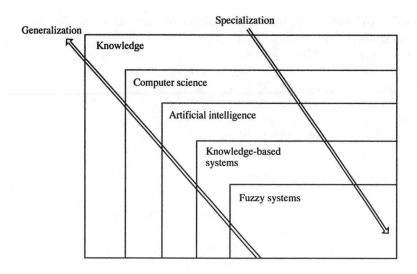

Figure 16.2 Directions of generalization and specialization.

abstracted away and the commonalties factored out as a more general superclass' (Bertino, 1991: 38).

The process of moving down in the hierarchy is referred to as *specialization*; each subclass is a particular specialization in its superclass. Thus the class of 'tables' is a subclass and hence a specialization of the class of 'furniture'. Going upward in the hierarchy is *generalization*. An example shown in Fig. 16.2 might help. It shows AI as an object that can be specialized into KBSs, which in turn are further specialized into fuzzy systems. Moving up the hierarchy from AI, we see that AI is part of a generalized concept of computer science, and computer science is part of the concept in the real world of what we may call knowledge. Note that we have used the term 'concept' in its day-to-day meaning without causing you confusion or anxiety, and yet it is a term used in the technical sense. Thus the circle in the real world as shown in Fig. 16.1 can be called a *concept*.

Generalization and specialization (its complement) are two mechanisms for reducing and decomposing complexity in the real world. 'Generalization enables us to say that all instances of a specific concept are also instances of a more general concept—but not necessarily the other way around' (Odell, 1992: 20). Another mechanism for reducing complexity is abstraction, discussed above. Without generalization and abstraction there would be no distinctions and resolution among objects. We would only know that everything is different, but not know how different.

We will now redraw Fig. 16.1 to be more specific, as shown in Fig. 16.3 with AI as an object. We can now say that an object is a representation, a

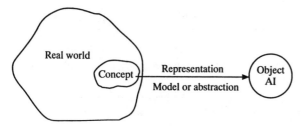

Figure 16.3 Object abstracted from a concept.

model, or an abstraction of a concept in the real world. For the object 'AI', we show a hierarchical diagram, as in Fig. 16.4, corresponding to the generalization and specialization shown in Fig. 16.2. In Fig. 16.4 we see that KBSs will inherit all the characteristics from its parent AI (and its parents, computer science, and other ancestor, knowledge) but not from its child: fuzzy systems. However, fuzzy systems will inherit all the characteristics from both its parent KBSs and KBSs' ancestors, computer science and AI, etc. Now if we invert this diagram we see the familiar shape of a tree, and so this structure can be referred to as the *hierarchical tree structure*. (We do not show all the other branches in order not to clutter the diagram.) This is a *single inheritance* structure, where each subclass inherits only from one immediate superclass.

The inheritance feature assumes that classes and subclasses of objects have been carefully outlined in the design phase of an OOS, for then the parent objects pass characteristics to subordinate classes (subclasses) in the hierarchy. The characteristics can include attributes, methods, behaviour, and messages.

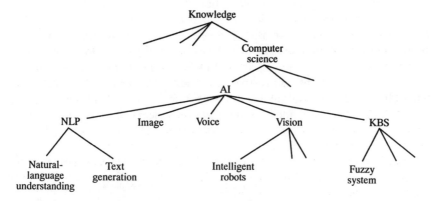

Figure 16.4 Inheritance in a hierarchical structure.

Inheritance enables reuse and specialization, where the programmer only adds new programming code to extend the existing function of the object. 'The creation of new classes of objects (also called *sub-classing*) results in class hierarchies and their collections become *libraries* of reusable components' (Friedman, 1992: 29–30).

Inheritance plays a crucial role in an OOS because it is used to transfer information from a more general class to a more specific class, thus resulting in an easier process of specification because many of the classes inherit large portions of their specification from the more general class (their parent class).

Besides a simple tree hierarchy, there is an extended form of inheritance in which a child object can inherit from more than just one parent object. This is called *multiple inheritance*.

Multiple inheritance is a powerful feature but can lead to conflicts. One type of conflict may arise because two or more superclasses might have an attribute with the same name but different domains. Or a conflict may arise when the name of an attribute explicitly defined in a class is the same as the attribute of a superclass. In such conflicts, the superclass is not inherited, i.e. the definition in the subclass overrides the superclass definition (Bertino, 1991: 38).

There are other conflicts to overcome and solve. One rule in the case of the domains in the superclass being related by inheritance relationships is for the most specific domain to be chosen for the subclass. If the domains are not related by inheritance, then the user can specify from which superclass the attribute must be inherited (Bertino, 1991: 38).

Another important idea is *polymorphism*, where the same name can be used to mean different things in different contexts. 'Polymorphism provides the ability to hide different implementations of a particular function behind a common interface. The same message can be used for several objects, each possibly providing its own implementation' (Friedman, 1992: 30).

Polymorphism greatly enhances the flexibility of OOSs. Using polymorphism, the developer can use the same code for different objects, thereby adding to the flexibility of the system. An example of polymorphism in OOSs is multiplication in mathematics as this function can be applied to a variety of object *types* (e.g. numbers, vectors, matrices, and functions). A message 'multiply A and B' should invoke different code, i.e. a different implementation of the 'multiply' method, if A and B were matrices rather than integers.

The process of selecting the appropriate method on the basis of an object's type is called *binding*. If the determination of an object's type can be deferred until run-time (rather than compile time), the selection is called *late binding*. Late binding is a useful feature in object-oriented systems because developers need not declare an object's type before execution. Used effectively, polymorphism and late binding add considerably to the overall maintainability and flexibility of an application.   (Weinberg *et al.*, 1990: 21)

(Note that late binding is not unique to an OOS and can be found in AI languages such as LISP.)

Polymorphism and inheritance are two essentials for an object-oriented environment. The other essential is *encapsulation*. This property refers to structure, where each object is a capsule of code and data characterizing an object in a single package; the actual code and data details are hidden from the other objects to insulate them from the effects of system modifications. This results in improved maintainability. Data is encapsulated with programs that operate on the data and enables the use of user-defined data types, on a par with the system-defined ones. An encapsulated object is accessed or modified only through the activation of its methods, i.e. the encapsulated code.

The *object* is a chunk of code that tightly binds attribute to action, making the object analogous to a complete sentence containing both noun and a verb. 'If procedures and functions are verbs and pieces of data are nouns, a procedure-oriented program is organized around verbs while an object-oriented program is organized around nouns.' In many conventional linear programs, nouns and verbs are developed separately, then linked through an application program.

OBJECT-ORIENTED DATABASES

Encapsulation, inheritance, and polymorphism provide the essential constructs of an object-oriented database system. These are shown graphically in Fig. 16.5.

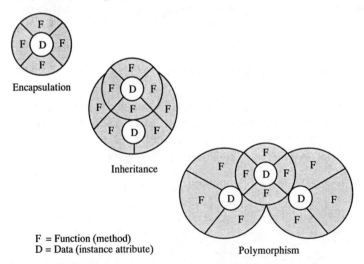

F = Function (method)
D = Data (instance attribute)

Figure 16.5 Fundamental object technology concepts. (From A. B. Friedman, 'Introduction to Object Technology on AIX', *AIXpert Journal*, May 1992, pp. 29–34.)

There are many differences between the traditional database and the object-oriented database. One significant difference is that the object-oriented model alone describes not only object structures but also their behaviour. Specifically (looking at an actual model), the CODASYL model lets complex objects be defined and supports some form of object identity, but does not provide concepts such as methods and class hierarchies. Looking at the relational model, it differs from the object-oriented model in that it (the relational model)

> does not provide the possibility of directly modeling complex objects (since attribute domains can only be primitive domains), and of defining inheritance relationships among sets of entities. Furthermore, it doesn't provide mechanisms to associate object behaviors with object definitions at schema level.   (Bertino, 1991: 40)

Another comparison that should be made is between an object-oriented database, which is a representation system, and an object-oriented programming system, which also claims some representation capabilities. However, object-oriented programming languages

> are not adequately concerned with the representation aspects of these objects and classes: they provide no formal, non-operational semantics for objects or classes, and thus lack an adequate representational basis for truly representing objects and classes; they are expressively limited, and thus cannot declaratively represent many aspects of domains; they allow user procedures to modify their data structures, and thus are hard to describe and understand.   (Patel-Schneider, 1990: 9)

What was designed for a programming system just does not prove appropriate for knowledge representation.

OBJECT-ORIENTED ENVIRONMENTS

A database is just one element in an object-oriented environment, central though this may be, as shown in Fig. 16.7. First to be discussed, however, should be the class libraries, which are compiled to form executable applications (Fig. 16.6). These include the many domain-specific libraries as well as some libraries that are function specific, which include the graphical user interface, the database, communication, and a base set. These function-specific libraries are in between the class libraries and the operating system set of objects. Each successive layer above the operating system builds on the one below it. The topmost layer, which has the domain-specific libraries, reflects objects that can be reused across applications but within a specific domain.

As shown in Fig. 16.6, the class libraries are stored within the *object management system* (OMS), and are managed under a configuration

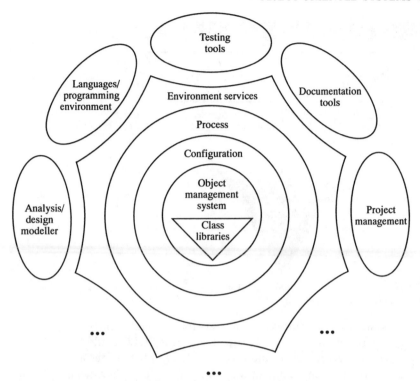

Figure 16.6 Object-oriented development environment. (From A. B. Friedman, 'Introduction to Object Technology on AIX', *AIXpert Journal*, May 1992, pp. 29–34.)

management discipline. Surrounding the OMS are environmental services, including the analysis and design tool, which supports the linkage representations and the notational representation of the objects in the OMS. The programming environment and programming languages are another important service and will be discussed later. The testing tools run validation tests on objects that have previously been validated but are tested again to ensure that no errors have crept in. And then there is the documentation tool, common and important to all information systems. Finally, we have the project management tool. This does not replace the project management techniques such as CPM, PERT, or GERT that are used in any SDLC for an information system but performs the supplementary functions unique to an OOS—such as new estimating techniques and project metrics needed for reusable components.

DEVELOPMENT OF OBJECT-ORIENTED SYSTEMS

Having discussed the object-oriented environment, we are now ready to discuss the development of an OOS, which is a complex process. Object-

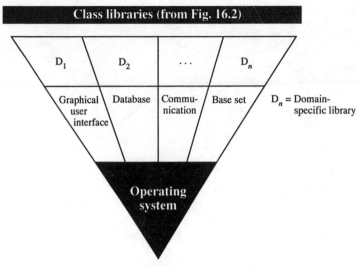

Figure 16.7 Class hierarchies. (From A. B. Friedman, 'Introduction to Object Technology on AIX', *AIXPert Journal*, May 1992, pp. 29–34.)

oriented systems development is not always incremental or interactive, hence prototyping is not always appropriate; instead the SDLC could be used (for details, see Henderson-Sellers and Edwards, 1990). Many of the activities for an object-oriented environment are similar to other environments in principle, especially in the planning and feasibility stages. Hence we start the discussion with the user specification and analysis stage, activity 9–10 in Fig. 16.8. (For more on this, see Bailin, 1989, and also Rubin and Goldberg, 1992.)

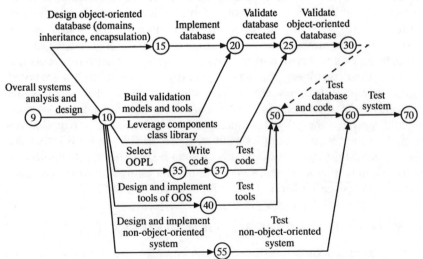

Figure 16.8 Activity diagram for the development of an object-oriented system.

In the initial design of an OOS, the essential focus for an object-oriented designer is not solving the problem but determining what objects are required in the problem domain, what functions each object has to perform, and how they relate to each other. There are, of course, the considerations of flow and control as in all information systems. To handle these functions effectively and smoothly, there are many techniques of analysis and design, some of which claim to be object-oriented. (For details, see Bailin, 1989; de Champeaux and Faure, 1992). There are also development techniques, which have been studied exhaustively by Sutcliffe who compared them with the object-oriented meta-model. Sutcliffe concludes that 'no complete OO method exists although the issues are addressed separately in different models' (Sutcliffe, 1991: 437). More specifically, Sutcliffe finds that hierarchical object-oriented design (HOOD) 'does fulfil most OO criteria, but does not completely support property inheritance'; object-oriented analysis (OOA) 'is more likely to identify actor as well as server objects. OOA meets many OO criteria and gives procedural advice'; structured analysis/structured design (SASD) does not support any object-oriented concepts because it 'separates data and process specification of functionally based systems components'; the structured systems analysis and design method (SSADM) does encourage data abstraction by conceptual modelling but it also supports functional modelling and hence it 'cannot be said to be truly object-oriented'; the structure analysis and design technique (SADT) does separate the process specification from data, making 'this method unsuitable for an OO approach'; information engineering (IE) encourages object modelling of the data components of a system and cross-referencing of functions to entities 'giving a partial OO specification'; information systems activity and change analysis (ISAC) emphasizes analysis and processes and are viewed as transforming data 'which encourages a partial OO approach'; Nijssen's information analysis method (NIAM) can be said to possess some object-oriented properties 'although it does not support inheritance'; and finally, Jackson systems development (JSD) 'has much in common with OO methods, although it does not explicitly support any OO concepts' (Sutcliffe, 1990: 437–439).

Sutcliffe should not be blamed for not mentioning all the techniques because there are so many of them. (For more on this, see Monarchi and Puhr, 1992; Nerson, 1992.) One that should be emphasized is SSADM, which is very commonly used in the United Kingdom. Like some of the other techniques, it is applicable to both analysis and design (activities 9–10 and 10–15, respectively). Such techniques supplemented by other methods for defining domains, polymorphism, and encapsulation of objects are used to create the object-oriented database. Once created, the database is implemented (15–20) and tested (validated) (20–25) with testing, models and tools developed in parallel (10–20). Also in parallel, objects already available in the class directories can be used (10–25). The object-oriented database is then complete and is tested (25–30). Also in parallel are the activities of object-oriented programming, which includes the selection of the programming language (10–35) and the writing of the code (35–37). These activities are important and complex enough to deserve a separate section and will be discussed later. The object-oriented code is tested (37–50), most likely with the help of a walkthrough method conducted by peers of the programmer. Further parallel activities are development of tools for the object-oriented environment (10–40), and its testing (40–50) followed by a test of the database and the code (50–60) for a validated object-oriented database (25–30). At the same time, the design and implementation of the rest of the system (the non-object-oriented systems: 10–55) can be pursued. All components are now ready for the test of the entire system (60–70). These tests follow the sequence of testing functions, subsystems, and then the entire system in order to catch errors or dysfunctions before they compound and make their detection and correction more difficult. This is, of course, not the only testing methodology that can be used but testing is a detailed subject for another time and another place. In this chapter we discuss only those activities that are more or less unique to the object-oriented environment and this brings us to the selection of coding with object-oriented programming languages.

OBJECT-ORIENTED PROGRAMMING

A study, on object-oriented programming languages (Saunders, 1989) found that of the 88 languages, 69 were stand-alone languages and 19 were incorporated into either multiparadigm or database languages. The growth of object-oriented programming languages (OOPLs) arose in three separate, yet interconnected, strains. These were LISP based (including LISP, Object LISP, FLAVORS, LOOPS, XLISP, and GLISP); C based (including C + +, Objective C, Inheritance C, and C-Talk) or Smalltalk based (the most prominent being Smalltalk, Distributed Smalltalk, and Smalltalk-80).

As you can see, without looking too closely, we did not call this section Smalltalk-80 but opted for a general presentation of *object-oriented programming* (OOP) as a style of programming. As to whether OOP is a programming paradigm in its own right, or more a style of programming that can be realized in conventional programming languages is a matter for debate as we have already inferred.

Advocates of the programming-style viewpoint can point to the many OOP options that exist for a wide variety of programming languages. There is, for example, a proposed extension to Common LISP known as the *Common LISP Object System* (CLOS).

But whatever the actual language selected, OOP is not like programming in FORTRAN, or COBOL, or any other traditional language. System development in the OOP style is typically tailoring a general system to specific needs by extracting particular substructures from the very general structures provided at the outset. By way of contrast, more traditional programming can be thought of in terms of building up the specific substructures required to perform the task at hand (i.e. constructing procedures and functions) from the set of primitive elements that comprise the language being used (i.e. the statements of the programming language).

Modularization is always a key strategy for managing the complexity of software system development. In traditional programming the programmer breaks the problem down into functional components and designs blocks of code to realise these modules. The particular modularization scheme chosen is dictated by consideration of the flow of control through the system as it is passed more or less explicitly from one module to the next. Subsequently, data structures are distributed through the framework of procedural modules as dictated by a strategy of localizing the data items to specific modules as much as possible. Data structures that are used by a number of different modules may be made 'global' so that a collection of modules may access a single representation of these data. In the more ancient programming languages the existence of such long-distance associations in a program was simply implicit in the overall structuring of the set of modules that comprised the program. In more modern languages (e.g. ADA and Modula-2) these long-distance connections must be explicitly signalled within each module, as well as restrictions on the nature of the association (e.g. information may be restricted to a one-way flow from the global data structure into the module).

In OOP modularization is still a key strategy, and there are many parallels with the caricaturization of traditional system design that we have just presented. But there are also many differences. The basic module of OOP is an 'object'. An object is an integrated collection of data and code (instance *variables* and *methods*, respectively, if you would like a dose of jargon). Superficially this does not seem very different from a traditional subroutine or function (and if you want to be awkward about it, we would find it hard to persuade you otherwise—after all, the OOP paradigm is not extraterrestrial; it did grow out of the procedural paradigm, and its ancestry, not surprisingly, is still apparent). But there are significant differences. There are differences of modularization criteria in system design, and there are differences of module use in the solution of a problem, and these two types of difference are, of course, closely related.

The use of an OOS to solve problems is typically an interactive one, whereas the traditional procedural paradigm arose in a batch processing environment—execution of the system was initiated, and the programmer was forced to take a back seat until it had worked its way through, being passed in a more or less predetermined way from procedure to procedure, to some end point. In an interactive environment the programmer is not forced to design for a monolithic approach to sequence control. The programmer can design a system in which problems are solved by a conglomerate of autonomous subcomputations by the machine, where much of the binding that results in the specific conglomerates that solve the problem at hand is supplied 'live,' as it were, by the human system user. In less pretentious prose, the user of an OOS has much scope to dabble in each execution of the system, and thus the system designer can, and should, take this into account during the design process. This consideration applies, of course, to any interactive environment, and is thus not a unique characteristic of OOP. It is, nevertheless, a characteristic of OOP that sets it apart from much traditional procedural programming. OOP can also claim much of the credit for what has become the standard style of interaction in modern computer systems: OOP initiated the age of WIMPs. This style of interaction with computers represents a considerable innovation for managers and other non-computer experts who can, nevertheless, expect to derive considerable assistance in their workaday tasks from the use of computer systems. Instead of having to learn the tedious details of a programming language (or even of a somewhat more friendly pseudo-English interface language), the manager can use a mouse to point to icons (simple pictorial representations of operations and objects) in order to achieve the desired results.

These are all OOP contributions to the human–computer interface; the use of this technology is what makes Macintosh computers, for example, usable tools for people who know no programming languages. Windows provide multiple views of a computation, e.g. a listing of the program, a trace of an execution, and a diagram of the inheritance hierarchy. Icons are pictorial representations of computational objects, and the mouse is a device that senses horizontal motion and is used to point to objects on the screen. Thus we might use the mouse to point to, say, a 'pencil' (i.e. an icon) on the screen in order to initiate line drawing in one of the screen windows. And pop-up menus provide a convenient 'choice' mechanism for the system user. A menu is a list of options, such as run, edit, or view a program. The mouse is used to point to and thus select the option required. Once an option has been selected, the next menu for the subsequent options, if any, pops up, and selection within its list of options becomes possible. This general style of human–computer interaction, pioneered in the OOP movement, is now widespread and commonplace in computer systems, even ones that are otherwise totally traditional in their approach to computation.

What is unique to OOP is the nature of primitive elements of sequence control. In OOP they are called *messages*. An execution of an OOS is composed of a collection of messages. A message tells an object to compute something (by say, applying one of its methods to some of its instance variable values). A message may be sent to an object and trigger a computation either directly by the system user, or indirectly as a result of a message received from another object that could not, on its own, deal with the message that it was originally sent. Objects exist in the well-defined context of more general objects and of more specific objects. This superclass-class-subclass hierarchy (it is, of course, not limited to three levels like the English language is) is known as an *inheritance hierarchy*, because both data and code in an object at one level may be used by a lower-level object—the lower level object is said to *inherit* a specific method from its superclass.

With the aid of the specific class hierarchy illustrated in Fig. 16.9, we can generate examples of the fundamental features of OOP. So, for a start we need to be able to create objects. Let us say we want to create an INTEGER object named X with the initial value 2. What do we do? We send a message to the class INTEGER telling it to use the NEW operation (*method*, if you want to be pedantic) and to associate the object that NEW generates with the name X and the value 2. We might do it as follows:

X INTEGER NEW 2   (creates an object X)

so now (as depicted in Fig. 16.10) we have an integer object named X whose value is 2. We have sent the message 'NEW 2' to the class INTEGER, and it has associated the result (i.e. a new object whose value is 2) with the name X.

Let us add 3 to the value of this object. We type:

X + 3   (which invokes X)

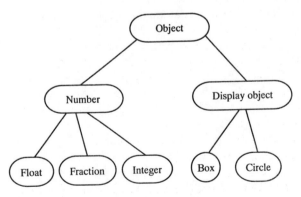

Figure 16.9 A three-level hierarchy of classes.

and the response, not too surprisingly, is:

5

Internally, the message '+3' was sent to the object X and its '+' method performed an operation that resulted in the value 5. One point to note is that the '+3' message gets its meaning (i.e. is associated with a specific operation) from the object that receives the message. Thus if '+3' were sent to a CHARACTER__STRING object, it might interpret '+' as concatenation and just add the character 3 to its current string value. Thus it is said that '+' is *overloaded* with more than one interpretation. This should not be too surprising, as the operator '+' is typically overloaded in conventional languages. Thus in FORTRAN the expression 'J=I+3' causes integer addition, while 'R=F+3.2' would cause floating-point addition. Internally, these are very different operations, and the computer system selects the appropriate one on the basis of the type (INTEGER or REAL) of the operands.

What is special about overloading in OOP is that this mechanism is generalized to all operators and is made available to the programmer (rather than acting as a system feature that the programmer cannot change, as in FORTRAN). But the fairly conventional language Ada, for example, offers comprehensive operator overloading facilities to the programmer as well as OOP-like class hierarchies, etc. Nevertheless, it is not classed as an OOP language.

It is time to look inside of objects. Suppose we want to create a DISPLAY__OBJECT, a BOX, that we shall call B1.

B1 BOX NEWAT:100@200

This message to the class BOX will produce a box (of default size) on the screen at location (100, 200), wherever that might be. In addition, this

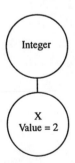

Figure 16.10

particular BOX object is called B1. Figure 16.11 is an illustration of the innards of the class BOX which, of course, is an object.

It might be worth noting a few features illustrated in Fig. 16.11. To begin with, it contains a link up to its superclass; this ties it into the inheritance hierarchy. Secondly, there are some *instance variables*—these are the variables needed to define and manage objects of this class, such as B1. Thus, B1 will have specific values for SIZE, TILT, and LOCATION. Thirdly, there are the *methods*, which are the legal operations on this class and objects of this class. It is these methods that will determine how messages are interpreted. Finally, you might note that the first method is somewhat different from the other two. The first method is a class method. It is used by the class to create new objects. The second and third methods are instance methods. They are used by instances of this class (i.e. specific

Class name	BOX
Superclass	DISPLAY_OBJECT
Instance variable names	SIZE TILT LOCATION

Methods

    NEWAT: INITIAL_LOCATION
        (code to generate a new object of default
        SIZE and TILT, and draw it on the screen
        at INITIAL_LOCATION; returns a pointer to
        the new object)

    SHOW:
        (code to draw a particular box)

    ERASE:
        (code to remove a particular box from the screen)

Figure 16.11

BOX objects like B1). Thus, SHOW would be used by B1 to display itself on the sreeen, and ERASE would be used for just the opposite purpose.

OBJECT-ORIENTED DATABASE MANAGEMENT SYSTEMS

Once an OOS is fully implemented and ready for conversion (transformation of old to new system) and operations, it needs to be tested (unless it is a stand-alone program) with an object-oriented DBMS (OODBMS). It is assumed that one is already up and running and does not have to be acquired and installed. An overview of the OODBMS in its operational mode is graphically shown in Fig. 16.12. The OODBMS now accesses an object-oriented database instead of a traditional data-oriented database. The OODBMS is supported by a knowledge object database dictionary, and an object and class directory, instead of a data dictionary.

An OODBMS performs all the functions that a traditional DBMS would perform. This includes many of the functions of an operating system (OS)—crash control, concurrency control, disk management, etc.—except that in an object-oriented environment the OS performs actions on objects instead of data elements, records, and files. Also, the OODBMS is not specifically designed or appropriate for queries as in a traditional database, though some OODBMSs have structured query language (SQL)-like constructs in addition to the programs and parameters necessary for input. Some OODBMSs have programming language features for end-user access that look much like OOPLs. However, because of the object orientation, the OODBMS does work at

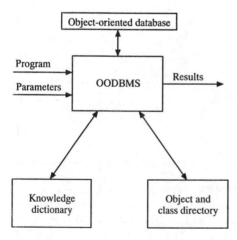

Figure 16.12 Operations of an OODBMS.

a higher level of abstraction and flexibility. It supports spatial, graphic objects, complex arrays, AI knowledge representations, engineering applications, and an office environment that handles compound documents requiring the integration of text, voice, video, pictures, graphics and alphameric data. And it allows the sharing of objects that were otherwise created for only one application but are now reusable, thereby increasing the use of modularity and decreasing costs of maintenance. The OODBMS also supports user-defined data structures and operations on them in terms of object classes and method inheritance.

OODBMS technology is still immature, and capabilities vary greatly. However, the OODBMS is typically a multi-user environment with some concurrency control and locking capability. It can support a variety of computer applications, including those that require managing and modelling complex nested entities with a rich set of data types, such as images, audio and textual documents, as well as semantic and temporal concepts.

An OODBMS usually offers multiple language support but its query support is quite limited and nothing close to the ANSI standards for SQL. This limitation is partly due to the complexity of the syntax necessary for the different types of data that have to be accessed.

OODBMSs have a spectrum of security mechanisms ranging from not even a log-in security facility to facilities that surpass many a relational DBMS. Another weakness of the OODBMS is that the standards for the OODBMS and its database languages are still under development, i.e. at the moment there are no standards.

Many OODBMSs are closer in nature to a hierarchical system than a relational one because of their structure (remember Fig. 16.4). OODBMSs employ navigational techniques and pointers, and therefore are not suited to handle certain query operations as well as the relational DBMS (RDBMS) is able to do. But navigational methods are more natural than the relational joins in a relational database. Because each object in a OODBMS requires a unique identifier, these databases may have greater inherent integrity than a RDBMS. Attempts have been made to marry the OODBMS with the RDBMS, notably by extending the relational model with OO features. SQL itself has been extended to encompass OO features.

beneath an object-oriented programming language. The buffering algorithm yields fast interactive performance while storing objects in a database. . . . The OO data models produce relational databases that match real-world applications and avoid the normalization problems associated with relational database design. . . . OO programming languages (OOPLs) improve code reuse, code maintenance, and modularity This approach combines the best features of both RDBMS and OO programming languages. (Premerlani et al., 1990: 107)

Whether by grafting a relational model to an OOPL or preferably by designing an RDBMS specifically for an object orientation, one can combine the database capabilities of persistence, transaction processing, concurrency, and query handling with the object-oriented concepts of abstract data typing, object identity and inheritance. OODBMSs will then supersede the current dominance of RDBMSs and may well lead us through to the next evolutionary step of a truly intelligent DBMS. (For more on OODBMSs, see Kim, 1991.)

CRITIQUE OF THE OBJECT-ORIENTED APPROACH

In critiquing the object-oriented approach, we shall start with its advantages, and not necessarily in the order of importance or priority. Some of the advantages have been explicitly or implicitly mentioned earlier. These include the improvement in the quality as well as the productivity of code generated, resulting partly because of the reuse of code (for objects that range from small routines to entire applications) that has been tested and refined over time. The reusable code encourages greater organization-wide sharing, which could result not only in monetary savings but also consistency and adherence to existing standards. There is also a flexibility in the object-oriented software that results from both encapsulation and polymorphism. The reuse and modularity possible in the object orientation also results in lower costs of both development and maintenance. The modularity has replaced the sequential code of many traditional systems. Modularity, object abstraction, and hierarchical reasoning may well lead to distributed problem solving for management in business and industry.

Object orientation enables the designer to model real-world problems of feature-rich and increasingly complex environments; hitherto this was not possible. Object orientation facilitates the development of applications that model solutions closely on the structure of real-world problems.

> Object-oriented systems can more closely reflect the behavior of elements in the problem domain itself, thereby reducing the loss of information, undesirable side effects, and spurious behavior that can affect conventional structured data processing solutions. This fundamental approach to problem abstraction gives the object-oriented paradigm great potential power. (Weinberg *et al.*, 1990: 20)

Object-oriented systems have been used successfully for complex tasks, such as inventory management; computer integrated manufacturing (CIM), including computer-aided design/manufacture (CAD/CAM); integrated office automation; multimedia systems; KBSs; AI applications (including natural language processing and image, voice, and vision processing); automated discovery and retrieval systems; and scientific applications.

On the negative side, it has been said that the object-oriented architecture is too slow. There are at least two reasons for this:

> The first is granularity. In Smalltalk, for example, an integer is an object; adding two integers involves sending a message to one of the two arguments. When the number of objects in the system is huge, overhead is considerable. The second is the number of procedure calls involved in a computation. When hardware resources are limited, the time spent on context swapping is also considerable. Again, we hope such difficulties can be overcome in the future.   (Ramamoorthy and Sheu, 1988: 14)

Ramamoorthy and Sheu also criticize OOPLs (1988: 14). They argue that programmers in these languages have to answer the following questions during the implementation stage:

1. What is the best way to decompose the system into a set of objects and classes?
2. What target systems element is to be an object, and what elements are not?
3. Which object and class provides methods that realize the required functions?
4. What is the best set of message protocols?

There are other criticisms which are not so wordy but just as telling: OOSs require more computing power to execute (sometimes up to 10 per cent more than traditional systems); OOSs require programming skills that are either not available or are too expensive; an OODBMS provides only limited support for integrating data in existing heterogeneous databases with databases maintained by the OODBMS; higher design integrity and quality control are needed for reusing existing software; the current crop of object-oriented programming products may be more trouble than they are worth for creating simple utility programs, or for persons who program infrequently; and there is little portability among object-oriented products, partly because there are no accepted standards for such products, or for object-oriented databases or programming languages.

Another criticism concerns the nature of object-oriented technology. It is often either an 'all or nothing' proposition. To benefit fully from this technology, one must not only have an object-oriented database with all its strong requirements but also know the relevant methods of design and development, and then be conversant with the rather specialized OOPLs. This may be difficult and expensive for an organization with an established computing environment and a large investment in a non-object-oriented computing environment.

Support for the object-oriented approach comes from Edward Yourdon, the author (and publisher) of many books on structured techniques. Structured techniques were hailed by some as the productivity solution of the 1970s and the 1980s. Computer-aided software engineering (CASE) was promoted in the same way during the second half of the 1980s. Some people are now suggesting that 'object orientation is the salvation of the 1990s' (Yourdon, 1990: 257). And Yourdon seems to be one of these people, for he concludes: 'Object orientation is the future, and the future is here and now' (Yourdon, 1990: 264).

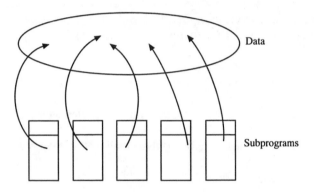

Figure 16.13 Program design in the early 1960s. From G. Booch, *Object Oriented Design with Applications*, Benjamin/Cummings, Redwood City, CA.

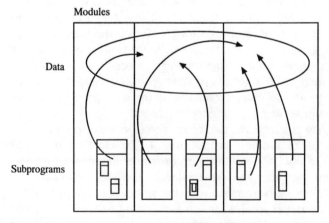

Figure 16.14 Program Design of the 1970s. (From G. Booch, *Object Oriented Design with Applications*, Benjamin/Cummings, Redwood City, CA.)

We conclude this critique with a comparison of the OOS with previous approaches as given by Booch (1991): those in the early 1960s are shown in Fig. 16.13; those in the 1970s in Fig. 16.14; early OOSs in Fig. 16.15; and finally, programming-in-the-large, which has grown into what Booch so nicely puts it as 'programming-in-the-colossal', where clusters of abstractions are built in layers on top of one another, in Fig. 16.16.

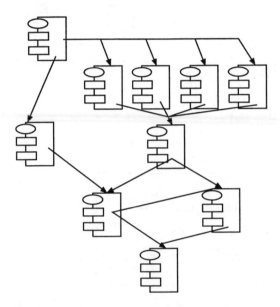

Figure 16.15 Early program design based on OOP. From G. Booch, *Object Oriented Design with Applications*, Benjamin/Cummings, Redwood City, CA.

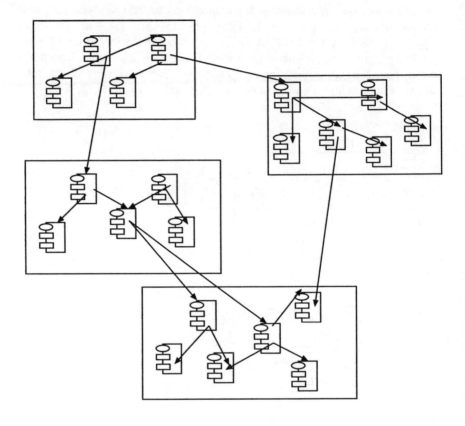

Figure 16.16 The OOP approach to programming-in-the-colossal. (From G. Booch, *Object Oriented Design with Applications*, Benjamin/Cummings, Redwood City, CA.)

SUMMARY AND CONCLUSIONS

An object-oriented environment implies the existence of objects, inheritance, encapsulation, and polymorphism. This environment results in a system with higher programmer productivity, and lower development and maintenance costs, and one that is able to handle complex real-world problems. Some of the advantages and limitations of the object-oriented environment are summarized in Table 16.1

Table 16.1 Summary of advantages and limitations of an object-oriented system

Advantages	Limitations
Greater object sharing	Slow in execution
Lower costs because of: —Higher productivity —Reusable code	Difficulties in delineating object, messages, and decomposition
Flexibility because of: —Encapsulation —Polymorphism	Object-orientation skills are expensive and rare in market place
Object-orientation reflects real-world problems	Object-oriented databases do not integrate well with non-object-oriented databases

Applicable to complex application problems:
—CIM (including CAD)
—Integrated office
—Multimedia
—AI applications
    NLP (natural-language understanding, text processing)
    Image
    Voice
    Vision
—Retrieval
—Scientific applications
	Higher integrity and control required for reuse of objects
	
	Object-orientation not worthwhile for simple problems
	
	Lack of standards for object-oriented
	—Databases
	—Analysis and design
	—Programming
	Little portability among object-oriented products
	OOSs require packaging
	—Object-oriented database
	—Analysis and design
	—OOPL

There are many differences between the object-oriented environment and traditional computing environments. These are summarized in Table 16.2.

Table 16.2 Comparison of object-oriented systems with conventional systems

Conventional systems	Object-oriented systems
Algorithmic abstraction	Object and class abstraction
No inheritance	Concept of inheritance is an important feature
Program module, subroutine, or program as basic building block	Objects as basic building block that is reusable
Abstract data types used	Complex data types supported
Early binding and some late binding	Late binding supported
Imperative programming languages used, e.g. —ALGOL —Pascal —FORTRAN —COBOL —PL/1	Declarative OOPLs used, e.g. derivations of —LISP —C —Smalltalk
DBMS based on models —Hierarchical —Network —Relational —Extended relational	OODBMS based on object orientation and describing —Structure —Behaviour
Effort and cost in writing code is high	Effort and cost in writing is relatively low
Linear sequence of steps for modification	Modification is relatively easy
Maintenance is high	Maintenance is relatively low

As objects become numerous and as the relationships between these objects are many and complex, object orientation and object management becomes necessary. As objects become more reusable, we may well approach an era that has been referred to as 'applications without programmers'. As sharing of the objects and applications increases, we may exploit the advantages of concurrency control and multiple files to approach *group-ware* and application sharing.

Were OOSs in the 1980s what structured design was to the computing community in the 1970s, as implied by Rentsch? To quote Rentsch more fully:

> My guess is that object-programming will be in the 1980s what structured programming was in the 1970s. Everyone will be in favor of it. Every manufacturer will promote his products supporting it. Every manager will pay lip service to it. Every programmer will practice it (differently). And no one will know just what it is.

Perhaps Rentsch was right in general terms. But Rentsch underestimated the time it takes and the difficulties along the path. Resistance among managers for changes in computing is well documented. Not so well documented is the resistance among the computer community to change, especially when years of investment in programming and in training for development methodologies may have to change. But programmers (and analysts) are very adaptable to new techniques and can learn to 'know just what [an OOS] is'. If the path of change towards an OOS is selected for the 1990s, it could still be long and tough going, but certainly exciting.

CASE 16.1 SPELLING DUTCH NAMES—2

Unlike many European languages, the Dutch language lacks cedillas, circumflexes, accents, and umlauts. However, thousands of Dutch family names are spelled with such diacritical marks. Should Dutch databases be designed to store such marks?

To many people, the spelling of a family name is a matter of personal pride. No wonder the decision by some 700 Dutch municipalities and the tax office to omit storing and processing diacritical marks in computer processing has caused offence. Richard Gütlich claims that his brother was buried under a name not his own, because the town registrar could not deal with the umlaut. A woman whose name is Hör (pronounced like the French word fleur) objects that her name is officially Hoer (pronounced whore), because the umlaut was replaced with an oe, as in the German usage.

An organization called the 'Up and Down' has been formed in The Netherlands of activists who want Dutch names processed by computer to be spelled as families write them. The group is planning a lawsuit to force modification of the name field in government databases.

Source: 'Spell that name again, please', *Time* (23 January 1989), p. 19.

Questions

1. The above application can be implemented as a transactional system. If implemented as a KBIS, how would the system be applicable to other languages like German, French, Scandinavian, and even Turkish, which all use the Latin script but have different diacritical marks?
2. Would you use an object-oriented approach for such an application, treating each name as an object?
3. Assuming that you decide to use the object-oriented approach, would you use an OOPL or would you use a shell, a toolkit, or a programming language environment?
4. What hardware demands would you face (if any)? Explain.

REVIEW AND DISCUSSION QUESTIONS

16.1 List the most important concepts that identify an OOS. Would you care to rank them?

16.2 List conditions necessary for the application of object-oriented concepts.

16.3 List generic applications appropriate for an object-oriented portfolio.

16.4 Why should methods of analysis and design and development be different for an object-oriented environment than for any other information system?

16.5 If you decided to use object-oriented methodology, how will it affect the following?
- (*a*)   Data.
- (*b*)   Analysis stage.
- (*c*)   Design stage.
- (*d*)   Programming language used.
- (*e*)   DBMS used.

In each case, explain why.

16.6 How is the administration of a knowledge-base for an object-oriented environment different from a non-object-oriented environment?

16.7 Will an OOS be more expensive to develop than say a relational system? Whether yes or no, please explain your position.

16.8 List the tangible *and* intangible benefits of an OOS. How would you justify each item to management?

16.9 List possible pitfalls in implementing an object-oriented system.

16.10 Does the proliferation of OOPLs help or hinder the following?
- (*a*)   Programmer.
- (*b*)   Analyst.
- (*c*)   End-user.

Explain.

16.11 How will an object-oriented environment affect the following?
- (*a*)   Analyst.
- (*b*)   End-user.
- (*c*)   Manager of IT (information technology)
- (*d*)   Corporate manager.

16.12 What are the costs of hiring and training a programmer in OOPLs?

16.13 Would you prefer hiring an OOPL programmer from outside or train a programmer already in your organization? Explain your reasoning.

16.14 What would you look for if you had to select a person for in-house training?

16.15 Is it easier or more difficult to manage the following aspects of an OOS as opposed to those of a transaction system?
- (*a*)   Development.
- (*b*)   Operations.

Explain.

16.16 'Object orientation is a fad. Given time, it will fade away.' Comment.

16.17 'Object orientation is too new. Wait until it is debugged before you use it.' Comment.

16.18 'Object orientation is too complex.' Do you agree or disagree? Discuss.

16.19 'An object-oriented system is abstract.' Explain.

16.20 How do you see the future of OOSs? Why?

16.21 Do you agree with Rentsch's (detailed) prediction about OOSs? Explain.

BIBLIOGRAPHY AND REFERENCES

Askit, M. and Lodewijk, B. (1992) 'Obstacles in object-oriented development', *ACM SIGPLAN*, **27** (10), 341–358.
Discusses obstacles to OOS development and evaluates them with respect to their pilot applications.

Bailin, S. C. (1989) 'An object-oriented requirements specification method', *Communications of the ACM*, **32** (5), 608–623.
This is a good tutorial on user specification for an object-oriented database.

Bertino, E. (1991) 'Object-oriented database management systems: concepts and issues', *Computer*, **24** (3), 33–42.
This article is not restricted to OODBMSs as the title suggests, but takes a much broader view of object-oriented technology.

Booch, G. (1991) *Object-Oriented Design with Applications*, Benjamin Cummings, Redwood City, CA.

de Champeaux, D. and P. Faure (1992) 'A comparative study of object-oriented analysis methods', *Journal of Object-Oriented Programming*, **5** (1), 21–33.
A good comparison of approaches of 10 sets of authors, each for a set of 14 criteria.

de Champeaux, D., D. Lea and P. Faure (1992) 'The process of object-oriented design', *ACM SIGPLAN*, **27** (10), 45–62.
Discussed are: abstraction, prototyping, bottom-up composition, delegation, interoperability, clustering objects into processes, resource management design, tuning and optimization.

Dittrich, K. R. (1990) 'Object-oriented database systems: the next miles in the marathon', *Information Systems*, **15** (1), pp. 161–167.

Fishman, R. G. and C. E. Kemerer (1993) 'Adoption of software engineering process innovations: the case of object orientation', *Sloan Management Review*, **34** (2) 7–22.
The authors conclude that object-oriented technology 'is not likely to be quickly adopted by large in-house business information systems groups'.

Friedman, A. B. (1992) 'Introduction to object technology on AIX', *AIXpert*, May, 29–33.
This is a superb introduction to object technology. Its source is an IBM in-house journal and is a good example of how excellent material is often hidden in an inaccessible publication.

Henderson-Sellers, B. and J. M. Edwards (1990) 'The object-oriented systems life cycle', *Communications of the ACM*, **33** (9), 142–159.
A discussion of the SDLC for an OOS.

Higa, K., M. Morrison, J. Morrison and O. R. Liu Sheng (1992) 'Object-oriented methodology for knowledge-based/database coupling', *Communications for the ACM*, **35** (6), 99–113.
The authors discuss how knowledge-bases can provide for exceptional handling, query optimization and some update constraints.

Kim, W. (1990) 'A new database for new times', *Datamation*, **36** (2), 35–42.
Kim argues that current data models, even the extended relational model, are not able to handle the complex business systems of today let alone tomorrow. He then makes the case for the OOS and even offers a set of eight rules that must be satisfied before a database can be called an object-oriented database.

Kim, W. (1991) 'Object-oriented database: strengths and weaknesses', *Journal of Object-Oriented Programming*, **4** (4), 21–29.

McLeod, D. (1991) 'Perspective on object databases', *Information and Software Technology*, **33** (1), 13–22.
McLeod discusses the 'principle underlying structurally object-oriented (semantic) database models' and compares it with record-based models.

Manola, F. (1991) 'Object-oriented knowledge bases, part I', *AI Expert*, **3** (3), 26–36.
A good discussion of an object-oriented database.

Monarchi, D. E. and G. I. Puhr (1992) 'A research topology for object-oriented analysis and design', *Communications of the ACM*, **35** (9), 35–47.
Twenty-three authors have been compared for handling process (in analysis or/and design), representation, and complexity management.

Nerson, J.-M. (1992) 'Applying object-oriented analysis and design', *Communications of the ACM*, **35** (9), 63–74.
An excellent walk-through of the analysis for an object-oriented car rental system with numerous good diagrams.

Odell, J. (1992) 'Managing object complexity. Part 1: abstraction and generalization', *Journal of Object-Oriented Programming*, **5** (5), 19–23.
Odell has a delightful way of simplifying difficult concepts into simple-to-understand diagrams.

Patel-Schneider, P. F. (1990) 'Practical, object-based knowledge representation for knowledge-based systems', *Information Systems*, **15** (1), 9–18.
This article makes a sharp distinction between object-oriented knowledge representation systems and object-oriented programming systems.

Peterson, G. E. (ed.) (1988) *Tutorial: Object-Oriented Computing*, 2 vols, Computer Society of the IEEE, New York.
This is a set of readings that makes an excellent reference besides being a good tutorial.

Premeriani, W. J., M. R. Blaha, J. E. Rumbaugh and T. A. Varwig (1990) 'An object-oriented relational database', *Communications of the ACM*, **33** (11), 99–108.
A discussion of a RDBMS combined with a OOPL.

Ramamoorthy, C. V. and P. C. Sheu (1988) 'Object-oriented systems', *IEEE EXPERT*, **3** (3), 9–14.
A good overview, including some discussion of hardware.

Rentsch, T. (1982) 'Object oriented programming', *SIGPLAN Notices*, **17** (9), 51–61.

Rubin, K. S. and A. Goldberg (1992) 'Object behavior analysis', *Communications of the ACM*, **35** (9), 48–62.
The authors focus on the *what*, *why* and *how* in the analysis of an OOS and justify 'the existence of a given result to the stated goals and objectives'.

Saunders, J. H. (1989) 'A survey of object-oriented languages', *Journal of Object-Oriented Programming*, **1** (2), 5–11.
A good survey of programming languages with their roots. Has a bibliography of 104 items.

Sutcliffe, A. G. (1991) 'Object-oriented systems development: survey of structured methods', *Information and Software Technology*, **33** (6), 433-441.
This article is a welcome survey of the basic concepts of object-oriented methodology plus a superb comparison of structured methods of systems development with object-oriented methodology.

Thomas, D. (1989) 'What's in an object?', *Byte*, **14** (3), 231–240.
Discusses how even 'limited object-oriented systems let you build your own integrated applications quickly'.

Wegner, P. (1989) 'Learning the language', *Byte*, **14** (3), 245–253.
'Object-oriented programming trades the ability to use individual operations for efficiency and conceptual simplicity.'

Weinberg, R., T. Guimareas and R. Heath (1990) 'Object-oriented systems development', *Journal of Information Systems Management*, **7** (4), 18–26.
Like Sutcliffe's article, this is a survey of object-oriented technology and includes a good discussion of the differences between traditional and object-oriented systems development.

Yourdon, E. (1990) 'Auld Lang Syne', *Byte*, **15** (10), 257–263.
The author who is a source of many a book and critique on structured methodology argues that it is time to say goodbye to the older methodologies and say welcome to the new and promising methodology: object-oriented methodology.

17

PERSONNEL MIX FOR A KNOWLEDGE-BASED SYSTEM

There are three major problems in systems development: people, people, and people.

Anon.

INTRODUCTION

We have mentioned KBIS personnel often in this book. In the discussion of project management for a KBIS, we compared the knowledge engineer with the domain expert in terms of functions to be performed and abilities that the two groups bring to a KBIS. In the same chapter, we examined the education and training of computer personnel for a KBIS. But many questions still remain. What are the functions of the knowledge engineer and domain expert during the different stages of development of a KBIS? How does the knowledge engineer differ from other personnel such as the analyst of the transactional system and the practitioner of OR/MS? How does the knowledge engineer and other AI personnel differ from other personnel in a corporation? Should the high-tech AI personnel be treated and managed differently? If so, how? These and other related questions are the subject of this chapter.

We start our discussion with the identification of the different information technology (IT), OR/MS, and AI personnel needed for the development of a KBIS. This discussion is a necessary background for our understanding of the background, satisficers/dissatisficers, motivation, educational needs, and relationships with the end-user of the different personnel involved in a KBIS.

PERSONNEL NEEDED FOR A KNOWLEDGE-BASED SYSTEM

Many personnel are involved in a KBIS. One rough classification would be to distinguish between technical personnel, responsible for system development, and the rest of the personnel involved in a KBIS. The organizational personnel would include management: the project sponsor, the project manager, or top managers who make the 'go/no go' decision for the project. There are also the staff of the planning department, which may include an economist, a financial person, perhaps a consultant, and other technical personnel such as a cost accountant. Then there is the domain expert, and finally, the end-user, who may be one of the persons listed above but not necessarily.

The technological personnel could include one of the traditional IT personnel such as a systems analyst responsible for transactional systems but well versed in systems development. Also included would be the OR/MS person most knowledgeable of the DSS aspects of the organization as well as of the decision-making power structure. And finally, there are the AI personnel, which in the case of a KBIS is the knowledge engineer. All of these personnel as classified above are shown in Fig. 17.1.

The personnel listed above do not all actively participate at the same time, but instead contribute their expertise to different stages of the development of a KBIS. One such distribution of effort of personnel in a KBIS is shown in Fig. 17.2; this should be self-explanatory in view of the development process discussed in earlier chapters.

THE KNOWLEDGE ENGINEER

The knowledge engineer plays an important (and even dominant) role in the development of a KBIS as illustrated in Fig. 17.2. In addition, the knowledge engineer is responsible for all the prototyping done in a KBIS. Prototyping is not new to a KBIS, as it has been used extensively in a DSS. However, there are differences in the interactions in prototyping for a KBIS as compared to that in a DSS. In prototyping a DSS, the stages of user specification, design, implementation, and testing are often lumped together in a tightly coupled set of interactions between the OR/MS specialist and the manager end-user. The prototyping of a KBIS is typically done separately for two modules (knowledge-base preparation and the presenta-

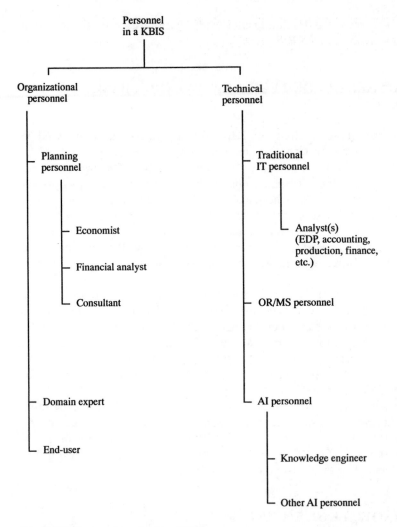

Figure 17.1 Personnel involved in a KBIS.

tion module), and the players in each case are different. In the case of knowledge-base preparation, the knowledge acquisition (and the testing of the knowledge base) is done between the domain expert and the knowledge engineer as shown in Fig. 17.2. In the case of the presentation module (not shown explicitly in Fig. 17.2), the knowledge engineer must interact with the domain expert in the testing phase in order to ensure the effectiveness and accuracy of the system, while the knowledge engineer must also interact with the domain end-user to ensure that the presentation module is user friendly and effective in its presentations and explanations. In the final

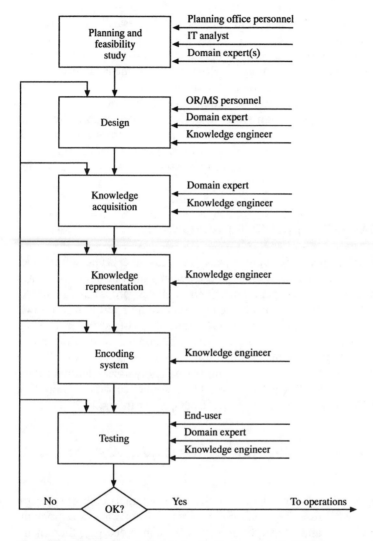

Figure 17.2 Distribution of effort during the development of a KBIS.

acceptance testing phase, the end-user will most likely participate in addition to the domain expert.

As for motivation of the players involved in the prototyping, the chances of cooperation by the players in a DSS prototyping exercise is high because the end-user is often the project sponsor and hence highly motivated. In the case of a KBIS, the cooperation from the domain expert may be less than enthusiastic and motivating. In some cases the human expert is assigned to the task and thus is not necessarily motivated or enthusiastic about the project.

A knowledge engineer is perhaps first and foremost a computer expert well versed in AI tools and techniques. However, he or she must also be able to interact effectively with human domain experts and induce them to articulate their expertise in a precise manner. The knowledge engineer must be able to translate the human expert's decision strategies into facts and rules of the appropriate form as well as translate problems with the functioning of the computer system into a form that the human expert can evaluate. The outcome should be results that the end-user can apply with ease and confidence.

ARTIFICIAL INTELLIGENCE PERSONNEL

In addition to the knowledge engineer, a KBIS needs other AI personnel—AI technology, like any new technology and especially high technology, brings with it the need for new personnel. This includes programmers in AI languages and specialists in knowledge representation in addition to knowledge engineers and specialists in AI applications like NLP, voice processing, image processing and vision processing. Also, the domain expert for a KBIS is closely related to AI personnel though some domain experts may wish to be associated only temporarily with AI and permanently associated with their domain professionals. The addition of AI personnel to other computing personnel is shown in its historical evolving perspective in Fig. 17.3.

THE KNOWLEDGE ENGINEER AND OTHER SYSTEMS PERSONNEL

There is a temptation to identify knowledge engineers with software engineers partly because they are both involved with software development. A study by Couger and McIntyre done in 1987 concluded that there is no significant difference between knowledge engineers and software engineers in terms of their perceptions of the importance of task identity, autonomy, and feedback from the job; but there were some significant differences in their perception of task significance and skill variety. These two groups are often considered part of the same breed, partly perhaps because they are both professionally educated as computer programmers and computer scientists even though their functions are somewhat different. In the early days of ES technology, it was naïvely thought that a human domain expert could simply explain the rules behind his or her expertise and the conventional programmer could then code them into an appropriate form

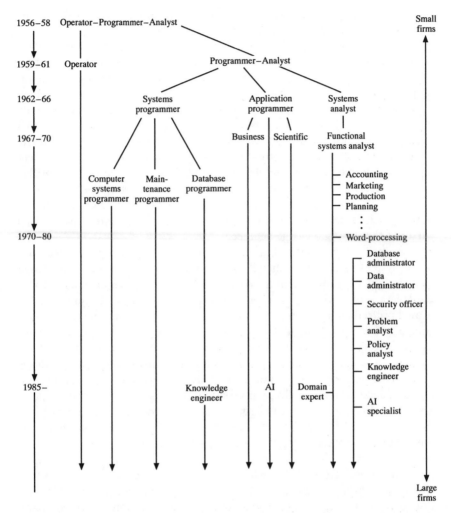

Figure 17.3 Correlation of temporal and size evolution in computing personnel configurations.

for the knowledge-base. We now know from experience of implementing ESs that the domain experts are not particularly expert at articulating the reasoning behind their expertise. The knowledge engineers have to 'extract' information from the human experts, which may involve an understanding of psychology and group dynamics.

In addition, building a KBIS is not like programming a mathematical function—there is typically not a correct implementation to aim for in any absolute sense. The goal is usually to reproduce (and perhaps exceed) the performance of human experts—and the best of them are never perfect, but their behaviour provides the basic data for validating a KBIS. What this means, in practice, is that KBISs are never 'finished' in the way that classic software may be. It is a matter of first producing a system that is good enough to satisfy a real practical need, and then of continually working on the system to continue the long-term, in-use validation process as well as to improve the system's expertise.

In order to be capable of building, validating, and maintaining or upgrading an ES, we must have available a computer expert. But this technologist is rather different from the traditional software person, for the software cannot, in many situations, be accurately treated as a correct implementation of some well-defined specification. The validity of a KBIS is largely determined by the judgements of human experts in the application domain. So the role of the technologist becomes one of a communicator in both directions, between the software system and the domain experts. This person is then the knowledge engineer.

Because of the important differences between a knowledge engineer and other systems personnel, including computer scientists, the knowledge engineer must be hired (or trained) for KBSs. An example of this need was the creation of a whole new group of employees when AI technology was brought into the factory in the Digital Equipment Corporation (DEC). This company was one of the first (and still perhaps one of the most successful) users of ES technology in business applications. The XCON system is used by DEC to help in the checking of complex computer configurations and is more accurate than the human experts that it replaced. The R1 system, developed at Carnegie Mellon University, is famous as the first of its type of ES that DEC commissioned. From our current perspective, the point is that, after DEC had embraced this new technology, despite the fact that they are a computer company with presumably many different sorts of computer technologists on hand, they were quite surprised by the need to set up a support group of knowledge engineers—people with expertise that was significantly different from that which they already had available, and thus persons who needed to be either employed from outside the company or retrained within it.

ARE ARTIFICIAL INTELLIGENCE AND COMPUTER PERSONNEL DIFFERENT?

Project management is a good one-time approach to organizing for an AI project—like a KBIS. But to have an available source of loyal and competent personnel, a firm must have a long-term plan for managing its AI and computer people. The question of course arises: why cannot AI and computer people be managed by the personnel department of the firm, along with the other personnel? One answer is that AI and computer personnel are different from each other and from the other personnel. How different? Are the satisfiers/dissatisfiers for each group different? And what personnel strategies are necessary to attract and retain personnel so that AI systems can be both developed and *sustained* through the necessary maintenance and enhancements that will be required in response to a changing technology (as well as to accommodate the 'unfinished' nature of AI systems).

The answer to the question—'Are AI and computer personnel different?'—depends on your classification scheme for personnel. One distinction is high and low tech. OR/MS, and even some management information systems (MIS) applications, may be said to be old tech, but advanced MIS applications, such as the integration of an electronic office or automated factory, must clearly be classified as high tech. And certainly the intelligent part of an information system (IS) and all of AI, including KBISs, must be classified as high tech. If AI is high tech, then one must recall John Naisbitt's book *The Restructuring of America*, in which he argues that one of the five necessary approaches to restructuring the United States is the high-tech/high-touch approach—i.e., successful introduction of any high-tech innovation (including computer technology) must be accompanied by a corresponding and compulsory human response, otherwise the technology will be rejected.

A study (Ferratt and Short, 1988) carried out on IS personnel concluded emphatically that IS people should not be treated differently from non-IS people. Another study by the sociologist Alvin Gouldner (1984: 70) separates people into 'cosmopolitans' and 'locals'. The cosmopolitans are loyal to their professions throughout their career and attach great importance to keeping up with their profession through reading technical professional journals and attending professional conferences. In contrast, the locals give all their loyalty to their organizations. In this classification scheme, both computer personnel and AI personnel are clearly cosmopolitans. They are known for their mobility, caused partly by higher economic rewards elsewhere (where they can market their newly won knowledge), partly because they have opportunities of growth in their career, and partly in response to a technological challenge of applying newer techniques to more complex problems.

Lack of qualified personnel is not the only staffing problem of computer, OR/MS, or AI personnel. Turnover is also a major concern. In the early 1980s, annual attrition of computing personnel was as high as 15–20 per cent in many organizations. Although there has been a drop in turnover in recent years—to an average of 5.6 per cent in the mid-1980s (Rifkin, 1985)—corporate managers remain concerned about turnover, because qualified computer personnel replacements are hard to find and expensive to train. They recognize the importance of identifying positive and negative motivational work factors so that they can improve the corporate environment in ways that will encourage employees to remain productive.

We do not yet have enough longitudinal and historical studies of computer personnel, especially programmers and analysts. These people are a major source of AI personnel, and hence their satisfiers and dissatisfiers may be similar to those of AI personnel. Only recently have studies of employee motivation addressed the question of whether factors motivating computer personnel are different from those for other employees in the work force. For example, 1500 computer personnel were questioned on how they ranked a list of job satisfiers and dissatisfiers (Fitz-enz, 1978) using criteria drawn from a study by Herzberg et al. (1959).

The rankings for three criteria (achievement, work itself, and advancement) are identical in the two surveys. However, significant divergence is apparent in some other rankings. Computer personnel list recognition and salary as much less important than Herzberg et al.'s respondents, whereas growth possibilities and certain other criteria are valued more highly.

In another study, Couger and Zawacki (1980) compared the attitudes of 2500 computer employees with the findings in another survey which used the same diagnostic survey instrument. The two main findings of Couger and Zawacki were that analysts and programmers express a greater need for personal growth and development than the 500 other occupational groups surveyed, and they express a lower social-need strength (i.e. a desire to interact with others) than any other job category analyzed. However, Couger (1988) hastens to add:

> Programmers and analysts are not anti-social; they will participate actively in meetings that are meaningful to them. But their high growth need also causes intolerance for group activities that are not well organized and conducted efficiently.

More recent studies agree that computer people seek personal fulfilment and growth from their work and are less motivated by money and job titles than other employee groups. In acknowledgement of such differences in personnel, corporate managers must develop new strategies to motivate and reward computer professionals, especially knowledge engineers.

END-USERS

The end-user has gained great recognition (as well as great respectability) with the emergence of the ES, which makes a clear distinction between the interface for the end-user and the development interface for the system developer. The end-user is no longer the passive receiver of information dished out by the system. Instead, the end-user now can confront the system and demand an explanation of justification of what the system does. This recognition of the end-user is partly the consequences of technological development like the PC and distributed processing. It is also the result of the end-user becoming more computer-literate, more willing to participate in computer processing and more able to manage computing resources. In the case of a KBIS, the objective of the system is to offer the end-user a system that is not only user-friendly (from the point-of-view of ergonomics and human factors) but also a system that is understandable and credible.

Another evolution for the end-user is the transference of responsibility from the computer professional to the end-user. An important reason for this shift to the end-user and to end-user computing is the desire of autonomy on the part of the end-user and a release from the 'tyranny' of the computer kingdom, which has resulted in many delays in development and much 'noise' in the development process. By assuming the responsibility, the end-users no longer have anyone to blame but themselves, and hence must be knowledgeable and literate in computing and AI before taking such a responsibility in a KBIS environment. The shift to the end-user is actually an evolving process in the responsibilities of computing, as is shown in Fig. 17.4.

There are, however, a number of risks associated with end-user computing that can readily be identified (Alawi and Weiss, 1985–86):

- Risks related to problem analysis. In developing applications, end-users may proceed without adequate problem specification and end up solving the wrong problem.
- Development risks. Persons who do not have systems development training and experience are more susceptible to modelling errors. They may fail to apply documentation standards and to test their solutions.
- Redundancy. End-users may spend time and effort developing applications that have already been developed.
- Unprofitable expenditure of time and effort. It is questionable whether people with professional skills should spend time developing applications rather than concentrating on their area of expertise.
- Waste of computing resources. End-users may be unaware of underlying operational costs as well as hardware/software costs. Without budgetary restraints, their use of computing resources may be uneconomical.
- Threat to data privacy and security. Physical access, custodianship controls, backup, and recovery issues are seldom addressed by end-users.

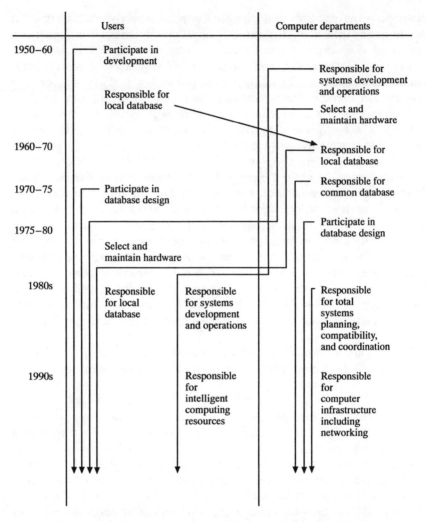

Figure 17.4 Changing responsibilities of end-users and computer departments.

- Lack of computing efficiency and effectiveness. Few end-users establish procedures for performance evaluation of their systems or subject them to audits.
- Incompatability of end-user tools and devices. Standards for acquisitions may be lacking.

The controls that need to be installed by management fall into three categories: preventive, detective, and corrective. The preventive category includes policies, procedures, and authorization structures to minimize the possibility that the risks will occur. For example, a cost–benefit analysis might be required before computer equipment is purchased by end-users; computer training might be mandatory; and rules on diskette access, storage, and backup might be promulgated. Detective controls might include procedures such as supervisory review of logs and performance. The changing of a password could be categorized as a corrective control.

SUMMARY AND CONCLUSIONS

The professional players considered in this chapter were the knowledge engineer, the IT analyst, and the practitioner of OR/MS. The important profession, somewhat neglected, is the AI person who is more than just a knowledge engineer. As more AI products relevant to a KBIS (such as voice processing, image processing, and NLP) become available and are integrated into a KBIS, AI personnel will become more numerous and more prominent within a KBIS. But there are no reasons to believe that this trend towards more AI personnel will substantially change the problems of personnel that have to be addressed in a KBIS. Corporate management must, however, constantly watch for changing satisficers and dissatisficers, as well as factors that lead to success or failure of a KBIS in order to ensure relevance, effectiveness, and efficiency of the organization using the KBIS.

A summary comparison of the current key technical players in the development of a KBIS is shown in Fig. 17.5.

Management, both corporate and IT, must be alert to the changing relevance of individual professions—some emerge, others exit, and yet others merge. Some may fall victim to automation. Decision making and problem solving may well become significantly automated, just as production and office management have both moved substantially out of human hands. This will not only result in the replacement of some white-collar workers but may also affect the role of corporate management, which must perhaps adapt from the management of people to the management of systems. They may even use software packages that have integrated inference engines, and then they will become knowledge engineers themselves and develop intelligent systems, just as opsearchers (operation research practitioners) now develop DSS subsystems in prototype mode.

The role of top and middle management relative to a KBIS (besides being a potential user) is crucial. They must define and declare technology and management of technology as important and of high priority if they are to use technology to maintain their competitive edge, not only through better morale or high motivation of staff, but also through shorter product cycles, higher productivity, and lower turnover. They must transform the priority for technology into policies that encourage motivation as well as

Personnel / Functions	IT specialist	OR/MS practitioner	Knowledge engineer
Prime problem-solving environment	Transactional	DSS	KBS
	Certainty	Probabilistic	Uncertainty
	Structured	Ill-/semi-structured	Ill-/semi-structured
Application orientation	Business	Business/industry	KBSs
Primary functional responsibilities	Transactional processing	Modelling Decision making	Knowledge acquisition
			Knowledge representation
			Knowledge systems programming
Programming languages used	3GL 4GL	3GL 4GL	3GL AI languages −PROLOG −LISP
Mother discipline	Business computing	OR/MS Decision sciences	Computer science

Figure 17.5 Comparison of IT specialists, OR/MS practitioners, and knowledge engineers.

attract and retain creative personnel (the potential innovators). Management must match jobs to individuals so as to meet the growth needs and potential of the professional employees. This can best be done through a careful plan and implementation of career paths and education, as well as training programs to allow AI-systems professionals to follow their chosen career paths. These professionals must be given the time to learn more about their technology or just keep abreast of it as it is continuously changing and becoming more complex. They must be trained and encouraged to be proactive. Above all, they must be made to share the same goals and vision as corporate management. There must be formal planning and attempts to integrate technology into the corporate culture and to develop interdisciplinary relations and attitudes necessary for successful deployment of AI technology.

What may well emerge, or should be fostered, is a new breed of professional who is not only up to the state of the art of high technology but also attempts to adapt it to the institution. This new breed must not only know the cognitive processes and problem-solving heuristics of the end-user and corporate management, but also appreciate the need for effective human interfaces. They must also be people-oriented persons and able to recognize that a KBIS is a human–machine system that is not just technological but also political. The new breed must also be interested and cognizant of power relationships in the organization and the success/failure factors unique to the organization.

The knowledge of technology and maturing attitudes conducive to technological innovation must be transferred, not only to the professional of a KBIS but also to the end-user. This can be accomplished through an *information centre*, through formal educational and training channels, or through a *technology 'watcher'*. Whatever the approach, there must be recognition that a successful KBIS depends on knowledge and attitudes and a close trust and working relationship between the end-users of the KBIS and its professional workers.

CASE 17.1 SURVEY ON USER PARTICIPATION

A survey was conducted by the University of Loughborough (UK) in 1987–88. One objective was to determine the degree of user participation in a KBIS. Fifty producers of ESs from academia, industry, and commerce were interviewed in depth. The results for user participation were as follows:

When users were consulted	%
At outset and throughout project	35
During and after system development	30
Varies according to project	23
Did not consult users	12

Source: M. O'Neill and A. Morris (1989) 'Expert systems in the United Kingdom: an evaluation of development methodologies', *Expert Systems*, **6** (2), pp. 90–91.

Questions
1. Do you think that the participation recorded in the survey did include prototyping or input to the design process or both?
2. Would you expect the high end-user participation to be from large organizations or small ones?
3. Do you think that the relationships with the end-users were well established or *ad hoc*?
4. Were the 12 per cent that did not consult end-users due to the fact that they were denied access or because they felt that the experts knew best?

Note: If you wish to know the comments of the authors of the article on this survey, then read the source but only after you have attempted the answers yourself.

CASE 17.2   R1/XCON—6: PERSONNEL

The model for development personnel for XCON reflected a broad perspective of involvement. It is a model of functions not individuals, and individuals playing one or more role. The roles played were as follows:

- The champion
- The sponsor
- The program manager
- The technical team
- The knowledge engineer
- The software systems integration engineer
- The domain experts
- The end-users

The integration of XCON into the manufacturing process at DEC was achieved by people with no previous experience with developing ESs.

There was a formal training program to ensure a supply of qualified AI engineers to maintain their AI systems.

> Students are first given a fourteen-week introductory course in AI, which is taught by both DEC personnel and university AI researchers. They then enter a nine-month apprenticeship in building expert systems at either a university or a DEC AI group. The aim of this program is not to produce AI researchers, but rather to provide a pool of people familiar with AI who can support the systems DEC develops.

Source: S. Polit (1985) 'R1 and beyond: the technology transfer at DEC', *AI Magazine*, **5** (4). This article (as well as the other articles on

R1 by McDermott and Barchant and McDermott quoted earlier) is printed in R. Engelmore (ed.) (1988) *Readings from the AI Magazine, Volumes 1–5, 1980–1985*, American Association of Artificial Intelligence, Menlo Park, CA, pp. 635–638.

Questions

1. Is the model of roles rather than individuals viable for a KBIS?
2. Does the fact that the integration of a KBIS into manufacturing was left to people inexperienced in a KBIS bother you? Would you prefer a systems integrator with experience in AI integrating the KBIS?
3. Is a 14-week period of training in AI sufficient for today, when AI is more multidisciplined and complex?
4. How is the management and integration of a KBIS more complex today than it was in the early days of XCON?

REVIEW AND DISCUSSION QUESTIONS

17.1 'Knowledge engineers are in short supply and high demand.' Discuss.

17.2 'AI people are scarce and thus expensive, but this will change soon.' Discuss and explain your position.

17.3 'AI personnel are different from computer personnel. Both are equally difficult to manage.' Discuss.

17.4 'It is better to hire good programmers and then train them for AI programming than to hire AI programmers.' Do you agree? If yes, why? If not, why not?

17.5 For successful AI applications in business two things are essential:
   (*a*) Top management support.
   (*b*) Corporate management knowledge of AI.
   Discuss.

17.6 'The overseeing of AI personnel in a business is best done by an MOT, manager of technology.' Discuss.

17.7 'It is logical to integrate AI personnel with computer personnel organizationally and not organize them independently.' Discuss

17.8 Describe and discuss the satisfiers and dissatisfiers of computer personnel. Explain why we might expect similar results for AI personnel and why this issue must still be largely conjectural at the present time.

17.9 'It is difficult to hire, train, and retrain AI personnel.' Explain this statement and discuss its validity.

17.10 'AI personnel should be organizationally integrated with computer personnel as well as with the OR/MS personnel in a business firm in order to provide organizational coherence and supervision, and at the same time avoid overlap and inefficiency.' Comment.

17.11 'The importance of systems specification by corporate management in an AI application is as important and crucial as in any non-AI application.' Comment.

17.12 'AI personnel and OR/MS personnel should be organizationally integrated in any business because they are both conversant with problem solving.' Comment.

17.13 There is some empirical evidence that the turnover of computer personnel is higher than for non-computer personnel in business and industry. Do you expect AI personnel to be like computer personnel in this regard? Explain your answer and suggest what might be done to decrease the turnover. Does it matter whether the firm is small or large? Does it matter where it is located (geographically) and in what industry?

17.14 If you were an MOT for a firm, which three main motivators (satisfiers) and demotivators (dissatisfiers) would you consider most important? Explain.

17.15 Is the problem of turnover and the consideration of satisfiers and dissatisfiers for AI and other computer personnel a matter of concern only to developed countries, or is it relevant (or more relevant) in developing countries? Explain.

BIBLIOGRAPHY AND REFERENCES

Alavi, M. and I. R. Weiss (1985–86) 'Managing the risks associated with end-user computing', *Journal of Management Information Systems*, **1**, 5–20.

Blender, E. (1987) 'The Knowledge Engineers'. *PC World*, **5** (6), 172–179.

Blender identifies the skills and relationships of the knowledge engineer and the human domain expert. He observes that a tension exists between the two reflecting the clash between the vernacular of the domain experts and the methodology of the knowledge engineer.

Couger, D. (1988) 'Motivating IS Personnel', *Datamation*, **34** (28), 59–64.

Couger continues reporting on his research relating to what motivates computer personnel. He argues that 'there is a critical need to motivate, not only the top performers, but all employees, particularly in an environment of stabilizing growth, slower promotion, and increased levels of maintenance of older systems'.

Couger, D. and R. A. Zawacki (1980) *Motivating and Managing Computer Personnel*, Wiley, New York.

Ferrat, T. W. and L. E. Short (1988) 'Are information systems people different? An investigation of how they are managed', *MIS Quarterly*, **12** (2), pp. 427–443.

Fitz-enz, J. (1978) 'Who is a DP professional?', *Datamation*, **14** (9), 125–128.

Gorman, L. (1989) 'Corporate culture', *Management Decisions*, **27** (1), pp. 14–19.

A good discussion of the significance of corporate culture to personnel management for the practicing manager, be it a corporate manager or a manager of high technology.

Gouldner, A. (1984) *Information Systems*, **9** (1), 70–78.

Herzberg, F., F. B. Mausner and B. S. Snyderman (1959) *The Motivation to Work*, 2nd edn, John Wiley, New York.

Igbaria, M. and J. H. Greenhaus (1992) 'The career advancement prospects of managers and professionals: are MIS employees different?', *Decision Sciences*, **23** (2), 478–499.

An on-going study examining the career advancement of MIS and non-MIS employees. Relevant to AI personnel too.

Igbaria, M., J. Greenhaus and S. Parasuraman (1991) 'Career orientations of MIS employees: an empirical analysis', *MIS Quarterly*, **15** (2), 151–169.

The implications on job dissatisfaction, commitment, and retention are discussed.

Lea, D. and R. Brostrom (1988) 'Managing the high tech professional', *Personnel*, **65** (6), 12–14.

The authors predict more and more high tech in organizations and a consequent increase in the need of special skills at managerial levels.

Morrison, M., J. Morrison, O. R. Liu Sheng and K. Higa (1992) 'Environment selection, training, and implementation in high-level expert systems environments: experiences and guidelines', *Journal of Systems Software*, **19** (2), 147–152.

The authors find an inverse relationship between complex software and developer productivity. The authors' experiences suggest that 'developers should use familiar development tools for projects involving firm deadlines and deliverables, and new environments should be investigated only when time pressure for product deliverables will not inhibit unbiased evaluation'.

Rifkin, G. (1985) 'Finding and keeping DP/MIS professionals', *ComputerWorld*, **19** (22), p. ID 15.

POSTSCRIPT

As we move from an industrial to an information society, we will use our brain power to create instead of our physical power and the technology of the day will extend and enhance our mental ability.

Naisbitt, *Megatrends 2000*

In this book we have considered KBISs, just one branch of AI and computer science that now has many potential applications in business, science, engineering, and industry. Unfortunately, we have been unable to examine some of the important implications of a KBIS, especially its important social and economic implications. We have also not discussed areas that are on the boundary of social and technological implications such as those of security and legal problems arising out of liability resulting from the harmful results of incorrect inferences and conclusions of a KBIS.

There are also many technological implications of KBISs that are just being fully recognized. One of these relates to the integration of a KBIS. This has organizational implications too, but there are also many problems in the logical integration of a KBIS with an organizational information-processing system, namely integrating the data system with the knowledge-base, especially for the transactional, executive, and decision support systems (Turban and Trippe, 1990). We need to forge links between the KBIS and the database management systems and hypertext systems. We need to integrate multiple knowledge domains and sources, especially for interactive and on-line/real-time and control systems. We also have the problem of integrating software and hardware, especially multimedia (O'Docherty, and Daskalakis, 1991). And then there is the problem of integrating the branches of AI related to a KBIS, especially those of voice processing, image processing, and natural-language processing, all (or any) of which can open up whole new dimensions for KBIS usage. Such integration will make the end-user interface more accessible and end-user friendly.

An important prerequisite for a successful integration of the type mentioned above is the need for standards—standards for the development of a KBIS (Gorney and Coleman, 1991); standards for validation of a KBIS (Harrison and Ratcliffe, 1991); standards on evaluating a KBIS (Beach and Gevarter); and perhaps even standards for end-user interfaces (Berry and Hart, 1991). These standards need to be developed in parallel with the on-going efforts at international standards for message formatting and network architecture. Then there are advances in technology that impact on a KBIS, both hardware (IEEE, 1994), and software technology (Lowry, 1992).

We have discussed the development of a KBIS, but there is still much research and development work needed in the areas of knowledge organization and representation as well as knowledge acquisition. In this relatively new domain (i.e. complex technology) whole new system development paradigms are still emerging—such as the object-oriented approach and neural computing. We are still in the process of fully understanding the new possibilities, and we cannot be at all sure that totally new, currently unforeseen possibilities will not emerge.

Expert systems and KBISs have made important contributions in making systems more user-friendly through presentation and justification facilities, but there is much more that can and must be done to make the systems more accessible to the casual and non-technical end-user. Natural-language processing through natural language interfaces (Copestake and Jones, 1990) is one important avenue.

Then there is the problem of training and educating the future designers (*Expert Systems with Applications*, 1992; Strok, 1992) and end-users of systems like the KBIS. We need to train not just the development specialist with knowledge of the ever-changing state of the art but also end-users who need to know how to use this technology. They need to know how to ask the right questions before they can get the proper answers. Both the end-users and the developers of a KBIS have a productive and exciting time ahead! The authors wish them well.

BIBLIOGRAPHY

Beach, S. S. and W. Gevarter (1991) 'Standards for evaluating expert systems tools', *Expert Systems with Applications*, **2** (4), 225–268.

Berry, D. and A. Hart (1991) 'User interface standards for expert systems: are they appropriate', *Expert Systems with Applications*, **2** (4), 245–250.

Bradley, E. (1993) 'Functional programming languages for AI problem solving', *Knowledge Engineering Review*, **6** (3), 223–235.

Coleman, K. (1993) 'The AI market in the year 2000', *AI Expert*, **8** (1), 34–44.

Communications of the ACM, **36** (3) (1993), pp. 46–100. Special section on personal perspectives of the Fifth Generation project.

Copestake, A. and K. S. Jones (1990) 'Natural language interfaces to databases', *Knowledge Engineering Review*, **5** (4), 225–249.

Data Communications, **16** S2–S29 (1991) Editorial supplement on the internetwork decade.

Expert Systems with Applications, **4** (2) (1992), 175–227. Special issue on 'Applied Artificial Intelligence/Expert Systems Program in Universities'.

Germain, E. (1992) 'Introducing natural language processing', *AI Expert*, **7** (8), 30–35.

Gorney, D. J. and K. G. Coleman (1991) 'Expert systems development standards', *Expert Systems with Applications*, **2** (4), 239–244.

Harrison, P. R. and P. A. Ratcliffe (1991) 'Towards standards for validation of expert systems', *Expert Systems with Applications*, **2** (4), 251–258.

Hsieh, D. (1993) 'A logic to unify semantic-network knowledge system with object-oriented database models', *Journal of Object Oriented Programming*, **6** (2), 55–67.

IEEE (1994) *Spectrum*, January, **31**(1) Special issue on technology.

Ketler, K. (1993) 'Case-based reasoning: an introduction', *Expert Systems with Applications*, **6** (1), 3–8.

Keyes, J. (1991) 'AI on a chip', *AI Expert*, **6** (4), 33–38.

Lowry, M. R. (1992) 'Software engineering in the twenty-first century', *AI Magazine*, **13** (9), 71–87.

Motiwala, J. (1991) 'Artificial intelligence in management: future challenges', *Transactions on Knowledge and Data Engineering*, **3** (2), 125–159.

Nash, J. (1993) 'State of the market, art, union and technology', *AI Expert*, **8** (1), 45–51.

O'Docherty, M. H. and C. N. Daskalakis (1991) 'Multimedia information systems: the management and semantic retrieval of all electronic data types', *Computer Journal*, **34** (3), 225–238.

Rowe, A. J. and P. R. Watkins (1992) 'Beyond expert systems—reasoning, judgement, and wisdom', *Expert Systems with Applications*, **4** (1), 1–10.

Strok, D. (1992) 'Teaching artificial intelligence: an IEEE survey', *IEEE Expert*, **7** (2), 59–62.

Turban, E. and R. Trippe (1990) 'Integrating expert systems with operations research: a conceptual framework', *Expert Systems with Applications*, **1** (4), 335–344.

Tryan, C. K. and J. F. Georga (1993) 'The implementation of expert systems: a survey of successful implementations', *Database*, **24** (1), 5–15.

INDEX